ENVIRONMENTAL DEMOCRACY

Michael Mason

Earthscan Publications Ltd, London

For my parents

First published in the UK in 1999 by
Earthscan Publications Ltd

Copyright © Michael Mason, 1999

A catalogue record for this book is available from the British Library

ISBN: 1 85383 617 6 paperback
      1 85383 618 4 hardback

Typesetting by JS Typesetting, Wellingborough, Northants
Printed and bound by Biddles Ltd, Guildford and King's Lynn
Cover design by Yvonne Booth

For a full list of publications please contact:

Earthscan Publications Ltd
120 Pentonville Road
London, N1 9JN, UK
Tel: +44 (0)171 278 0433
Fax: +44 (0)171 278 1142
Email: earthinfo@earthscan.co.uk
http://www.earthscan.co.uk

Earthscan is an editorially independent subsidiary of Kogan Page Ltd and publishes
in association with WWF-UK and the International Institute for Environment and
Development

This book is printed on elemental chlorine free paper

CONTENTS

Acronyms and Abbreviations

ALG	Association of London Government
BATNEEC	best available technology not entailing excessive cost
BPEO	best practicable environmental option
CFC	chlorofluorocarbon
CO_2	carbon dioxide
CORE	Commission on Resources and Environment (British Columbia)
CND	Campaign for Nuclear Disarmament
CPR	common-pool resource
CSD	Commission on Sustainable Development
EC	European Community
ECHR	European Convention on Human Rights
EMAS	ecomanagement and audit scheme
ENACT	Working Group on Environmental Action
EU	European Union
EWC	European Works Council
FAO	Food and Agriculture Organization
GATT	General Agreement on Tariffs and Trade
GFA	general forest area
GMB	General, Municipal and Boilermakers' Union
GNP	gross national product
HIA	high-intensity area
HMIP	Her Majesty's Inspectorate of Pollution
ICC	International Criminal Court
ICFTU	International Confederation of Free Trade Unions
IIASA	International Institute for Applied Systems Analysis
IPCC	Intergovernmental Panel on Climate Change
ISO	International Standards Organization
JEAC	joint environment advisory committee
KNU	Karen National Union
LETS	local exchange trading scheme
LGMB	Local Government Management Board
LRMP	land and resource management planning
LUCO	land-use coordination office (British Columbia)
NDP	New Democratic Party (Canada)
NEPP	National Environmental Policy Plan (The Netherlands)
NGO	nongovernmental organization
NO_x	nitrous oxide
OECD	Organisation for Economic Co-operation and Development
PLUS	provincial land-use strategy (Canada)
SEA	Strategic Environmental Assessment
SLF	secondary liquid fuel
SLORC	State Law and Order Restoration Council (Myanmar)
SO_2	sulphur dioxide
T&G	Transport and General Workers' Union
TUC	Trades Union Congress
UK	United Kingdom
UN	United Nations
UNEP	United Nations Environment Programme
US	United States
WATCH	Workers Against Toxic Chemicals
WHO	World Health Organization
WTO	World Trade Organization

ACKNOWLEDGEMENTS

This is as good a place as any to acknowledge my debt to several outstanding teachers who, in one way or another, encouraged me to reflect on and articulate my environmental interests in an informed manner – Chaloner Chute, Mike French and Simon James. As a university student, Derek Gregory, the late Graham Smith and Bill Adams helped me to develop this intellectual curiosity in the most rewarding way possible. Now a university teacher myself, the high pedagogic standard set by all these individuals is the true benchmark by which I judge my own activities in the midst of an ever-increasing array of performance indicators. Bill Adams served as my PhD supervisor and has provided valuable feedback on several chapters in this work. I want to acknowledge also the comments on the initial book proposal by Tim O'Riordan and those of an anonymous referee. I fear that the arguments in the book may not meet all their constructive criticisms and suggestions, but their scrutiny has been welcome.

The research on which the book is based stretches back over the past couple of years. Chapters 3 and 4 are informed by research in British Columbia, Canada: some of this work was assisted by a research grant from the Canadian government (administered through the academic section of the Canadian High Commission in London), and I would like to express my appreciation for that support. This Canadian research could also not have been completed without the assistance and hospitality of Joan Calderhead and Peter Marter, Kevin Park and Karen Snowshoe in Vancouver and, across the water in Victoria, Yasmeen Qureshi and Pat Hill. Their knowledge and experience not only helped to focus my efforts, but also kept everything in the proper perspective. I am fortunate that these individuals have become valued friends.

Chapter 5 owes a significant debt to the research of Nigel Morter on the Transport and General Workers' Union in what started off as a combined project on trade union environmentalism. This is a woefully neglected area in the literature on environmental politics and I am happy to acknowledge the contribution of Nigel to the research content of this chapter, without necessarily implying his endorsement of all the ideas expressed. Chapter 6 derives in part from my own involvement in a London Local Agenda 21 process. Again, while I take sole responsibility for the ideas expressed here, I want to mention a number of tireless, committed individuals who have shown me in practice what it means to engage locally to improve quality of life for all – Jeremy Corbyn, Beatriz Echeverri, Doug Gleave, Rosemary Jones, Lester Pritchard and Tom Rubens.

Chapters 3, 4 and 5 are based on material which originally appeared in the following academic journals respectively: *Environmental Politics*, Vol 5, No 4, 1996 (Frank Cass), *Environmental Values*, Vol 6, No 3, 1997 (White Horse Press) and *Capitalism, Nature, Socialism*, Vol 9, No 2, 1998 (Guilford Press). I want to thank the publishers of those periodicals for allowing me to draw on and revise that material here. At Earthscan, Jonathan Sinclair Wilson supported and guided my original book proposal, while Frances MacDermott provided invaluable editorial help in preparing the manuscript for publication – to both I am most grateful. Finally, the maps were very ably drafted by John Gibbs.

INTRODUCTION

We might imagine that, at the close of the 20th century, the case for both democracy and environmentalism has been successfully established. However difficult it may be to reach agreement on these terms in detail, our intuitive sense is that both relate to justifiable ideologies; the former suggests a way of organizing our social affairs in which we are able to participate equitably in decision-making affecting our interests, and the latter expresses a shared concern with maintaining and improving environmental quality (understood in a broad sense). Furthermore, while there is a notable late 20th century disposition to 'deconstruct' and deflate any notions that claim to ground arguments for improving quality of life on this planet, democracy and environmentalism stubbornly stand for a moral universalism. This is not to deny that these deconstructive tendencies often help us to unmask the particular behind the universal and the historical behind the natural. The contention in this book is that, even in the face of such necessary questioning, there remains a common normative space for democratic governance and environmental justice – a justification that extends across borders, resonating with all non-fundamentalist cultures: one also that reaches back through history to the nameless victims of past social and environmental injustices, and at the same time stretches forward to consider the interests of future generations. It is also my argument that the two political projects are mutually reinforcing; a democratic determination of collective choices requires necessary ecological (and social) preconditions, while only a socially inclusive environmentalism justifies long-term public support.

I will term the convergence of the two 'environmental democracy': this is the subject of the book and the first chapter will make explicit its theoretical outlines. In short, environmental democracy is defined as a participatory and ecologically rational form of collective decision-making: it prioritizes judgements based on long-term generalizable interests, facilitated by communicative political procedures and a radicalization of existing liberal rights. Environmental democracy is a normative conception that connects with intuitive presuppositions of ordinary language use; in particular, that communication is partly about coming to a shared understanding about something. It also describes existing political practices and institutions that respect the social and ecological conditions of communicative freedom. Of course the terms 'ecological democracy' and 'green democracy' have been used before to refer to a variety of philosophical positions ostensibly sympathetic to the dual challenge of democratic self-determination and ecological sustainability. There is a newly burgeoning literature on the democratic credentials of green political thought, as well as on the green challenge to prevailing ideas of liberal democracy (see, for example, Dobson and Lucardie, 1993; Doherty and de Geus, 1996; Lafferty and Meadowcroft, 1996). In Chapter 1 I will introduce some of the recurrent themes running through that discussion, registering my affinity with particular perpectives and outlining my own conceptual position – one indebted to discourse theories of democracy.

Until these recent theoretical exchanges around the relationship between environmentalism and democracy – the academic response in the English-speaking world to the upsurge in public environmental concern at the end of the 1980s – there had been little examination of the democratic self-understanding of environmentalists. Anna Bramwell's (1989) ideological and political history of the 20th century ecology movement provoked reactions from green activists for laying bare the anti-democratic beliefs of some of its intellectual forebears, although she noted the later leftward shift to more egalitarian beliefs. The understandable preoccupation of environ-mentalists with ecological campaigns, and the wish to be seen as apolitical, nevertheless left unexamined, at least in public, the assumption that the association between environmentalism and democracy was unproblematic. This study will examine those recent academic debates that have problem-atized this relationship, but in a methodological fashion that contrasts with their largely abstract exchanges. This introduction aims to provide an intellectual rationale for an approach that recognizes the need to combine theoretical commentary with reference to relevant empirical investigations in order to conjoin the general and the particular in a productive way. Before that, though, there is a need to demonstrate why there is a very pressing *practical* justification for bringing environmentalism and democracy together in political terms; and why we should want to make any expression of environmentalist values accountable to principles of human justice.

'SAVE THE RHINO: KILL THE PEOPLE': CREATING A BURMESE NATURE RESERVE

We found them deep in the Burmese jungle, east of the Tenasserim River. About 200 of them, hungry, exhausted and fearing for their lives. They have no money, no change of clothes, and they eat what they can find. They sleep under palm trees propped up teepee style against the trees. A sickly child is crying. An old woman sobs endlessly (Levy, Scott-Clark and Harrison, 1997).

The sight of fleeing refugees, the sound of crying: this description of members of the Karen ethnic group, recorded in March 1997 by journalists from the British *Observer* newspaper, sadly evokes a not uncommon scene of human distress in our time. In this case, however, the ethnic cleansing was in order to make way for a million-hectare 'protected area' – the Myinmoletkat Nature Reserve in Kayin (Karen) State in eastern Myanmar (Burma) (see Figure I.1). The launch ceremony for the 'biosphere' reserve had taken place the previous September in Rangoon, hosted by the forestry and energy ministers. Shortly after this announcement the Myanmar army, the *tatmadaw*, began the forced removal of Karen civilians and the political role of the nature reserve soon became clearer.

In February 1997 the State Law and Order Restoration Council (SLORC) – the military government of Myanmar – launched a large-scale armed offensive against the Karen National Union (KNU), an armed separatist movement (Amnesty International, 1997c, p 2). This was only the latest move in an eight-year campaign by the *tatmadaw* against the KNU in Kayin (Amnesty International, 1996). In its total war against the Karen ethnic minority, the *tatmadaw* has, according to independent observers, taken part in extrajudicial killings, forced labour and portering, looting and burning of villages, and forcible relocations (Amnesty International, 1997b). Two months after the start of the 1997 military onslaught, human rights groups claimed that 2000 Karen people had been killed, at least 20,000 had fled across the border to Thailand and tens of thousands – including children – had been driven into forced labour (Levy, Scott-Clark and Harrison, 1997).

The creation of the Myinmoletkat Nature Reserve thus served, firstly, as a cover for an attempt to eradicate the KNU by forcibly removing the Karen ethnic minority. Secondly, it provided the military regime with a cynical means of appealing for international environmental legitimacy in the face of an appalling human rights record. Given the very high levels of biological diversity in Myanmar, the country has attracted attention from prestigious international conservation organizations. Following a visit to Washington in 1994 from a representative of SLORC, the Office of Bio-diversity Programs at the Smithsonian Institution began working with the regime on its biodiversity conservation projects. According to senior policy advisors at the Myanmar Forestry Ministry, interviewed by *Observer* journalists in March 1997, the Smithsonian Institution and the New York-based Wildlife Conservation Society were both involved in helping to run the Myinmoletkat Nature Reserve. They had also been brought in to advise on the creation of the Lambi Kyun coral islands reserve – a combined marine national park and ecotourism venture (Levy, Scott-Clark and Harrison, 1997). The Myanmar forest policy, influenced by their advice, anticipates designating 30 per cent of the land area of the country as reserved forests and another 10 per cent as parks and wildlife sanctuaries under the national protected areas system.

The statements of representatives for the two American conservation organizations, when contacted for responses by the *Observer*, warrant direct

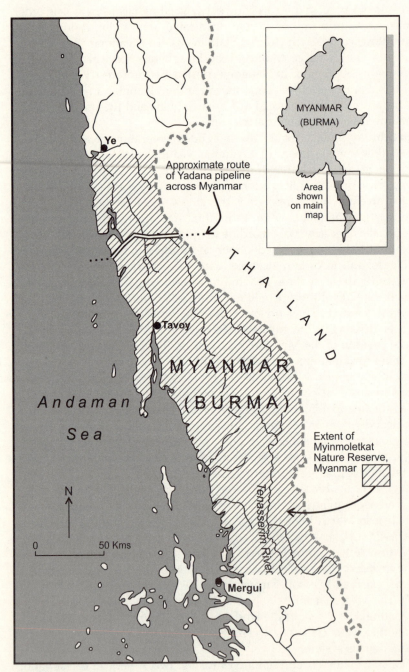

Approximate route
of Yadana pipeline
across Myanmar

MYANMAR
(BURMA)

Area
shown
on main
map

T H A I L A N D

Ye

Tavoy

M Y A N M A R

(B U R M A)

A n d a m a n

S e a

Extent of
Myinmoletkat
Nature Reserve,
Myanmar

Tenasserim River

N

0   50 Kms

Mergui

Figure I.1 *Myinmoletkat Nature Reserve, Myanma*

quotation (both in Levy, Scott-Clark and Harrison, 1997). Firstly, the science director of the Wildlife Conservation Society emphasized:

> *We do not sanction forced relocation, torture or killing. But we have no control over the government. We are in Burma because it is one of the highest biodiversity countries in Asia. We can walk away from it, but that wouldn't do any good for biodiversity. We are focused on biodiversity and conservation.*

In the same vein, the reported comments of a spokesman for the Smithsonian Institution in Washington were:

> *We are there to do important conservation work. We may disagree with a regime but it is not our place to challenge it.*

For these environmentalists concerned with the global biodiversity crisis – what Edward O Wilson correctly describes as 'one of the greatest extinction spasms of geological history' (1993, p 268) – the moral ledger can be drawn up in favour of involvement with a repressive regime. There is no question that Myanmar possesses an exceptional level of biological diversity, ranging across three zoogeographic zones: the Indian, Indomalayan and Palaeartic regions. While Rangoon sits in the rice-producing delta zone of the River Irrawaddy, extensively cleared of its monsoon hardwood forests by the British in the latter half of the 19th century (Myers, 1985, p 340), the Myinmoletkat Nature Reserve envelopes a remote jungle environment, isolated from adjoining Thailand by the densely vegetated slopes of the Dawma range. It includes the Heinza-Kaleinaung and Luwaing reserved forests which are believed to contain the rare, endemic Sumatran rhinoceros. The whole reserve area also stands in stark contrast to the Malay peninsular further south – one of the 18 conservation hot spots across the world identified by Norman Myers (1988), all with high levels of biological endemicity and where the danger of species extinction is deemed to be critical. Yet the tragic environmentalist irony of the Myinmoletkat Reserve creation is that it displaced a pre-existing network of unofficial community wildlife sanctuaries established by the Karen people and other ethnic groups. For those Western environmentalists seeking to convince such peoples of the value of protected natural areas, participatory examples of community park design and management have represented increasingly influential models of biodiversity conservation, both ethically fair and practically effective (Furze, de Lacy and Birckhead, 1996).

What then is the moral worth of a conservation programme seemingly indifferent to the political means of preservation? Have we come to regard the use of environmental science – in this case conservation biology – in such an instrumentalist manner that we are immune to the social consequences of its production and reception? Above all, how can the motives informing environmental concern seem to exclude, at great misanthropic cost, consideration of their inter-relatedness with fundamental human rights and interests? The above may be read as an 'extreme' example (an unhelpful category to the Karen victims of ethnic cleansing), but environmentalism cannot afford to ignore questions of political justice and civic self-determination. In other words, a fixation on natural attributes – the content of biodiversity – is not sufficient *anywhere*, I believe, to justify environmental preservation in the public realm. It must also be attached to universal human interests about self-determination and quality of life.

The practical necessity for a project of environmental democracy is in helping to redefine environmentalism as a humanistic programme for ecological and social change, with procedures of moral self-determination at its centre. Unless environmental preservation facilitates equitable decision-making, my claim is that it will lack the support of those suffering most from social and ecological injustices across the world. And without demonstrating this participatory democratic intent, it will not be a force for progressive social change in the 21st century. This book is concerned above all with showing how this presents challenges to the North American and Western European democracies – those countries responsible in the 20th century for the productive and consumptive excesses at the heart of global environmental problems, yet, at the same time, those countries which are often the most complacent about their green and democratic credentials. In making a case for a critical environmentalism, this book will explore several political projects, at different scales, that make a claim to combining meaningfully civic self-determination and ecological sustainability – that is, a claim to environmental democracy.

The violations of environmental democracy appear tragically clear in the Myanmar case. Ultimately, responsibility must be assigned to the authoritarian regime in Rangoon, although the rush of the *Observer* to charge the American conservation groups with a lack of conscience should not prevent us from a wider soul-searching. Crisscrossing the northern end of the national nature reserve is the route of a gas pipeline which, when complete, will pump natural gas from the Yadana gas field in the Andaman Sea across Burma to power plants in Thailand (see Figure I.1). The pipeline is being constructed by the French Total Company in partnership with an American oil company, Unocal Corporation, while Thailand's PTT Exploration & Production Public Co Ltd and Myanma Oil and Gas Enterprise have lesser stakes in the venture. According to Thai-based human rights groups, the gas project represents a grave threat to human and environmental interests in Myanmar (Mon Information Service, 1996; Greer, 1998). Allegations of the use of slave labour and forced relocation of ethnic groups – including Mon and Tavoyan communities as well as Karen people – have led, as we shall see in this book's conclusion, to a transnational human rights lawsuit launched against the energy companies in the United States in 1996. The *Observer* team gathered first-hand accounts on the rape, execution and enslavement of Karen villagers by the *tatmadaw* in the vicinity of the pipeline (Levy, Scott-Clark and Harrison, 1997).

According to human rights groups, there is corporate complicity in these systematic human rights violations because the pipeline, and its promise of US$400 million a year income for the Myanmar government, was the main reason for the security operation to establish the park. Behind the green zoning of the Myinmoletkat are the more sinister 'black areas' designated by the Myanmar army, signifying 'free-fire areas' against resident ethnic groups in the region. The French Total Company has reportedly directly paid the salaries of the SLORC military personnel responsible for securing the pipeline construction (Mon Information Service, 1996, pp 4–5). None of the ethnic groups have been allowed to participate meaningfully in the decision-making process of the pipeline project, even though it directly affects their interests: this includes the refusal of Total and Unocal to divulge the results of their environmental impact assessments for the pipeline (Greer, 1998, p 35). They claim that the pipeline route, following environmental field surveys of three suggested routes, is following the most environmentally responsible option. Neither Total nor Unocal have divested from the project, claiming that they are undertaking socio-economic development programmes for the principal villages in the pipeline region, while arguing more generally that economic development is encouraging democratization in Myanmar. For those ethnic communities not displaced, the only significant 'economic return' so far has been the reported pushing of young women, some only 13 or 14 years old, into giving their services as prostitutes to the French field personnel from Total Company in the region (Mon Information Service, 1996, p 8).

Whatever the veracity of the claims of the ethnic groups in eastern Myanmar, and many have been corroborated by independent observers, the clear absence of social and ecological accountability of private capital investment in this case is, as will be argued more generally in this book, inimical to environmental democracy. Furthermore, as will be mentioned at the end of the book, there is a failing of us as consumers in not being aware of – let alone questioning – the social and environmental costs of the profusion of products we incessantly demand.

What of the responsibility of other governments? Within Asia, Myanmar was admitted into the Association of South-East Asian Nations in July 1997, resting on a claim that engagement would encourage democracy, although the desire for greater political stability in the region was at least as important. But the human rights violations have continued (Amnesty International, 1998). The member states of the European Union proved slow in formulating a common response to the situation in Myanmar. Following repeated resolutions from the European Parliament, the Council of Ministers finally suspended preferential trade tariffs to Myanmar in 1997; but this limited measure has been the only action to ensue. In the United States, in contrast, federal financial sanctions introduced against Myanmar in April 1997, and renewed in May 1998, have been supplemented by 21 American state and city jurisdictions refusing to conduct business with companies operating in the country. These subnational American measures have in

fact been *opposed* by the European Commission, which has formally challenged them under World Trade Organization (WTO) rules prohibiting
governments from basing purchasing decisions on political grounds (the
WTO Government Procurement Agreement). European companies have
continued to invest in Myanmar – in Britain, for example, Premier Oil
moved in to replace the American company Texaco when the latter
withdrew from the Burmese gas fields – but they now face in return the
loss of US state and city procurement contracts. Opposed by a European
Parliament powerless to stop the action, the European Commission diplomatic challenge sharply exposed the democratic deficit in the union.

In December 1997, the United Nations General Assembly adopted by
consensus a resolution expressing grave concern at the continuing human
violations in the country (Amnesty International, 1997a, p 2). The absence
of an action-enforcing resolution, in contrast to the contemporaneous
security council obsession with weapons inspections in Iraq, seems to give
support to those who note the consistent subordination of international
justice considerations to geopolitical interests within the United Nations.
Insofar as the five permanent security council members remain the driving
force between enforcement of United Nations resolutions – choosing
strategically which ones to pursue and which to ignore – power politics
indeed plays a decisive role. Yet, as will be argued in this book's conclusion,
the inculcation of environmental equity at this level of governance, while
requiring a democratization of global institutions, nevertheless finds
support in existing international law and the efforts of nongovernmental
organizations pressing for transnational justice. However, this is to fast-
forward. The rest of this introduction will mark out the author's conceptual
and methodological frame of reference for environmental democracy.

THE DISCOURSE PRINCIPLE AND ENVIRONMENTAL DEMOCRACY

This study seeks to explore the environmental implications of a discourse
theory of democracy (Habermas, 1996). It is concerned with democracy as
a form of political communication that is both inclusive and rational. The
term 'discourse' relates to the importance of language in addressing political
phenomena: language, in this communicative approach, is a central medium
of political action (and of social reproduction generally). Discourse refers
to modes of communication between people in which understanding rests
upon, or presumes the possibility of, agreement motivated by convincing
reasons rather than by any form of coercion or deception. Applied to the
realm of politics, a *discourse principle* can be invoked to question the rightness
of socially binding decisions or the generalizability of different interests:
that principle, according to political philosopher Jürgen Habermas, states
that 'only those action norms are valid in which all possibly affected persons

could agree as participants in rational discourses' (Habermas, 1996, p 459). Democratic justification or 'legitimacy' can, through the employment of this discourse principle, be connected to communicative criteria of inclusiveness and impartiality. One of the key aims of this work is to examine some promising candidates for environmental democracy – both governmental and nongovernmental forms of social action – where environmental interests have been developed with explicit reference to participatory democratic norms.

This book claims that environmental democracy has both a normative and explanatory aspect. In normative terms, it describes a radical democratic project which extends and radicalizes existing liberal norms in order to include the ecological and social conditions for civic self-determination; in explanatory terms, it accounts for existing tendencies for noncoercive green communication found in various political forms and practices. The discourse principle encompasses simultaneously these logically distinct but inter-related normative and explanatory components.

The Normative Role of the Discourse Principle

At a normative level, the discourse principle enables us to specify and justify the institutional conditions for rational collective decision-making – conditions that *ought* to govern political communication about the environment. Chapter 1 presents the argument that environmental democracy is strongly participatory, extending democratic influence into all areas of social choice affecting our interests. This occurs not only in the formal political sphere: the collective, often nonsubstitutable nature of ecological structures and processes vindicates, however unwelcome to private corporations, the democratization of economic governance. The single greatest cause of ecological degradation remains private investment decisions, structurally bound to externalize or socialize environmental costs unless reined in by democratic controls. Of course, the feasibility of democratic incursions within corporate economic sovereignty currently seems to be beyond the bounds of democratic possibility. According to the 'economic fatalism' of dominant neoliberal thinking, there is no alternative to the unfettered rule of market forces and the increasing concentration of global wealth in the hands of a small minority (Bourdieu, 1998). Under these circumstances, the normative promise of the discourse principle seems hopelessly utopian, remote from the practical experience of all those across the world with little or no say in the collective political and economic decisions affecting their lives. Even for the liberal democracies of the global North, this means the overwhelming majority of citizens.

However, according to Habermas, the discourse principle finds practical currency in the conditions of reaching understanding that are faced by individuals in ordinary communication. This is commented upon as a philosophical source of environmental democracy in the first chapter, while its moral implications are elaborated upon in Chapter 4. All we need note here is the assertion that in everyday communication, individuals are subject to a set of unavoidable idealizations without which mutual understanding would be impossible. These presuppositions include conferring identical meanings on expressions employed and the expectation that interacting actors are mutually accountable – that is, they could, if requested, give good reasons that they are expressing something faithful to their intentions (truthfulness), recognizing a social norm as legitimate (rightness), and representing something accurately (truth) (Habermas, 1984, pp 18–21). Reasons to doubt any of these 'validity claims' can block or delay efforts at reaching shared understanding. Processes of reaching understanding ordinarily take place against a background of unquestioned, taken-for-granted knowledge, and the meaning of these validity claims, Habermas notes, is only ascertained from the way they are justified when they are problematic (1984, pp 100–101). Argumentation stands apart from everyday communication as a *reflective* continuation of action orientated to reaching mutual understanding. As a type of speech, argumentation involves participants focusing on contested validity claims and, under suitable circumstances, supporting or criticizing them. Discourse then means, more precisely, those attempts to resolve problematic validity claims by the force of the better argument alone, free of strategic motives of self-interest or coercion, aspiring to a rationally motivated agreement. Habermas concedes that discourses are improbable forms of communication, but reminds us that they are shaped by the idealizations built into everyday linguistic exchanges.

The preoccupation of the discourse principle with norms indicates the central role of *practical discourse* – the mode of argumentation concerned with claims to normative validity (rightness) – in political deliberation and decision-making. In short, the discourse principle provides us with a standard for impartial justification with which we can assess the validity of norms of action (Habermas, 1996, pp 108–109). Subcategories of practical discourse can be distinguished according to the relevant problem under collective discussion: *pragmatic* discourse refers to the determination of rational choices when the underlying values or goals are not up for question (for instance, the appropriate management techniques to enhance bio-diversity in a nature reserve); *ethical* discourse covers critical reflections on shared values – the space of collective understandings and cultural traditions (for example, obligations of humane treatment in our relations to domestic animals). Lastly, *moral* discourse relates to the regulation of competing interests in a just or impartial manner (such as deliberation over the distributional implications of a locational strategy for toxic waste dumps). The environmental examples merely illustrate the different types of argumentation at stake in each discourse. In practice, any given issue in environmental politics is, of course, likely to involve all three at different intensities: all forms of argumentation are only recognizable in connection with particular contexts and domains of action. While Habermas maintains that the validity claimed for particular norms transcends concrete locales, perhaps appealing to universal values, actual claims are always raised in specific contexts in which acceptance or rejection has practical consequences (1996, pp 20–21). Methodologically, we must therefore study their expression in particular forms of argumentation.

The discourse principle relates to action norms animated by moral, ethical and pragmatic concerns. However, in outlining the normative meaning of environmental democracy in Chapter 1, Habermas and also John Rawls (1988) are followed in arguing for the *political* priority of moral rightness (justice) over ethical ideas of the good. Moral discourse assumes primary importance in democratic decision-making on account of its concern with the impartial regulation of conflicts, where the interests of each person are given equal consideration. Justification of moral norms in argumentation relates, then, to generalizing or universalizing interests, while their application in practice takes into account their appropriateness for those relevant interests (Habermas, 1996, p109). Placing such an emphasis on moral questions – issues of ecological and social justice – might seem to downplay the very important ethical content of environmentalism and contrasts with discussion in environmental philosophy. Is not a concern with environmental quality predicated on distinctive environmental values, on how we see ourselves in relation to nonhuman nature, and on spiritual and aesthetic traditions of environmental respect and responsibility? In addition, we can all point to formative moments or relationships in our life histories that catalysed convictions about the way we should live. All these sources of ethical reflection and valuation inform political action addressed to environmental protection: they are a critical element of environmental politics. Nevertheless, the stress on moral questions is designed, at the normative level, to demonstrate the social relevance of environmentalism as a political project of environmental justice, implying institutional designs based on public participation and fairness. It is also intended to signal the cosmopolitan reach of environmentalism as a global political programme.

Democracy finds its universalistic green premise by connecting with the moral discourses of environmentalism. This book argues that these moral discourses are broader than commonly portrayed (at least in the northern hemisphere); they include the struggles of organized labour (Chapter 5) and multicultural inner city communities (Chapter 6), as much as environmental conservation and preservation (Chapter 4). The discourse principle is extended to the institutional framework of environmental democracy by addressing legal norms – norms that govern political decision-making, including their interpretation by the judiciary and their application by administrative mechanisms. A fundamental precondition for democracy is thus discursive procedures of legitimate lawmaking:

> . . .*the democratic principle states that only those statutes may claim legitimacy that can meet with the assent . . . of all citizens in a*

> *discursive process of legislation that in turn has been legally constituted*
> *(Habermas, 1996, p 110).*

Democratic legitimacy therefore rests on the claim that political deliberation and law-making is rational, and that this decision-making can be justified as recognizing all citizens as free and equal members of their political community. When related to the whole range of government activities, the belief of citizens becomes that public authorities will justly represent and consider all relevant interests. The formal political realization of the discourse principle, with reference to environmental problems, directs attention to the institutional environmental capacity of nation-states (Chapter 2) as well as regional experiments in institutional participatory practice (such as the one described in Chapter 3): how can public forms of communicative practice be encouraged? What are the criteria for judging the fairness of these? Furthermore, democratic legitimacy fans out wider still to institutions in the private sector. The social and environmental impact of capital investment decisions means that corporate governance needs to face meaningful democratic accountability. Applied to private economic choices, democratic legitimacy refers to the expectation on the part of citizens that capital investment does not, at the very least, undermine public environmental interests and minimally acceptable standards of social justice.

The Explanatory Role of the Discourse Principle

Attention to the notion of discourse in the academic literature on environmental politics has recently led to some innovative work on particular policy areas, notably Litfin (1994) on stratospheric ozone depletion and Hajer (1995) on acid rain, as well as more encompassing overviews of environmental discourses (Dryzek, 1997). These studies have cogently demonstrated the wide-ranging, often subtle, ways in which ecological politics involve competing discursive types. Their *explanatory* formulations of discourse – Hajer (1995, p 44) speaks of 'a specific ensemble of ideas, concepts and categorizations that are produced, reproduced and transformed in a particular set of practices and through which meaning is given to the physical and social realities' and Dryzek (1997, p 8) of a 'shared way of apprehending the world' – dwell on the ways in which the linguistic framing of environmental problems has wide-ranging practical consequences. Any comprehensive analysis of environmental discourses must cover both their communicative *functions* (of expression, interaction and representation) and their *formats*. It has been a significant contribution of discourse analysis in the social sciences that the significance of the latter is more fully acknowledged: to study discursive forms, as evident in the research on environmental politics, is to map out the narrative construction of environmental story lines, the role of emblematic motifs, the employment of metaphors and other rhetorical devices, and so on. Discursive forms are rich and complex.

In line with the discourse principle, the explanatory emphasis in this study is on the communicative role of environmental norms – particularly, for the reasons set out above, on moral norms. It means looking at actual political and policy examples of environmental communication. Discourses have a socially integrative force, actively shaping the constitution of political *actors*, *interests* and *institutions*. Each of these will be briefly taken in turn, referring above all to claims about their legitimacy or rightness.

Firstly, discourses mark out political agents or subjects, drawing on, and imputing, a variety of motives for action. Hajer (1995, pp 52–58) represents environmental politics as an argumentative struggle in which actors are configured in relational terms, politically constrained and enabled in unequal ways. These 'subject-positions' link personal goals and aspirations with wider political contests: they are reproduced through discourse. In practical discourses environmental norms either confirm or question those social rules and conventions that position actors in the field of ecological politics. Environmental philosophical debates interrogate the very conditions for moral and political agency – whether we can attach moral competence to nonhuman entities, whether a right to a safe environment is a valid claim even when restricted to humans, and so on. For questions of environmental democracy, the explanatory focus here is more on how environmental norms contribute to understanding ourselves as subjects of democratic citizenship.

Ranging over different geographical scales, this study examines the normative mix influencing the collective subject-positions of wilderness preservationists, organized labour and urban communities. How do they identify and justify themselves in the terms of environmental democracy? How compatible are green and democratic sources of political orientation? Politics, in this sense, is the power to craft group allegiances against competing sources of collective identity. The democratic legitimacy of ecological activism lies partly in demonstrating how regard for the social and environmental interests of others, including those not yet born, enlarges our understanding as self-governing subjects with responsibilities beyond conventional political boundaries. For environmentalism, it is both an opportunity and challenge thrown up by the fluid social and cultural bonds of late modern society that political identities are more open ended (Giddens, 1991; Berking, 1996).

Secondly, and linked to the creation of political subject-positions, discourses shape motives for political action, including actors' perceptions of social and environmental needs. In other words, discourses fashion political interests. Environmental interests, as other-regarding or public interests, pose a theoretical problem for those social scientists who seek to explain political action in terms of self-interest motivation. The rational choice tradition (see Weale, 1992, pp 38–46) argues that those ecological organizations classifiable as public interest groups must rely on selective benefits for their members in order to encourage political mobilization, otherwise there would be no incentives for individuals to contribute to environmental public goods (since others can always 'free-ride' on the environmental improvements they achieve). In contrast, appreciating the role of the discourse principle in motivating collective political action highlights the role of nonpurposive incentives – normative motivations – in environmental activism. This is more than incorporating additional motives for action: communicative political action collectively defines the context of interaction, creating new political spaces – for example, demonstrations and community visioning – through argumentation over environmental interests. Practical discourse featuring environmental norms redefines the nature of the political: what should be subject to collectively binding decisions.

Of course, ecological science has played an important part in constituting environmental interests, but this book's explanatory concern with environmental politics rests less on the content of that knowledge than its differential uptake and use by competing social groups. Giddens (1984, pp 342–343) pointedly shows how the possibility of discursively articulating interests is asymmetrically distributed in society. Those in the lower echelons, he claims, often face limitations – in terms of inferior educational opportunities, their more local milieux of action and their lack of access to relevant information – upon their capabilities to formulate, let alone pursue, their interests. And, to connect with environmental values, this may prevent them from influencing the long-term goals articulated by environmentalists (who, in advanced capitalist countries, are predominantly middle class), impeding their efforts to connect their interests to the political conditions for realizing environmental interests.

A last explanatory role for the discourse principle fixes onto this relationship between institutionally established relations of power and political argumentation. In the political field, more visibly than other areas of social action, linguistic relations reflect and reproduce dynamic relations of power. The sociologist Pierre Bourdieu (1990, pp 123–139) has developed the ideas of 'symbolic power' and 'symbolic violence' to explain how institutions endow certain communicative acts with authority, maintaining particular forms of domination. Objective power relations thereby tend to reproduce themselves as symbolic interactions. The concentration of political power in the state, with its 'monopoly of legitimate symbolic violence' (1990, p 136), permeates the official discourses of state representatives through authoritative classifications and names, hierarchies of rank, administrative prescriptions and so forth. Symbolic power presents as self-evident that which is historical, including liberal democracy itself. The practical import of oppositional environmental discourses depends upon the extent to which they convince social actors not only to question environmentally and socially destructive consequences accompanying 'legitimate' institutional practices, but also to push for these political (and economic) institutions to open up to environmental interests. In spite of the seeming proliferation of communication on environmental problems, it is still commonplace for there to be nondecision-making about the possibility for addressing these democratically (Crenson, 1971, pp 85, 117).

The discourse principle has emerged from an intellectual domain targeted on uncovering the rational characteristics of human interaction. Disciplines such as philosophy, linguistics, cognitive and moral psychology, and discourse analysis are, in this area, united by an academic interest in explaining the background intuitive knowledge used in everyday linguistic action. Habermas (1990, pp 31–42) terms this academic field 'reconstructive science' in recognition of the common goal of making explicit that which is taken for granted by communicative subjects, and includes his own theory of communicative action (1984, 1987) as a sociological attempt to account for the general and necessary conditions for validating communicative claims. While his democratic theory starts off from the premise that positive law and democratic constitutions embody the normative self-understanding expressed by the discourse principle, however imperfect its realization in liberal political institutions and practices, this discourse principle is logically related to the communicative presuppositions claimed for ordinary language use. What needs to be borne in mind, though, is that like any academic thesis, Habermas's claims pertaining to the universal structure of language use are open to falsification by work in the reconstructive sciences. Nevertheless, even if his philosophy of language is not sustained, the discourse principle may still be offered as a model for democratic legitimacy (Bohman, 1990).

This book's concern is not a detailed linguistic exposition of particular environmental discourses, analysing the linguistic rules operating within them. Rather, it is to account for various institutional and noninstitutional tendencies towards environmental democracy. The intellectual and research interest is in the discourse principle at the level of environmental policy and politics. Since this principle directs us to examine the social effects of its *existing* democratic influence, through prevailing norms of equal treatment, it therefore becomes a methodological technique for looking at the quality of democratic communication on environmental issues, whether applied to state structures and initiatives (Chapters 2 and 3), environmental preservationists (Chapter 4), organized labour (Chapter 5), or local communities (Chapter 6). This is where an explanatory interest in the actual reach of deliberative forms of communication meets up with a normative perspective in building discursive democracy. The discourse principle examines examples of ecological argumentation according to democratic criteria of responsiveness and fairness.

CASING THE DISCOURSE PRINCIPLE:
THE STRUCTURE OF THE STUDY

The theoretically informed empirical work that constitutes the bulk of this book reflects my professional background as a human geographer: this entails a sensitivity to regional or local context and, in my case, an intellectual preoccupation with the politico-ecological aspects of society–land relations. The case studies detailed in Chapters 3 to 6 reflect personal research over the past couple of years – a biographical thread governed by a motive to explore notable and innovative examples of participatory environmentalism. In 'casing' these examples (Ragin, 1992, p 217) – that is, in delimiting them as objects for practical research – I have followed a distinctive methodological strategy. Most obviously, the examples represent institutionalized systems of interaction and/or environmental discourses with internal claims to environmental democracy. They offer themselves, in their different ways, as either champions or models for a more ecologically rational and democratic society. As cases, they were therefore chosen as promising candidates aspiring towards the practical embodiment of environmental norms compatible with the discourse principle of equal respect for all. In each case, the coherence and consistency of these democratic claims are examined.

While the discourse principle is thus a common theoretical strand, allowing a deductive selection of case studies, they nevertheless represent differentiated subject matter according to their formal institutional status. If the survey of secondary literature in the second chapter is included, the book runs from nation states (Chapter 2) and a regional planning body (Chapter 3) to a variety of more autonomous political entities – interest groups (Chapter 4), a union (Chapter 5) and, at the more diffuse end of political action, community voluntarism (Chapter 6). The chapters also range across different (but inter-related) geographical scales – local (Chapter 6), regional (Chapters 3 and 4), national (Chapter 5) and cross-national (Chapter 2), while the international implications of environmental discourse are discussed in the book's conclusion. This organizational and geographical diversity of methodological choices is deliberate: it is designed to explore the range of application for the idea of environmental democracy. However, it should also be clear from each chapter that the intellectual focus is consistently on environmental institutional designs and/or ecological argumentation with reference to participatory democratic norms. A short summary of each will hopefully aid the reader in appreciating that fact, although I have also attempted to write the chapters so that they may be read in a self-contained manner.

Chapter 1 details a theoretical conceptualization of environmental democracy compatible with the normative benchmark of the discourse principle. It begins with a discussion of democracy and environmentalism as political categories, highlighting the naturalistic self-understanding of environmentalism. A more sociological perspective on environmental degradation and ecological politics precedes a critical review of models of green democracy presented by both reformist and radical environmentalists. Following this survey, four general characteristics of environmental democracy are defined: an orientation to long-term generalizable interests; communicative political structures and practices; ecologically rational decision-making; and the radicalization of existing liberal rights. These signpost the necessary communicative and institutional conditions that must be met by any polity committed to realizing the discourse principle.

Equipped with this conceptual understanding, the second chapter presents a preliminary survey of environmental decision-making in Western Europe and North America in order to identify institutional tendencies sympathetic to the idea of environmental democracy. The chapter begins with some general comments on the resonance of liberal democratic polities to communication on ecological values and interests. Of three theoretical perspectives discussed, one is employed, the structuralist approach, to elaborate empirically upon several political-institutional conditions for environmental decision-making: participative capacity, integrative capacity, strategic capacity, and the role of noninstitutional political action. This is then linked to an influential economic-technological development path deemed consistent with environmental quality improvements: ecological modernization. The structuralist perspective claims that environmental decision-making is both more effective and democratically legitimate when the state facilitates the development of the above framework conditions. And it holds up the European neocorporatist states as successful policy innovators in these terms. That position is critically reviewed, concluding with comments on why there is still some way to go before we can speak of environmental democracy for the advanced capitalist states.

Chapter 3 continues the thematic focus on institutional conditions for environmental democracy, but relates the interest in administrative openness and participatory decision-making to a regional experiment in environmental negotiation in British Columbia, Canada. The Commission on Resources and Environment (1992–1996) was an ambitious attempt to facilitate democratic deliberation on environmental interests, with a view to resolving protracted ecological conflict over land-use allocation and management. Of particular interest here was the commission's articulation of the idea of administrative fairness, suggesting independent normative criteria for evaluating the democratic legitimacy of environmental decision-making. The chapter examines the understanding of environmental administration developed by the commission and how it had to adapt to prevailing political and policy constraints. It also scrutinizes the performance of the commission itself according to its own procedural criteria of fairness.

In Chapter 4, for the same area of the world, the discourse principle is applied to the preservationist arguments of environmental activists. By critically interpreting the 'political morality' of wilderness preservationists – that is, the key normative principles motivating their political actions –

the focus is on their reasoning. This requires, firstly, an elaboration of the moral philosophical status of the discourse principle, and then its employment to question the ethical rationale underlying the twin strands of the preservationist political platform – increased protection of natural areas and the democratization of land-use decision-making. My claim is that, as expressed through the naturalistic presumptions of deep ecology and bioregionalism, this dual agenda lacks political coherence and democratic legitimacy. However, the critique is a constructive one: at the end of the chapter, a moral justification of wilderness preservation, compatible with the discursive nature of environmental democracy, is offered instead.

Pulling organized labour into the political compass of environmental democracy might appear provocative to those familiar with the common representation of unions as indifferent to ecological concerns. Nonetheless, with reference to the Transport and General Workers' Union in Britain, Chapter 5 describes a union that lays claim to a decentralized democratic structure and a wide-ranging environmental commitment across its recruitment, bargaining and campaigning agendas. A critical examination of the union's attempts to link environmental concerns with health-and-safety regulations in the workplace and its ecological campaigning supports the characterization of organized labour in this case as a key actor for environmental democracy. In order for this to apply to organized labour in Britain and elsewhere, the chapter suggests four strategic political options available to unions to realize the radical democratic demands implied by the discourse principle.

In Chapter 6, turning to the local political realm in Britain, a series of participatory forms that have been at the centre of recent experiments in democratic governance are examined. A foremost catalyst for innovation here has been the remarkable uptake in the country of Local Agenda 21 consultation processes. The chapter outlines something of the political context of structural reforms in British local government before engaging with Local Agenda 21 initiatives – nationally and, above all, in London. Extended reference is made to the development of environmental democratic forms in the London borough of Islington, notably neighbourhood democracy structures, the borough's Local Agenda 21 consultation process, and community-led regeneration planning. Islington has been associated with developments in participatory decision-making sympathetic to the principle of subsidiarity, but at the limit of existing local authority powers. After reviewing these community-based methods of determining social and ecological interests, their implications are considered in light of the mix of representative and participatory political structures. They have raised expectations of democratic accountability and fairness, challenging the national government to make good its commitment to renew local democracy; and in a way that goes beyond community voluntarism to the local devolution of power.

The book's conclusion offers some general comments on the preceding chapters before outlining the global scope for environmental democracy.

This entails, firstly, a brief examination of the development of international environmental agreements, highlighting one perspective within regime theory to investigate the relevance of democratic norms. The increasing participation of nongovernmental actors in global environmental governance, associated with an emerging global civil society, enables me to locate a parallel thesis to the one provided in Chapter 1 on the democratic interplay between state institutions and nongovernmental political action. The environmental rights approach adopted in this book faces particular challenges at the international level from state sovereignty and market sovereignty. Both are addressed before illustrating one suggestive pathway to developing transnational liability for environmental harm (which returns to the Myanmar example). Finally, the book finishes by outlining the opportunities for, and constraints to, the development of global environmental citizenship.

The overarching theoretical claim governing this work is that mutual understanding, whether taken for granted in everyday communicative interaction or reflectively developed as discourse, is a basic ordering medium of social life. Communicative underpinning of social existence also presumes relations of symmetry and reciprocity that give us an intuitive handle on what democracy as civic self-determination means. The discourse principle articulates this philosophically through the idea of moral self-determination, but its social currency can only be gauged by examining particular institutional designs or examples of ecological argumentation. This book's main methodological aim is to look at several empirical instances where environmental understanding is structured or articulated in communicative terms; and to contextualize, with these cases, the operation of the discourse principle in practice. Unlike recent relativistic currents in the social sciences, this does not imply abandoning the project of uncovering any generalizable features of social life. As Thomas Schatski (1996, p 18) notes:

> *Underlying and thus connecting all the particulars populating the social world is a web of understanding and intelligibility that establishes meanings and possibilities and thereby institutes agents while coordinating them with their milieus.*

That interpretive web, as theorized by Habermas, shows how understanding communicative claims implies evaluating the shared reasons animating them.

This communicative circle also encompasses the social scientist trying to make sense of social practice. Anthony Giddens (1984, p 348), among others, has demonstrated how the social sciences are inevitably involved in a 'subject–subject' relation, where the question of interpreting meaning is already taking place before the researcher intervenes as another party. The researcher starts off from the understanding of the participants involved in any given situation before proceeding to the unacknowledged

circumstances and unintended consequences of action. I take this interpretive character of research as given, which means that the book's 'case
studies' represent the results of qualitative research concerned with
investigating existing forms of political communication favouring the norms
of environmental democracy. As such, they are not necessarily representative or replicated elsewhere, although the egalitarian promise of the
discourse principle is prefigured in everyday communication. The dialogue
between geographical context and generalization that this implies is as
relevant to environmental policy as it is to scientific research (Trudgill and
Richards, 1997). What the social scientist brings to this situation are objective
but falsifiable claims to the validity that primary research findings are
faithful to relevant factual evidence and theoretical understanding. In the
dialectic of theory and practice evident in this work, I offer my own
investigations for empirical corroboration and critical examination, as well
as my own moral judgements for practical discussion.

1 CONCEPTUALIZING ENVIRONMENTAL DEMOCRACY

DEMOCRACY AND ENVIRONMENTALISM

Let us begin with a minimal but widely accepted definition of democracy – as a political system in which the opportunity to participate in decisions is widely shared among all adult citizens (Dahl, 1991, p 6). The more significant and comprehensive these opportunities are, the greater the level of democracy attached to a political system: political theorists discuss, in these terms, the 'widening' or 'deepening' of democratic decision-making. Ultimately, this extension of the democratic principle can lead to the questioning of the 'political' category itself and its insulation from social choices determined by a market economy. However, within prevailing conceptions of *liberal* democracy, this division between the polity and the economy is firmly defended: liberalism, after all, supports the rights of individuals and property holders *against* the state. The characteristic concern is thus with the political decision-making of representatives elected by a form of majority voting among the population. Representative liberal democracy describes the overwhelming majority of political systems in the world today, in which the central institutions of governance claim to provide equitable opportunities for citizens to shape the exercise of power, and where that influence is facilitated by a plurality of competing parties. Representative democracy is also the modern form of democracy, expressed firstly in the late 18th century founding statements of the American and French republics, where it emerged as the moral justification for the lawful authority of the state over large populations (Pitkin, 1967, pp 196–208).

The contrast is thus set up with the classical idea of direct democracy associated, of course, with the power (*kratos*) of the people (*demos*) in ancient Greece. Here in the *poleis*, there is no corresponding division between ruling and being ruled, in the way modern elected representatives govern a citizen body (Arendt, 1958, pp 32–33). Citizen assemblies and committees exercising power, making laws and implementing policies preceded the creation of a separate state apparatus, although the restriction of citizenship to a privileged minority – excluding, in the well-known example of the Athenian *polis*, women, slaves and those of non-Athenian origin – obviously runs counter to our inclusive notions of democratic self-determination. As will be noted in the next section, this has not prevented some radical green philosophers from appealing to the participatory ethos attributed to Athenian citizenship as a model virtue for direct democracy, and also from extolling the smallness of scale implied by face-to-face deliberations.

The distinction between representative and direct democracy highlights a central dilemma of modern governance: the functional need for effective political decision-making – achieved in increasingly complex societies through representative, often remote, structures – threatens to undermine the accepted conditions for democratic justification: that affected interests have had a fair opportunity to influence the relevant decisions, giving them good reasons to support democratic norms. John Dunn expresses this paradox bluntly: 'We have all become democrats in theory at just that stage in history at which it has become impossible for us in practice to organize our social life in a democratic fashion any longer' (1993, p 29).

In the first place, democracy announces that a state has good intentions, a tried and tested crowd pleaser in the marketplace of political ideas. Furthermore, such is the elasticity of the concept – short of blatant violations of universal suffrage, effective party competition and rights of free speech – the claim of a state to being democratic immediately suggests that it is responsive to the needs of its citizens. According to Fukuyama's (1992) popular 'end of history' thesis, there are no alternatives left anyway: the world historical triumph of representative forms of liberal democracy represents the exhaustion or moral bankruptcy of other political ideologies. As Dunn observes, though, there is actually very little indication of meaningful civic self-determination within liberal democracies. The alarming levels of social and economic inequality in individual democracies and across the world seem to make a mockery of notions of political equality; the global reach of capitalist economic processes weakens the sovereignty of nation states; and even these states themselves, with their complex, alienating bureaucratic forms, offer little for the individual to identify with, let alone support (1993, pp 13–23). The lack of opportunities for individuals to influence the decisions affecting their interests is reflected in the consistently high levels of political apathy recorded across the liberal democracies. And then, of course, there is the 'ecological crisis'.

The narrative here is well worn but sadly remains relevant. In the list of problems attesting to the continuing deterioration of ecological conditions of life, particular issues jostle for attention and those that come to prominence reflect cultural presuppositions and shifting social priorities. However, the collective evidence for human-induced environmental degradation seems overwhelming – stratospheric ozone depletion, global warming, acidified lakes, species depletion and extinction, deforestation and soil degradation (Goudie, 1997; Middleton, 1995). To map out the full historical geography of environmental degradation in the second half of the 20th century is to record the consequences of an ever-expanding extractive demand on nonrenewable and renewable resources, coupled with an increasing output of toxic substances, many of which – heavy metals, synthetic insecticides, chloroflurocarbons (CFCs), dioxins, radioactive waste, etc – are alien to the normal functioning of ecological cycles.

To be sure, the high levels of complexity and uncertainty characterizing these environmental risks render incomplete our current understanding of biological systems. Within the discipline of ecology some observers have recently noted a conceptual reorientation in keeping with a necessary scientific humility. This 'ecology of chaos' identifies fields of study that claim there is no determinate direction governing such ecological processes as succession, speciation and biomass productivity. Sophisticated computer modelling has allowed the ability to observe nature as an expression of chaotic dynamics, overturning classical ideas of ecological equilibrium and order (Pahl-Wostl, 1995; Botkin, 1990). It is perhaps more accurate to claim that, as for most of this century, ecology remains torn between different conceptions of biology (McIntosh, 1985, pp 21–27) – notably the contrast between the mechanistic nature of population ecology, informed by the individualistic notions of neo-Darwinian evolutionary theory, and the more purposeful homeostatic nature of systems ecology, including, on the disciplinary margins of the latter, the global Gaia hypothesis of James Lovelock and Lynn Margulis (Bowler, 1992, pp 535–546).

These divisions within ecology alert us to the fact that even in the academic arena, where we might expect consensus on the objective assessments of ecological problems, there remain debates and disagreements. Not surprisingly, there are also divergent metaphors of nature – nature as fractal geometry, as resource stock, as organism, and so on. In the mirror of nature, what we see reflects the society we live in and the values we live by. The relevance here is that ecology has had a remarkable cultural resonance through the seepage of its naturalistic concepts into the public self-understanding of ecological problems; but this popular impact has not included an appreciation of the discipline's self-doubts and institutional reflections. The end result is the dominance of a 'value-free' naturalistic framework in the public discussion of environmental problems that has actually prevented, until very recently, a serious investigation of their social and political nature. This applies, ironically, to the major political movement responsible for popularizing the message for ecological responsibility – environmentalism.

At its broadest, environmentalism refers to the diverse set of philosophies and practices informing a concern with protecting (natural and human) environmental quality. Lynton Caldwell has succinctly characterized the ethical challenge presented by the environmental movement (1990, p 86):

> *The movement is life centred, distinguished by a sense of moral imperative regarding human behaviour in relation to other life forms within the biosphere. . . Environmentalist values are species oriented and transgenerational, emphasizing personal and social responsibility.*

The birth of modern environmentalism is conventionally related to the ten years following 1962, between the publication of *Silent Spring* – the clarion call on pesticides poisoning from Rachel Carson (1962) – and the 1972 Stockholm Conference on the Human Environment, which led to the founding of the United Nations Environment Programme (UNEP) (McCormick, 1989, pp 88–105). In that formative decade several catalysts warrant historical attention, such as the countercultural backlash against materialist values, the influence of other social movements (notably the peace movement), and a sensitivity in the popular media to anxieties about resource scarcity and environmental pollution (McCormick, 1989, pp 47–68). Commentators attach different weight to the immediate causes, yet there is a shared recognition that the environmental movement is a truly global phenomenon, cutting across social, political and religious divides. There is also a common acknowledgment that, for all the organizational variety of the environmental movement, environmentalism represents a challenge – whether reformist or radical – to the Promethean belief that current patterns of economic growth can motor on regardless of their accumulating social and ecological costs.

The key ideological distinction within environmentalism relates to the valuation of nonhuman nature. Tim O'Riordan (1981, 1989b) remains the most helpful guide to the complex and competing strands of thought making up the two modern worldviews of environmentalism – techno-centrism and ecocentrism. The division is ideal-typical because individuals may well favour elements from both modes according to the institutional setting, the nature of the issue, and the socio-economic context (O'Riordan, 1981, p 2). Moreover, the two ideological themes both have autonomous and inter-related dynamics of conceptual change warranting detailed historico-geographical exposition (Pepper, 1996, provides an excellent over-view). It is sufficient here to outline their broadest characteristics.

The reformist worldview, *technocentrism*, recognizes the challenge posed by environmental degradation but, on account of its technological optimism regarding the problem-solving ability of modern society and the rationing efficiency of market-based social choice, addresses ecological problems through managerial means. Chapter 2 discusses an influential contempo-rary manifestation of technocentrism – ecological modernization – which is associated with policy shifts to anticipatory environmental management. Within technocentrism, O'Riordan differentiates a confident 'interventionist' credo from a more cautious 'accommodative' strain: the contrast also lies in the willingness of proponents of the latter to entertain proposals for institutional reform to incorporate environmental interests.

However, while such proposals may endorse increased democratic accountability in political decision-making, there is no appetite for recasting existing structures of political and economic power (O'Riordan, 1989b, pp 85–89). Overall, the efficiency-oriented agenda of technocentrism leaves unexamined prevailing notions of the good life in advanced capitalist societies. By accepting the dominant instrumentalist metaphor of nonhuman nature as a storehouse of resources, technocentric environmentalism is more concerned with means than with ends. In this worldview, environmental problems belong to the domain of professional expertise; given their prominence in high managerial or executive positions, this strata of environmentalists – for all their participatory rhetoric – are determined to maintain their technical authority when negotiating environmental risks. The political problem is that accommodative moves to open up environmental decision-making are inadequate to keep in touch with the global scale of many current environmental problems and insufficient to satisfy the persistent demands for public empowerment coming from the ecocentric heart of the environmental movement.

Ecocentrism rejects the political reformism of technocentric environmentalism, outlining instead a range of radical demands for redistributing power. These projects all share a 'nurturing' or 'nature-regarding' view of society-nature relationships, and are profoundly sceptical of large-scale technology, corporate commitments to environmental management and existing systems of professional expertise (O'Riordan, 1989b, pp 82–86). Their underlying philosophy of nature is informed by an ecological model of internal relatedness in which the dividing lines between the human and the nonhuman are dissolved: humankind is embedded in biophysical relationships and, like any other species, subject to ecological laws (Eckersley, 1992, pp 49–55). This results in two defining features of ecocentrism – a practical concern with limits to material and demographic growth coupled with ethical concerns about the nonhuman world (Dobson, 1990, p 205). The latter encompasses a variety of 'natural attributes-based' value theories (Goodin, 1992, pp 24–25). and Chapter 3 discusses the challenging ethical ideas of deep ecology and bioregionalism. More generally, ecocentrism can be subdivided into a left-inclined communalism and a more conservative Gaianism: both tend to favour decentralized political structures and economically self-contained communities; however, anarchist and socialist influences on communalism have given it a participatory democratic flavour. As is often the case at the radical end of an ideological spectrum, there are numerous nuances of deep green thinking and no lack of agitated disagreements – something that applies, as we shall shortly see, to their competing notions of green democracy.

In his overview of environmentalist ideologies, O'Riordan identifies 'a picture of contradictions and tensions dominated by a failure to agree over cause, symptom, and action' (1989b, p 93). This accounts for the imaginative dynamism of the environmental movement. Nevertheless, both technocentric and ecocentric strains, informed by ecological concepts, share a naturalistic understanding of environmental problems. Both presume that the environmental risks generated by modern life are 'external' threats to our well-being, while the impacts of our productive and consumptive processes render vulnerable a realm of independent, nonhuman nature. This is not to deny that there are competing representations of natural science at stake. The international policy currency of technocentric environmentalism has established the modelling of human environmental impacts as a leading research priority – for example, through the scientific working groups of the Intergovernmental Panel on Climate Change (IPCC). These attempts to make sense of environmental degradation reflect a managerial confidence in the predictive capacity of natural science, but leave unexamined crucial links between the generation of environmental knowledge and social structures of scientific authority and credibility (Wynne, 1994). From ecocentric environmentalism, the Gaia hypothesis – that life on Earth provides a cybernetic, homeostatic feedback system – would seem to present a more radical challenge to the observations, models and methodologies of environmental science (Schneider and Boston, 1991); but for all its interdisciplinary ambitions, scientific discussion of the Gaia concept has yet to include any significant sociological input.

Why should this 'loss of social thinking' (Beck, 1992, p 25) concern us? An immediate reason is that it misconstrues even the natural scientific understanding of environmental problems. The development of environmental knowledge, like science generally, has not cumulatively converged on a permanent or fixed truth, but been forged in volatile conditions of historical change and intellectual struggle (Kuhn, 1970). The fact that scientific change is shaped by institutional allegiances, and wider social and economic power relations, is to recognize the underdetermination of any theory by empirical data. Science may be instrumentally progressive, increasing the practical possibilities of predicating and controlling natural processes through technological applications; but the scientific statements rendered truthful through such technical utilization are always relative to limited data and local phenomena (Hesse, 1980, p xi). Joseph Rouse claims that our laboratory-oriented natural scientific methods have actually encouraged, in their application, the damaging simplification of natural environmental processes, as is evident from the 'Green Revolution' in agriculture (1987, pp 322–323). Others push this claim further still to consider the ways in which scientific knowledge of environmental problems naturalizes and reinforces particular cultural and moral values or identities (Wynne, 1994, p 186); they even construe natural science as no more than a story-telling practice governed by a particular aesthetic realism and ethic of progress (Haraway, 1989, pp 4–5).

It is not necessary to agree with the more relativistic perspectives in order to accept a general *political* point here – that the conventional natural scientific understanding of environmental problems displaces a necessary role for democratic negotiation over claims to the truth of scientific knowledge, making explicit underlying social interests and moral norms (Wynne, 1994, p 188). This is a self-evident objection to technocentric environmentalism, perhaps; but ecocentric notions fall prey to the same criticism. The preoccupation of ecocentric environmentalism with 'objective' ecological limits to growth erases the practical character of natural scientific practices. By accepting that the determination of ecological interests in the case of 'limits' is a technical project, ecocentrism undermines its participatory democratic claims elsewhere. The more that environmental interests are defined as objective, the less reason there is to enable people to determine these according to collective debate and decision-making: the task is for expert policy prescriptions as guided by our political representatives (in line with the liberal democratic tradition of civic passivity). If, on the other hand, we accept that natural science has shaped the world we live in and the terms in which we might come to understand ourselves (Rouse, 1987, p 265), environmental knowledge becomes no different from any other social space where the norms of democratic participation are applicable.

The absence of social thinking in conventional environmentalist under-standing is all the more remarkable given that environmentalism is, above all, a social movement. Indeed, with its emphasis on post-material values and personal lifestyle choices, environmentalism shares similarities with other so-called 'new social movements' – for example, feminism and the peace movement – that have emerged in advanced capitalist countries since the 1960s. Placed in contrast to older forms of protest groupings, such as organized labour, new social movements lack formal organization and ideological unity, expressing diffuse concerns with quality of life, human rights, individual self-realization and participatory democracy (Habermas, 1987, pp 392–396; Dalton and Kuelcher, 1990). In this academic literature, environmentalism is conceptualized in terms of value change, notably with reference to Ronald Inglehart's (1977) identification of a 'silent revolution' – a long-term shift to post-material values among the Western public, especially in the younger and more educated groups of the new middle classes. Cotgrove and Duff (1981) have further narrowed the highest environmental value propensity to public welfare and educational occupational categories. From this focus on changing values comes the cultural character-ization of environmentalism, articulating aesthetic and ethical issues tradi-tionally excluded from mainstream political debate, and doing so through noninstitutional means of political action – typically unconventional means of collective protest – which are themselves often expressions of lifestyle choices: for example, the 1990s anti-roads protests in Britain.

Influenced by Inglehart's value change thesis, the major source of social thinking on environmental politics has come from professional sociology. In order to make intellectual sense of environmentalism, social theorists have recast ideas about modern forms of social life (Goldblatt, 1996). The most suggestive attempts have conceptualized environmentalism, along-side other social movements, as symptoms of, and reactions to, far-reaching cultural and institutional change in the late 20th century. At the risk of oversimplification, I shall state several overlapping theses on the modern origins of environmentalism offered by three European thinkers: Ulrich Beck, Anthony Giddens and Jürgen Habermas.

Firstly, there is the common acknowledgment by all three that environ-mentalism is partly a resistance to an unbalanced pattern of political and economic modernization – one felt most fully in advanced capitalist societies. This refers to the development and invasive reach into everyday lives of an economic system predicated on ever-increasing material growth and commodification, coupled with representative systems of political decision-making bereft of democratic responsiveness. Habermas employs the term 'lifeworld colonization' (1987, pp 318–331) to describe the way in which both capitalist economic imperatives and invasive norms of political governance push us to adopt, in a seemingly uncontrolled manner, instrumental attitudes to each other and to nonhuman nature. Environmentalism, most clearly in its ecocentric form, represents a backlash against reducing natural values to consumptive preferences and, as Beck emphasizes, against the undemocratic way in which decisions on environmental quality are ceded to the technical calculations of policy experts (Beck, 1995, pp 158–184). There is, above all, the charge that the prevailing instrumental attitude to nature violates our widely held moral-aesthetic valuations of the natural environment rooted in lived experience and cultural traditions. Environmentalism has responded to economic and technical intervention within our lives in a largely defensive manner, mapping out the 'ecological dangers' and railing against industrial technologies; however, to understand this in a naturalistic manner is to downplay the social origins of environmental problems (Giddens, 1994, pp 206–207; Habermas, 1987, pp 393–394). It also, therefore, underestimates the importance of political and economic democratization in addressing these problems.

Secondly, the socio-cultural exploration of ecological politics by these theorists results in a particular interpretation of the political interests at stake in environmentalism. For Habermas, the lifeworld colonization thesis points to the reduction of individual freedom because the moral and practical elements of politics – rights, responsibilities and duties – are squeezed out of collective decision-making or, in the case of environmental choices, often not even recognized as relevant. The popular discontentment expressed by ecological activists invites a 'withdrawal of legitimation' from the state, where large sections of the public regard as invalid its policy justifications (Habermas, 1987, pp 140–148), particularly if environmentalists draw together single issue concerns into more far-reaching criticisms of political authority. Beck argues that the need for democratic legitimation of decisions is strengthened as political responsibility is taken by governments for dealing with environmental problems; however, this may paradoxically let polluting industries off the hook by removing from scrutiny their culpability for ecological degradation (1992, pp 212–215). There is, then, the odd coupling of political responsibility for environmental problems and the 'organized irresponsibility' of industry (Beck, 1995, pp 63–69) – a division compatible with the liberal separation of the polity from the economy, with democratic governance only applying to the former. For Beck the naturalistic understanding of environmental problems evident in the ecological movement fails to give us the conceptual tools to attribute responsibility for environmental degradation to *particular* social interests (as opposed to 'humanity' in general).

Both Habermas and Beck acknowledge an intellectual debt to Inglehart's theory of post-materialist change in accounting for environmental interests, while the notion of 'life politics' formulated by Giddens, anticipating 'post-scarcity' circumstances in which economic criteria no longer delimit our political interests (1990, p 165), is not dissimilar. We may still be subject to capitalist economic relations, but for all three theorists material motives have lost their saliency as markers of political identification. This is, of course, neither to deny the environmentalist concern with our planetary survival as a species, nor to lessen self-regarding health or economic motivations behind the mobilization of ecological concern. Rather, environmentalist discourse, as Goldblatt suggests, has 'led to a redefinition of self-interest and a narrowing of distance between self-interests and the common interest due to the shared necessity for ecological survival and environmental quality' (1996, p 144). So material interests are entwined with concerns about the environmental consequences of our lifestyles – existential questions about how we should live and our responsibilities to nature (Giddens, 1991, pp 209–231). Giddens and Beck are sensitive to the close relationship between our instrumental attitudes to nonhuman nature and the way in which technology redefines our very notions of subjectivity. Human or 'inner' nature is as much a site of social conflict and political choice as 'outer' nature, now that reproductive technologies and human genetics have abolished the option of not making decisions about the natural foundations of human life (Giddens, 1994, pp 212–219; Beck, 1995, pp 17–35).

For Beck, Giddens and Habermas, whatever their theoretical differences, modern environmental degradation reveals a series of social relationships. A third common thesis, therefore, is that environmentalism is not simply a response to 'natural dangers' because nature is now thoroughly socialized. Modern industrial processes, informed by scientific knowledge and technology, have rendered all parts of the planet subject to human involvement and control (whether direct or indirect). Most modes of living now take place in 'created environments' or 'ecosocial systems' where our environment of action is no longer external to social organization (Giddens, 1990, p 60; 1994, p 210). Beck quips that even nature is no longer nature, but 'rather a concept, norm, memory, utopia, counterimage' (1995, p 38). Along with Giddens, he is strongest on the particular role ecological and high-technological dangers play as part of a distinctive risk profile characterizing modern social life. High-consequence environmental risks pose a novel set of hazards: reaching out across the globe, they present the possibility, however much talked down by establishment scientists, of irreversible, incalculable consequences – for example, nuclear accidents, mass biological extinction and chemical warfare/terrorism. And they are politically legitimated or 'excused' as unintended consequences, thus displaying responsibility for their effects onto society as a whole (Beck, 1992, pp 19–50; Giddens, 1990, pp 124–134). Such is the omnipresence of these risks that Beck labels contemporary social life as a 'risk society': environmentalism is understood as an example of a wider reflexive modernization, where modern society becomes aware of, and preoccupied with, contesting and managing risk (1992, pp 6–8). As Giddens also emphasizes, the nature of modernity is deeply bound up with our trust in systems of professional knowledge to address risk (1990, pp 79–100). Environmentalism reflects a dissatisfaction with managing risk that requires either an ecologically revised application of expertise (technocentrism) or a rejection of orthodox scientific and bureaucratic authority (ecocentrism).

Fourthly, all three social theorists have offered a participatory supplement to reigning liberal ideas of democracy. The scope of democratic influence, they argue, must expand to keep up with, and infiltrate, those complex and interdependent sources of collective choice affecting our interests – the areas of corporate decision-making, state power (including the internal and external use of force) and administrative control. All three understand democratic will-formation in terms of noncoercive political communication rather than the formal mechanisms of majority rule. In other words, democracy relates to fair procedures for inclusive decision-making which promote relationships of mutual tolerance (Giddens, 1994, p 115) or, more ambitiously, mutual understanding (Habermas, 1996, pp 298–302). Beck is most explicit on the ecological turn that democracy must take, exploring the scope for democratizing 'techno-economic' development, including the very definition and burdens of proof attached to environmental risks (1992, pp 228–231; 1995, pp 178–183). There are other significant differences of emphasis: both Beck and Habermas emphasize the necessary role of basic political rights in facilitating equal participation in democratic decision-making, while Giddens is more preoccupied with the freedoms necessary to allow individuals to develop their own identities. Nevertheless, their overlapping normative arguments are characterized by a bold commitment to universal norms and values: a position which this author has much sympathy with. Indeed, the idea of environmental democracy developed later in this chapter owes an intellectual debt to the strongest universalist of the three.

The work of these theorists has thus alerted us to the need for political and social thinking on environmental degradation and ecological politics. Environmentalism is ill-served by an ecological naturalism that deflects attention from the social organization – and competing cultural understandings – of nonhuman nature and, therefore, also away from illuminating the asymmetrical structures of political and economic power that undermine both democracy and environmental quality. Other social theorists have pushed this interpretive claim further still, offering a more thoroughgoing social constructivist reading of environmentalism and nature (for example, Eder, 1996; Macnaghten and Urry, 1998). In these analyses, the unavoidable symbolic mediation of nature through social practices licenses the ungracious dethroning of ecology as the lead discipline in understanding environmental degradation: the theoretical discourse of environmental science is neither value neutral nor politically innocent. As Kate Soper has argued (1995, pp 155–160), 'nature' is called upon to play multiple, often conflicting, roles in ecological discussion, including nature as the nonhuman (the meta-physical concept), nature as causal physical processes (the realist concept), and nature as the nonurban (the lay concept). However, these various meanings, she maintains, should not prevent us from recognizing extra-discursive reality: 'it is not language that has a hole in the ozone layer' (1995, p 151). We need to navigate carefully between the Charybdis of naturalism and the Syclla of culturalism as we turn to survey briefly the political varieties of 'green' democracy.

GREEN DEMOCRACIES?

Environmentalism, in all its organizational and ideological diversity, has presented a number of challenges to existing models of democratic politics. Along with the other new social movements (today, not so new), ecological activists have redrawn political boundaries – questioning accepted values and interests, developing noninstitutional forms of political action, and deepening ideas of democratic self-government. The particular contribution of environmentalism has been in making political space for nonhuman nature and the interests of future generations. Of course, the ecocentric end of the environmental movement, as ecologism, claims to represent a sepa-rate political ideology – one that strongly questions the limited, state-centred forms of civic self-determination under liberal democracy. This cuts to the individualistic, human-centred heart of liberalism and its contention that the state has no role in constituting and defending common environmental interests or in prescribing some type of ecological good life. It is instructive to note, though, that in the flurry of recent academic debate on the relation-ship between ecological problem-solving and democracy (notably, Doherty and de Geus, 1996; Lafferty and Meadowcroft, 1996), key ecocentric propo-nents of 'green political theory' have been less concerned with alternatives to liberal representative structures than ways of modifying them according to new environmental constituencies (for example, Eckersley, 1995; Dobson, 1996).

There is no simple correspondence between environmental politics and democracy: what can be asserted is that both the technocentric and ecocentric strands of environmentalism maintain a commitment to democratic strate-gies for political and social transformation (whether defined in radical or reformist terms). This commitment does not always sit comfortably with a passionate advocacy of ecologically informed social choices – an apparent tension between democratic means and green ends that reveals less an inherent contradiction than the need for a more politically rounded concept-ualization of environmentalism. The theoretical definition of environmental democracy that is sketched in the next section at least explicitly recognizes democratic political processes and values in environmental choices. Before that, however, a brief survey is warranted on the key environmentalist positions regarding democracy. The following classification shares the taxonomic rationale of Pepper (1993, pp 45–58) in interrogating environmentalist ideas with a more or less conventional typology of political ideologies. While this sometimes blurs the technocentric-ecocentric division, it assists in the politicization of environmentalism.

Conservatism

According to Anna Bramwell (1989), the first mature, albeit small-scale, expression of ecologism as a political ideology took place in Britain and Germany in the 1930s. Biological, economic and literary ecologism converged in a proselytizing manifesto for ecological awareness and rural regeneration. To Bramwell, this creed was intrinsically conservative: she labels the English version 'High Tory' to capture its atavistic mixture of anti-industrialism and nationalism, combined with an organic defence of traditional social hierarchies (1989, pp 104–105). British ecologism was much influenced by the parallel German 'blood and soil' movement, sharing ideas about soil conservation, organic farming and racial health. That these ecological themes were picked up by the Nazis (and more recently by European neofascist groups) is beyond doubt, although Bramwell disputes the existence of generic fascist ecologists, noting that most European variants had a future-oriented, urban and technological focus (1989, p 173). The conservative influence on interwar ecologism is more consistent and, rather than the fascist disdain for democracy, is associated with an elitist understanding of democratic decision-making.

Pepper (1996, p 48) notes the compatibility of traditional conservatism with conservation and (landowner) stewardship. Deference to a natural order, to the perceived continuity and stability in ecological systems, offers a direct analogy for society: social change should be organic, respecting the overarching goal of stability. Political authority derives from the 'natural' superiority of established institutions, proven by their longevity and their embeddedness in traditional ways of life – hence the continuing conservative emphasis on identification with, and allegiance to, all existing forms of authority. This casts a restrictive net over democracy. Conservatives traditionally adhere to Burkean notions of political representation, where a government thrives on the wisdom of the rulers rather than popular will-formation. Democratic representatives take care of the wishes of their constituents by exercising the appropriate political wisdom and judgement (Pitkin, 1967, pp 168–189). Democratic responsiveness to public concerns may be perceived as a weakness, in that it invites an active citizenry rather than the body of passive subjects deemed conducive to political stability. The conservative idea of democracy as elite representation, by leaving authority unexamined and denying the historicity of social structures, always threatens to empty the democratic idea of all effective meaning. Historically, the conservative practice of opposing attempts to extend democracy attests to powerful anti-democratic instincts.

Given the democratic strategies favoured by modern environmentalism, conservative political notions have had little ideological impact. Yet there are conservative strains to be found, most obviously linked at the ecocentric end to some high-profile paternalistic thinkers. Perhaps the most well known are the economist Garrett Hardin (1993), through his survivalist prescriptions on resource management and population control, and the long-standing editor of *The Ecologist*, Edward Goldsmith. From the *Blueprint for Survival* (*The Ecologist*, 1972) to the most recent formulation of his ecological worldview (Goldsmith, 1992), Goldsmith has displayed affinities with earlier 'High Tory' ecologism, notably on the role of traditional social hierarchies and cultural rituals in inculcating ecologically responsible attitudes. For Goldsmith, the 'vernacular society', in order to respect Gaian processes, must be governed by small-scale settlements, economic self-sufficiency and a ritualized use of technology (1992, pp 287–331). Inspired by pre-industrial tribal models, the political upshot is a distaste for current examples of democracy, compromised as they are by destructive concentrations of political and economic power: the vernacular alternative, following anthropologist Pierre Clastres, offers a 'society against the state' (Goldsmith, 1992, pp 336–338). The obligation on 'man' to follow *the* way claims political legitimacy based on religious wisdom rather than civic self-determination, and therefore finds no resonance with the post-traditional self-understanding of modern democracy.

Ecological appeals to restoring traditional values and decentralization find favour with the cultural agenda of *neoconservatism*, which shares a critique of the 'desanctifying' effects of modern economic and political institutions (Giddens, 1994, pp 30–33; Paehlke, 1989, pp 217–242). Indeed, Giddens claims that, despite its elitist political morality, the conservative values of protection, conservation and solidarity have a very real relevance for any radical political programme attuned to the ecological crisis. In an era of intensifying globalization and cultural uncertainty, the conservative scepticism about modern ideas of progress strikes a chord with those concerned with maintaining acceptable conditions of life (Giddens, 1994, pp 27–37, 41–50). What this glosses over, of course, is the consistent conservative indifference to the social costs of environmental degradation on the poorest in society – whether domestically or overseas – and the glaring inadequacy of an organicist worldview for progressive political thinking. One reason why the recovery of social thinking is crucial to environmentalism is that the democratic ideas of free will and autonomy can only sensibly be predicated on a cultural understanding of human nature: 'Civil rights are much more difficult to defend in a discourse that purports to explain human nature in biological terms' (Lewis, 1992, p 39). It is no coincidence that the established conservative hostility to the notion of positive political rights exists alongside a sense of the 'natural' place of traditional social hierarchies and vernacular landscapes.

Neoliberalism

While neoconservatism preaches caution in the face of economic globalization and rapid social change, neoliberalism boldly embraces the forces of modernization. Above all, neoliberalism announces a return to the 19th-century free market thinking of neoclassical economics, applying these ideas indiscriminately to political decision-making. This means that the purported allocative and productive efficiency of economic markets, achieved through the free play of the price mechanism, secures the conditions of individual freedom; the freedom to buy and sell, encouraged by material incentives, allows people to carve out their own life paths according to their own interests. Through the 'invisible hand' of the market, the aggregation of these individual preferences maximizes social welfare, and all the state needs to do is guarantee internal and external security, protecting private property rights. In its political philosophy, neoliberalism combines two classical sources – the liberal constitutionalism of John Locke and the radical individualism of Thomas Hobbes (Dunn, 1993, pp 38–44), resulting in a picture of the individual as the cause of all actions and the subject of rights against the state ('negative' freedoms). Not surprisingly, this philosophy has historically been conditioned by, and also been functional to, the evolution of capitalist markets (Shapiro, 1986, p 302). Neoliberalism is the theoretical apologia for those who profit most handsomely from current capitalist economic processes.

Updated to engage with ecological problems, the neoliberal approach finds fault only with the state. The economic theory of democracy associated with the so-called public choice school maintains that self-interest predominates in all forms of political or administrative decision-making – voters follow their pocket-books, politicians try to maximize their votes, and bureaucrats are only interested in maximizing their budgets (Lewin, 1991). Ecological problems, insofar as they are conceded to exist (and many neoliberal writings are preoccupied with denying their magnitude or gravity; see, for example, Ridley, 1995), are the result, it is claimed, of illegitimate state interference in the market – state ownership of environmental resources, command-and-control regulatory instruments, environmentally destructive state subsidies and so on (Block, 1990). Environmental policy bureaucrats come in for particular criticism for supposedly masking their selfish careerist ambitions behind a 'public service' commitment to environmental quality (Stroup and Baden, 1983). Only when private property rights are more thoroughly established in the environmental resource realm, according to the neoliberals, will truly democratic decision-making about environmental quality be possible – a democracy with the state firmly pegged back. Environmental liberty means business as usual, except now the market, responding to consumer preferences for increased environmental quality, meets that demand through 'green' goods and services (Elkington and Burke, 1987). The stress on market innovation and technological ingenuity in meeting environmental challenges makes this philosophy attractive to the optimistic technocentric end of the environmental movement; but the true political home of neoliberal environmental thinking is wise-use environmentalism.

Wise-use environmentalism proclaims itself in a variety of, ostensibly, community-based coalitions for protecting private property resource interests, taking in such diverse groupings as the US Wise-Use Movement, the Canadian Share Group network and the UK Countryside Alliance. The US Wise-Use Movement served as the organizational template for these political mobilizations *against* mainstream environmental interest groups (in the UK example, against anti-hunting and countryside access groups) when, in the late 1980s, it united a wide-ranging constituency of organizations opposed to environmental regulations and wilderness preservation in the US, notably in the extensive tracts of federal land in the west and Alaska (Dowie, 1995, pp 93–98; Gottlieb, 1989). Although employing a populist rhetoric of community democracy, the US Wise-Use Movement is mostly funded by resource extraction corporations. Similarly, in western Canada, the Share Group movement, which sprang up as opposition from forest resource-sector-dependent communities to wilderness preservation groups, has been financially supported by mining and logging companies; the more recent UK Countryside Alliance, defending the 'rural communities' of Britain, has attracted significant funding from gun manufacturers and the fieldsports industry. There are, of course, different issues at stake within the three alliances, mediated through contrasting political cultures; but it is possible to observe a common championing of private property claims against the state. The American property rights or 'takings' backlash, facilitated by the Wise-Use Movement, has forced federal agencies to review the impact of environmental regulations on private property and seriously disabled much environmental legislation (for example, on wetlands protection). In western Canada, forest and mining companies have pushed for the privatization of Crown environmental resources; and in Britain, the Country Landowners Association has vehemently resisted proposals for a public right to roam in the countryside.

Wise-use environmentalism, for all its populist community rhetoric, is behoven to a neoliberal understanding of democracy: that is, the political system as instrumental to the smooth functioning of the capitalist economy, limiting its representatives to protecting private property rights and market structures. For the state to presume to know more than the market about the environmental quality preferences of individuals, expressed through billions of daily transactions, is merely one more example of 'the fatal conceit of socialism' (Hayek, 1988). However, this truncated notion of democracy runs up against three major objections.

Firstly, its anthropological assumption that egocentric behaviour dominates political decision-making is not borne out by *empirical* research, at least in Western democracies, where public interest motivations seem to be of greater importance (Lewin, 1991, pp 98–112). Environmentalism, in particular, is hardly a movement preoccupied with material self-interest. Related to this, as will be noted next for welfare liberalism, the provision of environmental public goods (such as clean air and water, and biodiversity) is characterized by pervasive market failure – the inability of the price system to impart collective ecological benefits. Secondly, the neoliberal political philosophy soon becomes entangled in its own *conceptual contradictions*, not only through the tension evident in its defence of traditional identities (family, community, nation) at the same time as it champions those market forces undermining these forms of social integration (Giddens, 1994, p 9), but also through its disingenuous critique of the state. The wise-use attack on the state for encroaching on individual property rights is not matched by a willingness to relinquish public subsidies to private property owners, whether for natural resource extraction in North America or agricultural subsidies in Britain (and the rest of the European Union). Consideration of such inconsistencies soon uncovers the sectional interests behind the bogus universalism of 'our communities'. Lastly, there is the *moral defeatism* of a democratic theory that removes any understanding of politics as collective discussions over shared environmental norms; a defeatism that erases, also, the democratic ideal that we have political choices, and that we can improve the quality of life for those in greatest need.

Welfare Liberalism

Welfare liberalism recognizes that, left to its own devices, capitalist enterprise cannot guarantee the range of public goods necessary for a flourishing society. In welfare economics, public goods refer to those collective social and environmental benefits commonly provided, or protected, by public institutions. Businesses have no incentive in delivering these because their collective nature resists attempts at rationing use through price. Environmental economics concentrates on questions around the monetary valuation of environmental values and the internalization of negative environmental externalities. With its typical technocentric prescriptions for market-based environmental policy instruments (green taxes, tradeable pollution permits, cost-benefit analysis), the subdiscipline has found a receptive audience in North American and European governments seeking policy solutions for ecological problems. Since the Brundtland Report (World Commission on Environment and Development, 1987) and the United Nations Conference on Environment and Development in Rio de Janeiro in 1992, the idea of sustainable development has provoked environmental economists into considering the *distribution* of environmental goods. Sustainable development implies positive socio-economic change geared to meeting the needs of present generations, particularly those least well off (intragenerational equity), while at the same time ensuring that we pass on the ecological and economic means to future generations to meet their needs (intergenerational equity) (Pearce, 1992).

There are two influential economic interpretations of sustainable development (see Turner, 1995). The first defines sustainability as nondeclining natural capital stock (the set of all ecological assets) over time. This 'strong' notion of sustainability, based on the understanding that there are limits to which economic production processes can replace natural assets with human capital, claims that reductions in aggregate natural capital represent an unacceptable loss in sources of well-being for present and future generations. It implies community-led political planning and binding policy measures for safeguarding irreplaceable ecological assets (O'Riordan, 1996), although its practical impact has so far been negligible. The 'weak' sustainability approach assumes that much of the ecological contribution to human welfare can be substituted by physical or human capital (with the exception of such nonsubstitutable natural capital as stratospheric ozone protection and biodiversity), so that conditions for sustainability are satisfied as long as losses of the former are compensated by losses of the latter. For example, the loss in future welfare represented by a semi-natural habitat bulldozed to construct a road may be compensated by the future economic value flowing as a result of this development. Weak sustainability chimes more harmoniously with orthodox liberal welfare notions of development-led progress tempered by compensatory transfer payments. In the environmental policy area, it has so far been the dominant sustainability discourse, giving rise to a variety of institutional experiments across the world for integrating environmental interests within sectoral decision-making, though even here the wider political impact has remained minimal.

Without entering the economic debates about sustainability, we can note that both approaches assume that meaningful monetary values can be placed on disparate ecological entities, gauging these through consumer preferences rather than the collective discussion of public preferences (Jacobs, 1996c, p 63). However, strong sustainability at least suggests the potential for a more participatory political structure of needs-determination – the freedom and capability of communities to meet well-being requirements. Furthermore, both these economic interpretations of sustainability endorse sustainable development as a concept of intra- and intergenerational justice, accepting the ethical position that 'if future generations are to be left the means to secure equal or rising per capita welfare, the means to maintain and improve the well-being of today's poor must also be provided (Turner, 1995, p 7). Wouter Achterberg (1993; 1996a; 1996b) has shown how this conception of justice is compatible with the contemporary liberal political philosophy. Building on John Rawls's (1987) liberal conception of political justice, which accepts that moral and cultural diversity is an inescapable feature of modern democracies – but nevertheless states that shared democratic values (liberty, equality, fairness) provide the common ground for an 'overlapping consensus' in support of liberal democracy – Achterberg views sustainability as a principle fundamental to the long-term durability and legitimacy of liberal democracy (1993, pp 91–99). Furthermore, in order to achieve sustainability, he argues for an institutional supplement to liberal representative political structures – *associative democracy*.

The associative democratic recommendation, drawing on the work of Hirst (1994) and Cohen and Rogers (1995), refers to a revived civil society of self-governing voluntary groups and communicative networks which extend the scope for political self-determination – including, of course, areas of environmental regulation and coordination. For Achterberg, unless this sort of civic renewal takes place, the constituency of support for sustainability will not be strong enough. Taking intragenerational and intergenerational justice seriously will require the social acceptance of substantial resource redistribution, and democratic agreement to such transfers is more probable if mutual identification between citizens is strengthened and there is a greater awareness of social continuity with future generations (1996a, pp 172–173; 1996b, pp 173–179). Bronislaw Szerszynski (1997, pp 151–154) makes a similar argument in noting how voluntary associations evince more civic trust and other-regarding behaviour among their participants than that typically induced by the state. Both these political expressions of welfare liberalism investigate the democratic conditions for realizing the sustainability principle developed in environmental economics – although, in their siding with strong sustainability, they recover an older liberal scepticism about economic progress. Their institutional imagination and communitarian sensitivity also lead to an appreciation of individuals in their social and cultural context. Szerszynski explicitly addresses the role of associations in displacing more consumerist forms of motivation, in advanced capitalist societies, by promoting mutuality in the social and psychological shaping of human needs (1997, pp 156–158).

The associative agenda of Achterberg and Szerszynski usefully directs our attention to the role of civil society in environmental governance, and this will be discussed in the conceptualization of environmental democracy, albeit from a more radical participatory perspective. The difference with welfare liberalism lies, firstly, in a more realistic appraisal of the political weight of existing corporate interests, which unravels the pluralist assumptions of the associative democratic model. With its emphasis on maximizing the range and number of voluntary associations, the associative perspective entails a laissez-faire attitude to political representation seemingly oblivious to the structural asymmetries in the public sphere which favour capital (for example, corporate media ownership and property law). Secondly, whatever the potential gains in the democratic communication of needs, this group differentiation in itself is unlikely to capture the full set of environmental interests that must inform programmes for sustainability (for instance, who will promote the vital photosynthetic services of phytoplankton?). As will be argued, environmental democracy must acknowledge the critical, irreplaceable role of formal political institutions (and environmental planning) in making collectively binding decisions, however much these are shaped by changing environmental attitudes and values in civil society – in other words, the ecological role of the state (Chapter 2). This conception of the democratic process, in stressing the interplay between political institutions and voluntary associations, carries stronger *critical* connotations than the liberal perspective.

Ecocentrism

Ecocentrics are ambivalent about liberal democracy. On the one hand, they are impatient with the openness of a majoritarian decision rule that offers no guarantee of green outcomes. The procedural neutrality of liberal democratic institutions leaves it to the citizens to decide which notion of the good life to subscribe to; and in the thick of political bargaining processes, long-term public concerns with environmental protection are deemed to fare badly against short-term material interests. On the other hand, liberal democracy has facilitated the political mobilization of ecological concern, while green political forms – from protest groups to green parties – rely on the maintenance of basic liberal freedoms (Eckersley, 1995, pp 169–172; 1996, pp 212–214). Robyn Eckersley labels this the 'democratic paradox' facing the green movement: any practical attempt to move towards a stronger and more ecologically informed democratic alternative to liberal democracy must begin by utilizing existing liberal democratic institutions and regulative ideals (1996, p 213).

Formulations of ecocentric democracy reflect this dilemma, but have tended to converge on recommendations for more participatory decision-making structures, typically focusing on small-scale communities. They also commonly stress a *remoralization* of democracy, where ecocentric values provide a means for democratic institutions to prioritize environmental protection. The philosophical reliance is on an ethical position that confers intrinsic or inherent value on nonhuman lifeforms, although articulated in a variety of ways – from holistic notions of 'ecosystem integrity' (Westra, 1994) to individualistic expressions of environmental value (Taylor, 1986). Holistic ethical positions, particularly influential in deep ecology, create the furthest distance from the liberal democratic emphasis on individuals. For some ecocentric thinkers, the imperative of ecological survival cannot therefore avoid 'checks' on current forms of majoritarian rule (Westra, 1993), while others argue that nonindividualistic forms of ecological identity are compatible with a continued stress on existing liberal freedoms (Matthews, 1995, pp 94–95). Chapter 4, in relation to deep ecological and bioregionalist appeals for wilderness preservation, explores the tensions that exist between ecocentric ethical claims and the norms of participatory democracy. There is an obligation on deep ecologists to make clear the relationship between their environmental values and their democratic self-understanding: this connects to the communicative political philosophy embraced in this book, where advances in participatory democracy depend upon a commitment to openness and rational justification.

For Goodin (1992) and Saward (1993) the clash between ecological values and democratic norms is a contradiction at the heart of ecologism.

Goodin identifies democratic participation as the central principle for green political action – in the sense of increasing civic self-determination over all areas of social life – and contrasts this with the ecocentric theory of environmental value. The moral basis of the latter, he claims, leads to a principled all-or-nothing commitment to ecocentric political outcomes that must, ultimately, claim priority over the means of political transformation (1992, pp 120–123). One consequence of this, according to Goodin, is a discounting of traditional political action in liberal democracies (electoral campaigning, lobbying, making deals), although this does not square with, to take an obvious counterexample, the growing political realism of European Green parties (O'Neill, 1997). Nevertheless, the democratic paradox remains: there is no guarantee that democratic procedures will yield ecocentric outcomes. For Saward (1993, p 77), the political priority accorded to green imperatives by ecocentric value theory results in an *instrumental* rather than a principled attachment to democracy – one, therefore, that leaves open the possibility of authoritarian prescriptions. Only if ecocentric environmentalists abandon their dependence upon naturalness as the lexical source of value can they, he contends, offer a stronger democratic justification for green political action.

According to Goodin and Saward there is, at best, a contingent relationship between core ecocentric values and democracy. Ecocentric thinkers have responded directly to this claim by arguing that there are grounds for connecting green values and democracy at the level of principle. Two of the more interesting proposals have come from Eckersley (1995, 1996) and Mills (1996), which involve, respectively, radicalizing existing liberal democratic notions of autonomy and political representation. Eckersley maintains an ecocentric ethical premise – respect for the intrinsic value of all lifeforms – by extending the idea of autonomy to 'the freedom of human and non-human beings to unfold in their own ways' in a manner that accords a moral priority to the bodily and ecological needs that enable this freedom to be exercised (1995, pp 179–180; 1996, p 223). She then argues that the liberal rights discourse could likewise be enlarged to include not only environmental citizenship rights for humans but also rights to moral consideration of selected nonhuman populations and species (1995, pp 181–193; 1996, pp 228–233).

While accepting the same contention that democratic will-formation should include consideration of the rights and interests of the nonhuman world, Mills dwells on the reforms to democratic procedures needed to achieve this. These include widening rules of legal standing, opening up political opportunity structures and changing the nature of political representation; for example, he suggests the creation of multimember constituencies in which some of the representatives would be expected to represent the interests of nonhuman constituency members. In this way, Mills claims, the democratic process would as a matter of principle incorporate the interests of nonhuman nature and future generations (1996, pp 107–112).

The above proposals develop ideas of ecocentric democracy in a provocative but suggestive fashion. There are, of course, considerable, perhaps intractable, conceptual problems when liberal norms and values are stretched to these limits; questions include the boundaries for ascribing moral concern, the administration of appropriate principles of harm and equity, and the paternalistic way in which humans would have to determine the interests of ecological entities. Moreover, it is surprising that few of the formulations of ecocentric democracy have elaborated upon transformations required of collective decision-making rules (Rolston, 1988, pp 246–289, is an engaging exception). This is certainly not for the lack of innovative organizational forms and policy suggestions within the environmental movement itself. My philosophical reservations about ecocentric democratic claims, as expressed in Chapter 4, side with humanistic critiques of naturalistic ethics (for example, Soper, 1995); but the idea of environmental democracy outlined in the next section by no means ignores the political value of ecocentrism in questioning existing democratic parameters.

Social Ecology

Aside from bioregionalism (see Chapter 4), recent anarchist thinking within radical environmentalism has been dominated by social ecology and associated, above all, with the work of Murray Bookchin. Social ecology posits a holistic understanding of ecological systems and evolutionary processes to account for humanity's relationship with the natural world. In short, the 'dialectical' development of humanity in nature reveals a tendency to ever-increasing complexity and diversity which provides the ecological *logic* for universal political values (Bookchin, 1990). From an appreciation of unity in diversity, spontaneity and mutualistic relationships comes the vision of an ecological society in harmony with natural processes. The ecological crisis, according to Bookchin, results from a way of life that actively frustrates the evolutionary tendency to self-determination or *freedom*. In his classic work *The Ecology of Freedom* (1982), Bookchin explores the historical roots of the social hierarchies that account for relations of domination between humans and, in turn, human attempts to dominate 'external' nature. While the technical forces and institutional forms developed by capitalism have brought the social domination of nature to an unprecedented level, accelerating environmental degradation at an alarming rate, Bookchin insists that practical liberation must focus upon social hierarchy as much as class exploitation. Domination according to age, gender, race and physical qualities can all be traced back to pre-capitalist forms of hierarchy. According to social ecologists, the ecological crisis is rooted in these relationships of social domination, so any emancipatory project must therefore abolish all concentrations of political and economic power. Ecological renewal implies the creation of human-scale communities founded on nondomination and ecotechnologies that respect environmental diversity and complexity.

For social ecologists the most appropriate political form for their eco-anarchist vision is direct democracy. The inspiration here is the classical

Athenian *polis* with its active notion of citizenship and the principle that sovereignty is exercised directly by the (free) citizens (Fotopoulos, 1997, pp 184–194). Bookchin (1995, p 6) thus rejects the liberal representative model in favour of political self-management, in line with the ecological principle of self-determination:

> *Democracy generically defined . . . is the direct management of society in face-to-face assemblies – in which* policy *is formulated by the resident citizenry and* administration *is executed by mandated and delegated councils.*

Takis Fotopoulos (1997), who develops most fully the social ecological understanding of political self-management, stresses democracy as a process of 'social self-institution' which requires an equal sharing of political and economic power. Following Bookchin, he argues that this is only possible at the community level: the principles of confederal municipalism therefore prioritize local economic self-reliance, municipal ownership of productive resources, and democratic allocation of goods and services (Fotopoulos, 1997, pp 224–274). These are the material conditions that enable municipal assemblies – and, on a regional scale, confederal councils – effectively to determine their collective choices. Democratic authority resides at the level of face-to-face assemblies which mandate delegates, on a rotating basis, to express their preferences directly, avoiding the need for independent political representatives: indeed, the participation of all citizens, building up levels of civic consciousness, removes the rationale for separate political or administrative expertise. True to anarchist intentions, the creation of such community-based decision-making is ultimately directed at replacing the state completely through establishing popular local bases of political and economic power (for example, neighbourhood assemblies, local currencies and tax systems, workplace assemblies: Fotopoulos, 1997, pp 282–301). The projected vehicle to achieve this is a mass popular movement, drawing in current green and social justice groupings, and combining radical political demands with a revolutionary cultural commitment to nonhierarchy.

The bold utopian strokes making up the social ecological conception of democracy claim justification in the evolutionary potential for differentiation and mutuality. Human responsibility to the environment, claims Bookchin, reflects the 'thrust toward reflexivity' (1990, p 216) embodied in nature, even if the capacity for conceptual thought and moral empathy is unique to our species. This means that moral norms, including democratic ones, have an 'objective' ethical basis in evolutionary processes (1990, pp 206–210). Without entering the debates in environmental philosophy about whether or not social ecology supports an ecocentric value theory, I reject the claim that political norms are prefigured in nature in such a way. The validity of moral norms depends upon mutual recognition rather than translating objective ecological properties. To argue otherwise, to justify a political form on its ecological 'authenticity' in an age when we have become used to the fallibilism of scientific knowledge (including ecological theories), is to become a hostage to the fortunes of evolutionary thought. And recent evolutionary science has been amassing support for the claim that there is *no* purposive direction in long-term environmental change (see Dennett, 1995).

Of more immediate practical relevance is the fact that the moral conviction behind the social ecological support for direct democracy leads to the total, indeed arrogant, rejection of all other democratic forms (liberal, social democrat or socialist) as 'statist'. Since the state is considered by social ecologists to be hierarchical and oppressive by definition, the whole range of proposals for democratizing the state are dismissed (Pepper, 1996, p 322). We might add that this includes a rejection of the notion of human rights because these rights only make sense, it is claimed, against the state (Fotopoulos, 1997, p 232), thereby stripping us of a critical emancipatory resource. Moreover, as Eckersley convincingly argues (1992, pp 173–178), democratically accountable states are, on account of their regulatory and legal reach, better placed than anarchist governmental forms to negotiate international environmental agreements, promote integrated and international redistributive justice, and protect fundamental human rights and freedoms. This is not to deny, of course, the need ecologically to restructure the state, but to recognize the necessary role of democratically organized administrative power in translating collective interests into binding decisions.

Ecosocialism

The total opposition to the state registered by social ecologists is rejected by ecosocialists who argue that an ecologically sane society will require formal political institutions. Indeed, Frankel (1987, p 263) warns that, in contrast to the social ecological vision of harmonious face-to-face community assemblies, participatory democracy would not survive the abolition of state institutions, since the democratic empowerment of citizens must be supported by a framework of legal, cultural, educational and administrative structures. Ecosocialist discourse on the state reflects democratic socialist expectations that, as political and bureaucratic institutions are unavoidable in modern, functionally differentiated societies, the practical imperative becomes their *democratization* (Pepper, 1993, pp 215–217). There remains in ecosocialism the classic socialist ambivalence about a state that, on the one hand, represents so firmly the interests of capital but, on the other, has historically, as a result of working class struggle, established social citizenship rights and systems of social welfare. This contradictory character, for ecosocialists, of the *capitalist* state diverges from the orthodox Marxist view that it is purely an instrument of class domination, destined to wither away with the transition to communism. An appreciation of the extra-local reach of social and ecological problems has led ecosocialists to a more sophisticated political conceptualization of the state, including the role of democratic decision-making.

Frankel's proposals for a semi-autarkic society, combining both representative and direct democratic structures, restricts the functions of centralized planning to the minimum necessary to coordinate social choices at the national and international level in order to secure a fair distribution of social income, raw materials and capital goods. At regional and local levels, democratic decentralized planning steers employment choices and self-organized workers' cooperatives, alongside an autonomous market-based sector of individual and family producers. The focus of democratic control is on natural resource allocation and income maintenance, with ongoing public deliberation to determine the exact reach of strategic planning (Frankel, 1987, pp 252–260). For Frankel, the ecological virtue of a semi-autarky strategy arises from the short- and long-term objective of maximizing self-sufficiency. This means a scaling down of production processes combined with a qualitative shift to socially useful production for democratically determined needs.

In their ecological interrogation of productive activities, the ecosocialists mark their greatest distance from the socialist 'productivism', with its uncritical faith in economic growth and technological progress. Recent ecosocialist debate has dwelt, in this way, upon an ecological resurrection of Marxism, running against the grain of its instrumental approach to external nature. For example, Benton (1989) and James O'Connor (1997) have supplemented the classic Marxist formulation that capitalism is subject to internal crises of overproduction with the argument that the expansive dynamic of capital accumulation also leads to an 'ecological crisis tendency'. The structural contradiction here is between the social organization of production and its ecological preconditions. This contradiction is accentuated by prevailing forms of economic valuation, which allow corporate interests to offload external environmental costs onto society as a way of lowering their own costs of production, thereby degrading public environmental goods. To be sure, other ecosocialist writers, such as Grundmann (1991) and Harvey (1996), have criticized these revisions as conceding too much to the 'natural limits' discourse of environmentalism, losing some sense of how these are constituted by prevailing social relationships or how the human domination of nature actually *allows* the possibility of collective control over human affairs.

Whatever the difference, the common thread feeding into ecosocialism more generally is the contention that capitalist institutions – governed by the profit imperative, technological dynamism and mass production and consumption – provide the main structural causes of environmental degradation in the modern world. Furthermore, this has shaped the nature of democratic politics in capitalist societies; offering or promising levels of material affluence that, until the arrival of the Greens, meant opposition to economic growth was absent from party political discourse, and placing substantial constraints on the scope for environmental regulation of private investment.

Ecosocialists have acknowledged the important political role of radical environmentalism in questioning the ecologically destructive growth of advanced capitalism, but remain uncomfortable with what they perceive as ecocentrism's preoccupation with opposing industrialism and high technology per se, rather than the capitalist organization of production. Yet this common socialist objection, while certainly valid for the resource scarcity debates of the 1970s, finds less correspondence with contemporary green positions where there tends to be an acceptance of the negative ecological and social consequences of capital accumulation processes (for example, Eckersley, 1992, p 121). It also ignores the consistent support given by ecocentric political projects to worker cooperatives, even if the institutional arrangements advanced have begged elaboration (Carter, 1996). Green interest in democratic self-management in the workplace has recently widened into a creative embrace of community-based production and exchange networks, drawing upon a wide range of existing experiments in informal economic allocation, such as local currencies and barter-based schemes (Douthwaite, 1996). While ecosocialists have applauded these micro-scale initiatives in alternative production, and also expressed support for the green idea of a universal basic income decoupled from a market-based valuation of labour, they are viewed as insufficient to secure democratic economic governance. That requires, they claim, an international social movement challenging capitalist relations of production. At this point, the ecosocialist insistence that organized labour remains a key catalyst for progressive social and ecological change attracts very little sympathy from mainstream Western environmentalists who, sometimes with justification, see unions as wedded to a productivist worldview. However, Chapter 5 provides evidence from a UK case study to argue that organized labour can indeed play a crucial part in the movement for achieving environmental democracy.

The global hegemony of the capitalist labour contract and the accelerating commodification of nature – now invading, through biotechnology, the genetic structures of life itself – means that the need for cooperation between the labour movement and environmentalism is even more pressing. Ecosocialists rightly stress that the everyday living and working conditions of most people are environmental issues. Since half of the world's population now lives in urban areas, those issues include inner city decay, poverty and unemployment, vehicle pollution and accidents, street and domestic violence, access to social services, and local democracy (Pepper, 1993, p 234). The challenge to unions, as outlined in Chapter 5, is to appreciate the relevance of wider 'social wage' concerns to their members, and to realize that historical gains in money wages and working conditions are threatened by new employment patterns and quality of life issues. Feminist arguments about the traditional burden loaded onto women for maintaining basic conditions of human existence are central here. Capitalist production processes are as parasitic on the 'free' contribution of nonpaid domestic labour to workforce reproduction as they are on the socialization of environmental costs. 'In societies throughout the world it is women who fight to sustain

some semblance of family and community life when all else has failed'
(Mellor, 1992, p 251). The responsibilities disproportionately assumed by
women for meeting the basic needs of their families become, by societal
default, an issue for environmental politics.

To regain a socially just control of needs-determination from this 'imposed
altruism' on women requires us to make democratic inroads into the economic sovereignty of corporate capital, which continues to dictate exploit-
ative production choices and to stoke up nonsustainable consumption
patterns. The notion of environmental democracy that is now introduced
acknowledges the influence of ecosocialist conceptions of justice that *radicalize* liberal democratic ideals. Pushing notions of equitable participation into
the realm of production decisions breaks the liberal taboo that this arena is
exempt from the democratic principle. When related both to the ecological
conditions and consequences of these production decisions, it also affords
us a critical tool to expose the social, spatial and temporal inequalities
governing the use of environmental resources and services throughout the
world (Martinez-Alier, 1995).

ENVIRONMENTAL DEMOCRACY

Never has a democratic principle been more disregarded, claims political
theorist Noberto Bobbio (1987, p 29), than that of political representation.
The political promise of modern democracy, as representative democracy,
was that those elected to serve the people would be free to take part in
rational parliamentary deliberation unimpeded by sectional interests. They
would not, therefore, be subject to any binding mandate predetermining
their choice in political decision-making. Bobbio judges the prohibition of
a binding mandate as one of the historic agreements at the French Constituent Assembly that informed the 1791 constitution. Since that time, freedom
from a binding mandate has featured in all the constitutions of representative democracy, in principle protecting them from a substitution for, or
integration with, a mechanical representation of interests. Yet the liberal
ideal of a sovereign people composed of free individuals has been comprehensively refuted by historical practice, no more so than in the modern
liberal democracies in which party-dominated politics and government
reflect more a constellation of organized sectional groupings and sharply
asymmetrical power relationships. In the political arena of competing
groups, where is the basis, Bobbio asks, for distinguishing the public interest
from sectional interests? And, we should add, where does this leave the
political determination of general environmental interests traditionally
ignored by liberal political systems?

To be sure, Bobbio's distaste for current structures of political representation should not be read as the classic conservative argument for precluding
democratic responsiveness to the electorate between elections. His claim,

after all, is that the progressive development of democratization increases the number of spaces where citizens can exercise their right to participate in decisions concerning them (1987, p 32) – a perspective that, for environmental interests, excludes no area of decision-making incurring significant ecological or social consequences. Above all, this means, to follow Bobbio's more general line, that the process of democracy cannot be considered complete until the advanced capitalist societies' two great power blocs from above – capitalist enterprises and the administrative apparatus – are breached by democratization (1987, p 33).

Given the widespread public acceptance that environmental quality (or, at the very least, ecological life support) represents an area where corporate and administrative decision-making frequently generates impacts that negatively affect our interests, the temptation is to ignore Bobbio's fears about the absence of open-ended decision-making. Surely preserving healthy ecological systems is the clearest candidate for a binding mandate that should apply to all those with relevant decision-making power? However, if we wish to avoid ecoauthoritarian prescriptions, the problem here is more the incomplete representation of environmental interests, allied with the lack of environmental accountability of current state-centred political systems. How do we take into account the new environmental constituencies – nonnationals adversely affected by the environmental practices of democratic polities, members of future generations and nonhuman species (Dobson, 1996b)? The next chapter considers the resonance of formal political institutions to environmental problems, which is described by the fragmentary environmental record of even those advanced democratic countries most lauded for their ecological policies.

A parallel challenge to the democratic generalization of environmental interests occurs *outside* the formal political sphere and relates to the political mobilization of environmental groups. Unlike sectoral-based lobbying and campaigning organizations, environmental interest groups tend to lack a firm social-structural basis, both vertically to their grassroots support and horizontally to other organized political and social interests. Without firm institutional continuity, their long-term strength relates to the general growth in public environmental consciousness. In other words, the appeal to common ecological interests by environmental groups demands an energy-sapping continual commitment to agenda-setting in the public sphere. Robert Paehlke captures neatly the structural asymmetries in the liberal democracies that this reveals (1989, p 210):

> *Interest group liberalism is really a formula for a politics of incremental-ism and compromise between* organized *interests. In such a system the less organized and the unorganized lose ground, particularly in hard economic times. The elderly, the poor, the unemployed, and the ill are grossly unrepresented. So too, of course, are future generations and other species.*

The limited political response to environmental concerns is, then, a reflection of a democratic decision-making process most receptive to economic self-interest and powerful sectoral interest groups. Even if we were to accept the contention that there are now too many environmental voices fighting to be heard (Eder, 1996, p 165), particularly now that corporate interests have discovered the benefits of 'greenwashing' their identity and products, the question remains of the democratic validity of competing political claims – the extent to which any particular representation of environmental interests accords with the discourse principle.

A central claim of ecocentric environmentalism is that ecological degradation and the social dislocation that invariably accompanies it affects everybody, so that we all share a common interest in addressing environmental problems (Dobson, 1990, p 23). Beck makes a similar point: the production of global environmental risks in modern society strikes everybody. In a 'world-risk society' even the rich and powerful are not safe from the hazardous side effects of industrial production: 'smog is democratic' (1992, p 37). At the same time, Beck accepts that environmental risks are often distributed in a socially stratified or class-specific way (more than he is prepared to admit), but the universalization of ecological hazards ultimately means that the environmental movement cannot avoid expressing a common good, regardless of age, gender, ethnicity and nationality. This suggests the first of four defining characteristics of a discourse theory of environmental democracy.

Prioritizing Moral Judgements Based on Long-term Generalizable Interests

If we accept that interests relate to the needs of individuals, and that they provide relatively durable motives for social action, a democratic coordination of our social relationship to nonhuman nature would be expected to respond to environmental interests that are constitutive of our physical survival and well-being. The basis of a government's democratic legitimacy resides partly in the expectation of citizens that it will fairly represent and consider all relevant interests (Levi, 1997, p 204). One of the achievements of environmentalism has been to extend standards of fairness to ecological concerns so that government trustworthiness or responsiveness now includes its performance in environmental policy areas. Indeed, one of the purposes of this book is to suggest means in which this could be strengthened or extended. However, as indicated above, an immediate problem is that prevailing patterns of interest representation in the liberal democracies militate against those concerns not serving the immediate material interests of a specific constituency. One challenge is thus to redefine material well-being in a way that meshes in with ecological concerns, bringing to the fore the often latent environmental interests that we have in common with others – including those individuals not yet born.

Michael Jacobs (1997) argues convincingly that 'quality of life' represents a valuable concept for demonstrating to people how they are made better off by environmental policies. Improvements in environmental quality arising from regulatory policies may involve curbs on private consumption – for example, road pricing for private vehicles in urban areas – but highlight alternative collective good sources of well-being. To continue the example, in countries such as Britain which suffer from heavy traffic congestion and air pollution in urban areas, Jacobs claims that conventional measurements of economic health fail to reflect that the value of public goods is becoming increasingly redundant in communicating living standards. Public or social goods (such as community safety and anti-poverty strategies) allow a broader understanding of environmental quality, helping to craft a more socially aware environmentalism. Under the umbrella of Local Agenda 21, Britain has recently seen an encouraging range of community initiatives informing the development of alternative quality of life or sustainability indicators (see Chapter 6). Another key point made by Jacobs is that even when the provision of certain social goods may not make us better off on an individual level (I may not have children at school, or use the local open space), they nevertheless enhance our collective well-being as a society.

A wider social identification with quality of life, of the sort promoted by environmentalism, encourages not only a recognition of generalizable interests but also their logical linkage to democratic processes of public deliberation:

> ... the concept of quality of life seeks not just an expansion of the objects of well-being, from private goods to social goods, but of the subject of well-being too. It asks people to consider themselves not just as individuals, with private interests, but as members of society, with social interests too (Jacobs, 1997, p 59).

The political goal here – reasserting, against dominant neoliberal norms, the role of individual as community member rather than consumer – is, of course, deserving of the support of all those wanting a more just society. However, it is not necessary to accept Jacobs's stronger conclusion that this repositions environmentalism as a *communitarian* project, where the burden of interest generalization falls more exclusively on community traditions, because this move, in my view, threatens to blunt the cosmopolitan critical potential of environmental democracy.

For example, John O'Neill (1993) shares with Jacobs the Aristotelian premise that environmental responsibility, like concern with social well-being, is likely to follow socialization into a culture that places priority on care for human and nonhuman life. In the way that citizen engagement in the classical Athenian *polis* is assumed to have imparted political judgement and wisdom, more participatory structures of decision-making in modern society promise to educate citizens about their common interests (obviously in a much more inclusive manner than the *polis*). O'Neill makes more explicit than Jacobs the reasons why this form of political life would be conducive to ecologically rational decision-making: it would nurture an appreciation of existing forms of human and nonhuman life, develop an awareness of the historical continuity between pro-environmental traditions, and demonstrate the limits to equating the acquisition of material goods with the good life (1993, p 180). While O'Neill gives no illustration of social solidarity approximating this exemplary form, others have pointed to the lessons available from surviving indigenous cultures – for example, the Andean peasantry (Apffel-Marglin, 1998) – as well as, in advanced industrial societies, the recovery and reworking of pre-industrial configurations of 'customary consciousness' with stable material expectations (Thompson, 1991, pp 13–15). The emphasis is on ethical and cultural forms of self-understanding that provide an alternative to market-based evaluation of environmental interests, although still rooted in human capabilities. An ecological future-oriented democracy is thus enriched by the widening political, educational and aesthetic learning of its citizens, feeding what Castoriadis (1995, pp 34–35) terms a 'passion for public affairs'.

From this approach, then, we gather the important insight that identifying generalizable ecological interests may be *encouraged* by a participatory form of democracy in which citizens' preferences can be changed by ethical reflections on the good life. That much is in accord with the notion of environmental democracy put forward here. This book differs in claiming that the democratic principle of self-determination, in the diverse ethical mix of modern societies, is necessarily wary of depending too much for political legitimacy upon *particular* community traditions and cultures. Environmental democracy also invites *moral* judgements based on long-term generalizable interests: this refers to democratic decisions justified by interest universalization across different cultures as opposed to ideas of worth within a culture. This is influenced by John Rawls's (1988) argument for the priority of right – of a democratic conception of justice ('justice as fairness') – in determining the role played, and limits, of ideas about what constitutes a good life. It is, as Rawls stresses, not a claim that ethical questions are unimportant, or that democracy does not invoke its own virtues of appropriate political behaviour. What the priority of (moral) right over (ethical) good implies is the normative antecedence of a common justification for democratic institutions. If democratic principles are to have a global legitimacy, they are best expressed through a discourse or procedural approach which, apart from requiring a commitment to democratic norms of communication (and other basic freedoms), is neutral to the rich detail of competing cultural traditions.

The crucial supplement is that basic democratic freedoms include the right to secure living conditions, so that neutrality is amongst cultural worldviews supportive of this (see the section below on extending and radicalizing liberal rights). This does not preclude the ethical consideration of ecological interests as generalizable within particular political communities and cultural traditions, both of which are crucial to imparting ecological responsibility and providing regionally distinctive reasons for environmental protection. What it achieves, by attaching one set of generalizable interests to the sum of humanity, is to afford environmental democracy a moral priority independent of nonglobal collective identities. This is illustrated by Klaus Eder's comment that modern environmentalism extends moral universalism by directing attention to fairness in the contribution of collective environmental and social goods (Eder, 1996, pp 162–165). Fairness in providing healthy ecological conditions of existence means that the social justice component of sustainability can be recovered, as we pay attention to intra- and intergenerational justice. By understanding ecological interests in moral terms rather than only in ethical terms, we also have a stronger basis for criticizing cultural forms of life hostile to environmental democracy, because we are dealing with what is equally good for all rather than just particular groups or communities. Such common interests include, alongside existing human rights and the right to a safe, healthy environment, an attitude of respect towards other living things, nonviolence and global forms of democratic self-understanding.

Centring Environmental Democracy on Communicative Political Structures and Practices

This second defining characteristic of environmental democracy relates to the distinctive *deliberative* underpinning of environmental democracy – that is, the role in collective decision-making of reasonable and impartial arguments (Elster, 1998, p 8). Whatever the level of agreement reached by citizens about the validity of generalizable interests, democracy requires collectively binding decisions with legal force. Governments have to act according to more than moral reasons – environmental (and other) policy decisions also draw upon particular cultural preferences (for example, for the protection of a 'heritage' building or landscape) and power-oriented practical positions (for example, negotiating with business and labour representatives over appropriate levels of health-and-safety cover in the workplace). In these examples, the state may well cite a public interest motivation for actions, although the reasons involved are less conducive to generalization. In addition, the political decisions themselves can clearly demonstrate strategic motivations, such as a pre-election tax cut or a policy concession to a favoured constituency. Given the complex mix of values and interests informing political decision-making, the democratic organization of institutional power, in order to respect its core norm of civic self-determination, places a premium on procedures for free and open communication:

> . . . *democratic procedure makes it possible for issues and contributions, information and reasons to float freely; it secures a discursive character for political will-formation, and it thereby grounds the fallibilist assumption that results issuing from proper procedures are more or less reasonable (Habermas, 1996, p 448).*

The discourse theory of democracy presented by Habermas (1996) represents the most important statement of this proceduralist perspective. It is intimately related to his wider theory of communicative action (1984; 1987), which conceives of social coordination through language use. For Habermas social practice is held together by action oriented to reaching understanding (communicative action), where individuals share knowledge, mutual trust and common definitions of a situation. This is achieved because, in their everyday interactions, individuals cannot avoid implicitly raising a number of validity claims (to truth, truthfulness and rightness) that are assumed to be justified. Of course, individuals may also act in an egocentric way, seeking mastery of aspects of the social and physical environment (instrumental action), or in a self-interested, calculating way with others (strategic action); however, these are parasitic on communicative action, Habermas maintains, because the latter is innate to language use (1984, pp 100–101). Everyday communicative practice thus involves unavoidable presuppositions of shared meanings and the expectation that any claims made can be supported with good reasons. The associated concept of communicative rationality expresses the condition that actions oriented toward reaching understanding must be open to rational justification. The discussion and resolution of problematic validity claims, free of strategic influence or coercion, by the better argument alone, constitutes discursive forms of communication (Habermas, 1984, pp 18–23). For the discourse theory of democracy, the most important questions concern the rational basis of political authority; therefore, the emphasis is on the extent to which political action norms have given adequate consideration to the interests of all those possibly involved. On this criterion is based the judgement of their democratic strength, whether for moral, ethical or practical reasons.

Rational public deliberation contrasts with the liberal democratic model, where a stable system of governance rests on limited channels of influence afforded through elections and interest groups. Most citizens remain uninvolved in public affairs while the state is preoccupied with aggregating the political preferences expressed through voting or lobbying. As already mentioned, the economic sphere also stands insulated from any democratic interrogation. Both result in a weak normative role for civic opinion-formation and self-determination. Against this, discourse theory proposes a participatory, democratic self-understanding based on the idealized validity that political norms would hold if all affected by them had an opportunity to shape them or accepted them only on the basis of good reasons. Following Habermas, David Held (1995) has outlined 'a democratic thought experiment' which makes explicit the demanding conditions for political participation and communication necessary to realizing such civic self-determination. Such an 'ideal deliberative situation' invites reflection on the conditions necessary for democratic dialogue – 'the framework that might allow conflicting interpretations of value, interest and judgement to be explored without resort to coercion, force or violence' (Held, 1995, p 167).

For example, citizens would be freed from time and resource constraints, have equal access to information, and be able to reflect upon how their interests affect others: as posited by the discourse principle, a cooperative search for agreement would be the only legitimate motive. Although Held does not share Habermas's view that these counterfactual conditions are presupposed in linguistic interaction, he demonstrates their value as a means of 'imminently critiquing' existing political institutions and practices. They are therefore in accord with the Habermasian view of democratic legitimacy as the justifiability of current political institutions according to equal respect for all interests.

This critical theory is the conceptual setting for my understanding of environmental democracy: it extends the 'ideal intersubjectivity' associated with mutual understanding to political opinion-formation and decision-making on issues in need of environmental regulation. The difference with deep green notions of democracy is that the political norms governing environmental protection are not pre-given by a naturalistic philosophy or by 'reading off' an evolutionary logic from nature; rather they are the result of uncoerced social choice about environmental interests. An additional divergence from blanket green condemnations of Western cultural values and political organization (for example, Atkinson, 1991) is the suggestion of a learning potential in the universalistic promise of moral representations of constitutional democracy (and also environmentalism itself). The normative heart of Habermas's critique of uncontrolled growth in political and economic systems is that such systems sacrifice the democratic learning potential residing in communicative action (Habermas, 1987, pp 307–313). Deliberative political procedures are oriented towards developing that potential through, firstly, the *institutionalization* of procedures and conditions for free political communication, and, secondly, the *interplay* of these institutionalized communicative processes with informally developed public opinions (Habermas, 1996, p 298).

The *institutional* design of new forms of public participation and new arenas for practical deliberation is, under a discourse theory of democracy, to be determined by the citizens themselves in specific social contexts; there is no institutional blueprint. However, there are general guidelines and 'discursive designs' for consideration. To address, firstly, the classical locus of decision-making power in parliamentary law-making, including its interpretation by the judiciary, the stress is on increased opportunities for articulating needs and meaningful involvement in decision-making. Chapter 2 notes some of the more promising constitutional tendencies in participatory environmental governance at the national level. For legal decision-making, Habermas advances a parallel discourse theory of law to suggest ways in which courts would have an additional responsibility for normative justification – for example, before an enlarged 'legal public sphere' subject to public questioning (1996, p 440). In the environmental policy field, Hajer has similarly recommended that regulatory action should be exposed to normative arguments rather than an often technocentric preoccupation with the practicalities of specific cases. Discursive law would link legal argumentation with wider societal debates on environmental interests (Hajer, 1995, pp 292–293).

Secondly, selected democratization of the administration would also encourage opportunities for public deliberation. This is particularly important where administrative decisions, such as environmental ones, are bound up with social values and have important effects on future choices (Reich, 1985). Such a communicative role for administrative choice departs from the classic liberal restriction of normative questioning to the legislature and the judiciary, according the administration merely the instrumental role of implemented preselected decisions. More than any other political theorist, John Dryzek has discussed the institutional potential for discursive designs, locating a number of incipient examples in the real world. These include discursively designed public inquiries, regulatory negotiation and environmental mediation: all are characterized by the communicative scrutiny of collective values, searching for reasoned agreements on social choices (Dryzek, 1990a; 1990b; also, Renn, Webler and Wiedemann, 1995). I agree with Dryzek that, however imperfect in practice, these deliberative exercises in institutional design reveal a wide potential for communicative rationalization. Chapter 3 discusses a western Canadian experiment in participatory environmental planning noteworthy for its geographical scope and its explicit articulation of normative criteria for democratizing environmental decision-making.

According to the discourse theory of democracy, the communicative rationality – hence democratic legitimacy – of political decision-making depends on an *interplay* between formal political will-formation and a surrounding environment of public discussion and associational activity. This core-periphery model attaches distinctive normative contributions to both – the former, as above, offering democratic procedures for making collectively binding decisions, but only legitimately insofar as it is receptive to the latter: a vibrant, autonomous public sphere (Habermas, 1996, pp 354–358). The political public sphere comprises communicative networks rooted in everyday interaction, associational activity and the mass media, which serve to relay information about issues to the formal political system. Once again, the discourse principle enables us to gauge the democratic health of this feedback:

> *The political public sphere can fulfill its functions of perceiving and thematizing encompassing social problems only insofar as it develops out of the communication taking place among those who are potentially affected (Habermas, 1996, p 365).*

As a normative benchmark, this assists us in picking up those who fall through the gaps of existing associational activity – the blind spot of the associative democratic position noted earlier in the chapter. It also serves to reveal the asymmetrical nature of political communication within civil society more generally: for example, selective access to expertise and the lack of a strong, independent media. In recent years, environmental problems have been extensively aired in the public sphere, in no small amount due to the tireless efforts of environmental interest organizations, but not always in a manner sensitive to those groups suffering most from ecological degradation. Environmental democracy, through a communicative perspective, sets procedural conditions for a more inclusive interpretation and determination of needs (Chapter 6 provides a case study of attempts to ascertain needs democratically in an inner-city environment). There have been representative instruments suggested for encouraging this: deliberative interviews and opinion polls, electronic town halls, citizens' juries and representation vouchers (Gundersen, 1995, p 206; Fishkin, 1991, pp 81–104). However, all these rely upon formal political structures for sponsorship. Historically, collective efforts at broadening political discourse to accommodate new norms and new need-interpretations have come from social movement activism (Cohen and Arato, 1993, pp 523–532), and this has been the case with radical environmentalism. Civil society thus remains as much a space for democratization as formal political institutions.

Promoting Ecologically Rational Decision-making

At first, a discourse theory of democracy would not appear to be a promising starting point for advancing ecologically rational decision-making. Both human centred and procedural in orientation, it is twice removed from environmentalist concerns with nonhuman values and substantive ecological goals. Not surprisingly the ecocentric critique is forceful: Eckersley (1992, pp 109–117) addresses communicative action theory at source, arguing that its normative project precludes consideration of the 'emancipation of nonhuman nature' and that its theoretical handle on nature is instrumental. It is possible to sympathize with the latter point, for Habermas has remained wedded to a Eurocentric understanding that natural scientific knowledge is necessarily predicated on notions of technical mastery and control. Eckersley gives a series of examples, from medical anthropology to biodynamic farming, to demonstrate how noninstitutional motives can inform knowledge which, when applied, leads to productive yet ecologically benign resource uses. Environmentalism is partly a reaction to the social and ecological bankruptcy of overly instrumental interventions – for example, the Green Revolution (Eckersley, 1992, p 114). In addition, as feminist critiques of science have shown, the internal logic of the natural sciences is by no means value free: it is legitimately subject to cultural and political evaluation (Haraway, 1989; Harding, 1986). Theoretical knowledge on the natural environment, an important resource for political communication, is therefore by no means exclusively based on cognitive-instrumental attitudes. That point accepted, this book nevertheless defends the claim that ethical and moral justification of environmental interests necessarily relates to human valuation and valuation criteria. Indeed, the very basis for human responsibility to nature rests on our detachment from it, obliging us to extend moral consideration to it in a nonreciprocal way (Chapter 4).

The philosophical faithfulness here to the Habermasian idea of *human* intersubjectivity differs from Dryzek's (1990b, 1995) green recasting of communicative rationality through recognizing agency in nature. For Dryzek, 'ecological democracy' allows rational communicative interaction with the natural world because nonhuman entities, though short of the self-awareness that constitutes human subjectivity, give off ecological signals – for example, non-verbal communication in the body language and facial displays of other mammals or the biophysical changes evident in wider ecological processes, such as nitrogen and carbon cycles. In short: 'the nonhuman world can communicate, and human decision processes can be structured so as to listen to communications more or less well' (Dryzek, 1997, p 200). The gain over liberal conceptions of democracy is that ecologically receptive political communication extends not only beyond the aggregation of human preferences but also beyond traditional political boundaries. Dryzek draws upon his earlier principle of *ecological rationality* (1987) – an evaluative notion concerned with conserving low entropy in human systems as they combine with natural systems – to demonstrate how enhanced ecological communication can increase the 'symbiotic problem-solving intelligence' of political decision-making. The democratic learning potential of communicative political procedures thus converges with an ecological learning potential.

One reservation about this communicative derivation of ecological democracy is that it imparts a naturalistic conception of meaning that is incompatible with communicative rationality. Ecological signals are always mediated through human social activity, notably language. Meaning does not simply reside in nature, or words simply apply to (ecological) objects; the communicative orientation to *mutual* understanding means that non-human nature can only communicate meaningfully to us insofar as we communicate about it to each other. This is not to deny the reality of nonhuman nature but to stress that all or any part of it lacks a communicative competence sufficient to qualify as a *participant* in the negotiation of political choices.

Dryzek is more successful in developing from the other direction – from discursive democracy – the connections between the communicative rationality of politics and ecological problem-solving. In the same way that the communicative rationality of decisions would be enhanced in principle by the reciprocal recognition of public interests in a discursive democracy, so too, he asserts, would their ecological rationality. In the first place, the human life-support capacity of natural systems is better placed to be recognized and defended as a generalizable interest when political and policy institutions are structured along discursive lines. And secondly, he claims, nonexclusive processes of public communication are conducive to solving complex ecological problems inasmuch as they spread the cognitive burden of decision-making among the cooperative efforts of many individuals (Dryzek, 1990b, pp 69–73, 124–126). These points support his prescriptions for decentralized, participatory democracy where regular deliberations are possible that have immediate and identifiable weight within discursive communities (which may be local to international in scope). Empirical support for the thesis that public deliberation enhances ecological rationality is provided by Gundersen (1995, pp 150–192) who, in 46 in-depth interviews with a cross-section of Americans, demonstrates that problem-oriented discussion strengthens a commitment to collective environmental values, encouraging also holistic thinking, a long-term view and a clarification of environmental ends (of course, the cross-cultural validity of his conclusions awaits corroborative research within the US as well as in other political cultures).

Environmental democracy, in agreement with the above, allows communicative political procedures to provide much of its green content. Andrew Light and Eric Higgs (1996) have shown this with regard to ecological restoration – the renewal of ecosystem health. For them, the democratic potential for ecological restoration lies in the scope for public participation in restoration projects, cultivating human-nature relationships. In the terms of our discourse principle, the extent to which ecological restorations are determined by public deliberation and participation provides the measure for environmental democracy; the fuller the relevant communicative contribution, the more democratic the restoration. This stance removes political legitimacy from a simple engineering justification of restoration projects – that is, their technical success in effectively producing selected environmental attributes. Light and Higgs mark out well the critical gains involved in attaching a participatory democratic meaning to ecological restoration, opening up the social criteria under which restoration projects are discussed. This allows a critique both of corporate-sponsored ecological-renewal projects which produce natural attributes on the whim of private capital interests, and of state-led restorations impervious to participatory inputs. Only restorations approximating meaningful conditions of effective public participation and communication could legitimately claim to be practical instances of environmental democracy. In other words, environmental democracy *socializes* the definition and negotiation of ecological interests.

The argument adopted here is that communicative political procedures promote ecologically rational decision-making, firstly, through identifying ecological sustainability as a generalizable interest. From Dryzek (1990b, p 55), this can be extended to recognizing the democratic legitimacy of state action in maintaining or renewing the supply of environmental social goods on account of their role in providing the preconditions for discursive democracy. It has been pointed out, though, that this second argument implies no logical linkage with *democratic* decision-making; the functional need for an ecologically viable society is as much a prerequisite for authoritarian political communication as noncoercive communication. Dobson

(1996a, pp 136–139), who makes this observation, correctly notes that this 'argument from preconditions' must therefore be supplemented by a joint appeal to the democratic principle of *autonomy*. A fourth defining characteristic of environmental democracy relates to the necessary connection between the (social and ecological) conditions for democratic decision-making and the freedoms stipulated by the principle of autonomy. However, while this book accepts the argument of Dobson and other green political theorists that this requires a radicalization of liberal democratic freedoms, it stops short of their naturalistic theories of justice.

Extending and Radicalizing Existing Liberal Rights

David Held (1995, p 147) provides a clear formulation of the principle of autonomy as a key concept for liberal democracy:

> . . . *persons should enjoy equal rights and, accordingly, equal obligations in the specification of the political framework which generates and limits the opportunities available to them; that is, they should be free and equal in the determination of the conditions of their own lives, so long as they do not deploy this framework to negate the rights of others.*

The principle of autonomy relates the rightness of collective decision-making to the freedom of self-determination based, in principle, on equal opportunities for participation. From the democratic thought experiment described above, the *normative* meaning of autonomy is anticipated as the ideal conditions which citizens would accept as necessary to realizing their status as equally free members of their political community. Autonomy also has an empirical grounding in the historic accomplishments represented by the widening of political inclusion in liberal democracies (Held, 1995, pp 159–161). Rights have been enacted or recognized by the state to strengthen the democratic framing of political deliberation and decision-making, typically after active struggles by those disempowered. The benchmark of ideal autonomy remains the conceptual tool for demonstrating the continuing shortfall from the communicative and participatory conditions under which all areas of social choice respect the principle of autonomy. How does the idea of environmental democracy alter the application of this principle and its realization in a system of rights?

Liberal political philosophy defends a restrictive notion of rights: the subject of rights is the individual and the substance of rights is a *negative* libertarian view of freedom (Shapiro, 1986, pp 275–279). In this constrained space of private autonomy, rights are attached to the individual and exercised as claims for noninterference against other individuals and public authorities – for example, restricting incursions against free speech, freedom of association and so on. Ted Benton's (1993) ecosocialist critique of this liberal–individualist conception highlights incisively its social and ecological shortcomings. Firstly, there is the familiar charge that these rights are not realizable under prevailing circumstances of sharply asymmetrical and mutually antagonistic relationships of economic power; and, secondly, they serve an ideological function in excluding from moral consideration sources of harm which fall outside individual human agency or acts of public power. The liberal-individualist view of rights presumes a human-centred, atomistic conception of well-being that is abstracted from social and ecological conditions of life. We are left with a moral vocabulary seemingly incapable of addressing environmental problems. At the same time, however, those gains in environmental quality that have been accomplished through legal and regulatory advances in many countries might be interpreted as heralding a positive extension of liberal rights, in the same way that various rights to social security accompanied the construction of the welfare state.

Environmental democracy bypasses this liberal inconsistency by presenting rights and democracy as internally linked. Under the discourse theory of democracy, a system of rights is a necessary precondition for institutionalizing noncoercive and reflexive forms of public communication. In principle, rights maintain the levels of reciprocal recognition and equal participation among citizens that are required for rational political deliberation, while democracy ensures that this mutual recognition is inclusive. Both are essential for the democratic legitimacy of law-making and public policy. Autonomy becomes those private and public spaces which are protected by basic rights, shorn of individualistic connotations. Private autonomy, moving beyond the minimal recognition of negative liberties, relates to those individual liberties, associational freedoms and legal protections which, guaranteed by rights, recognize citizens as *addressees* of law. Political autonomy, the public space where citizens recognize themselves as *authors* of democratic decision-making, is secured by basic rights to equal opportunities to participate in processes of opinion- and will-formation (Habermas, 1996, pp 104, 120–123; Ingram, 1994, pp 93–117). For Habermas, the two are mutually supportive or 'co-original': according to the discourse principle of democratic self-determination, the addressees of law are simultaneously the authors of their rights. Crucially, the notion of autonomy is extended further still by showing how the exercise of these civil and political rights depends upon healthy social and ecological conditions of life: this implies 'basic rights to the provision of living conditions that are socially, technologically and ecologically safeguarded' (Habermas, 1996, p 123). Habermas himself does not expound on the nature of these social and ecological rights. However, I now offer some introductory comments on environmental rights which are taken to be compatible with a communicative notion of environmental democracy.

Environmental rights are human rights: they are basic rights which may not actually be recognized in a positive legal sense by a particular state or set of states, but which nevertheless have a moral authority that appeals to a common humanity. The normative strength of a discourse theory of democracy is that, in justifying these rights through communicative processes of interaction, it broadens out the principle of autonomy in a cosmopolitan way. In the case of recent suggestions for a right to a clean, healthy or viable environment, the sources have actually been international in scope, including nongovernmental human rights and ecological organizations, intellectuals, global and regional environmental treaties, and the United Nations – notably the 1994 report on human rights and the environment by the UN Subcommission on the Prevention of Discrimination and Protection of Minorities (the *Ksentini Report*). The draft principles on human rights and the environment proposed by the latter include the universal right to a secure, healthy and ecologically sound environment (Boyle, 1996). Extending international human rights to environmental protection endows those interests which are universal (the obvious candidates are ecological life-support systems and common heritage environments) with a powerful claim to moral consideration.

The crucial political move, then, is from moral prescription to becoming an international obligation, whether by means of formal legal instruments or binding customary rule (such as the Universal Declaration of Human Rights, 1948). Michael Anderson (1996, pp 21–22) has suggested that this would in principle allow environmental protection to trump short-term motives or sectoral interests in bureaucratic decision-making, buttressed by extensive procedural rights. Furthermore, an environmental rights framework could increase the coordination of environmental decision-making by bringing local, national and international issues within the same legal framework, while perhaps also stimulating more internationalist strands of ecological activism. However, Anderson's is a qualified endorsement recognizing that there remain numerous questions of definition and legal application, many related to the extent to which formulations of environmental quality hold cross-cultural validity. The position here is that the more relativist arguments which equate environmental rights with particular conceptions of the good life (for example, du Bois, 1996), thereby clamping these rights to national legal systems, effectively empty them of their cosmopolitan scope and weaken their normative claim to respect and consider the interests of all. They also fly in the face of the diplomatic internationalization of environmental interests: from the UN Conference on Environment and Development (1992) to the Kyoto Climate Change Conference (1997), the 1990s have seen numerous global political gatherings designed to thrash out common environmental concerns (however imperfect the ensuing agreements have been). Like the communitarian reduction of environmental interests to cultural valuations, interpreting autonomy and rights in terms of national judicial traditions shortchanges the global reach of an environmental democracy discourse.

A more practical objection raised by Boyle (1996, pp 53–57) is that creating a right to a decent environment may be redundant given the rapid development of international environmental law. This criticism recites the emergence of multilateral legal instruments and institutions that promise a more effective regulatory regime than reliance upon a diffuse generic right to environmental quality. This book's conclusion will illustrate how these two need not be mutually exclusive, arguing that transnational public-law litigation is at least one nascent channel by which a human right to environmental quality could be democratically vindicated. For the foreseeable future, though, the greatest political promise for advancing environmental democracy lies with reinterpreting existing human rights standards in environmental terms – for example, the right to adequate health care recast to support the right of citizens not to suffer from preventable environmental risks (Saward, 1996) – and, as Boyle (1996, pp 59–63) stresses, on procedural environmental rights, noting the key ones identified by the *Ksentini Report*:

- the right to information concerning the environment;
- the right to receive and disseminate ideas and information;
- the right to participation in planning and decision-making processes, including prior environmental impact assessment;
- the right to freedom of association for the purpose of protecting the environment or the rights of persons affected by environmental harm;
- the right to effective remedies and redress for environmental harm in administrative or judicial proceedings.

These principles expand on the comprehensive participatory rights contained in principle 10 of the Rio Declaration and, notes Boyle, are also informed by existing human rights law and international environmental law. In terms of the discourse theory of environmental democracy, they express the environmental force of the basic civil and political rights grounding civic self-determination, reinforcing a basic entitlement to democratic governance as a transnational human right (Franck, 1992). This places corresponding duties on individual states to provide minimal levels of support for public participation in environmental decision-making (against a general redistributive background of equitable social provision; see Ingram, 1994, p 188). Rights must, of course, be mediated through existing institutions, but their dynamic character (Raz, 1986, p 171) means also that deepening communicative democracy will create new duties for facilitating democratic environmental governance (for example, participant funding in environmental mediation).

An exclusive focus on human rights to environmental protection would appear to offend the naturalistic sensibilities of those green political theorists uncomfortable with its human-centred framework. Benton (1993) and Eckersley (1995; 1996) both extend the principle of autonomy further. For Benton, this turns on a needs-based conception of justice which stresses those common environmental, developmental and bodily needs that humans share with other animals (although he attempts to do so without endorsing any type of evolutionary psychology; compare, for example, Dennett, 1995, pp 452–510). Eckersley goes further, offering an ecologically reworked notion of autonomy – 'the freedom of human and nonhuman beings to unfold in their own ways and live according to their "species life"' (1995, p 180) – connected to her ecocentric value theory. While she argues in support of human environmental rights (1996), her programme for a properly 'ecocentric democracy' also includes moral rights for domestic and captive animals (obliging a positive duty of care on humans) and negative rights for wild animals (obliging duties of noninterference from humans). Beyond these 'human analogous' cases for sentient, conscious beings, she recognizes that the rights discourse will not stretch to the rest of nonhuman nature, becoming morally and practically unworkable (1995, p 193). Nevertheless, both Eckersley and Benton defend a naturalistic interpretation to green the democratic principle of autonomy.

Environmental democracy extends and radicalizes liberal rights in a *nonnaturalistic* fashion. The green extension of autonomy to nonhuman beings breaks the internal relationship between private and public autonomy, along with its expression in democratic will-formation, because the nonhuman addressees of legal duties are neither participants in the authorship of their rights nor, as is the case with future generations, anticipated participants needing proxy representation. They cannot pursue values or take part in discursive processes of civic self-determination. At most, the arguments that all living entities self-produce as ends in themselves (Eckersley), or that there is an objective commonality in some of the needs shared with other animals (Benton), suggest that nonhuman entities can be objects of moral consideration but not shared subjects of autonomy. Is this not just 'blatant speciesism' (Regan, 1985, p 23)? This is only the case if nonhuman nature is then valued in an instrumental way. There is no reason why the exclusion of nonhuman entities as rights-holders logically entails that environmental interests cannot be championed in political arenas. The argument here is that rights claims are 'strong' moral entitlements attached to those who can be both addressees and authors of autonomy. This means, again, that the strongest moral claims to ecological sustainability are human rights to a healthy, safe and decent environment coupled with environmental participatory rights. These rights should be given legal recognition by democratic governments because they underpin civil and political freedoms: this is a necessary radical extension of existing liberal rights. It does not prevent us from marshalling other ethical or practical reasons for environmental protection based on noninstrumental environmental values.

The radical force of a strong participatory human rights discourse is that those without a legal recognition of basic freedoms in their domestic political situation, or suffering economic and social deprivation in clear violation of existing rights, never lose their claim to self-determination (amongst other basic freedoms). Furthermore, according to human environmental rights, they are invited to interpret *themselves* the gap between the circumstances under which they live and decent social and ecological conditions. This applies even to the most established liberal democracies insofar as they maintain insufficient environmental and social conditions to realize democracy across all spheres of life and, through their networks of political and economic influence, across the world; the radical force of human rights lies in their unforgiving universalism.

The above characterization of environmental democracy refers mainly to positions and debates in political theory. This chapter has stressed its *normative* dimension as a committed and future-oriented project seeking to realize universal principles of freedom and justice. The idea of environmental democracy is to communicate the ecological and social conditions for civic self-determination, as well as individual self-realization. One indicator of that linkage becoming central to our democratic self-understanding is that we no longer accept as 'democratic' political systems that deliberately or inadvertently undermine basic social and environmental rights and freedoms. This is perhaps no more than a hope, resting on the outcome of numerous practical and political engagements with very powerful interests. However, environmental democracy also describes the existing potential for inclusive communication embodied in democratic practices and institutions. The rest of the book will describe some of the more promising tendencies towards environmental democracy, starting in Chapter 2 with institutional designs at the state level.

2 ENVIRONMENTAL DECISION-MAKING IN WESTERN EUROPE AND NORTH AMERICA: DEMOCRATIC CAPACITY-BUILDING?

If it is to have any explanatory value, the notion of environmental democracy must be able to refer to empirical instances of ecological communication which pay serious attention to the discourse principle – that is, processes of opinion-formation and decision-making which, at first sight, seem to be concerned with discovering shared environmental interests. The thesis that free and inclusive political communication on environmental issues can facilitate collective agreement and effective action on policy choices is therefore open to empirical verification (or falsification). Of course, this presumes that we will be able to specify criteria for evaluating the quality of political communication and participation as well as the effectiveness of environmental policy decisions. Even if restricted, firstly, to the standards necessary to distinguish a healthy democratic order, there are important differences (compare, for example, Dahl, 1989, pp 106–118 and Ingram, 1994, pp 168–192).[1] And given the diversity of regulatory structures and practices within and between jurisdictions, what scope is there, secondly, for comparative observations about environmental policy choices?

The explanatory task for the discourse principle, then, is to account for the processes and outcomes of environmental decision-making according to its deliberative idea of justice – what is right or justifiable which all those affected could, in principle, agree upon. To recall a claim from Chapter 1, inclusive political communication aids ecologically rational decision-making by encouraging the mutual recognition of environmental interests and values. In order to investigate that conjunction, this chapter identifies selected discursive democratic tendencies at the state level in the European Union (EU) and North America, offering some preliminary comments as to whether these have any bearing on national progress in environmental protection. The aim is not to provide a comprehensive cross-national survey of environmental decision-making for these states, but to pick out nascent aspects of environmental democracy. Furthermore, the focus on advanced capitalist countries by no means disregards the social and environmental plight of the global South, including the culpability of the former in shaping that order. Examining those countries with the most developed institutions for environmental decision-making, who have claimed authority on the basis of that institutionalization during international environmental negotiations, means that the onus on them for facilitating environmental democracy is even greater.

After reviewing alternative perspectives on the environmental resonance of liberal democratic polities, this chapter considers various organizational and institutional tendencies towards environmental democracy informed by the concept of *environmental capacity* (Jänicke and Weidner, 1997). This enables comparison, with reference to selected countries, on the role of organized proponents of environmental protection and political-institutional framework conditions for environmental policy. In keeping with the discourse theory of environmental democracy, this chapter pays particular attention to the openness (participative capacity) and coordination (integrative capacity) of policy processes. It also flags up several principles for ecological reform that are making inroads into environmental planning and management in Western Europe and North America, paying attention to their compatibility with the discourse principle. Finally, the collaborative shaping of environmental interests promoted by these procedural innovations and principles has invited positive appraisal according to the idea of *ecological modernization*. While this captures much of the rationale for those governments engaging in green administrative reforms, it downplays the continuing democratic deficit of environmental decision-making. This democratic failing is expressed by direct-action environmentalism, which – by politicizing the identification and negotiation of environmental risks – exposes the distributional blindspots of ecological modernization discourse: locally, nationally and internationally.

POLITICAL RESONANCE TO ENVIRONMENTAL PROBLEMS

The formulation of environmental democracy governing this book, as outlined in the last chapter, rests on the premise that current forms of political communication do not represent satisfactorily those social and ecological conditions necessary for self-government. This chapter's focus on environmental interests rather than environmental values reflects an acceptance of one tenet of liberal democracy – political discourse is properly concerned with generating collectively binding decisions that citizens have good reason to accept, even if their own particular preferences lie elsewhere. In terms of environmental protection, this means that respecting ecosystem health is not merely an ethical choice available to individuals but a collective concern deserving constitutional protection, hence the emphasis on human environmental rights. The right to a safe and healthy environment – supported by concomitant procedural rights – becomes a strong moral claim for enabling the political autonomy of individuals and groups in democratic societies, and anticipates adequate protection of the relevant ecological conditions of life. Environmental rights are therefore designed, in part, to make it more difficult for political communication to ignore important ecological problems. They highlight general environmental interests which citizens could, in principle, agree upon as part of the supporting framework of a sustainable democracy. However, the discussion of environmental rights in the last chapter stressed their moral character as human rights, holding authority regardless of whether they are recognized within existing liberal democracies. It is clear that even in those advanced capitalist societies noted for the political salience of environmental communication, there remain structural impediments to ecologically rational decision-making. What are these blockages?

According to the *systems* theoretical approach to political communication, which understands politics as just one subsystem in a complex and interdependent social order, it is no surprise that liberal democratic polities have exhibited sluggishness in responding to calls for integrating environmental interests (Luhmann, 1989; Papadakis, 1996, pp 32–35). Niklas Luhmann, who is most associated with this perspective, argues that each of the different subsystems within society is defined and constituted by its own form of binary communication – payment or nonpayment for the economic system; power or lack of power for the political system; legality or illegality for the legal system, and so on. These subsystems can only react to communication about ecological facts in terms of their own structures and codes, so that ecological communication will resonate differently amongst them according to their specific functions (Luhmann, 1989, pp 15–21). For liberal democratic polities, whose fundamental communicative coding is political office – the holding (government) or nonholding (opposition) of positions of political authority – environmental interests are registered through collectively binding decisions based upon power. Luhmann's thesis is that this functional order militates against the development of preventative environmental policy.

In the first place, the political system 'observes' environmental problems indirectly through public opinion – that is, environmental concerns registered by the voting public. Popular demands for environmental decisions in any given area are only likely to result in durable policy responses from the political system if the chance of re-election is enhanced for the government (Luhmann, 1989, pp 88–89). Within the competitive party systems of liberal democracies, a high threshold of public concern is needed to trigger political attention by the party in power. The institutional inertia of the system favours nonintervention, especially if the environmental policy action perceived necessary threatens to upset a favoured constituency of support. Only those ecological problems that become 'urgent', that impinge directly upon the material interests or moral consciousness of enough voters, invite more than a token political response. This means, of course, that more diffuse environmental concerns threaten to fall by the political wayside. Naturally, different party systems can make an important difference to the weight accorded to green votes; the classic contrast here is between the German system of proportional representation and the UK system of simple plurality voting, which Weale (1992, pp 72–

73) suggests is one important reason why German environmental policy has advanced systematically more quickly than Britain. This need not necessarily mean, as in the former case, that Green parties have better chances of reaching political office and winning political concessions from other parties, since the increased environmental resonance of representative systems based on proportional voting may also 'green' traditional parties to the detriment of Green party progress (such as in Denmark).

Nevertheless, even with an electoral system more effective in representing environmental values and interests, these concerns must still compete for political attention against more defined economic interests with clearer links to citizens' material circumstances; the same reasons were mentioned in the last chapter to explain why environmental campaigning groups face an uphill struggle in championing public ecological interests. Luhmann concedes that political sensitivity to environmental communication may be increased by the awareness-raising efforts of individual politicians or bureaucrats, but that they are constrained by the adversarial logic of the political system. Moreover, there are fundamental spatial and temporal limits to ecologically rational decision-making imposed by this logic. In the absence of effective international regulations, territorial sovereignty restricts politics to the ecological communication of direct jurisdictional impact, while the short-term structure of electoral cycles fails to mirror the temporal rhythms of key ecological cycles (1989, pp 91–92).

The political system is also limited in its capacity for environmental problem-solving, Luhmann claims, because policy interventions have to be translated into the language of other subsystems – notably the legal and economic subsystems – and these place their own constraints on ecological communication. By generating new regulatory structures and practices, the state might hope to address ecological problems in a definitive way; but ecological problems are often too complex, interlinked and unpredictable to be managed by the rigid prescriptions of legal norms and rules (1989, p 73; Dryzek, 1987, pp 132–148). In fact, an expansion of regulations can overburden the political system with monitoring and enforcement responsibilities. Luhmann's conservatism becomes even clearer with his warning that the policy utilization of economic instruments for environmental aims may undermine the stability of the economic system. The attempt by government to employ economic incentives (grants, subsidies) or disincentives (taxes, charges) to correct the externalization of environmental costs by companies threatens the autonomy of private investment decisions, disrupting the productive and allocative functioning of the economy (1989, pp 61–62).

Governments are, of course, constrained in their ability to intervene in existing capitalist market practices, which are protected by 'natural' private-property relations and limited liability laws. The threat of disinvestment or capital flight is a real possibility for environmental regulations potentially injurious to the 'business climate'; not only is the state fiscally dependent upon taxation revenue from the private sector, but an unwavering commitment to economic growth is viewed by all mainstream political parties as a prerequisite for winning electoral support for their programmes. The discourse of 'ecological modernization' discussed later in this chapter suggests that there is room for manoeuvre, and that the state can redefine growth in qualitative terms and convince citizens that reductions in material expectations can be justified by the better provision of public environmental goods. This chapter will address whether this has a place in environmental democracy. Firstly, however, it is important to note further theoretical support for Luhmann's pessimistic appraisal of political resonance to eco-logical risks. This conceptual approach moves focus from the system's theoretical preoccupation with the dichotomous, power-based logic of political choice to the more concrete realm of political institutions.

Political and administrative institutions are the key structures for integrating environmental interests within sectoral decision-making in liberal democracies. This applies even to those countries where market-based social choice is dominant, because these economic exchanges are still legally protected by the state. Institutions can be defined as 'enduring regularities of human action in situations structured by rules, norms and shared strategies, as well as the physical world' (Crawford and Ostrom, 1995, p 582). A recurrent claim guiding recent institutional analysis of environmental politics is that in order to understand the resonance of political systems to environmental problems, it is necessary to recognize the various parts of the state – the legislature, bureaucracy and judiciary – as institutionally rich in their own right, bound up with the constitution and negotiation of various interests (Papadakis, 1996, pp 25–35). This *new institutionalism* has marked out well the range of incentives and sanctions employed, in practice, to support environmental policies. State institutions have to aggregate a diverse range of individual and group preferences, working up durable policies in the face of competing claims. Informed by rational choice theory, new institutionalist analysis is particularly attuned to the interplay of (constitutional to customary) rules, information availa-bility and physical constraints affecting policy outcomes. Perhaps its most significant contribution to the area of environmental governance, developed impressively by Elinor Ostrom, relates to the institutional provision of collective environmental goods.

Ostrom (1990) argues that public and common-pool environmental resources pose a particular problem for political decision-making, with governments facing difficulties in creating institutional rules which secure cooperation over the sustainable provision of collective ecological benefits.[2] The theory of collective action, familiar in natural resource-management debates, addresses the perverse incentive structure that seems to undermine the sustainable use of such common-pool resources (CPRs) as fisheries and groundwater basins. The well-known 'tragedy of the commons' thesis (Hardin, 1968) affirms that individuals allowed unrestricted access to a common-property resource will seek to maximize the private benefits of productive or consumptive use. In contrast, any individual investment in maintaining or enhancing the ecological integrity of the resource in question bears an altruistic burden of personal cost for a generalized benefit: it is not possible to exclude provision of benefits to those unwilling to contribute to their upkeep. With no selective incentive to maintain its quality, and assuming the dominance of those who maximize selective benefits accruing from material extraction or consumption, the result is overuse and resource depletion. This negative consequence becomes more serious, the less the resource or ecological service is substitutable or renewable. At the vulnerable end, the frequently cited examples include stratospheric ozone and biological diversity.

Now, given that political regulation is typically proposed as the solution to CPR problems – we expect political authorities to impose institutional rules to protect environmental resources – what is the nature of state failure in this area? According to the new institutionalists, there are many occasions when, in regulating CPRs, political authorities have not managed to reorient the incentives and behaviour of actors in an ecologically rational manner. The obvious example, to recall Luhmann's point on the spatial limits to political action, might seem to be at a transnational or international level where large-scale CPRs fall outside the jurisdictional purview of any one state. There is no central political authority to enforce rules for cooperation between states on environmental commons issues. In the absence of such a political regime, institutional arrangements for effective environmental protection and management must come from inter-state cooperation where all the temptations remain for states to 'free-ride' on the environmental investments of others. The protracted difficulties encountered in creating effective international environmental agreements would seem to bear this out (see this book's conclusion). What is more significant here is the new institutionalist exposure of state failure to solve local or regional CPR problems which fall squarely within the authority of a particular government.

This analysis has highlighted the conceptual and practical shortcomings of regulatory strategies that assume that the rules and legal norms centrally prescribed can simply be translated into effective policy, when the common environmental resource itself, or its usage, may actually be misunderstood by government authorities. The policy instruments employed do not therefore have the intended effects on individual and group behaviour. In fact, state institutions can exacerbate the overexploitation of CPRs. The nationalization of communal forests in Thailand, Nepal and India has led to extensive deforestation. And this situation is not restricted to developing countries. One of the more dramatic instances of this in recent years was the collapse of the Canadian East Coast cod fishery, where the federal government undermined established networks of customary rules and regulations within its 200-mile fishing grounds by imposing a licensing system favouring capitalization of the industry (Ostrom, 1990, pp 173–177; Matthews, 1995). Not only were the diverse forms of community fishing and harbour rules ignored, and sometimes overturned, by the state, but the inshore fishermen's knowledge of fish movements was not incorporated within the national fisheries department's estimates of fish stocks. The warnings of the former that stocks were collapsing failed to influence licensing policy, leading ultimately to the closure of the fishing ground in 1992 (Matthews, 1995).

The presumption of the federal government in the above example that the inshore fisheries were (like patterns of offshore exploitation) open access, and that only top-down formal rationing could ensure sustainable use of the resource, illustrates for institutionalists the type of one-dimensional understanding of regulatory practice inimical to effective environmental management. Interestingly, Ostrom raises the same criticism of simplistic reasoning against the blanket privatization prescriptions of the public choice theorists, who advocate breaking up CPRs through the creation of private and transferable property rights (1990, pp 21–23). In this latter case, for most common environmental resources the problem of excluding free-riders remains even if it proves possible to agree upon property boundaries (and the responsibility of policing these boundaries is still with political and legal institutions). Ostrom argues that all policy analysts who recommend a uniform prescription for common-resource problems have failed to appreciate the diverse operational workings of institutional arrangements.

From the new institutionalist scepticism at top-down management designs for local and regional CPRs comes perhaps their key contention – that self-managed CPRs have a strong claim to environmental sustainability. Drawing upon examples from across the world, including high mountain communal pastures in Switzerland and irrigation institutions in Spain, Ostrom has developed an institutional theory of self-governing forms of collective action, positing that participatory forms of CPR management have a proven record of sustainable use. The success of these customary regulatory practices, she argues, reflects mutually supportive networks of cooperation and trust – an accretion of 'social capital' which reinforces the rules governing resource appropriations. This community solidarity helps to overcome the difficulties with compliance, monitoring and enforcement often encountered by centralized regulatory regimes (Ostrom, 1990, pp 182–190; 1995). In the language of environmental democracy, relying upon communicative action for collective management agreements generates shared environmental rules and norms which are more likely to meet the discourse principle. However, enthusiasm for such arrangements must be tempered by the recognition of their marginality in advanced capitalist countries. In a neoliberal era, when all local and regional forms of environmental self-governance face a global political economy hostile to common property regimes, their future survival remains precarious. Addressing these framework conditions of collective action is the strength of a third theoretical approach: *structuralism*.

The important explanatory contribution of structuralist political analysis is in demonstrating more clearly than the system's theoretical and new institutionalist perspectives the political and economic inequalities holding back the democratic negotiation of environmental interests. Significantly, there is a broad agreement with the institutionalist claim that the public good or CPR characteristics of ecological resources present difficulties in delivering collectively binding decisions on environmental protection; but the theory of state failure expands to address the context of political and administrative decision-making (Jänicke, 1990, pp 31–40). There is also an overlap with Luhmann's observations about the mismatch between the adversarial logic of the political system and the weak, diffuse interest representation of ecological interests. The theoretical difference arises from the structuralist appreciation that political communication is more than a self-referential circuit between formal political institutions. Indeed, structuralists argue that the representation of the political system in such hermetic terms actually reflects the continuing sway of capitalist interests in keeping economic decision-making off-limits to democratic governance. The structuralists bemoan the impotence of the state in the face of increasing social and environmental inequalities. Unwilling and unable to take on the economic sovereignty of corporate actors, state institutions find themselves dealing with the symptoms rather than the causes of environmental degradation. Jänicke claims that this failure to take preventative action is actually self-reinforcing, for the more it is drawn into costly remedial action, the stronger is its fiscal dependence upon taxation revenue from economic growth (1990, p 35).

Even if the environmental resolve of government is strengthened, Jänicke argues, it still has to force the relevant policy measures through a powerful, conservative bureaucracy (1990, pp 11–18). In the advanced capitalist countries, there are what he terms 'structural affinities' between industrial and bureaucratic organizations, restricting their resonance to common environmental interests. What is most relevant here is that neither side has a need to demonstrate democratic legitimacy (1990, p 27). Furthermore, experienced bureaucrats can employ their expertise to dilute or block the sort of cross-sectoral environmental initiatives that threaten to weaken their own departmental strengths. Of course, as critics of this position have rightly pointed out, bureaucrats are subject to numerous means of political and legal accountability (Papadakis, 1996, pp 30–31); but the problem with greening administrative systems is widely acknowledged. Conventional administrative decision-making – centralized, hierarchical and closed – is ill-equipped to register complex, dynamic ecological signals and to offer coordinated policy responses (Dryzek, 1987, pp 96–109; Paehlkle and Torgerson, 1990). Environmental decision-making typically entails the consideration of divergent interests and values; yet administrative institutions are, by most constitutional traditions, strictly separated from the political representation and negotiation of interests. They are designed to implement rather than facilitate collective decisions.

Political structuralists offer a plausible thesis as to why public administration, in the area of environmental protection (as well as the provision of other public goods), is compelled to engage in environmental interest intermediation and more participatory decision-making. According to Claus Offe (1985, p 310), for straightforward functional reasons – in order to secure effective policy and actions – administrative bodies have to involve citizens and interest groups as sources of assistance in the delivery of policy: 'the outcomes of administrative action are in many areas not the outcomes of the authoritative implementation of pre-established rules, but rather, the result of a "co-production" of the administration and its clients'. Offe applies this *co-production thesis* to policy areas where citizen compliance cannot, at a reasonable cost, be secured by traditional positive and negative incentives: traffic safety improvements, reducing car use in favour of public transport, preventive health care, the enhancement of environmental protection, and so on. In these areas, individuals may well be required to incur personal costs or inconvenience (at least in the short term) for a long-term public benefit; therefore, the administration needs recourse to communicative policy procedures and instruments to help alter existing environmental attitudes and behaviour.

There are parallels here with the new institutionalist recommendations for self-governance for local and regional CPRs, except that the former finds cooperative motives in individual gains and customary social ties. The co-production thesis is closer to the communicative understanding of politics informing environmental democracy, where democratic deliberation offers the possibility of identifying and agreeing upon environmental interests which *cross* community boundaries. That is why this chapter will focus on its more recent articulation in structuralist accounts of 'environmental capacity-building'.

POLITICAL CAPACITY-BUILDING FOR ENVIRONMENTAL DEMOCRACY

A very suggestive body of work on capacity-building in environmental protection and management has emerged from the structuralist analysis of state failure in ecological problem-solving. Undertaken by the Berlin school of environmental policy research, this has entailed a series of cross-cultural studies on the conditions for 'successful' environmental decision-making, encompassing both public and private actors and a diverse range of ecological risks (Jänicke, 1992; Jänicke and Weidner, 1995; 1997).[3] The Berlin school combines an explanatory and normative interest in successful environmental policy innovations, defining policy success in terms of improved environmental quality outcomes. A political system's capacity for environmental policy – its ability to identify and solve ecological problems – is constituted by the strength of organized governmental and nongovernmental proponents of environmental protection constrained, or enabled, by the structural framework of political action (Jänicke, 1997, p 8). Structuralist analysis of environmental decision-making has consistently stressed the resource configurations and institutional arrangements which frame the opportunities for proponents of environmental protection (see Kitschelt, 1986). The Berlin-directed research on environmental capacity has thematized more precisely these structural framework conditions, distinguishing between cognitive–informational conditions (the availability and application of environmental knowledge), political–institutional conditions (the prevailing norms and rules set by constitutional, institutional and legal systems), and economic–technological conditions (economic strength and technological expertise) (Jänicke, 1997, pp 11–14). And in response to criticisms that structuralist accounts offer only static representations of decision-making, it has developed a more nuanced appreciation of the 'situative contexts' – short-term action conditions – which mirrors the new institutionalist concern with immediate and dynamic decision environments.

It is not possible here to convey the scope of the Berlin work on environmental capacity-building. Rather, this chapter will look more closely at the political–institutional framework conditions, since this research suggests a positive relationship between discursive institutional structures and environmental policy success. This chapter also follows Jänicke in his finer subdivisions of conditions for *participation, integration* and *strategic* (long-term) action. Institutional arrangements enhancing these capacities concur with the procedural definition of environmental democracy offered in the last chapter: identifying empirical instances of each enables an elaboration of Offe's co-production thesis. Is democratic capacity-building conducive to successful environmental policy outcomes? In addition, since the discourse theory of democracy directs us not just to the character of formal political institutions and organizations, but to their communicative interplay with civil society, capacity-building for environmental democracy must also provide conditions favourable for public deliberation on environmental interests by citizens, informal associations and an open-mass media: the area of *noninstitutional* action.

Participative Capacity

Jänicke (1997, p 12) refers to participative capacity as 'the openness of the input structures of the policy process'. The structural conditions for participating in environmental decision-making encompass the range of political and policy institutions for collective choice, from constitutional frameworks for democratic governance to routine levels of administrative choice. The development of environmental policy, Jänicke observes, is usually associated with an increase in participative capacity cascading through the political system (1997, pp 17–18). The increasing participatory expectations of citizens, anticipating opportunities for meaningful involvement in environmental decision-making, test the democratic legitimacy of all parts of that system. In such a governance transition, the traditional liberal democratic restriction of participation to elections and largely symbolic public consultation exercises is found increasingly wanting. How can participative capacity improve upon the representation and negotiation of environmental interests?

At the constitutional level of political representation, the universal franchise is the distinguishing feature of liberal democratic states. While the universalization of the right to vote only reached North American and Western European countries in the 20th century, to the extent that all adults qualified for an equal vote at elections, it is commonly accepted in these democracies that citizenship status now appropriately includes all (aside from those deemed to have forfeited that right, such as prisoners). The universal franchise might thus seem to satisfy the discourse principle regarding the election of political representatives. However, Andrew Dobson (1996b) argues that the capacity of this franchise system to represent environmental interests is insufficient in democratic as well as ecological terms. For any democratic polity, the full representation of interests affected by environmental risk would have to include: those inhabitants of other countries experiencing negative ecological consequences as a result of productive or consumptive practices in the domestic political system; future generations, who can be assumed to favour the continuation of viable ecological conditions; and nonhuman species. Without taking into account these new constituencies, Dobson claims, national political systems lack the conditions to represent fairly environmental interests: their criteria for political membership remain arbitrary. He recommends that more inclusive ecological representation may be achieved by the election of proxy or substitute representatives, competing for reserved seats in national legislatures (1996b, p 136).

Dobson recognizes the immense practical difficulties associated with such an extension of political representation, although there are theoretical flaws enough with proxy representation to rule it out as a means of pushing forward constitutional participative capacity. Chapter 1 noted the inadmissibility of nonhuman species or individuals as moral participants in political discourse, and in the interplay of private and public autonomy that constitutes democratic will-formation (see also Chapter 4). It is perhaps enough here to note that determining different species' representation, which goes against the grain of species diversity and ecological interdependence, cannot avoid a conceptual quagmire at odds with transparent democratic decision rules. Proxy representation of the interests of future generations seems no less problematic, given the speculative nature of democratic accountability for those not yet born – although suggestions have been made by environmentalists for the direct representation of children's interests in national legislatures. A more sensible option is that adult citizens learn to represent more seriously their interests as future citizens (not forgetting that children also have interests as children). With the notion of strategic capacity, shortly to be discussed, there is more scope for this in long-term environmental planning. Finally, representing the environmental interests of nonnationals in national parliaments already exists, in part, through continental and international treaty obligations; and it would seem more promising to reinforce and extend these existing institutional channels rather than graft onto domestic political systems a complex mechanism for registering the concerns of nonnationals. As Dobson (1996b, p 131) indeed recognizes, there are further institutional conditions for capacity-building here, relating to the development of transnational parliaments, which would influence national polities.

David Held (1995, pp 273–275) proposes the creation of a new democratic international assembly, either a reformed United Nations General Assembly or a complementary 'second chamber' as a 'framework-setting' institution able to examine those global social and ecological problems neglected by nation states. Representation of environmental interests would be promoted by securing electoral opportunities for environmental nongovernmental organizations (NGOs), while an international chamber more sensitive than the United Nations to the concerns of developing countries might be able to register more clearly their burden of social and ecological justice. The international arena of environmental decision-making will be returned to in the conclusion to this book.

For the advanced capitalist countries under consideration, the only existing example of transnational parliamentary decision-making is the Parliament of the European Union (EU), which has been elected by general election since 1979. Since the Maastricht Treaty on European Union entered into force in 1993, there has been an expanded role for the European Parliament in shaping EU-wide environmental policy. This is consolidated by the environment committee of the European Parliament and encouraged by a unified group of European Parliament Green members. Restricting remarks here to the participative capacity facilitated by this electoral body, there remains a problem with the relative weakness of the Parliament in the EU policy-making process, since it is subordinate to the European Commission and the Council of Ministers. Thus, the opening up of the Parliament in recent years to lobbying by environmental interest groups has not closed the oft-noted democratic deficit of the EU's legislative process (Baker, 1996, p 221). For some, the extent to which the Parliament can ensure representation of nonnational environmental interests in the environmental policies of member states is compromised further by an EU executive preference for framework directives and voluntary instruments in the environmental field as opposed to the more binding use of regulations. It has been countered that the regulatory flexibility this affords member states in implementing environmental measures actually renders the EU formula as a best-practice model for transnational environmental law-making (Kramer, 1996, p 316), but this still begs the question of democratic legitimacy.

In keeping with the conceptual framing of environmental democracy in the last chapter, my claim is that the strongest *constitutional* support for the political representation of environmental interests is through the greening of human rights. A fundamental right to a safe and healthy environment could be employed by individuals and groups to prize open political decision-making on environmental concerns. Despite the diffuse and complex character of any such substantive right, there have been positive assessments of its potential in Europe – for example, in 1994 environmental protection was incorporated within the German constitution as a state objective (Ladeur, 1996) – alongside, as might be expected, a more developed debate in North America. US discussion in this area was first sparked by the Tanner versus Armico Steel Corporation case in the early 1970s, and has since wrestled with the scope for identifying a constitutional right to a decent environment in terms of existing bill of rights provisions or as the basis of a new constitutional amendment (Hoborn and Brooks, 1996, pp 49–59). Some states (Minnesota, New Jersey) have indeed developed their own environmental bill of rights. However, no such explicit national right has emerged, although the keynote environmental legislation of the 1960s and the 1970s has been construed as establishing statutory rights to a clean environment through the setting of exposure limits for pollutants (Pulido, 1994, p 917).

The Canadian discourse on environmental rights, built up over the past two decades, has drawn inspiration from the American public trust doctrine, which attaches legal recognition to common environmental resources as a collective right (Hoban and Brook, 1996, pp 169–187). This has achieved statutory expression at a subnational level in the Northwest Territories Environmental Rights Act and Ontario's Environmental Bill of Rights. In the jurisdictional tussle between federal and provincial governments that represents Canadian environmental decision-making, legal reform proposals for clear environmental rights have particular force. And they have started to impact upon the judiciary. In a recent Canadian Supreme Court decision addressing federal environmental powers, R versus Hydro-Quebec, 1997, the reasons cited in support of the national government's criminal law power to protect the environment include reference to the Law Reform Commission of Canada's formulation of 'the right to a safe environment' (1985a, p 8). This right is identified by the court as both an extension of existing rights and values – sanctity of life, the inviolability and integrity of persons, protection of human life and health – and the expression of newly emerging values about quality of life and stewardship of the natural environment (Supreme Court of Canada, 1997, p 44).

It is still too soon to assess the enduring impact of the R versus Hydro-Quebec decision on national environmental decision-making in Canada and the status of federal environmental authority vis-à-vis the provinces. In terms of participative capacity, though, it marks an important step towards the constitutional recognition of a right to a safe and healthy environment.

Of course, statutory support for participative capacity encompasses the numerous provisions for public participation in environmental decision-making in North American and European countries. Here the extensive American raft of access rights to government information and decision-making processes still stands out, in principle, as a model framework for democratic transparency and accountability. The seminal US National Environmental Policy Act, 1969, requires public involvement in preparing environmental impact statements by federal agencies and allows citizen lawsuits to challenge administrative decisions – powers that are evident in other environmental statutes, such as the US Clean Water Act and the US Emergency Planning and Community Right-to-Know Act. Accountability for environmental decisions is also facilitated by the general procedural disclosure rights created by the US Administrative Procedures Act and the US Freedom of Information Act (Andrews, 1997, pp 36–37). Whether these rights have meaningful purchase in practice is another matter. In the area of environmental assessment, for example, Wood (1995, p 240) claims that the formal rights for public participation in The Netherlands under its environmental management act are more effective than those in the US, in part due to the availability of public intervenor funding.

Assessed according to access criteria, Wood (1995, pp 236–237) also favours the Dutch system over the Canadian public information and participation procedures for environmental assessment. Canada's Environmental Assessment Act features access to information and public participation provisions, including a participant funding programme for resource-poor groups; but these are only triggered for contentious development proposals at the discretion of the federal government. There are no formal rights to public participation and a series of broad exemption powers have diluted the act's participatory potential (although legal challenges by environmental groups to the discretionary downgrading of the act have partially reversed this as a result of several federal court rulings). Interestingly, the design of the Canadian environmental assessment process by national department of the environment officials was influenced by a fear of the administrative logjams associated with the legalistic regulatory style of American environmental decision-making (Doern and Conway, 1994, pp 190–210). Yet a result of this bureaucratic caution has been a level of administrative discretion at odds with democratic openness and responsiveness.

The general rights to public participation contained in The Netherlands' Environmental Management Act contrast with the overwhelming Western European pattern of interest-based rights to public involvement in environmental decision-making. Notwithstanding differences in political systems and political cultures, this commonality can be related to shared principles of administrative fairness, requiring that those whose direct interests are affected by the decision of a public authority should be accorded a fair hearing (Lambrechts, 1996, p 95). In his review of public inquiry processes in the UK, France and Germany, Lambrechts (1996) notes that the French system is nominally the most open, with the freedom to participate on behalf of public interests (though usually entailing no public debate), while the German inquiry process is deemed the most closed because of the narrow interpretation of affected interests. While embracing an open right to participate, the UK system has traditionally distinguished between the legal rights of private and local general interests on the one hand, and third parties on the other, giving serious consideration only to the former – a situation that has recently become more ambiguous as a result of legal rulings on standing (Hilson and Cram, 1996). It is noteworthy that, even when required, environmental assessments seem to have made little or no difference on public inquiry decisions in the UK (Jones and Wood, 1995), casting doubt on the ability of public authorities to take into account ecological interests.

Lambrechts (1996, p 100) records the public ambivalence accompanying the inquiry process in these three countries:

> *Everywhere, the attitude of the public towards public inquiries is rather ambiguous: on the one hand there is a strong demand for participation; on the other hand there is a general feeling that public inquiries are only a mock-consultation – a means to give legitimacy to a decision made beforehand by the responsible authorities.*

Environmental democracy meets this public expectation with the institutionalization of meaningful public participation early on in the decision-making process (see the section on strategic capacity). It implies a relaxation of rules of standing for affected parties to promote the discursive identification of environmental interests. Increasing participative capacity in this way obliges a recognition of access rights regardless of personal legal interest. Supportive steps in this direction within the European Union include EC Directive 90/313 on Freedom of Access to Environmental Information (giving uniform information access rights), and proposed legislation on extending standing to individuals and groups across the EU to challenge alleged breaches of environmental legislation.

Of course, as is evident from the environmental policy gridlock and reversals in the US, general rights to participation in environmental decision-making may not necessarily lead to durable, effective decisions. In an adversarial system of interest representation, a high participative capacity can accentuate environmental conflict. This has led to the development of regulatory negotiation techniques in environmental decision-making which invite representatives of affected interests (widely defined) to come together and attempt to agree upon a proposed rule or decision (Fiorino, 1995). Their novelty arises from the pooling of authority amongst the representatives of relevant interests, with public authorities also participating as substantive negotiators.[4] Public accountability is protected by overarching regulations and existing legal norms of procedural fairness; therefore, regulatory negotiation is seen more as a complement than a replacement to conventional environmental decision-making. To be sure, there remain concerns about the exclusion of unorganized interests (Fiorino, 1995, p 34); yet with its emphasis on the communicative resolution of environmental problems, regulatory negotiations have attracted attention as representing participatory institutional designs – what Williams and Matheny describe as a 'dialogic model of social regulation' (1995, pp 36–65; see also Webler, 1995).

This is certainly the closest regulatory approximation to the discursive intent of environmental democracy, even if its still limited use in North America (and a growing interest in Europe) caution against immediate judgements. There is a need for further research on particular examples of regulatory negotiation.

The next chapter assesses a large-scale Canadian experiment with environmental negotiation, focusing upon its institutional commitment to administrative fairness in land-use governance. What this example reveals is that the democratization of environmental administration, as shared decision-making or co-production, ultimately presents a far-reaching choice to liberal democratic governments concerning the location of decision-making. The potential of environmental democracy rests upon their ability and commitment to redistribute that political and economic authority. But before we can address that point in this chapter, the other framework capacities for political action must be described.

Integrative Capacity

Opening up the political system to the representation of ecological interests will not, in itself, boost environmental capacity: collective decisions must bind all relevant actors. Jänicke has labelled as 'integrative capacity' those political-institutional framework conditions conducive to integrating environmental interests in sectoral decision-making (1997, p 13). The structuralist co-production thesis states here that those advanced capitalist countries with the most notable progress in environmental protection (Japan, The Netherlands, Sweden, Norway) are those with 'consensual' or 'neocorporatist' structures for negotiating interests – that is, they benefit from cooperative political styles where environmental interests have been incorporated within traditional sectoral bargaining processes (Jänicke, 1992, pp 52–55). These policy styles are long established and not restricted to environmental decision-making, hence their integrative potential when allied with an openness to environmental concerns (we shall leave to the side, for the moment, the fact that the impetus for including environmental interests typically comes from political mobilization in civil society). The institutional contrast is with those Western countries less successful in environmental policy-making, where interest mediation is more adversarial, encompassing both pluralistic (such as in the US) and closed (for example, the UK, France) systems of policy-making. These are broad-brush general-izations, of course, but their heuristic value is in offering explanatory propositions in support of movement towards environmental democracy. Open and inclusive structures of policy-making seem to achieve more significant improvements in environmental quality.[5]

An immediate objection to this thesis might be that it misconstrues environmental decision-making, downplaying the existing integrative mechanisms in those countries who 'underperform' in environmental quality terms. For example, David Vogel (1986, pp 269–276) interprets the British environmental policy style as 'corporatist' on account of the traditional regulatory negotiations between government officials, industry and those interest groups accorded consultative status. He cites policy-making on pollution, planning and environmental health as evidence of this cooperative working. Yet, it has been a regulatory style historically closed to environmental protection interests and, until recently, undermined by bureaucratic fragmentation (Smith, 1997). It is noteworthy that the need for intrapolicy coordination in the area of pollution control was identified in a report by the independent Royal Commission on Environmental Pollution in 1975, which articulated the best practicable environmental option (BPEO) methodology for integrating pollution licensing across environmental media (Royal Commission on Environmental Pollution, 1976). However, the uniform regulation promised by integrated pollution control had to wait 15 years for full statutory recognition and five more for institutional embodiment in a central administrative agency. Even in recent years, under an integrated regulatory regime, the problems of regulatory deference to industrial interests and administrative secrecy have continued (as noted in Chapter 5 with reference to the cement industry). The missed opportunity for a consensual policy-making process goes back 25 years to the same Royal Commission report; this recommended a more participatory approach to environmental regulation, open to the scrutiny of public interest groups (O'Riordan, 1989, p 116).

Interpolicy (interdepartmental) integration of environmental interests within the UK government has also seen a false dawn. The 1990 white paper *This Common Inheritance* announced a government commitment to greening all policy areas, led to the establishment of various cabinet and interdepartmental committees to achieve that end, and set up an annual environmental reporting system for all government departments. In practice, the committees rarely met and the annual reports on progress of administrative greening have lacked detail (Weale, 1997, p 104). The new Labour government elected in 1997 declared a firm interest in integrated environmental decision-making, creating new cabinet and parliament environment committees as well as a combined department of the environment, transport and the regions. Whether these more recent institutional innovations will kick-start interministerial environmental decision-making remains to be seen.

More progress has been made in Canada in moving away from a similarly closed regulatory approach – termed 'bipartite bargaining' by Hoberg (1993a) – towards multistakeholder negotiations over national and provincial environmental policy (a provincial example, in the area of land-use planning, is discussed in the next chapter). At the national level, the federal department of the environment, partly in response to environmentalist pressure, facilitated a series of meetings in the mid 1980s – the Niagara process – between representatives drawn from government, industry, organized labour and the environmental movement. These exploratory sessions in the discursive identification of shared environmental interests actually led to consensus-based development of toxics legislation (which evolved into the Canadian Environmental Protection Act) and the formulation of long-term environmental management plans on nitrogen oxide and volatile organic compound emissions. They also prompted the formation of broad-based round tables on sustainable development, both at federal level and in most provinces (Doern and Conway, 1994, pp 107–116). And in 1990 the federal government introduced an ambitious Cdn$13 billion Green Plan as an integrative framework for environmental policy initiatives, including recommendations for intersectoral environmental decision-making. If the latter, subsequently weakened by budget cuts, has not achieved the institutionalization of environmental integration envisaged for depart-mental decision-making in Ottawa, the government's selective use of discursive designs for environmental decision-making nevertheless deserves recognition as a modest advance in environmental democracy.

For the development of integrative environmental capacities, the neocorporatist states demonstrate the most progress, with The Netherlands most often cited as the exemplar. The Netherlands' National Environmental Policy Plan (NEPP), first published in 1989, has been lauded as 'the most serious attempt to integrate environmental concerns into the full range of public policy' (Weale, 1992, p 124; also Straaten, 1992) on account of its innovative policy instruments and ambitious environmental quality targets. To be sure, the promotion of internal policy integration by NEPP built on established indicative multiyear plans designed to tackle pollution on a cross-media basis (Weale, 1992, pp 137–138), which led to integrated licences for industrial discharges not dissimilar from the British pollution control system. Yet NEPP consolidated this cross-sectoral approach to environ-mental management and extended it into other policy spheres, proposing source-oriented pollution reduction (through recycling, renewable resource use and energy efficiency), investment in environmental technologies and management systems, and the widespread use of voluntary agreements as environmental policy instruments (the 'target group' approach). The latter entailed the cooperative negotiation of sector-based ecological objectives with key economic interests (for example, agriculture, traffic and transport).

The national environmental planning heralded by NEPP can be under-stood as an example of Dutch cooperative decision-making (though the first NEPP was a casualty of political opposition to a proposal to abolish tax breaks for commuters). Despite cabinet-level endorsement of its content, its optimistic aspirations to interpolicy integration have not been realized, and this implementation gap reveals something of the constraints to voluntary-based environmental coordination. In the agriculture and transport sectors, results have been the most disappointing: these are the policy areas where strong sectoral lobbying maintains a clear subordination of environmental interests to economic development interests (Bressers and Plettenburg, 1997, p 128). This also reflects the maintenance of existing ministerial boundaries, since NEPP never entertained structural reforms to administrative decision-making. Behind the use of target groups, environmental partnerships and regulatory negotiations, traditional administrative boundaries and responsibilities have been maintained. Bressers and Plettenburg (1997, p 129) astutely point out that the use of cooperative environmental policy instruments – particularly the target group approach to self-regulation – has served to boost integrative capacity, delivering some significant environmental quality benefits (notably by the industry, refineries and construction target groups), but that there is a *democratic* danger that collective environmental interests are removed from public deliberation. For the mixed but undoubted gains in policy effectiveness, NEPP's neocorporatist bargaining is not yet inclusive enough.

Dutch environmental policy-making has always taken place against a background of governmental understanding that it will not undermine economic competitiveness or clash with the direction of European integration, hence the state's vigorous lobbying to ensure that Dutch environmental planning instruments are at the forefront of European Union policy development and its sponsorship of environmental technologies (this type of subsidy is a legitimate derogation from the standardizing provisions of the Single European Market). It is no coincidence, then, that the European Union's Fifth Environmental Action Programme, introduced in 1992, established a general consultative forum composed of governmental representatives, nongovernmental organizations and business interests, alongside intra- and interpolicy forums on implementation and environmental policy review. This promotion of integrative environmental capacity has support under article 130r(2) of the Maastricht Treaty, which stipulates that environmental protection requirements must be integrated within the definition and implementation of all EC policies (Wilkinson, 1997, p 155). This carries no direct legal implications for member states, but the influence of such a defining principle on national environmental policies through Europe-wide decisions is potentially very significant.

So far, though, the consultative and coordinating bodies set up under the Fifth Environmental Action Programme have failed to achieve satisfactory external integration of environmental concerns across other policy areas, and in April 1997, following a review of the programme, the Council of Ministers resolved to address this failing as a priority area for action. To some commentators, this deficiency has not been surprising for two chief reasons. Firstly, the programme is neither binding on member states nor on the ministers or directorates general in the European Commission. Without this formal power, the environment directorate general has had to rely on bottom-up integration methods, trying to persuade other parts of the European Union political and policy system to embrace its programme (Wilkinson, 1997). The absence of resources and high-level commitment to build integrative capacity is indicative of the overall weakness in environmental capacity at the federal European decision-making level. Secondly, environmental issues are being marginalized in the push towards economic and monetary union. Such is the seeming inexorability of this project, supported by powerful sectoral groupings across the European Union, that environmental proposals incompatible with those economic interests are consistently weakened – for example, the undermining of the EU preventative waste policy by the waste management industry (O'Brien and Penna, 1997, pp 190–192). The lack of integrative capacity at the European level is compounded by, and in turn reinforces, the democratic deficiencies in representing, and being accountable to, collective environmental interests. This does not bode well for developing environmental capacity in Western European states.

Strategic Capacity

Integrating long-term environmental interests in sectoral decision-making marks out a third aspect of the political–institutional framework conditions necessary for effective policy outcomes: strategic capacity. According to Jänicke, this refers to 'the capacity to implement comprehensive and long-term objectives in a well-coordinated manner with sufficient staying power' (1992, p 55; 1997, p 13). Strategic environmental capacity is a necessary institutional precondition for environmental democracy, locking ecological objectives into all levels of formal decision-making. As with integrative capacity, there are good theoretical and empirical grounds for suggesting a noncontingent link between strategic ecological decision-making and discursive institutional designs. So while Jänicke claims that the North American and Western European democracies have much ground to cover in strategic capacity-building, he still maintains that those with cooperative political and regulatory styles have travelled the most. In countries where neocorporatist interest mediation and public deliberation on ecological issues is well established, environmental decision-making benefits from long-term political support and democratic legitimacy. Once again, Dutch environmental policy-making attracts plaudits in this regard (Hajer, 1995), although the accommodative style of the Swedish political system is also cited as conducive to strategic environmental capacity-building (Lundqvist, 1997).

Why should the co-production of collective choices within neocorporatist political systems be responsive to extending the time horizons of environmental decision-making? Chapter 2 stated that discursive democratic designs encourage the identification of – and subscription to – environmental protection as a generalizable interest. To recall, the discourse principle informing environmental democracy stipulates that such universal interests are those which everyone affected could, in principle, agree upon. The democratic legitimacy of human environmental rights is that they command protection of those vital ecological interests which make such autonomous decision-making possible. The more open and inclusive will-formation of the West European social democracies, and their active shaping of the 'public' interest through interest negotiation, suggests a receptiveness to environmentalist arguments that social cooperation between successive generations is as important as intragenerational cooperation in delivering shared environmental benefits. Another suggestion is that regulatory constraints on private investment decisions are widely accepted as legitimate in these countries. This gives rise to a discourse on environmental protection indebted to social democratic motifs of long-term planning and interest mediation. It is also why the difficult institutional move towards preventative environmental decision-making found resonance, first, in the West European social democracies. In other words, strategic environmental capacity-building has developed most, albeit haltingly, in those states which are comfortable with indicative planning and fared poorly in those countries under the sway of neoliberal short-termism.

An influential German innovation in strategic environmental planning and management illustrates this relationship with state intervention. What has become known as the precautionary principle, expressed in the Rio Declaration on Environment and Development as the state obligation to address serious environmental threats even in the absence of full scientific understanding (principle 15), owes much to the German adoption of *Vorsorgeprinzip*. In Germany this principle of precaution was introduced by the Social Democratic administration in the first federal environment programme in 1971, initially justifying the preventative policy action against air pollution but evolving in the 1980s as central to the national discourse of sustainable development. Boehmer-Christiansen (1994) sites the precautionary principle within the German corporatist tradition of consensus-based interest consultation and negotiation. As a result of public ecological concern and activism, environmental protection interests have successfully entered into these bargaining structures. Boehmer-Christiansen stresses that this means only a procedural opening: the precautionary principle must still compete with sectoral economic interests in policy-formation processes. In other words, political commitment to, and legal entrenchment of, the principle is critical:

> The duty of precaution endows public authorities with responsibility for the protection of the natural foundations of life and of maintaining the physical world intact for future as well as present generations. It can therefore be used to counter the short-termism endemic in all democratic, consumption oriented societies (Boehmer-Christiansen, 1994, p 55).

To be sure, as Boehmer-Christiansen recognizes, the generality of the precautionary principle actually provides little guidance on selecting and using policy instruments. More relevant here, the association of strategic capacity-building with democratic bargaining reveals, in practice, the continuing gap between neocorporatist structures and environmental democracy. The latter denotes institutional procedures geared towards the mutual recognition of generalizable interests (including environmental ones), whereas the German championing of the precautionary principle as a state-sponsored collective interest throws ecological concerns into the bargaining ring with economic growth interests. In other words, the opening up of corporatist interest mediation to (long-term) environmental concerns only goes half way. There has been no political commitment to redesigning bargaining structures so that they are more oriented towards communicative agreements rather than power brokering. Without such a restructuring, the much vaunted 'consensus' of neocorporatist policy-making often turns out to be no more than a tactical compromise between different groups, and may well exclude those social and ecological interests not meeting with state interests.

In fact, the German policy-making system is not short of procedural safeguards designed to ensure that decisions are publicly accountable. There are various mechanisms for making sure that administrative actions abide by due process and are explicitly justified (Weale, 1992, p 74). What is missing is an *enabling* role for government in bringing to the fore environmental interests. This has become apparent with regard to the lack of German progress in embracing the participatory implications of sustainable development. The federal government has not seen any need to create public forums to elicit the type of bottom-up input into sustainability structures envisaged by Agenda 21, nor to reorganize administrative structures to increase integration of environmental interests within decision-making (Beuermann and Burdick, 1997). Ironically, the early German adoption of the precautionary principle has thus acted as a brake on further institutional innovation by hightening government complacency about its environmental credentials. As is argued at the end of this chapter, only a political commitment to decentralization in environmental decision-making promises to marry strategic capacity with democratization.

Whatever the deficiencies displayed by the German system of environmental decision-making, it remains the case that neocorporatist countries seem to have higher levels of strategic environmental capacity. Their relative success may be contrasted again with the closed system of British environmental interest representation and the open but adversarial US system. For the former, we can note that the precautionary principle was absent from environmental policy discourse until the mid 1980s and was then limited in terms of its administrative articulation and application to policy areas (Haigh, 1994). Unlike Germany, there has been a flurry of government pronouncements and rhetorical commitments on the subject of a national sustainable development strategy but, as Voisey and O'Riordan (1997) point out, little in the way of evidence that policy-making structures are shaking off their limited spatial and temporal horizons. As is discussed in Chapter 6, the most encouraging signs of a revisioning towards long-term environmental interests are to be found in the diverse voluntarist streams of the British Local Agenda 21 process, generating new participatory forms. The source of strategic thinking has been the associative and communicative activities of civil society rather than political institutions.

In the US, several of the key environmental statutes introduced by the federal government in the 1970s have precautionary intent – for example, the margin of safety provisions prescribed for the setting of pollution emission levels by the US Clean Air Act or the even more risk averse provisions of the US Clean Water Act and the US Endangered Species Act (Bodansky, 1994). Such has been their onerous legislative burden, Bodansky claims, that they helped to spark the subsequent anti-regulatory backlash against environmental legislation by economic development interests (1994, p 205). Like Britain in the last 20 years, the American right has been dominated by an uncompromising neoliberal ideology hostile to environmental protection, and on reaching political office has attempted to disable ecological statutes, first at the White House and then in Congress.[6] Against this political tide, the strategic potential of such administrative innovations as the President's Council for Sustainable Development and the US Environmental Protection Agency's National Environmental Goals Project has been not been fulfilled. In addition, the continuing preoccupation in both the US and the UK with the monetary evaluation of environmental risks and regulatory burdens pulls policy planning away from precautionary restraint and strategic capacity-building.

Across North America and Western Europe, there is little sign of anything other than hesitating, incremental steps towards strategic environmental decision-making. At the cross-national level, one initiative worthy of note is the European Union's proposed Directive on Strategic Environmental Assessment (SEA). The planned directive extends environmental assessment procedures to the development plans and programmes of public authorities, requiring the preparation and public circulation of impact assessments prior to development decisions (Commission of the European Communities, 1997). There is a stress on the openness and accountability of the process, although there is no obligation on the development authority to facilitate public input when determining the policy and programme alternatives for the initial impact statement. Thus, the intended cross-sectoral integration of environmental considerations within strategic policy choices is more a matter for interdepartmental bargaining than participatory decision-making. This implies a limited, consultative idea of democratic responsiveness (Kornov, 197, p 180) that is at odds with the discursive democratic notion that citizens must have the opportunity early on in the policy process to shape the alternatives affecting their interests. It is perhaps symptomatic of EU environmental policy-making that even the modest ambitions of the SEA directive have not found universal favour with member states, and the proposal has been subject to a protracted process of negotiation.

The Role of Noninstitutional Political Action

So far this section has elaborated upon the thesis of the Berlin school of environmental policy research that certain political–institutional framework conditions are conducive to developing effective environmental decision-making. With reference (albeit briefly) to a series of recent institutional developments in North America and Western Europe, several examples of environmental capacity-building have been selected which seem to offer at least some substantive support for the claim that discursive democracy is good for the environment. Those neocorporatist political systems with more deliberative procedures for environmental interest mediation have more developed and more effective (according to the criteria of the Berlin school) processes of environmental policy-making. From the formulation of environmental democracy in the last chapter, though, it is evident that recasting formal political decision-making along (more) discursive lines is not enough. Those institutional procedures for making collective decisions can only begin to approximate the discourse principle if they are open to public communication on ecological problems. The diverse and dynamic civil space of concerned citizens, interest groups and media networks is the source of noninstitutional communicative and associative activity geared towards influencing the political system in such a way.

One reason that this book adopts a strong, rights-based notion of environmental democracy is that it takes citizenship seriously, enjoining actors in civil society to make an input to, and to impact upon, the political system. A platform of autonomy-based rights – from civil and political freedoms to rights to decent social and ecological provisions – gives individuals and groups an invaluable political resource for civic self-determination. Cohen and Arato (1993, pp 18–26) correctly point out that protecting the public and associative spheres of civil society is a prerequisite for meaningful deliberative democracy, where citizens can form collective preferences in an open and inclusive fashion. Once again, this highlights the link between the communicative determination of environmental interests and the democratic legitimacy of decisions shaped in this way. Public reasoning over environmental choices with the aim of identifying common ecological concerns (as well, of course, as the mutual recognition of those environmental preferences which resist generalization) nurtures environmental citizenship. The development of that citizenship competence rests on the inroads made by proponents of ecological democratization; and although the structuralist approach has surveyed thoroughly the development of environmental institutions, there is also a clear recognition that using existing environmental capacity depends on political agency and short-term political opportunities. Indeed, Jänicke claims that the most decisive *democratic* contribution of Western countries to environmental sustainability will come from the expansion of those constitutional civil rights which facilitate noninstitutional political action (1996, p 83).

Comparative cross-national research on environmental politics sympathetic to the structuralist perspective but preoccupied with explaining the public mobilization of environmental concern has come to be known as the *political process* approach. Its methodological interest in environmental activism has employed the structuralist notion of political opportunity structures – 'the specific configurations or resources, institutional arrangements and historical precedents for social mobilization' (Kitschelt, 1986,) – but with the aim of accounting for political agency. In practice this has meant a sensitivity to the noninstitutional aspects of national political contexts – enduring ideological cleavages, informal political strategies and action repertoires, the construction of norms and interests, and so on (Joppke, 1991; Kriesi et al, 1995; Heijden, 1997). The collective action studied is still 'political' insofar as its objectives would have to be formulated and implemented as legally binding decisions by public authorities. It is relevant here because, having discussed political-institutional conditions above, it addresses the other side of the dualistic thesis of environmental democracy presented in the last chapter: a discursive interplay of political communication between formal political institutions and civil society is vital to the effectiveness and democratic legitimacy of (environmental) decision-making. Two relevant explanatory claims of the political process work are that the nature of the political opportunity structure in a state determines to a large extent, firstly, the profile and impact of noninstitutional political mobilization (Heijden, 1997, p 33) and, secondly, its subsequent integration within the political system – how actors shape the nature of the political opportunities they encounter (Kriesi et al, 1995, p 245). If confirmed by further research, these claims have important implications for understanding the activities and effectiveness of environmental groups.

According to the first claim, social movement activism is more likely to achieve durable policy responses if the political structure is inclusive and the state strong. More expansively, sustained (ecological) protest is, other things being equal, likely to be more effective when a democratic system is open to environmental interests and when institutional decision-making structures have strong integrative and strategic capacity. This predictive model has been used to explain the relative effectiveness of anti-nuclear protest in several Western democracies (Kitschelt, 1986; Kriesi et al, 1995, pp 218–225). In The Netherlands and Sweden, which are both characterized as having open political input structures and closed output structures, the mobilization of anti-nuclear protest is recorded as having had the greatest policy impact (in terms of a reduction in nuclear capacity). In contrast, on the participative side, the closed political opportunity structures associated with France and, to a lesser extent, Germany led to more confrontational political strategies and fewer political gains for anti-nuclear movements.[7] Finally, the US offers relative openness to articulating environmental interests, but the fragmented state of its political and administrative institutions means that novel political demands, often successfully aired, nevertheless are likely to be dissipated by changing political agendas or weak implementation structures. For the anti-nuclear energy movement, political mobilization in the 1970s helped to reduce the size of the national nuclear programme; but as Joppke (1991, pp 48–51) observes, this energy campaign quickly collapsed in the 1980s as public issue-attention shifted under Reagan's militarism to nuclear disarmament. Anti-nuclear discourse was appropriated by a separate disarmament movement, suggesting that the American tendency towards competitive, issue-specific activism rather than progressive alliance-building makes protest movements less effective in the long run.

This leads to the second claim of the political process theorists – that the degree of institutionalization of the environmental movement (its organizational growth, professionalization and its repertoire of political action) is also strongly related to national political opportunity structures (Heijden, 1997; Kriesi et al, 1995, pp 244–247). Heijden (1997), noting the growing institutionalization of the environmental movement in Germany, The Netherlands and Switzerland, observes that these are political systems attuned to new political cleavages and accommodative interest intermediation (note Germany's move from 'closed' to 'open' system as the discourse of environmental interests shifts from anti-nuclear to ecological protection). A consistently high level of unconventional protest actions (82.9 per cent of environmentalist actions from 1975–1989) in the French democratic system is explained with reference to the noninclusive political opportunity structure (1997, pp 43–44).[8] Interestingly, Heijden also records a high level of confrontational and violent political actions in the German political system, which he reasons is partly to do with a tradition of repressive police tactics against protesters despite the state's greater participative capacity (he is more at a loss to explain a high level of violent and confrontational actions in The Netherlands). In addition, he states that, aside from Switzerland, the organizational growth and professionalization of mainstream environmental organizations is increasingly thrown into sharp relief against a proliferation of direct action groups. Nowhere in Western Europe is that more so in recent years than in Britain, as attested to by a series of anti-roads and animal welfare protests – a grassroots activism stoked up by a closed, centralized political system and the perceived cooption of mainstream environmental groups by government and industry (Macnaghten and Urry, 1998, pp 62–68).

Heijden (1997, pp 45–46) makes a parallel observation about the gap between the high levels of environmental concern registered by publics in the above countries and the modest numbers involved in comprehensive green behaviour. Across the European and North American democracies, this behavioural shortfall seems to question the sincerity of public environmental attitudes, implying expressive rather than normative concern. For example, in Britain the heightened concern in recent years about road-building, traffic growth and air pollution has not yet connected with a widespread acceptance of the need to temper personal car use (Taylor, 1997). This seems to demonstrate that the environmental movement still has communicative work to do regarding public support for appropriate policy measures. However, caution is needed in interpreting environmental attitude surveys. Macnaghten and Urry (1998, pp 75–103) offer an incisive critique of a 'polling culture' which assumes that opinion polls faithfully record and represent individual preferences, pointing instead to the complex interplay of environmental beliefs, attitudes and behaviour. The critical point is their stress on the discursive construction of environmental attitudes and value in relation to a variety of mediating connections – the mass media, science, political and policy communities, corporations, and so on. These make environmental attitudes a much more problematic notion than traditionally appreciated.

The obvious mediating influence relevant to the discussion here is *political context*; in particular, individual and group appraisals of political agency and community. There is much academic support for the proposition that environmental awareness and responsibility is strongly related to people's perception of political efficacy and their sense of moral community (Eden, 1993; Witherspoon, 1996; Macnaghten and Urry, 1998). Sharon Witherspoon (1996) employs this thesis to explain why the European social democracies – Norway, The Netherlands and Sweden – have progressed furthest in preventative environmental decision-making. This is not just because of their transparent and neocorporatist political opportunity structures, but also due to enduring political traditions of social provision and redistributive justice. To the structuralist support for environmental democracy – that these systems benefit from moving towards democratic deliberation in institutional terms – we can add the cultural support arising from democratic political cultures attuned to generalizable social and environmental norms. And this means their populations are more willing to countenance the curbing of their consumptive preferences for the common good – for example, the finding that there is a greater public acceptance in The Netherlands than in Britain for environmental policies which increase tax and price burdens (Witherspoon, 1996, p 65).

Recent British public opinion research seems to confirm Heijden's account of noninstitutional political mobilization, where a low trust in the ability of government to respond to public demands nevertheless combines with high levels of self-confidence in personal political efficacy to generate societal tolerance for unconventional (nonviolent) political activism (Curtice and Jowell, 1997), including the recent flurry of direct-action environmental protest. Yet environmentalist arguments are running against a neoliberal political culture (and noninclusive system of government) that remains at best indifferent to questions of ecological and social redistribution. For the US, the cultural bias against common environmental interests predates the neoliberal assault on government. Matthew Cahn (1995) argues that the strongly individualistic, historically entrenched strains of American liberalism have resulted in a political culture at odds with the representation of environmental interests as a collective good:

> *In the absence of an explicit language of communal rights, there is little prospect of limiting concrete property rights for an abstract public good. The narrow Liberal definition of communal good has consistently allowed individual and corporate claims of property rights to outweigh the need for serious environmental regulation (Cahn, 1995, p 7).*

It may be argued, of course, that various global influences are reducing the importance of national political cultures at the level of political communication, of which the most obvious one is global mass media. The global media, Macnaghten and Urry (1998, pp 97–101) explain, have not only been instrumental in communicating environmental information to national publics, but in actively 'constructing' environmental issues through a variety of discursive strategies. To take perhaps the dominant discursive framing: through the activities of the leading transnational environmental organizations, based in Western Europe and North America, the environmental agenda has become a global one – international ecological problems threatening a vulnerable planet (Jamison, 1996). This is a construction contested by much of the media, and numerous environmental groups, in the global South (Chapman, Kumar, Fraser and Gaber, 1997), since international environmental risk definitions can be tracked back to subglobal political structures and networks. The continuing dominance of nation states in setting opportunities for, and constraints to, noninstitutional political action means that national political cultures, however nebulous, will still impinge upon the activities of ecological activists at all geographical scales.

The political challenge for environmental democrats at the agenda-setting stage of political communication is to ensure that the dominant transnational environmental groups will open up to the concerns of the global South (a loaded term itself), and to oppose the concentration of corporate media power. An urgency attends both political tasks, although without the regulatory taming and democratization of the corporate media, the contribution of environmental groups to public discourse will wither away against the management of public opinion by giant economic interests (McChesney, 1997).

The maintenance of a free and independent media can only be secured effectively by formal political institutions; yet the pressure for such democratization comes from citizens groups. This indicates, finally, the self-limiting (Cohen and Arato, 1993, p 526) role of noninstitutional political action: its objective is to generate influence rather than to acquire political office. The critical democratic weight of that influence, according to the discourse principle, is the extent to which the political communication exposes unjust social practices and promotes the identification of common norms (Cohen and Arato, 1993, pp 15–26). Collective environmental interests acquire democratic legitimacy in civil society insofar as they are shown to support existing rights or public environmental needs. It is an axiom of the discourse theory of democracy that the strength of the communicative interplay between formal political institutions and civil society rests upon their retaining separate identities. For those environmental groups drawn into political bargaining structures in Western Europe, and increasingly in North America, there is likely to be a democratic price – the loss of oppositional freedom (Dryzek, 1996; Jamison, 1996). A democratic political culture is an independent and unashamedly critical one. And the discursive health of democracy depends upon this. We now need to see whether an awareness of the role of democratic deliberation in environmental decision-making has a place in the increasingly dominant economic rationalization of environmental policy in the Western democracies.

ECOLOGICAL MODERNIZATION

The research into environmental capacity associated with the Berlin school builds up a picture of policy success on the basis of favourable framework conditions for decision-making. From this perspective, institutional and noninstitutional political action for environmental protection is most effective when the state facilitates participation, integration, strategic planning and a thriving civil society; and when the relevant governmental and nongovernmental actors participate in the decision-making process cooperatively. The diffuse, complex nature of contemporary ecological problems means that they are not amenable to traditional, top-down state intervention; as a result, they must be addressed through inclusive policy networks. Common environmental interests can then be identified and decisions reached in a shared fashion. According to Jänicke and Weidner (1995, pp 23–24), if states want to get on top of ecological problem-solving, and keep up with the rising democratic expectations of citizens, they will need to continue, and in some cases accelerate, their environmental capacity-building. They describe this challenge as *political modernization*; however, this cannot be divorced from the economic-technological conditions for environmental policy-making: economic productivity, technological standards and resource attributes. National economic performance is an important determinant of environmental capacity (Jänicke, 1997, pp 7, 14). The prospect of a mutually reinforcing axis of environmental and economic policy has, since the late 1980s, become the dominant preoccupation of the advanced capitalist states in the area of environmental decision-making. This is the project of ecological modernization.

Ecological modernization, as understood by Jänicke, denotes a particular economic development path available to a country – one that entails a transition to 'ecologically better-adapted production structures' (1992, p 53). By this he means a greening of production processes through technological innovation and structural reorganization. These strategies offer cost savings to industry from more efficient resource and energy use, while also generating environmental benefits for the workplace and beyond (such as pollution reduction). Insofar as the cost reductions of 'clean production' are self-evident to industry, they are no more than part of the conventional corporate drive towards increased competitiveness. Where the state enters is in encouraging the corporate sector to internalize external environmental costs for long-term gains in economic growth. The carrot typically encompasses tax relief for ecotechnological investments, state-sponsored research and development assistance, and the prospect of a share of the profitable green consumer market. For the state, there is the promise of a more effective, preventative environmental policy alongside the political gains associated with continuing economic growth. As Jänicke cautions (1997, p 14), their connection is not assured since the relationship between environmental capacity and a country's economic performance is complex and indirect. However, it is no coincidence that the win-win rhetoric of political modernization has found a receptive audience with the policy elites of Western Europe's social democracies.

This correspondence with neocorporatism arises not only because ecological modernization presupposes a consensual and interventionist policy style (Dryzek, 1997, p 151), but also because these countries have had the economic resources to invest more in environmental technologies and amenities. They have tended to subscribe to economic growth models which, against the neoliberal free market orthodoxy, stress the competitive advantages from state investment in skills, technologies and infrastructure developments. It is a logical extension of this strategic economic model that environmental quality becomes drawn in as an additional attribute for attracting high-value capital and labour. In an environmental-economic classification of European Union states according to per capita income and environmental quality indices, Giannis and Liargoras (1998) identify a group of high-productivity countries – Sweden, Finland, Germany, Denmark, Austria and The Netherlands – that offers supply-side benefits from their above-average environmental quality:

> ... this above-average productivity effect is reflected in the ability of producers in these regions to pay above-average incomes and rents for having at their disposal a greater than average level of environmental quality (Giannis and Liargoras, 1998, p 90).[9]

Only the UK also possesses an above-average level of environmental quality, but its below-average per capita income means that there are no associated productivity benefits (it is 'high amenity'). The other member states all have relatively low levels of environmental quality, although there is a division between those with higher per capita incomes (the 'low amenity' countries: France, Belgium and Luxembourg) and those with lower than average incomes (the 'low productivity' countries: Italy, Ireland, Spain, Portugal and Greece).

This theoretical framework is only a preliminary attempt at an environmental–economic ranking and carries numerous simplifying assumptions – for example, that environmental quality is tradeable against income. Nevertheless, its correlative isolation of the neocorporatist countries is striking. Qualitative corroboration of the priority accorded to the environmental-productivity effect in these states is wide ranging; taking just government investment in green technologies, we can note, for example, the pivotal role of the Dutch National Environmental Technology

Programme (with its network of regional, state-funded innovation centres), the industrial research and development emphasis of the Swedish Foundation for Strategic Environmental Research, and Germany's impressive state funding for research and development into renewable energy technologies. A more systematic cross-national examination is not possible here, but there are several important studies on the differential development of ecological modernization discourse between selected European countries – for example, Hajer (1995) on the UK and The Netherlands and Weale (1992) on Germany and the UK. Hajer and Weale both examine the marked contrast between the early policy uptake of ecological modernization in the neocorporatist political systems against the institutional resistance to it in Britain.

The contemporary political and policy currency of ecological modernization in Western Europe (with a growing interest in North America) may be related to a particular convergence of interests between governments, nongovernmental organizations (including mainstream environmentalists) and businesses (Hajer, 1995, pp 73–103). At the international level, Hajer notes seminal ecomodernist statements by the Organisation for Economic Co-operation and Development's (OECD's) *Environment and Economics* (1985) and the Brundtland Report (World Commission on Environment and Development, 1987), which highlight the communicative interplay between ecological modernization and the more wide-ranging ideas of socio-economic change addressed by debates on sustainable development. Analyses of ecological modernization as a discourse have emphasized a variety of recurrent motifs – social partnerships, precautionary and prudent decision-making, nature as a public good, technological progress, and so on (Hajer, 1995, pp 24–36; Dryzek, 1997, pp 137–152). What is commented upon briefly here, employing the Habermasian discourse principle outlined in the introduction to this book, is its normative validity – specifically how it measures up against the deliberative notion of democracy. Ecological modernization, like sustainable development, claims to capture a mutuality of interests between economic growth and environmental protection. Its discursive democratic legitimacy rests upon the implicit claim that ecological modernization, as embraced by public and private institutions, would command sufficient support of the people (its impact is societywide) if subject to rational debate. What are its democratic credentials?

According to the proponents of ecological modernization, it extends environmental responsibility into economic decision-making by incorporating third-party environmental costs within private and public investment decisions. Through such principles as the polluter pays principle, cost-benefit analysis and ecological liability, public authorities are able to tailor policies to reduce the extent to which citizens are exposed to the external environmental risks generated by collective economic choices. The sub-discipline of environmental economics is concerned with demonstrating how environmental values can be expressed as monetary preferences for environmental quality, thereby quantifying ecological risks for market-based decision rules and policy objectives. It is then able to define, in line with (Pigovian) welfare economics, a 'Pareto optimum' of economic efficiency, where external environmental costs are taken into account in resource allocation decisions. In such an equilibrium state (where price = marginal social cost: Pearce and Turner, 1990, pp 62–67), production and capital investment can no longer bank on unloading environmental damage onto individuals and communities without at least handing over adequate compensation. In practice, technical difficulties in calculating the economically 'optimal' level of pollution have led to a more pragmatic employment of economic techniques as policy instruments – environmental taxes and charges, pollution-emission trading markets, deposit-refund systems and financial subsidies (Myrick Freeman III, 1994; Bandi, 1996). As Weale (1992, p 157) observes, even if these techniques have not been geared to achieving optimal economic efficiency, they have provided more cost-effective environmental decision-making, harnessing the flexibility and responsiveness of market incentives for politically or administratively set objectives.

Now, the employment of economic policy instruments is, by itself, only a weak indicator of ecological modernization, and an even weaker claim to a more democratic representation of environmental interests. Only neoliberalism (see Chapter 1) identifies in the increasing use of market-based incentives an expansion in the freedom of individuals to express their environmental quality preferences. Its economic theory of democracy is particularly vulnerable to the scrutiny of the discourse principle, because it ignores the asymmetries of economic power – how those without property rights and higher incomes are marginalized by decision rules based upon market valuation (such as cost-benefit analysis). The deliberative space of environmental democracy invites, in principle, the participation of all those affected by collective choices, whatever their market strength. Given current distributional inequities, and the seeming unwillingness of Western governments to reduce income polarization, the use of economic policy instruments to combat the socialization of environmental costs in private and public development decisions is at least a modest step towards more democratic accountability in environmental decision-making. Yet, this is only as a subset of all those policy tools available to society to achieve environmental objectives, and where those overarching goals are set by deliberative democratic procedures (Jacobs, 1997, pp 67–68; Holland, 1997). The determination of collective preferences, oriented towards identifying shared values and interests, is worked through by constructive dialogue rather than anonymous market transactions.

It is tempting to observe again in the European neocorporatist political systems the closest institutional designs to democratically negotiating environmental interests, where economic and non-economic policy instruments serve policy objectives. For those countries, internalizing environmental danger takes on a broader political sense to refer to the emergence of explicit decision-making and management processes for incorporating environmental quality concerns (M O'Connor, 1997, p 456). There are differences of emphasis, of course. The Scandinavian social democracies have

embraced the use of economic instruments the most; for example, environmental (including energy) taxation provides 12 per cent of state income in
Sweden and 8 to 10 per cent in Denmark (Lundqvist, 1997, p 60; Andersen,
1997, p 171). Political opposition to such taxes has prevented them from
becoming as significant in The Netherlands and Germany; but these
countries have pioneered other nonregulatory instruments in the delivery
of national environmental objectives. The Dutch target-group technique has
already been mentioned. In Germany an environmental liability law makes
important inroads into the traditional 'no-fault' immunity of corporations
with regard to legal action for environmental harm, shifting the burden of
proof away from the injured party for certain industrial processes (Grant,
1996, p 228). While this is still some way from the more extensive liability
provisions of the US Comprehensive Environmental Response, Compensation and Liability Act, the German law has helped to spur discussion on
European environmental liability legislation. Indeed, closer still to the
participatory intent of the discourse principle, recent Dutch law has
extended rights to environmental organizations to commence proceedings
against polluters on the basis of damage to the affected interests they
represent (Grant, 1996, p 231). The opening up of environmental liability
laws to citizen challenges is thus another policy instrument nudging economic
governance in the direction of environmental-democratic accountability.

Overall, though, the project of ecological modernization falls within the
institutional parameters and technological problem-solving worldview of
the advanced liberal democracies. Maarten Hajer (1995, p 279) claims that
rather than opening up environmental decision-making, it reinforces 'a
techno-corporatist tendency where policy-making practices aim to control
and subsequently solve a specific set of predefined problems rather than
leaving space for competing problem definitions and rival scenarios of
resolution.' His criticism bites deeper still: ecological modernization may
also be interpreted as a political strategy to blunt the critical challenge of
radical environmentalism by accommodating both ecologically innovative
sections of corporate capital and technocentric environmentalism (1995,
pp 32–33; Harvey, 1996, p 282). This conjunction of interests commands
attention from political parties in the advanced capitalist countries because
it simultaneously pretends to meet the dual state imperatives (Dryzek, 1996,
p 479) of maintaining conditions for productive capital investment (by
facilitating economic growth through high-value technological change) and
securing citizen consent (by being seen to respond to public concern about
environmental quality). The result, Dryzek (1997, p 146) claims, is a 'discourse of reassurance' for the citizens of those countries, because economic
growth and environmental protection are seen as mutually supportive.
There are no problematic trade-offs suggesting the need for a more far-
reaching scrutiny of production and consumption patterns. It is also an
expert knowledge domain, rather than a discursive space open to the
democratization of environmental knowledge.

Another political subtext of this discourse is that ecological modernization is very much a Western development path, predicated on maintaining the economic advantages of the advanced capitalist states. Without discussion of technology transfer and environmental justice (such as debt write-off) for the developing world, it violates the discursive democratic condition that all affected parties should be able to participate in decisions affecting their interests. In an interdependent world, the national economic policies of the North American and Western European states significantly impact upon the development conditions and possibilities of those in the global South. Ecological modernization is environmentally incoherent if it allows advanced capitalist countries to offload unsustainable practices onto developing countries, while still sourcing them for raw materials and energy supplies.

In short, ecological modernization highlights again the distance from environmental democracy of even those Western democracies that have made the most progress in environmental capacity-building. It would be churlish to dismiss the real environmental improvements achieved by the neocorporatist European states; but as a development strategy, ecological modernization as it has been articulated disappoints on both democratic and ecological grounds. Several commentators noting the limited, but significant, gains in environmental planning and management associated with ecological modernization have called for its radicalization to further its potential for environmental democracy. 'Strong' (Christoff, 1996, p 490) or 'reflexive' (Hajer, 1995, pp 279–294) ecological modernization names an approach more closely allied with a discourse notion of democracy – one explicitly addressed to open, inclusive deliberation on environmental values and norms across all forms of collective choice. And one that therefore takes seriously the calls for environmental justice which come from ecological activists across the world. It would throw into critical relief not just societal goals for economic development, alongside their environmental and social consequences, but also the political institutions by which we govern ourselves. This brings us back to the concern in this chapter with democratic capacity-building: what further institutional restructuring is needed to lay out the conditions for more participatory forms of environmental decision-making?

DECENTRALIZATION: THE NEXT STEP

This chapter has been concerned with identifying, at the national level across Western Europe and North America, institutional tendencies towards more democratic environmental decision-making. It has addressed at length the suggestive claims of the Berlin school of environmental research about the political–institutional conditions deemed conducive to effective environmental policy; and, in particular, it has addressed the thesis that communicative decision-making forms are a prerequisite for sustained environmental policy success. It should be clear that elements of the various political framework conditions for environmental capacity are found, to a greater or lesser extent, in all the countries mentioned. As a combination, and on the basis of including all affected parties (at the national level), these conditions offer the best structural backdrop for effective and democratically legitimate decisions. Of course, in practice it is not possible to dip into the menu of institutional forms, constructing an ideal model of environmental decision-making to which all countries should subscribe. Each democratic state is shaped by its own historical path of political and administrative development, as well as a domestic political culture. None-theless, as the example of the European neocorporatist states shows, some cross-national generalizations seem feasible with regard to political–institutional conditions amenable to development in an environmental–democratic direction. And they give empirical support to the argument that more inclusive regulatory styles oriented towards generalizable interests are more suited than closed styles to addressing environmental degradation.

In other words, *fairer* decision-making – that which is committed to realizing the discourse principle by allowing the participation of all relevant interests – leads to environmental governance that is more democratic and ecologically effective. Citizens are more likely to support a decision-making process that is demonstrably fair. Standards of fairness are not static. Margaret Levi (1997, pp 205–214) has shown how an extension of democratic institutions, such as the extension of political, civil and economic rights (one of the defining characteristics of environmental democracy), can raise public expectations of fairness from government. Raising the ability of citizens to participate in political action and decision-making encourages them to engage in the shaping of shared environmental interests. This is one response to the familiar conservative criticism that broadening democratic participation in decisions might well lead to less reasonable or less tolerant choices because of the improved access for 'parochial' interests. Rather, the direction implied is further democratization in environmental decision-making. Ultimately, it means a devolution of decision-making authority that is more rational in ecological terms. In many complex environmental challenges a clear case can be made for greater decentral-ization, in part to incorporate local knowledge, cooperation and motivation (Paehlke and Torgerson, 1990, pp 293–294; Dryzek, 1987, pp 216–229). One of the important contributions of the new institutionalist perspective has been to show how community norms and patterns of reciprocity – 'social capital' – afford effective responses to the problems of commitment and mutual monitoring for collective environmental resources; but this is only if power is devolved to institutions of self-government (Ostrom, 1990).

Decentralization in accord with the discourse principle would obviously not be restricted to environmental governance, but encompass all forms of collective decision-making impacting upon regional and local interests. Here, finally, is the greatest institutional obstacle to environmental democracy

– the current insulation of economic life from requirements of democratic responsiveness and accountability. It may seem that the European neo-corporatist states even offer a progressive example here, given discussions on their social-democratic stakeholding model of corporate governance, where companies are held accountable for their actions by a variety of stakeholder groups alongside their legal responsibilities to shareholders (Gamble, Kelly and Kelly, 1997). However, this other-regarding concern is at most a matter of corporate good manners, nurturing public–private partnerships in a locality or region to maintain the type of high-value investments mentioned above with regard to ecological modernization. Endogenous economic growth, in this model, benefits from neocorporatist relationships of mutual understanding and trust, but this involves no more than a voluntarist set of norms (evident in the various environmental management systems employed by companies) and makes no substantial democratic inroads into the economic sovereignty of private capital.

Democratic management of economic activity implies, at least, the participation of worker–citizen and community representatives on company boards. Following the discourse principle to its logical conclusion, it means that the democratically appointed representatives of employee and community interests (including, of course, environmental concerns) have an equal right to participate in production and revenue allocation decisions. In Chapter 5 the important but neglected role of unions as actors for environmental democracy is discussed, holding businesses to account for the social and ecological impacts of their activities. And this is not just within nation states. There is the crucial question of environmental destruction and social dislocation in developing world countries, aided by global capital exploiting regulatory differences between national jurisdictions (O'Riordan, 1996, p 151). Democratic decentralization suggests here forms of economic self-governance within the global context of a socially and ecologically regulated market. Following Carol Gould (1988), we can imagine the national establishment of democratically elected regulatory commissions, functioning at the lowest most effective level possible, which would indirectly steer production to meet social and ecological needs (for example, through making funds available for new environmental investments, perhaps financed by a Tobin tax on international currency transactions and global resource taxes; see the conclusion to this book).

This is a radical democratic extension of the already existing decision-making structures in the neocorporatist countries, but somewhat beyond the confines of mainstream political debate in the global North. Social and environmental justice activists across the world are, nevertheless, already cultivating a critical political discourse receptive to such ideas, exposing the historically arbitrary exclusion of the democratic idea from corporate governance. When will formal political institutions respond to *that* communication? How will economic sovereignty be wrested from those powerful vested interests who gain so much from the current asymmetries of social power? These are questions answered only by political practice.

3 ADMINISTRATIVE FAIRNESS AND FOREST LAND DECISION-MAKING: A CANADIAN EXPERIMENT IN PARTICIPATORY ENVIRONMENTAL PLANNING

'Land use is a major governance challenge in British Columbia'

(Commission on Resources and Environment, 1994c, p 1).

Attention to administrative process is key to reconciling competing interests in environmental policy-making and implementation. Chapter 2 argued that administrative openness and participatory decision-making are institutional prerequisites for environmental democracy. The notion of environmental capacity-building, referring to the degree to which political and administrative structures are able to address ecological interests and issues, allowed comparative observations on national regulatory frameworks. Those countries that promoted collaborative environmental policy styles seemed to approach most clearly our procedural concept of democracy, which locates political self-determination in the communicative interplay between formal decision-making institutions and the noninstitutional expression of environmental interests. It was also clear that even these environmental policy 'leaders' still have some way to go in democratizing environmental decision-making. However, there are also various initiatives in environmental capacity-building at the subnational scale in North America and Europe. This chapter will look at one of the most ambitious – the British Columbia Commission on Resources and Environment (1992–1996). This Canadian innovation in participatory environmental planning attracted international attention as a precocious embodiment of environmental democracy.

The creation, in July 1992, of the Commission on Resources and Environment (CORE) signalled a commitment by a new provincial government to restructure the land-use planning system. As a planned permanent advisory body, CORE was given a unique statutory mandate to develop a province-wide land-use strategy, including related resource and environmental management guidelines.[1] Alongside other strategic planning initiatives in British Columbia during the 1990s, such as the Forest Resources Commission and the BC protected areas strategy, the commission embraced broad principles of economic, environmental and social sustainability; but it represented the most far-reaching experiment with public deliberation in environmental decision-making.

A more immediate impetus behind the formation of the commission involved the widely acknowledged dysfunction in provincial land-use decision-making, as evidenced in several high-profile wilderness preservation disputes. From the early 1980s, the major source of environmental conflict had been the clearance of old-growth forest areas for timber. Without a firm legal and administrative basis for wilderness decision-making, the provincial government struggled to accommodate growing public support for preserving natural areas. Although over 90 per cent of British Columbia is Crown (public) land, the 81 million hectares designated as provincial forests have historically been allocated to long-term licences prioritizing timber production. The preservationist campaigns of environmental interest groups thus increasingly centred on park or wilderness reallocation for areas of commercial forest land, drawing support from a resurgence of public environmental concern in the late 1980s and early 1990s.

Substantive conflicts concerning land-use interests therefore prompted CORE fundamentally to review the institutional forms for deciding Crown land-use allocation and management – that is, the means of land-use governance. While the provincial government committed itself to completing an ecologically oriented protected-areas system, while implementing a comprehensive forest practice code, the commission identified a continuing need for more coordinated, preventative land-use planning in the province. Moreover, as embedded in a CORE land-use charter, an integrated planning approach is firmly tied to consensual notions of procedural fairness and participatory decision-making. This charter guided regional land-use negotiations and community-based resource planning processes undertaken by the commission – the heart of its work. Following these pilot planning exercises and extensive public consultation, CORE released the four volumes of its proposed provincial land-use strategy (CORE, 1994d and e; 1995a and b).

There is a clear debt in these recommendations to well-established principles of interest-based negotiation informing public-policy consensus processes in the US, notably environmental mediation and negotiation techniques (Cormick, 1989; Susskind and Cruikshank, 1987). Their common premise, and one borne out in Canada by the experience of Round Tables on the Environment and Economy as well as earlier experiments in environmental negotiations, is that, by satisfying public demands for increased participation in decisions affecting quality of life, consensus processes can generate fair and lasting responses to the complex challenges of sustainable living (Round Tables on the Environment and the Economy in Canada, 1993; Dorcey and Riek, 1987). Public participation, in the form of joint problem-solving, both draws on a great range of relevant knowledge and encourages a creative accommodation of diverse values in order to realize a common interest. Open communication between public agencies and stakeholder groups encourages agreement on the merits or, in more optimistic rhetoric, on a win–win situation where cooperation has replaced confrontation. Above all, the sensitivity to underlying values and interests rather than strategic positions invests environmental negotiations with a shared sense of ownership. And this, the proponents of consensus decision-making claim, makes for fairer, more prudent and more durable solutions to environmental conflicts (British Columbia Round Table on the Environment and the Economy, 1991; McDaniels, 1992).[2]

In a Canadian context, prior to its abrupt winding down in March 1996, CORE represented an ambitious attempt to generalize principles of environmental mediation on a province-wide scale – principles which addressed both the resolution of long-running land-use conflicts and negotiated settlements on land-use allocation. This planning experiment reflected a national trend towards multipartite bargaining as an environmental policy style, away from natural resource management regimes traditionally based upon closed, bipartite bargaining between government and private corporations (Hoberg, 1993b, pp 6–13). What distinguished CORE, in contrast to other multistakeholder environmental initiatives in western Canada – for example, the Alberta–Pacific Task Force (McInnis, 1996) – was its geographical scope and independence. After briefly outlining the structure of Crown land planning in British Columbia, this chapter assesses the commission in terms of its commitment to consensus decision-making – in particular, according to the criterion of *administrative fairness*. This makes explicit, in a normative sense, the minimal conditions for rational legitimacy that political authorities must meet if they are to implement environmental policies in a democratic fashion, highlighting the need for neutrally administered decision-making processes open to the participation of all interests. Administrative fairness is thus a key regulatory principle for environmental governance, informed by – and illustrating – the participatory notion of democracy that is advanced in this book.

CROWN LAND PLANNING IN BRITISH COLUMBIA

Along with the rest of Canada, British Columbia saw environmental concerns attain political saliency during the 1970s. Pollution control measures and attempts to protect threatened wildlife habitat shaped initial environmental policy debates; but the province has since experienced a series of protracted land-use disputes revolving around campaigns for wilderness preservation. For an economy traditionally based on timber extraction and a seemingly endless supply of other natural resources, the growing public demand to establish more park areas has questioned accepted resource management values (Wilderness Advisory Committee, 1986, p 131). As support for wilderness preservation has gathered momentum in the province, successive administrations have seen the traditional extractive goals of forest land allocation and management contested by environmentalists. Continued conflict throughout the 1980s and the early 1990s exposed serious flaws in the institutional framework for Crown land planning in the province.

For natural resources and environmental management, the basic distribution of legislative powers between the provinces and the federal government has remained constant since the 1867 British North American Act. By virtue of their proprietary rights (section 92) to public lands and natural resources within their boundaries, including the direct mention of timber rights, provincial legislatures hold the primary environmental management powers. In 1982 the Constitution Act confirmed this jurisdictional authority, clarified through a specific resources amendment (Lucas, 1987; Vanderzwaag and Duncan, 1992). Since 93 per cent of British Columbia is Crown land and only 1 per cent comes under federal ownership, the major resource planning responsibilities facing the provincial government on its 86 million hectares are substantial. The provincial ministry of forests assumes a lead role in planning and managing the 80.7 million hectares (84.5 per cent of the province's total area) designated as provincial forests by the British Columbia Forests Act.[3] About half of this area is classified as productive forest land (43.3 million hectares) where the stated objective is the sustainable use and management of timber, range, recreation, wildlife, fisheries and other resources. Just over half of this land is available and suitable as commercial forest, where timber harvesting has traditionally been the policy priority (Ministry of Crown Lands, 1989).

The dominant position of the ministry of forests in Crown land planning and management is reinforced by its broad legislated responsibilities over the provincial forests, assigned by the Ministry of Forests Act. Under section 4 the ministry is charged with encouraging maximum productivity and efficient utilization of the provincial forest and range resources in consultation and cooperation with other ministries and the private sector.[4] This extensive discretionary authority contrasts with the prescriptive legalistic approach provided by the US National Forest Management Act (Hoberg, 1993; Nixon, 1990). It is from this mandate that the ministry has committed itself to integrated resource management – in theory, a comprehensive process guided by the principle of sustained use, taken to mean a land-use and management emphasis based on the equitable consideration of social, economic and environmental factors (Ministry of Forests, 1990; 1994, p 1). In practice, a focus on timber resource planning has supported the agency's historical emphasis upon economic development of Crown forest land, promoting, in particular, the growth of a domestic-forest products manufacturing sector through secure land tenure rights. The consequence of prioritizing timber production uses on Crown land is borne out by the present complex system of public forest tenures, where corporate timber harvesting interests are entrenched. Not surprisingly, forest companies have been reluctant to relinquish resource rights without substantial compensation, reinforcing the predisposition of the provincial forest service not to redesignate commercial forest areas away from a timber production emphasis.

This has promoted the widespread view that the agency retains a pro-exploitation bias toward resource extraction industries, supported by charges of procedural unfairness in forest land-use planning. The perception of bias has undermined its claim to be representative of nontimber values such as wilderness, wildlife and recreation (Cabinet Planning Secretariat, 1993; Gunton, 1993). A land-use planning review undertaken by CORE supported this claim with two major findings. Firstly, a lack of neutrality exercised by planners in the ministry of forests was related to planning responsibilities and mandates lacking legal clarity and consistency, as well as inadequate referral systems – that is, other ministries with jurisdiction over Crown lands (notably the ministry of environment, lands and parks) not having an effective input when consulted by the forest service over resource plans affecting areas under their management authority. Secondly, CORE concluded that integrated resource management was weakened by the lack of meaningful public involvement in Crown land decision-making. Lacking a legally mandated public-participation process, opportunities for public involvement have been limited and ill defined, left to the discretion of the relevant resource agency officials (CORE, 1994e, pp 20–22; 1995a; see also Brenneis, 1991; Vance, 1990).

THE LEGITIMATION DEFICIT OF LAND-USE DECISION-MAKING

In its first annual report to the British Columbia Legislative Assembly in June 1993, the Commission on Resources and Environment identified a serious 'dysfunction' in Crown land-use decision-making, expressed as 'a widespread public cynicism about government effectiveness and fairness and a resulting dissatisfaction with the actions and directions of government' (CORE, 1993, p 10). The commission cited the rejection of the results of provincial planning processes as evidence of this procedural dysfunction. This was manifest across the spectrum of land-use interests, not only in terms of campaigns orchestrated by environmental preservation groups, but also established sectoral interests lobbying against administrative land-use decisions and seeking judicial redress. It is in these terms that we can characterize Crown land-use decision-making as facing a withdrawal of legitimation or, in other words, a *legitimation deficit* – a situation where large sections of the public regard as invalid the policy goals and justifications of government agencies (Habermas, 1987, pp 144–148; Finkle, 1983).

Within normative democratic theory, legitimacy refers to 'the convincing character of reasons that justify political decisions or, more generally, validate practices and institutions' (Bohman, 1990, p 95). As presented in the last chapter, democratic legitimacy is firmly tied to our procedural understanding of democracy as a deliberative process of collective will-formation – one that promotes reasoned agreement over practical-political questions through the acknowledgement of a common or general interest. In the next chapter this notion of legitimacy will be employed to scrutinize the normative claims of wilderness preservationists in British Columbia; here the claims under examination are those of the state. For society, the legitimacy of the legal principles and political or policy goals of a democratic state is dependent upon discursive procedures for positing and justifying norms. Consent to political authority is legitimate only if there are good (sufficient) reasons to enable people to accept administrative directives as binding on their behaviour (Benhabib, 1994; Dryzek, 1990b).

The legitimation deficit of the administrative system can therefore be 'measured' to the extent that it falls short of institutional procedures for free public deliberation on collective needs. As Bernard Manin notes, this idea still recognizes the necessity for decision, and the fact that collective choices must be made within particular resource and spatial–temporal constraints. All deliberative procedures offer is the likelihood of more reasonable decisions (Manin, 1987, p 363). In the case of Crown land-use decision-making in British Columbia, this refers both to the quality of public communication or discourse, and the scope of public participation procedures. To the degree that communication and participation rights are legally institutionalized, the basis of democratic legitimacy is, in principle, strengthened. As recognized in the CORE diagnosis of dysfunction in public policy decision-making, this is presented as a pressing need given the complexity of society and the increasing authority delegated to public representatives. It imposes a duty on government to make public at an early stage its plans and policy proposals, as well as a duty to publish the reasons for any significant decisions reached.

It was the absence of participatory deliberation in Crown land-use policy that spurred on wilderness activists in a spate of nonviolent civil disobedience over protecting specific natural areas. Blockades of logging roads, often in tactical alliance with aboriginal groups, culminated in the summer of 1993 with the arrest of over 800 people in Clayoquot Sound – a 262,000-hectare area of lowland temperate rainforest on the west coast of Vancouver Island (Hatch, 1994; MacIsaac and Champagne, 1994). This is the volatile context in which the provincial government explored new institutional structures for environmental conflict resolution in the early 1990s. The New Democratic Party (NDP) had swept to electoral victory in October 1991, promising increased democratic accountability in forest land-use policy and a legislative commitment to doubling the land allocated to natural areas protection in British Columbia. CORE is notable as the key strategic planning initiative established by the NDP to address the governance implications of this land-use conflict.

ADMINISTRATIVE FAIRNESS AND THE COMMISSION ON RESOURCES AND ENVIRONMENT: SOCIAL SUSTAINABILITY IN LAND-USE PLANNING

CORE's mandate was set out in the Commission on Resources and Environment Act which became law in July 1992. This established the commission as a permanent body, independent of the provincial ministries. The act required the development of a province-wide strategy 'for land-use and related resource and environmental management issues' (section 4.1), the development of participatory planning processes for implementation at regional and local levels, and the formulation of a land-use dispute resolution system. While independent, the commission also had an additional responsibility to coordinate resource and environmental management initiatives within government, as well as an explicit mandate to give due consideration to aboriginal land-use interests (without prejudice to treaty negotiations).

Within Crown land-use planning this statutory mandate had no precedent. It was similar to provincial Ombudsman legislation (the 1979 Ombudsman Act) in that it made the office independent of government ministries and agencies, provided full investigative and public hearing powers akin to a standing commission of inquiry, and gave the responsibility to report directly to the public alongside the legislature and the executive branch. The clear commitment to public inquiry and discourse underpinned the goal of enhancing the legitimacy of land-use decision-making, by increasing public participation in the planning process and encouraging an effective balance of economic, social and environmental interests in substantive land-use decisions (CORE, 1993b, pp 8–9). Administrative independence and absence of decision-making authority were viewed by the commission as essential to this task.[5]

After establishment and in response to cabinet directives, the commission concentrated its initial planning efforts on creating regional negotiation processes in areas of high land-use conflict. The first step in compiling a provincial land-use strategy was the publication of a land-use charter defining key principles of sustainability. This acknowledged the formative influence both of global statements on sustainability (World Commission on Environment and Development, 1987; United Nations, 1993) and of two provincial advisory forums established before CORE to review aspects of Crown land decision-making – the Round Table on Environment and Economy and the Forest Resources Commission. Both advisory bodies, following different land-use mandates, had in major reports advocated a comprehensive land-use planning process for the total land base of the province (Round Table on Environment and Economy, 1992; Forest Resources Commission, 1991).[6] These recommendations implicitly endorsed *administrative fairness* as a principle of governance, one explicitly articulated in the CORE land-use charter and actively supported by the first commissioner of CORE, Stephen Owen, who had previously served as the ombudsman for British Columbia from 1986 to 1992. In that capacity he had already defined seven rules of administrative fairness designed to improve Crown land-use decision-making in the province:

- access to information;
- opportunities to be heard by public officials;
- decision-making open to the participation of all relevant interests;
- explicit legal basis for decision-making authority and clear policy standards criteria;
- public accountability of decision-makers;
- written reasons for decisions affecting people's interests in a significant way; and
- an independent appeal process (Ombudsman of British Columbia, 1989, pp 30–31).

There is a debt here to common law rules of natural justice. In law a general duty to act fairly when using administrative powers is conventionally related to two procedural safeguards: the right to a fair hearing (*audi alteram partem*) and the rule against bias (*nemo judex in re sua*) (Wade and Forsyth, 1994, pp 471–575). What distinguishes the CORE formulation of administrative fairness is its application to public agency decision-making over and above the legalistic focus of traditional land-use appeal procedures in the province. These existing means of redress, available under the Judicial Review Procedure Act, are restricted to implementing administrative decisions, with limited criteria for standing to appeal. Although a 'public interest standing' category for challenges to statutory authority in administrative acts has been successfully demonstrated in British Columbia by a wilderness preservation group, the courts have not actively intervened to secure administrative fairness in forest land decision-making.[7] Indeed, as will be shown, Owen regarded such a legalistic approach as inappropriate to the Crown land-use planning context. Administrative fairness is represented in more autonomous terms as a normative principle of governance facilitating effective and nonexclusive decision-making.

For the CORE land-use charter, fairness requires an expansion of public participation and application of principles of sustainability to Crown land planning processes. Adopted in principle by the provincial government in June 1993, the charter commits it to protecting and restoring environmental quality, and securing a sound, prosperous economy for present and future generations (Owen, 1993, p 363). The province, it is asserted, will respect the integrity of natural systems and conserve biological diversity (environmental sustainability) while also promoting competitive and efficient economic development – deriving greater social benefits from the use of fewer environmental assets (sustainable economy). Such principles are, of course, difficult to operationalize, with obvious tensions – not least between recognizing non-negotiable ecological constraints on resource extraction and waste absorption on the one hand, and the intra- and intergenerational improvements in human welfare predicated on revived economic growth on the other. For land-use policy, the conflict is all the more acute when planning processes have been shaped by a long-standing presumption in favour of development. In British Columbia the provincial government has historically promoted export-driven industrial development, particularly natural resource extraction and processing activities through state-led expenditures on social and economic infrastructure (Howlett and Brownsey, 1988; Marchak, 1986). This tradition of state intervention on behalf of resource development interests has fuelled public scepticism about the ability of resource management agencies to incorporate, within their planning processes, a public interest in ecological sustainability.

The social dimension of sustainable development, as interpreted by CORE, has therefore become crucial to recovering public confidence in Crown land-use decision-making. Here an explicit connection is made to democratic rights of self-determination and participatory decision-making. The CORE land-use charter equates social sustainability with social equity – in terms of a fair distribution of the costs and benefits of land-use decisions, community stability, access to opportunities for a good quality of life, and the requirement that land-use decisions be made in a fair and open manner (Owen, 1993, pp 364–365). Processes for land-use decision-making must, according to the charter, be neutrally administered and open to the participation of all relevant interests. The egalitarian intent here is pushed further still. Decision-making should be shared, and based on consensus-building amongst the various stakeholders involved so that those with decision-making authority and those affected by such decisions are empowered jointly to accommodate all interests concerned (CORE, 1994c, p 20).

This land-use charter provided guidance for the regional land negotiation processes and community-based resource planning pilot schemes undertaken by CORE. Regionally the commission had, by the end of 1994, made public recommendations to cabinet for large-scale land-use zoning of four major regions of the province – Vancouver Island, Cariboo/Chilcotin, West Kootenay/Boundary and East Kootenay (see Figure 3.1) – following intensive public consultation and multiparty, consensus-based negotiations. For each CORE regional report, the government endorsed the bulk of the land-use (re)allocation recommendations. The commission also studied community-based models of participatory land-use planning and, following a number of successful pilot projects, reported in 1995 on options for environmental negotiation and mediation at a local level (CORE, 1995c).

It should be noted that a subregional integrated resource planning process was developed to complement the CORE-directed provincial land-use strategy, with the objective of providing specific management directions for Crown land. Land and resource management planning (LRMP) shares a commitment to principles of resource sustainability and public participation, incorporating environmental values and interests in consensus-

Figure 3.1 *Commission on Resources and the Environment: Regional Planning Processes, 1992–1995*

based negotiations (Integrated Resource Planning Committee, 1993). While formulated in cooperation with CORE, the LRMP programme has, however, been overseen within the land-use bureaucracy by an integrated resource planning committee, representing existing resource and environmental agencies. Indeed, senior resource planners at the provincial forest service and parks branch argued that the policy shift to shared decision-making predated CORE.[8]And since the termination of the commission in 1996, the CORE processes have been subsumed within the LRMP process. However, only with the creation of CORE was a participatory planning model, attuned to sustainability concerns, explicitly articulated and implemented. In addition, the scope of participatory resource planning and management in British Columbia still has no parallel in any other jurisdiction. By 1997 the whole province was covered by CORE-initiated regional plans and LRMP combined. The following sections will focus on the recommendations for a province-wide land-use strategy put forward by the commission, suggestions that build upon the experience of this innovative experiment in land-use planning. To what extent have they secured administrative fairness as a central principle of land-use governance in British Columbia?

TOWARDS A PROVINCIAL LAND-USE STRATEGY

The publication, in 1994–1995, of four volumes detailing CORE's recommendations for a provincial land-use strategy (PLUS) represented the culmination of two and a half years of extensive public consultation and commission-sponsored research. Released in December 1994, the first two reports – *A Sustainability Act for British Columbia* and *Planning for Sustainability* – offered a general framework and planning principles designed to seek cooperative agreement on land-use choices. As a mechanism for durable social choices, the land-use planning system was diagnosed as ineffective, in part due to its jurisdictional complexity and the lack of coordination between resource-use planning on Crown land and growth management in urban areas. Suggestions for improved efficiency encompassed clearer planning sequences, consistency in land-use designation and more uniform data standards and systems (CORE, 1994e, pp 13–23). The crucial point is that, for CORE, this increase in effectiveness was firmly predicated on procedural fairness in decision-making: only by making land-use planning more accountable and representative could planning results attain greater stability. In short, democratic legitimacy promotes policy longevity. This instrumental rationale for participatory planning represented the political pitch to a provincial administration not convinced of the need for a radical overhaul of environmental governance.

For CORE, though, the enactment of a sustainability act was critical to ensuring the long-term effectiveness of a planning system based on sustainability and participatory decision-making, overriding more immediate economic and political trends (CORE, 1994d, pp 19–21, 39–40). While the land-use charter was seen as the philosophical heart of such an act – describing its general statutory goals – according a legal status to sustainable planning on Crown land implied immediate, far-reaching reforms for achieving administrative fairness.

Firstly, a sustainability act would have entrenched neutrality in the institutional system for delivering, monitoring and reviewing land-use decisions. This would have given land-use planning more legal formality, reducing the discretionary scope for administrative favouritism of development-oriented allocation and management options. Cabinet would have been empowered to approve integrated land-use policies and goals, clarifying the provincial interest, while ministries would be directed in the formulation and administration of strategic land-use plans conforming to a legally binding designation and zoning system. Above all, there would have been a legal mandate for ensuring effective and balanced interministerial coordination, whether by a secretariat, ministry or independent commission akin to CORE. The envisaged act would also have established independent land-use review and appeal procedures on a more uniform and publicly accessible basis (CORE, 1994d, pp 40–53; 1994e, pp 46–47).

Secondly, administrative fairness informs the recommendation by CORE that a sustainability act place public participation in Crown land decision-making on a legislative footing, affirming the general right of members of the public to participate meaningfully in land-use decisions 'where such decisions may have a significant impact on a person's interests' (CORE, 1994d, pp 8, 48). The commission identified an acute need for increased public input to resolve competing land-use interests, reduce environmental conflict and provide stability in Crown land-use planning. Only from a representative planning process, CORE argued, can the political executive attain all the relevant information to fashion a public interest in social, economic and environmental sustainability (CORE, 1994e, p 77; 1995a, pp 25–27). The philosophical touchstone here, then, is a belief in partici- patory democracy, meant not as a replacement of existing representative procedures or an abdication of statutory authority, but rather a 'democratizing supplement' (Hirst, 1994, p 37) characterized by decentralized bargaining structures representative of all interests.

It is important to note that the sustainability act recommended by CORE contained no detailed, statutory codification of administrative fairness in the manner of the administrative procedure acts found in Alberta and Ontario, both of which present standards and criteria for measuring bureau- cratic performance (Macdonald, 1980b, pp 550–563). Rather, the proposed act would have stated only broad rights of participation and appeal regarding land use and related environmental planning. The political function was, as Macdonald (1980a, p 7) and Finkle (1983) have argued, one of securing the effective participation of persons likely to be affected by administrative decisions, thus rebuilding public trust in government institutions. This more general legislative commitment was purposively distanced from highly prescriptive land-use allocation and management policies, mindful in particular of the perceived weaknesses of US legalism – excessive costs, time delays and institutional rigidity (Hoberg, 1993, pp 24–27). While acknowledging the need for giving land-use planning in British Columbia more legal formality, the commission stressed the importance of flexibility to reflect local and regional variations (CORE, 1994e, p 22).

What needs to be shown now is how CORE's ambitious vision of a sustainable future, informed by a deliberative idea of democracy, had to adapt to prevailing political and policy constraints. This will be addressed with reference to the five primary components of the provincial land-use strategy presented by CORE:

- provincial direction;
- coordination;
- participatory planning;
- independent oversight; and
- dispute resolution.

Provincial Direction

A sustainability act would, according to CORE, have defined the provincial interest in Crown land planning and management, providing a clear statutory articulation of land-use decisions pertaining to resource lands, human settlement, protected areas, coastal and marine areas, transportation, energy, sustainable economic development, environmental sustainability, outdoor recreation, cultural heritage and aboriginal people (CORE, 1994d, pp 71–76). The recommendation of sustainable land-use goals by CORE in 1994 actually prompted the provincial government to accept them in principle, establishing an interministry committee to refine their cross-ministry policy viability, although this group ignored the commission's argument for a sustainability act.

Policy direction for forest land decision-making has also been shaped by other significant government initiatives. A forest practices code, legis-lated in 1994, outlining a comprehensive range of environmental regulations and standards for commercial timber operations in the province, established regional-scale resource management zones for translating higher-level strategic planning goals into specific management objectives. Provincial lands covered by the forest practices code encompass Crown forest land and privately managed forest lands, both protected from conversion to other uses by the 1994 Forest Land Reserve Act. The provincial commitment to forest resource development and management is consolidated by the 1994 British Columbia Forest Renewal Act – a long-term investment plan, financed through increased stumpage rates (the fees licensees pay for Crown timber), for the silvicultural and environmental improvement of forest lands, as well as investment in value-added manufacturing, forest worker training and research. Finally, the ministry of forests began a timber supply review in April 1992 to provide accurate, up-to-date information for integrated resource management within the 36 timber supply areas in the province.

Popular support is viewed by the provincial government as critical to the long-term purchase of commercial forest-sector policies and these strategic initiatives have, to that end, invited public input while flagging their collective allegiance to 'ecosystem management'. However, given the high level of public support for natural areas protection, demonstrated during an extensive public consultation exercise on parks and wilderness preservation, *Parks and Wilderness for the 90s*, the political executive initially accorded priority to the reallocation of Crown land for environmental preservation interests. The New Democratic Party administration that came to power in 1991 established a protected areas strategy to implement its manifesto promise to protect 12 per cent of the provincial land base by the year 2000, doubling the then existing figure. This strategy aims to set aside Crown land representative of the biodiversity, cultural heritage and recreational diversity of the province, the greatest weight given to the protection of ecological integrity (Province of British Columbia, 1993a, pp 5–8). Designated protected areas are inalienable; all industrial extraction and resource development activities are prohibited. Despite this political commitment, the status of candidate and existing parks within CORE land-use negotiations led to preservation groups questioning the fairness of the protected areas component of the provincial land-use strategy. Political leadership on parks and wilderness was perceived as wavering as soon as difficult reallocation decisions emerged.

Early in the CORE land-use negotiations, as a sign of government faith in consensus-based decision-making, each regional table was given the authority to make protected areas strategy recommendations within their geographical areas of multistakeholder bargaining. This caused a withdrawal of wilderness (and watershed protection) groups from a CORE local planning process – the Slocan Valley Pilot Project – in the West Kootenays in May 1993, charging the CORE process with 'substantial imbalances and inequities' (Sherrod, 1993b, p 7). They cited the refusal of CORE to preclude existing park boundaries from the consideration of regional land-use negotiating tables as having encouraged mining and logging interests to challenge existing park uses at CORE regional tables (Sherrod, 1993a). What further eroded the credibility of the CORE claim to balance, for wilderness advocates, was the simultaneous exclusion of large-scale resource extraction tenures as a legitimate concern for CORE-sponsored environmental mediation. Given the substantial capital withdrawal threatened by corporate interests had this been the case, the NDP claimed that this was a necessary pragmatic imposition on CORE land-use negotiations processes. What the government had not anticipated was that logging and mining companies consistently vetoed the consideration, by regional tables, of new candidate areas for parks, viewing such park zoning as de facto expropriation of their resource claims on Crown land. This was most starkly exposed in the Cariboo-Chilcotin regional process, where a resource industry alliance – the Cariboo Communities Coalition – effectively blocked any serious consideration of park proposals (Careless, 1997, pp 214–222).

Furthermore, the CORE regional zoning recommendations for land outside protected areas, establishing buffer areas with lower impact forestry, proved unpopular with the provincial administration who quickly baulked at the cost of the extensive implementation of ecosystem management (Rayner, 1996). Although the government initially declared its intention to incorporate these 'special management zones' within the forest practices code to make them legally enforceable, these were early casualties of intense corporate lobbying against the code. For preservationists, all this has represented an abdication of government responsibility for parks and wilderness protection.

The absence of executive direction for the protected areas strategy exposed a wider strategic deficit in provincial land-use planning – one that impacted negatively on the effectiveness of CORE. According to the then commissioner on resources and environment, the lack of crucial parts of the policy framework for land use made it very difficult for strategic planning processes to operate fairly.[9] For example, representatives of forest and mining companies facing restrictions on resource extraction rights as a result of official endorsement of CORE land-use recommendations objected to the ambivalence of policy statements on tenure reform and compensation. Furthermore, CORE was perceived as one of several strategic land-use processes, all with different planning regions and timetables: even senior resource agency bureaucrats expressed concern over the complexity of the planning situation. The CORE land-use charter, although accepted in principle by the government in 1993, has still not acquired binding status through policy directives or legislation akin to a sustainability act. Following its review of the CORE provincial land-use strategy recommendations, the government opted for selective endorsement, retreating from the more far-reaching proposals for legislating the land-use charter.[10] This piecemeal approach ensured that the subsequent implementation of recommendations coming from CORE and the various other provincial land-use planning processes was seriously delayed (Dunsmuir III Steering Committee, 1997, p 4), while the strategic line of communication between the commission and cabinet was severed with the axing of the commission in 1996.[11]

Interministerial Coordination

The protected areas strategy served as a model for interagency planning processes in British Columbia, prompting the government to create a land-use coordination office (LUCO) in 1994 to provide integration within government for the wider land-use planning delivery system. This was in response to the chaotic number of strategic planning initiatives and the absence of a single agency responsible for overseeing these processes. As the facilitator of interagency coordination with respect to land-use policy development and planning, LUCO supplied cabinet with an integrated government response to CORE land-use recommendations. In addition, LUCO has since taken over policy direction for the protected areas strategy, the CORE-derived planning processes and provincial land-use and natural resource inventory initiatives. Nevertheless, LUCO remains a small office within the resource bureaucracy. An assistant deputy minister of land use oversees three LUCO directors responsible for different planning regions and policy issues. The bulk of the technical work is at regional level through seven intermanagement committees composed of existing resource agency officials.[12]

In its review of provincial land-use planning, CORE claimed that coordination among government agencies has been enhanced substantially in recent years, noting the contribution of LUCO, but observed that the various interministry processes had taken place without clear legislative sanction. To hold the necessary degree of decision-making authority, such coordination, CORE argued, required statutory authorization through a sustainability act (CORE, 1994d, p 50). The commission recommended creating an agency solely responsible for interministerial coordination and integration, backed up by a legal mandate. As an organizational criterion for revising existing land-use institutions, administrative fairness demands that planning mechanisms operate in a neutral and unbiased manner, free of any sectoral alignment. CORE maintained that an external land-use planning commission would best satisfy the *fairness* criterion, by separating plan authorization from resource agency-based implementation and management functions. The neutrality of the commission, as with CORE itself, would be underpinned by its independence from government (CORE, 1994e, pp 41–45).

Yet, CORE opted instead for an enhancement of existing planning structures, acknowledging that radical reform would incur substantial implementation costs and would associate an independent land-use planning commission with a possible major loss in coordinative capacity and public accountability. Instead, the commission outlined a structural model for the provincial land-use planning system based on a legal formalization and increased resourcing of LUCO as a secretariat reporting to cabinet (CORE, 1994e, pp 45–46).[13] The CORE recommendations removed the obligation for integrated resources planning away from a ministry of forests long since targeted for charges of development-oriented bias. In reality, the uncertainty over interagency planning favoured the ministry of forests as a well-established administrative power base. Opposition to CORE from within the forest service executive effectively undermined the commission, and ensured that the ministry maintained lead agency status for land-use planning. By moving LUCO into the ministry of government services in February 1995, the government chose a far less radical means of bureaucratic formalization. By affording LUCO statutory authority, the CORE land-use planning suggestions, had they been implemented, would have represented a more serious challenge to the lead agency status of the forest service.

In according some weight to existing agency structures, CORE recognized the need to trade off maximizing fairness against other planning criteria: coordination, cost-effectiveness and accountability. While the focus here is on fairness, CORE placed emphasis on these other criteria. The commission judged that, while essential, administrative fairness should not be an overriding criterion of evaluating land-use decision-making. This concession to existing planning structures proved costly though. It ultimately allowed the ministry of forests to reassert its dominance, whereas the legitimation deficit in land-use planning identified by the commission necessitated more radical reforms to institutionalize administrative fairness in Crown land decision-making.

Participatory Planning

A shared decision-making approach was adopted by the participants in each of the four regional land-use negotiations initiated by CORE, under the guidance of commission-appointed facilitators. For each regional table undertaking this mediation, the aim was to develop a set of zoning recommendations to the commission regarding regional land-base allocations and mitigation strategies for those bearing the negative distributional consequences of forest land reallocations. The claim to fairness in these negotiation processes rests, firstly, on the procedural guarantee that all interests were accorded equal discursive status, regardless of their authority or power. Participation was open to all 'legitimate' interests, encompassing those with the authority to make land-use decisions and those affected by such decisions in the region, which thus included provincial and local government, labour, aboriginal groups and a range of nongovernmental organizations. Moreover, alongside determining their own representatives, all parties or 'sectors' were involved in the design and evolution of the negotiation processes themselves. This self-design element would build, it was hoped, mutual understanding by clarifying interests, roles and responsibilities. With the ground rules established, the commitment to collaborative negotiation of the issues through the voluntary participation of all parties promoted fairness, secondly, in the substantive outcome. To reach consensus, any agreement had to be acceptable to every party, pressing those concerned, it was argued, to incorporate all interests.

While not offering here a comprehensive appraisal of the CORE experience with shared decision-making, four areas will be highlighted where the effectiveness and the fairness of commission-directed land-use negotiation processes invited criticism. The centrality of participatory planning to the provincial land-use strategy reinforces their relevance.

Firstly, media response to the completion of the regional land-use negotiation tables, fuelled by the high expectations raised at the start of these initiatives, generally dwelled on the failure of all four processes to achieve full consensus land-use plans. On this outcome-based evaluation, portraying the CORE planning initiatives as ineffective, the East Kootenay table offered the greatest progress: sector representatives reached agreement on land-use zoning for 90 per cent of the regional land base. An East Kootenay table report published in June 1994 also contained land-use policy recommendations and a socio-economic transition strategy. As with the other three regional tables, though, even here the commissioner on resources and environment had to complete a land-use plan for submission to cabinet; and the cabinet-approved plan released in March 1995 had involved direct negotiations between sector representatives and the provincial government. Both the Vancouver Island and West Kootenay/Boundary tables failed to achieve any consensus on zoning recommendations, despite agreed policy objectives addressing land use and resource management, and economic restructuring. The Cariboo-Chilcotin regional process saw agreements on similar components of its planning mandate dropped, because their acceptance was contingent upon a consensus on land-use allocation for the whole region (CORE, 1995a, pp 50–51; 1995c, pp 35–39).

The community-based pilot projects in public participation sponsored by CORE were not required to deliver land-use designations, and were charged instead with the development of resource management guidelines. CORE promoted them as demonstration models of consensus decision-making at the local level. The withdrawal of environmental groups from the Slocan Valley Pilot Project has already been noted, which prevented the agreement of a resource management plan. However, the commission trumpeted the success of the Anahim Round Table, a pilot project initiated in the western part of the Cariboo-Chilcotin region in July 1992 to address forest management conflicts. Eventually comprising 29 self-defined interest sectors and facilitated by a professional mediator and a CORE associate, the table reached agreement on a community-based resource management plan in January 1994 for an area covering 650,000 hectares (Anahim Round Table 1994; CORE 1995a, pp 118–126). This achievement is partly attributable to the definition of consensus established by the table – 'agreement on a package of issues and solutions' (Anahim Round Table, 1994, p 12; Round Table on the Environment and the Economy, 1991, p 4) – allowing differences of opinion on aspects of the package at the same time as encouraging support of the overall agreement. This avoided, therefore, the all-or-nothing approach which undermined the Cariboo-Chilcotin regional table. Indeed, the first commissioner on resources and environment argued against treating a signed consensus agreement as the key indicator of success in land-use negotiations. Given the CORE mandate to promote participatory planning, there is validity in his claim that, even in the absence of consensus, the equitable inclusion of all relevant interests will generate a better outcome: 'It will be better informed, more balanced and more acceptable even though it is not a consensus.'[14] Such a process-oriented evaluation therefore identifies long-term gains in both effectiveness and fairness arising from the educative involvement of citizens in shared decision-making (Buckle and Thomas-Buckle, 1986).

A second, more real, constraint to the effectiveness of CORE land-use negotiations was the inability of the provincial government properly to support them. The commission registered its concern that the ad hoc diversion of ministerial resources to land-use negotiations led to a variable quality of assistance to these processes. Technical difficulties, including a shortage of relevant expertise in mediation, and information constraints, were compounded by the lack of one bureaucratic agency responsible for the range of provincial land-use negotiation approaches (CORE, 1995a, p 40). Forest service officials, eager to make political capital from this situation, pinpointed how this generated structural weaknesses in regional negotiation processes – in particular, the lack of clearly defined terms of reference for such planning areas as boundary demarcations, methodological guidance and product types: lessons subsequently taken on board by CORE

(CORE, 1994a, p 29). The central responsibility for the faltering of the early regional negotiation processes falls squarely upon the political executive. As already highlighted, the absence of strategic direction in key policy areas placed a major obstacle to developing full-consensus land-use plans. For example, forest union representatives walked away from Vancouver Island table negotiations when the provincial government proved unable to offer a comprehensive transition strategy. Without assured compensation and training they had no reason to consent to land-use reallocations which would result in the loss of forestry jobs. This withdrawal effectively disabled the process.

Thirdly, those environmental groups previously underrepresented in forest land decision-making, whose very inclusion in land-use negotiations had been targeted by CORE, questioned the fairness of the mediation undertaken on two counts: that an inadequate amount of time had been left within the time frames of the process to deal with substantive land-use issues, and that conservation stakeholders were not given adequate resources to support their attendance and information needs (Reardon, 1993).[15] Given the asymmetry of resources between the major forest land stakeholders in British Columbia, the degree of *transformative* mediation – that is, procedures designed to enhance the ability of resource-poor groups to protect and promote their interests (Ozawa, 1993) – disappointed environmentalists. In order to avoid advocacy over rival expert knowledge claims, the commission tended to favour the provision by interministerial working groups of independent technical and scientific support to the tables in general, with only a limited participant assistance policy. Not satisfied that there existed a fair incentive structure, those preservation groups that withdrew from CORE processes argued that nothing less than the full legislative enactment of the land-use charter and forest land tenure reform could have guaranteed real negotiating currency to the environmental sector (Sherrod, 1993b, p 52). The Western Canada Wilderness Committee, the leading wilderness advocacy group in the province, pulled out early from CORE negotiating processes (on account of the exclusion of Clayoquot Sound from consideration by the Vancouver Island table), charging the commission with a fundamental failing in public consultation and education: 'They relied on the elite – the elite of the environmental movement and the elite of industry sitting down and being gentlemen around a table.'[16]

Lastly, the commission struggled to ensure fairness to aboriginal peoples in its various policy and planning processes, even though the direct participation of First Nations had been actively encouraged as part of its legislative mandate. Despite a clear statement in the Commission on Resources and Environment Act that any such involvement be 'without prejudice' (section 4.4) to aboriginal rights and recently established treaty negotiations, aboriginal people participated only tentatively in the CORE regional planning processes, fearing that these negotiations would have prejudiced their land claims.[17] The design of an appropriate framework for aboriginal participation in land-use planning became a priority for the commission

(CORE 1995a, pp 59–63; 1995c, pp 63–67). Where aboriginal rights or interests may be affected by land-use decisions, the commission favoured the formulation of interim management agreements with First Nations until treaties are signed. Different resource ministries and the province as a whole have since begun negotiations with First Nations on a number of interim agreements. Only demonstrating a continued political commitment to the needs of native people at this government-to-government level will secure their greater participation in land-use planning, provided, of course, that the wider treaty negotiations are viewed as fair and just by First Nations.

Independent Oversight

In its provincial land-use strategy recommendations, the commission made it clear that it envisaged a future role as an environmental ombudsman, drawing on its statutory powers of public inquiry and reporting. CORE would have assumed more prominently an independent oversight function, investigating administrative performance and problems after the exhaustion of internal review processes, all the more necessary in the polarized political context of land-use planning and management in British Columbia, where in recent years the fairness of public administration has been regularly disputed (CORE, 1995c, pp 74–76). As part of the shift in emphasis to monitoring the sustainability strategy, CORE also began work on a sustainability reporting system for the province.

While CORE always acknowledged that its involvement with hands-on planning would be limited, the provincial government elected not to initiate any further regional negotiation processes, opting instead to expand the scope of subregional planning within existing resource agency responsibilities and terminating the commission. Within the political executive it was decided that the commission had fulfilled its mandate; the assumption was that there now existed more public confidence in Crown land-use decision-making with procedures for public participation firmly established (if not yet legislated). However, the independence of CORE from government ministries, and its principled commitment to participatory planning and sustainability, constituted a major political asset for provincial proponents of consensus decision-making. Without it, the New Democratic government, reelected in May 1996 with a slim working majority, proved more susceptible to pressures from resource industries to weaken environmental regulations in British Columbia. In particular, the provincial forest and mining industries have both lobbied hard for a reduction in their taxation and regulatory cost burdens, concerned about their competitiveness in global markets. The absence of entrenched structures of participatory planning and a high-profile environmental ombudsman threatens a reversion to traditional bipartite (government/industry) bargaining in the land-use policy area.

Dispute Resolution

CORE had the specific duty, under its statutory mandate, to develop and implement a 'dispute resolution system for land use and related resource and environmental issues in British Columbia' (Commissioner on Resources and Environment Act, Section 4.2(c)). Volume 4 of the provincial land-use strategy contains both an evaluation of the existing review and appeal procedures and recommendations for fairer, more effective dispute resolution (CORE, 1995b). The suggested reforms are closely tied to the philosophy and practice of shared decision-making, in that meaningful public participation in land-use planning, through the production of more informed and more balanced decisions, serves as a mechanism for *preventing* land-use disputes. Administrative fairness in this context is directed towards evaluating the nature and conditions of participation (Macdonald, 1980b, p 8).

Alongside the other four components of the provincial land-use strategy, administrative fairness is thus a key criterion informing the assessments by CORE of the dispute resolution system in British Columbia. The commission report relates a definition of fairness by the Law Reform Commission of Canada – 'according appropriate recognition to the interests that may be affected by an administrative decision' (CORE, 1995b, p 14, after Law Reform Commission of Canada, 1985b, p 9) – arguing that public officials have a delegated responsibility fairly to interpret and apply public policy. As the political executive itself is accountable for approving strategic land-use plans, which may, of course, be informed by partisan interests, the appropriate focus of review and appeal procedures is those administrative decisions concerning implementation of the intent of approved plans (CORE, 1994d, p 91). Contained in the various land-use and related resource statutes in British Columbia are review and appeal provisions establishing public accountability for such administrative choices. CORE reviewed 40 relevant pieces of provincial legislation, concluding that there exists a confusing and inconsistent array of adjudicative dispute resolution mechanisms, with very limited public access. Against established principles of administrative fairness – opportunities for review and appeal, notification of decisions, standing to appeal, jurisdictional clarity and reasons for decisions – these rules and procedures fare poorly.

Nowhere is this more apparent than for forest planning and management where, even with the extended appeal provisions of the forest practices code, the provincial forest service has far less accountability than equivalent US federal and state agencies. A permanent forest appeals commission created under the Forest Practices Code Act of British Columbia is still only accessible to those subject to forest service decisions, precluding the public right of appeal and administrative review characterizing the US forest service appeal system (notwithstanding the success of the Sierra Legal Defence Fund in 1996 in obtaining a recognition of intervenor status for environmental groups from the appeals commission). The act also established an audit body, the forest practices board, which has an ability to bring an appeal before the forest appeals commission for a limited range of forest land decisions, including development plans. However, the complaints structure is undermined by the absence of any predecisional notice requirement for agency or forest company decisions. This weakness is compounded by narrow time limits imposed upon the forest practices board when requesting an administrative review of planning and management decisions (Haddock, 1995, pp 71–78).

As a general principle of administrative fairness, the right to be heard shapes the CORE prescriptions for a reformed dispute-resolution system. The recommended shift to preventative dispute resolution implies due planning processes that involve public participation. The commission claimed that opportunities for negotiation and mediation should be formalized in legislation as a supplement to a set of simplified review and appeal procedures, ultimately merged into a comprehensive sustainability board served by a common secretariat (CORE, 1995b, pp 57–61). Yet CORE avoided embracing the adversarial emphasis on adjudication processes evident in American forest land use and environmental policy. Commissioner Owen deemed a legalistic model inappropriate to resolving the type of complex, dynamic land-use conflicts experienced in British Columbia, judged as too costly and time consuming. Indeed, as has been noted, the planning experiments with interest-based negotiation directed by CORE mirror an increasing employment of alternative dispute-resolution techniques in the US. After the release of the CORE report on dispute resolution, the provincial government consolidated land-use appeal and review structures by combining in a single secretariat the appeal board services for the forest appeals commission and the environmental appeal board. However, without the legal recognition of participatory planning and a proven system for delivering negotiation support services, the preventative dispute-resolution system favoured by CORE has still to be realized.

What needs to be shown now, before concluding on the contribution of – and challenges to – the CORE process are the concerns of those corporate and community interests who will bear negative effects of land-use reallocations resulting from CORE land-use plans. These distributional consequences relate directly to the commitment of the commission to principles of administrative fairness.

Crown Land-Use Reallocations: Fairness to Resource-Based Corporate and Community Interests

The commitment of the provincial government to double the amount of protected areas in British Columbia to 12 per cent of the land base had far-reaching implications for each CORE regional process and subsequent cabinet-approved land-use plan, in terms of increases in the area of Crown land designated as protected areas – notably a twofold expansion for the Cariboo-Chilcotin and almost 59 per cent for the West Kootenay/Boundary region.[18] The loss of public resource rights that this entails for corporate and community resource interests is compounded by the additional regional land-use designation of special resource management zones. Ranging in coverage from 8 per cent for the Vancouver Island regional plan to 26 per cent for the Cariboo-Chilcotin plan, these separate areas will result in a curb on resource development activities in order to protect environmental, recreational and cultural heritage values. As such they depart from more development-oriented integrated resource-management lands (Low Intensity Area Review Committee, 1995, pp 32–33; Land Use Coordination Office, 1997).[19]

CORE acknowledged that, as a design principle for the provincial land-use planning system, fairness must include the equitable treatment of those with existing resource rights (CORE, 1994e, p148). While the commission clearly articulated the requirement for procedural fairness, it failed to ascertain the equity implications of land-use decisions made in the public interest, other than embracing the principle that there should be a fair distribution of the benefits and costs of substantive decisions, with those stakeholders made worse off entitled to compensation and economic mitigation measures (CORE, 1994e, p 124; Gunton, 1993, p 285). Nevertheless, this represented a key test of fairness for CORE. In one of its first reports, reviewing Crown land-use options for the Tatshenshini/Alsek region, where planned development of a rich mineral deposit clashed with high wilderness values, the commission strongly urged that there is 'fair treatment and appropriate compensation' (CORE, 1993a, p 96) to the mining company involved if the provincial government favours a park option for the area.

With reference to the CORE regional planning tables, however, sectors dependent upon timber and mineral resource extraction questioned the fairness of the procedures and of the land-use decisions generated by them. The major criticism directed at the process itself has been that it lacked accountability in inviting environmental stakeholders to regional round tables who were not answerable to a clear constituency; in making land-use recommendations affecting local communities without the agreement of municipal authorities; and in suggesting radical institutional reforms inappropriate to a non-elected body: 'they are cherry-picking legislative styles under the illusion of finding a new style of governance'.[20,21,22] Several logging-dependent communities in CORE regional planning areas faced significant employment losses as a result of land-use reallocations. Their civic leaders mobilized pro-industry community coalitions to oppose, in particular, the protected areas strategy component of CORE land-use plans (Brunet, 1994; Vanagas, 1994). This lobbying prompted boundary adjustments to park use recommendations in the regional planning areas, but the provincial government chose not to alter its original endorsement of the four CORE land-use plans, rejecting the process criticisms levelled at the commission. Commissioner Owen also responded firmly to the charge that CORE regional processes neglected local concerns, pointing out that each land-use negotiation entailed intensive public involvement, but that the commission also had a responsibility to consider province-wide interests. Nevertheless, CORE did acknowledge procedural weaknesses in early regional negotiation processes – for example, the failure to brief local governments properly, the lack of effective communication between the regional CORE tables and the general public, and often unclear lines of accountability between sector representatives and their constituencies (CORE, 1995c, pp 54–55).

These imperfections are not serious enough to warrant the charge that resource extraction interests were not accorded a fair hearing or the opportunity to participate in the land-use negotiations. A second claim that the regional land-use plans themselves confer unfair distributional consequences has more merit, not least because of the uncertainty about their total economic impact. Forest-industry sector representatives argued that the provincial government did not anticipate the full cumulative impact of all its strategic land-use planning initiatives, noting that CORE, the forest practices code and the timber supply review will all significantly reduce the amount of forest land available to harvest every year (Price Waterhouse, 1995). On Vancouver Island in particular, several logging-dependent communities – Gold River, Tahsis and Zeballos – are facing major employment losses as a result of implementation of the Vancouver Island land-use plan.[23] In a leaked cabinet memo, the government itself estimated that provincial forest and land-use policy reforms will eventually reduce the annual allowable timber cut on Vancouver Island by 35 per cent – of which CORE recommendations are responsible for 8 per cent of the anticipated timber supply reduction. Even with planned public investment in silvicultural and environment-related employment creation in affected areas, the administration forecast a major reduction in worker income levels and a negative impact on economic confidence (Palmer, 1995).

Although the Vancouver Island table failed to agree upon an economic transition strategy, CORE formulated a programme for mitigating the negative impacts of its land-use allocation decisions, listing objectives for providing forest-dependent communities with alternative related employment. This outline strategy has informed direct discussions between the provincial government and affected parties, and has clear regard to the principle that the costs (and benefits) of landuse reallocations should be equitably distributed across society (CORE, 1994a, pp 209–219). But the official concern about future investment has been reinforced by forest industry forecasts that the economic impacts may be greater than estimated, prompting the government to make significant economic concessions to both forest companies and the timber unions (the 1997 Jobs and Timber Accord). Yet, while CORE was charged with undertaking incorrect cost-benefit analysis of its own planning recommendations, there is no agreed methodology in the province for assessing the economic and social impacts of Crown land-use decisions (Marvin Shaffer and Associates, 1992; Province of British Columbia, 1993b). In general, the commission was judged in resource industry circles to have had little economic accountability, with no detailed costings of its recommendations and contributing – despite its pronouncements to the contrary – to the tenure insecurity of forest licence holders.

A key source of the dissatisfaction expressed by corporate interests and associated community representatives over resource withdrawal decisions actually lay outside the responsibility of CORE – that is, the lack of a clear compensation assessment process. The provincial government has proved slow in developing this as a necessary strategic land-use policy, even though it created a commission of inquiry in 1992 to recommend a fair and efficient compensation policy for the taking of mineral and forest resource interests (Commission of Inquiry into Compensation for the Taking of Resource Interests, 1992). This commission formulated a strong American or 'takings' interpretation of public resource rights owned privately in the province, arguing that the range of forest and mineral tenures can all be broadly construed as akin to private property interests (also Bauman, 1994). Yet this view – one shared by industry – has been strongly contested; and, without any explicit constitutional or legislative direction, compensation assessment still retains great uncertainty, undermining corporate confidence in Crown land-use planning. The issues are complex; but if such a policy is fully to embrace administrative fairness, it would have to include provisions to balance the legal rights of other resource users and owners as well as, less conventionally, those workers whose livelihoods are negatively affected by Crown land-use reallocations even if they lack a direct property interest (Andrews, 1993, p 3; Bankes, 1993, p 6). Furthermore, against the recommendation of the commission of inquiry that public interest groups should not have standing in compensation cases (1992, p 146), as a matter of fairness decision-making regarding compensation for the loss of public resource rights must include opportunities for public participation (Andrews, 1993, pp 8–10; McDade, 1993, p 36). Only this would be consistent with the idea of nonexclusive decision-making governing the provincial land-use strategy recommendations of CORE.

CONCLUSION

Within Canada, CORE was unique in the geographical scope of its process and highly innovative in the procedural recommendations it developed for promoting fairness in Crown land decision-making. The commission maintained a strong commitment to entrench communication and participation rights in provincial land-use planning. However, the provincial government represented the political authority for all CORE processes and the ultimate arbiter of the public interest in land-use decision-making. It is at this level that a more participatory form of governance would have had to be legislated. For Commissioner Owen, greater public participation in land-use planning constituted a necessary supplement to representative government, not least in order to restore democratic legitimacy to resource agencies. However, he also maintained that the nature and scope of this input had to be determined by elected, accountable politicians (CORE, 1995c, pp 60–61). Those politicians, fearing the precedent that would have been set by CORE's recommendations on ongoing public involvement, and swayed by the lobbying of civil servants from the dominant land-use agency – the forest ministry – soon moved to weaken the participatory proposals of the commission. This left unchallenged the development biases within the provincial resource bureaucracy and has so far blocked the advance of environmental capacity-building envisaged by CORE.

In other words, the long-term impact of the participatory experiment represented by the CORE environmental mediation processes has been compromised by the unwillingness of the government to generalize its inclusive and deliberative planning forms. There was never any expectation that the regional tables would be more than time-limited structures; but the commission itself made province-wide procedural planning recom-mendations which would have started to institutionalize environmental democratic decision-making within the political sphere. And given the dependence of corporate interests upon state licensing for extractive activities on Crown land, it may have opened up private investment decisions in natural resource sectors to a more effective and equitable integration of environmental interests over the long term.

Provincial political commitment to implementing the type of reforms laid out by CORE therefore continues to be the key to the long-term effectiveness of the commission's ideas for institutionalizing administrative fairness. An incomplete strategic framework in key policy areas, allied with a lack of public agency expertise in shared decision-making, certainly hindered the regional land-use negotiation processes; but both these issues were eventually addressed. The major challenge to the communicative resolution of land-use conflicts in British Columbia remains the absence of a comprehensive sustainability act, including an explicitly legislated public-participation process and fundamental changes in the legal mandates governing Crown land-use planning. The New Democratic administration has yet to demonstrate a durable commitment to shared decision-making as the new paradigm of land-use planning in the province. Indeed, under a premier (Glen Clark) prone to anti-environmentalist rhetoric, the promise of consensus decision-making is threatening to drift away.

From the perspective of environmental preservation groups, the commission itself failed to realize that the competing interests evident in provincial wilderness disputes reflect incommensurable values. In such land-use conflicts, consensus may not necessarily be benign, according to wilderness activists, if it is a requirement blocking the political protection of an ecologically vital public interest – the preservation of natural areas beyond the levels of the protected areas strategy (Western Canada Wilderness Committee, 1996; Greater Ecosystem Alliance, 1994). For the environmental sector, legislative enactment of a sustainability act would properly recognize certain ecological parameters as nonnegotiable, countering the economic power of extractive resource-based corporations.[24] What can be maintained is that the ecological parameters of the protected areas strategy were somewhat arbitrary, with the 12 per cent target lacking scientific justification in conservation biology and thus restricting its authority to anticipate the ecological needs of future generations (Rayner, 1996). This implies that the regulative ideal of open discourse in this context needs to have been accompanied by improved communication about ecological signals (Dryzek, 1995, pp 24–26). While CORE rejected the preservationist claim that a deep ecological valuation of the land – one that implies radical tenure reform (see Chapter 4) – reflects a balanced consideration of economic, ecological and social interests, it nevertheless made clear, in principle, the correspondence between local and regional democratic deliberation and the incorporation of environmental interests in decision-making. The problem was that the novelty of the process, leading in practice to considerable time spent on deciding deliberative structures, left little scope for substantive discussion of environmental interests.

Notwithstanding the communicative value of its environmental mediation processes, the CORE process demonstrated that provincial decision-making over land use remains an area inevitably subject to strategic lobbying and pressure. The adoption of the land-use plan presented by each regional table was thrashed out more in conditions of sectional bargaining than mutual understanding. What the commission highlighted in its provincial land-use strategy retains saliency – that the institutionalization of participation rights in land-use planning offers a more effective and non-discriminatory means of resolving environmental conflicts than the strategic pursuit of sectional interests. The criticism that such a communicative vision, weighed down with universal premises, asks too much of democratic deliberation (see Williams, 1994, pp 4–5) misses the point. It demands, as the commission pointed out, a long-term educative process of social dialogue about sustainability based upon a participatory notion of citizenship. The commission successfully identified a willingness to participate in consensus-based decision-making, inviting acceptance of the virtue of mutual respect within the wider public culture (Chambers, 1996, pp 206–208). In addition, even without legislative embodiment in a sustainability act, the CORE articulation of administrative fairness also established independent normative criteria for evaluating the democratic legitimacy of environmental governance. This is of critical relevance to other regional and national contexts where public agency decision-making must mediate between diverse, often opposing, interests. The political challenge, as the CORE experiment illustrates, is in embedding such principles of environmental democracy within administrative structures.

4 DEMOCRATIZING NATURE? THE POLITICAL MORALITY OF WILDERNESS PRESERVATIONISTS

Is radical environmentalism, as expressed in deep ecological demands for wilderness preservation, compatible with our discourse notion of environmental democracy? Wilderness preservationists normally combine a commitment to protect large natural areas with an allegiance to participatory democratic norms – typically expressed in recommendations for self-governance of environmental resources. But what if the two are not mutually reinforcing? This is relevant to recent discussions in environmental philosophy on the democratic credentials of green political thought; however, this issue also carries wide-ranging practical implications for the political claims of the wilderness preservation movement in North America and Australasia. The interest in exploring preservationist arguments in this chapter lies less in the organizational form or tactics of the wilderness protection movement than its general value orientation – in particular, the logical consistency and moral justifiability of its normative premises. By 'political morality' this chapter refers to those key moral principles motivating green political action.

Insofar as we can identify a green theory of value anchoring radical environmentalism, it has been argued both by wilderness activists and environmental philosophers that wilderness preservation provides the strongest ethical basis for an ecologically enlightened relationship with nonhuman nature. This ecocentric position, it is claimed, draws its clearest inspiration from the contemporary experience of 'wild nature' in affluent post-frontier societies facing the imminent destruction of remnant wilderness areas. In contrast to European countries, where left-radical political traditions have fashioned the green response to losses in environmental quality, the wilderness preservation movement in North America and Australasia is portrayed as the main impetus for a deep ecological position attributing moral consideration to nonhuman nature (Hay and Hayward, 1988). The ethical stance adopted implies a fundamental opposition to the central tenets of industrial society. It challenges orthodox models of economic growth, the faith in a scientific or technological fix to current ecological problems, and the dominant instrumental mode of relating to nature in western culture – that is, as a storehouse of resources (Heidegger,

1977). In this sense, deep ecology refers to those in the environmental movement who 'go deep in their argumentation patterns' (Naess, 1995, p 149), drawing upon a distinctive philosophy of nature.

This chapter explores the tension between, on the one hand, a moral commitment to wilderness preservation, framed by deep ecological principles and bioregional political programmes, that is oriented towards a 'natural attributes-based' value order – to use Robert Goodin's (1992) terminology – and, on the other, the universal procedural norms of participatory democracy. This chapter returns to the theoretical arguments of Jürgen Habermas, as a representation of the normative meaning of the democratic process, although it also draws on the ideas of Karl-Otto Apel and Klaus Günther (collectively known, for this disciplinary area, as the Frankfurt school of moral philosophy). This creates a position for critically evaluating the claim, made by environmental activists, that wilderness preservation constitutes a common interest deserving of legal protection and administrative recognition in land-use policy. In examining this claim to normative rightness, this chapter will draw substantively upon western Canadian arguments for natural areas protection and associated prescriptions for democratizing land-use decision-making. The aim is ultimately to clarify a moral perspective that locks the preservation of biological diversity within a participatory notion of democracy – one that builds up the normative argument for environmental democracy. Firstly, though, it is important to elaborate on the moral meaning of the discourse principle and its relationship to democratic norms.

DISCOURSE ETHICS: A NORMATIVE FOUNDATION FOR DEMOCRATIC LEGITIMACY

Habermas introduces the principle of discourse or communicative ethics as a formal procedure where claims to normative rightness can be judged impartially ('redeemed discursively'). This procedure – practical discourse – is an argumentative enterprise where the validity of rightness claims is, in principle, determined by reasoned discussion. An important distinction immediately arises between the social purchase and validity of normative claims. The factual prevalence of a norm does not establish its validity as such. In addition, we can neither appeal to historical traditions nor to our evolutionary makeup in order to support controversial norms and practices. Instead, universal rules that contest norms are justified only when all those affected by them accept their consequences. Valid norms are thus limited to those that embody a common or general interest. The condition of inter-subjective recognition is designed to guarantee true impartiality and egalitarian reciprocity in moral choices. From this requirement Habermas states the central principle of discourse ethics (1990, p 66):

> *Only those norms can claim to be valid that meet (or could meet) with the approval of all affected in their capacity as participants in a practical discourse.*

The core idea here, of course, is the discourse principle already introduced at the start of this book, but now tied to an explicit moral theory. Discourse ethics employs the same argument about language use to justify the ideal principle of rational consensus-formation. This calls up a central thesis in Habermas's wider theory of social action, which makes a key analytical distinction between strategic action oriented towards success (effective action) and communicative action oriented towards consensus or mutual understanding. Practical discourse, it is claimed, is always anticipated in everyday contexts of communicative action (Habermas, 1990, p 130):

> *Argumentation is a reflective form of communicative action and the structures of action oriented toward reaching understanding always already presuppose those very relationships of reciprocity and mutual recognition around which* all *moral ideas revolve in everyday life no less than in philosophical ethics.*

In other words, in social interaction where human beings must share meaning to seek understanding, the normative presuppositions of ideal communication are intuitively grasped. When communicating, we normally assume – unless alerted otherwise – that all parties have good reasons for recognizing as right certain values and norms. Practical discourse reconstructs the universal character of these moral intuitions in order to show how they assume consensus: that the condition for asserting normative claims is their *potential* for rational justification (Ingram, 1993, pp 295–298). For Habermas these 'universal pragmatic presuppositions' belong to the know-how of all competent social actors in the modern world and this is their connection to practical discourse. Therefore, relations of symmetry and reciprocity presupposed in communicative action are expressed as fundamental moral principles of justice and solidarity. *Justice* postulates equal respect and equal rights for the individual, whereas *solidarity* concerns the well-being of the community to which the individual belongs. These are closely linked in discourse ethics: moral norms cannot protect the one without the other (Habermas, 1989–1990; 1996, pp 98–99).

What are the implications of this discourse theory for wilderness preservation politics? For environmentalists its immediate relevance stands as a regulative idea that enables criticism of existing institutional arrangements for land-use planning and management in any jurisdiction, insofar as these underrepresent or exclude preservation interests. And there are a priori grounds for suggesting that natural areas protection is a generalizable interest. The moral priority given to wilderness preservation by environmentalists rests, minimally, on an anthropocentric life-support rationale. Natural (largely unmodified) ecosystems provide essential protective and waste-assimilative functions through the ecological processes that stabilize climate, regulate air and water cycles, recycle essential elements and so on. The positive value attached to these processes has become all the more obvious in an era of global pollution and climate change. Similarly, the interconnected importance of protected areas in conserving genetic strains and wild species is also important. Both the World Commission on Environment and Development (1987, p 166) and the United Nations Conference on Environment and Development (United Nations, 1993, pp 230–232) noted the accelerated depletion and extinction of species resulting from human activities, stressing the economic (commodity) values at stake as reason enough to justify the preservation of biological diversity in situ.

In paying attention to the normative 'rightness' of wilderness preservation, translating from communicative ethics to the political realm is, however, by no means straightforward. As formulated at the philosophical level, discourse ethics does not imply a detailed model for the organization of (land-use) decision-making or the adjudication of environmental disputes over core values. Clearly, no argument concerning practical conflicts of interest can ever completely correspond to an ideal form of communication – that is, a rationally motivated dialogue under conditions of perfect transparency unlimited by time and space. Both institutional and noninstitutional political actors are subject to strategic considerations of political power, where coercion may be as important a means of influence as discourse (Apel, 1990). Strategic principles capture the obvious motives of instrumental effectiveness shaping the political behaviour of interest groups, whatever the constituency they purport to represent.

Habermas makes clear that when only particular interests are at stake – and whether environmental interests are cast as particular or general is, of course, the outcome of political debate – conflicts of interest must be settled through bargaining and compromise. For a strategically settled compromise of interests, the more modest role for practical discourse is to unmask false claims to represent a general interest, withdrawing legitimacy from the privilege of one party (Habermas, 1993, pp 176–177). This is where the discourse principle serves its critical function on behalf of environmental democracy by scrutinizing arguments about environmental interests according to its demanding criteria of social inclusion. Obviously, there are powerful sectional interests implacably opposed to proposals for natural areas protection that are inimical with industrial resource development, and they actively counter the claims of environmentalists to represent a public ecological interest. In a situation where the resources and political influence commanded by the former undermine the conditions for democratically determining environmental interests, the discourse principle must first expose these constraints to free and inclusive debate.

Furthermore, even if an agreement on common interests is not possible, collective decisions have to be made, and the state-led procedures adopted to reach these may also be judged with regard to environmental democratic criteria. Chapter 2 discussed a range of political–institutional conditions conducive to environmental decision-making that are both more effective and democratically legitimate, and these could be applied to wilderness decision-making. For example, with reference to strategic capacity, the notion of 'all affected interests' embodied by the discourse principle high-lights the relevance of precautionary motives in the area of wilderness decision-making. Although the exact ecological benefits of wilderness preservation remain uncertain, as a matter of fairness to present and future generations the onus of proof falls on those who develop natural areas to demonstrate that their actions will not cause irreversible losses in environ-mental quality (O'Riordan and Jordan, 1995).

Switching to the wider political system in this way, discourse ethics reminds us that the critique of existing environmental decision-making according to communicative criteria is immanent. It is connected to already existing tendencies towards democratic self-determination protected by rights. For political institutions, this means procedures in which universality is promoted through the equal participation of all those affected (Günther, 1993, p 169). Apel refers to the anchoring of executive decision-making authority in an independent legislature and judiciary as a means of ensuring democratic accountability (Apel, 1990, pp 49–52). The progressive realiza-tion of practical discourse embodied in the democratic constitutional state is the starting point for environmental democracy. Existing participation and communication rights attempt to realize the conditions for open and free discussion on moral-practical (and other) concerns. The argument for environmental democracy is that this only becomes meaningful when social and ecological rights are included. Healthy social and ecological conditions of life are necessary for the exercise of civil and political rights (see Chapter 1).

It falls to the political public sphere – the communicative network of voluntary associations and wider public debate – to scrutinize the state in the light of practical discourse (Habermas, 1996, pp 373–379). The communi-cative potential of environmental interest groups in this respect is to boost public discussion on justifying contested norms. The scope for practical discourse is central to the political legitimacy of democratic states since the public generally expects decisions on controversial norms to be based on inclusive forms of public deliberation and fair bargaining processes. For wilderness preservationists, considering the possible claims of all those who could be affected by the protection of large natural areas can enhance their own democratic credibility. The generalizability of wilderness preser-vation as a land-use prescription could therefore be enlarged (or possibly constricted). This chapter adopts this standpoint to assess the central moral claims made by preservation groups, while recognizing that, in practice, these are intermixed with strategic considerations. Behind their support for participatory democracy is the expectation of radical environmentalists that, as the movement for wilderness preservation is reinforced by public communication and participation, the ecological imperative for natural areas protection will become even more transparent. But this chapter will show that this outcome is by no means guaranteed by the support for rational procedural norms, and that this accounts for the tensions between core preservationist concerns and democracy.

WILDERNESS VALUES: ANTHROPOCENTRISM AND DEEP ECOLOGY

From the standpoint of discourse ethics, morality refers to practical questions which can be decided with reasons – in other words, normative conflicts amenable to communicative agreement. This signals, according to its proponents, a narrow or 'weak' concept of moral theory. It is directed, firstly, to the *justification* of norms and actions according to a principle of generalizability that embodies common interests, and, secondly, to the *application* of morally justified norms according to whether they are appropriate in a particular situation. The latter relates the meaning of impartiality to a specific context, where the acceptability of norms depends upon particular cultural traditions and values, societal institutions and biographical particularities. Just as universal justification is necessary to establish the validity of a norm, so the context of application, as judged by the participants involved, fills out the content of such a norm (Günther, 1993, pp 59–72). The recent appreciation of the importance of context in discourse ethics has helpfully corrected an earlier tendency to understand questions of justice only in terms of justification; this needs to be borne in mind when evaluating the substantive contribution that communicative ethics can make to the moral discourse of wilderness preservation.

An immediate objection to its relevance concerns the restriction of the ethical domain, encompassed by morally acting subjects, to human relations. The egalitarian relations of reciprocity presupposed in communicative action, which give rise to the moral principles of justice and solidarity, cannot be directly carried over into the relation between humans and nature (Habermas, 1982, p 248; Krebs, 1997, p 272). For some critics the principle of universalization therefore misses the central ethical thrust of biocentric or ecocentric environmentalism which attaches intrinsic value to 'nature in itself' (Eckersley, 1992, pp 106–117). The contrast is marked between a thoroughly *anthropocentric* discourse ethics and ecocentric attempts within environmental ethics at articulating a nonanthropocentric value theory.

Bryan Norton's inclusive definition of anthropocentrism (1987, pp 6–20, 221–239) affords a more useful category for classifying environmental preservation rationales than the (widespread) narrow equation of anthropocentric values with utilitarianism – the obligation to promote the greatest happiness for the greatest number. Norton accepts the general characterization that anthropocentrism confers instrumental value on nonhuman life according to human ends, but offers a useful distinction between 'strong' and 'weak' variants. Strong anthropocentrism restricts the value of nonhuman species and other natural entities to consumptive preferences. These demand values are typically expressed by market prices, such as arguments for wilderness preservation based upon the economic benefits of adventure tourism. Weak anthropocentrism countenances a broader range of human values; in particular, it assigns a qualitatively different transformative value to nonhuman nature. Transformative value refers to the altering and ranking of preferences that follows from discursive examination. Upon reflection and rationally motivated agreement, 'considered' preferences are the hypothetical desires or needs that may override demand values, such as moral or aesthetic ideals attributed to the human experience of nature.[1] Norton refers to a similar argument by Mark Sagoff in the context of social regulation, where 'community-regarding' values expressed by citizens through the political process justify environmental protection and preservation. These include such shared values as well-being, health, and respect and reverence for nature. The rational basis of their public interest credentials rests on their achieving intersubjective agreement (Sagoff, 1988, pp 1–23).

Neither Sagoff nor Norton refer to discourse ethics but their arguments can be interpreted as bringing cultural valuations of nature, over and above consumer preferences – expressed as prices – into the realm of intersubjective debate. This emphasis links communicative ethics relevant to wilderness preservation issues to weak anthropocentrism. It recognizes that all valuation is necessarily human-based, where moral choices are not philosophically pregiven, but subject to argument and debate; and that this moral pluralism can only be guaranteed by democratic institutions, universal human rights and, as will ultimately be argued, healthy and diverse ecological systems. Discourse ethics thus democratizes environmental valuation processes, opening up debate in a nonexclusive fashion, uncovering barriers and latent values, and allowing a critical reconstruction of ecological decision-making (O'Hara, 1996).

Nonanthropocentrism stands distinct from an anthropocentric axiology in conferring 'intrinsic' or 'inherent' value on nonhuman lifeforms. A range of nonanthropocentric approaches has been offered as grounds for the moral standing of nonhuman natural entities or systems (Nash, 1989). The first formulation of modern ecocentric ethics has been credited as one of the most influential for leading Canadian environmentalists, and is often cited by wilderness activists in western Canada as informing their philosophical perspective. This is the normative commitment to ecological integrity that Aldo Leopold encapsulated in his well-known maxim (1966, p 224):

> *A thing is right when it tends to preserve the integrity, stability and beauty of the biotic community. It is wrong when it tends otherwise.*

Indebted to Darwin's evolutionary account of ethical phenomena and community ecology, this environmental ethic derives norms from an organic or holistic conception of ecological interests. Darwin portrayed the sociobiological evolution of ethics as expanding modes of cooperation between interdependent individuals. Leopold's seminal contribution was to enlarge the boundaries of the moral community to include animals, plants, water and soil. This radical notion of ethical extension places human beings within a biotic community that accords both a 'right to continued existence' of its individual members and, more significantly, an intrinsic right to the compositional and functional integrity of ecosystems. The value of the healthy biotic community takes precedence over individual organisms. This approach, conferring intrinsic value on natural ecosystems and the integrity of ecological processes (Callicott, 1987; Westra, 1994), has had an obvious appeal for wilderness preservation advocates, reinforced by Leopold's historical role in promoting wilderness protection in North America (Nash, 1982, pp 182–199; Flader, 1974).

If the influence of a Leopoldian environmental ethic is acknowledged by wilderness activists, rationalizations for preservation founded on intrinsic value are more likely to refer to motifs of deep ecology. Deep ecological ideas share the process-orientation of a Leopoldian ethic; but this emerges as a metaphysical exposition and a logical difference from scientific ecology is maintained. The Norwegian philosopher Arne Naess introduced the term deep ecology in 1972 and his characterization has shaped its subsequent articulation in western Canada by wilderness preservationists. Deep ecology is presented as heralding a new philosophical and religious worldview for human-environment relations. Naess clarifies the approach by contrast with the 'shallow ecology movement' – reform environmentalism concerned with pollution abatement and resource conservation but subscribing to an anthropocentric value theory and the 'dominant technological paradigm' of modern industrial society (Naess, 1973). As a social movement, deep ecology envisages a shift in consciousness toward *ecosophy* – ecologically wise action and wisdom. Ecosophy represents a 'philosophical worldview or system inspired by the conditions of life in the ecosphere' (Naess, 1989a, p 38; Drengson, 1990). As a personal philosophical system, the details of an ecosophy are formulated by 'deep questioning', according to an individual's life context and background. Yet all ecospheric attitudes and practices recognize a broad ontological system which posits no division between human and nonhuman realms. From this ontology are derived common intuitions of the intrinsic value of nonhuman nature.

Naess presents the term 'self-realization' as his logically ultimate norm or intuition, although others have interpreted this as a fundamental norm of deep ecology in general. This core normative statement is conceived as a developmental process and fundamental goal, relating to an expanding identification of the self with all lifeforms. For Naess, the norm appeals beyond the narrowly self-centred, isolated 'ego-realization' of the modern Western self to a relational field-like conception of self. The Australian philosopher Warwick Fox (1990) has related this idea to advances in transpersonal psychology, although Naess has led recognition of the ecological self, linking identification with the total unfolding of life. Whereas the shallow ecological perspective retains an objective disengagement with nature, deep ecology stresses the integration of human individuals with the whole of nonhuman nature. This ecocentric cosmology indicates the highest level of maturity or growth for the self (Naess, 1989a, pp 84–86; 1989b).

From the top norm of self-realization, which denotes a universal right to self-unfolding, Naess derives the correlative norm of 'ecological egalitarianism' – the intrinsic value of every life form. This gives rise to the image of a 'democracy of lifeforms' but for obvious reasons is presented as a principle or guideline rather than a practical norm for conduct. Even in wilderness, Naess explains, full self-realization implies the acceptance of hurting and killing among lifeforms. The basic intuition nevertheless remains the unity of life and the right to self-unfolding (1989a, pp 167–177). Bill Devall and George Sessions name this intuition 'biocentric equality' (1985, p 67):

> *[All] things in the biosphere have an equal right to live and blossom and reach their own individual forms of unfolding and self-realization within the larger self-realization.*

Wilderness preservation assumes great importance as a manifestation of human restraint. The protection of large natural areas for their intrinsic value becomes central to the type of consciousness change envisaged by deep ecologists. Holmes Rolston has presented a nonanthropocentric theory of value, identifying an intrinsic worth in wilderness as ecological process. Individual organisms have an objective value arising from their genetic autonomy of self-maintenance; but, in a deep ecological fashion, the most important values belong to the speciation process itself – acknowledging wilderness as a 'generating matrix' of life (1988, pp 216–239). Other environmental philosophers have attempted to demonstrate an intrinsic value in wilderness – for example, Simonsen (1981) and Oelschlaeger (1993) – and, though their theoretical efforts may be subsumed under the general label 'deep ecology', Naess has not endorsed moves to justify this norm through practical discourse.[2] Rather than expressing self-realization or intrinsic value in terms of formal argumentation, as normative terms morally binding on others, Naess refers to the former term as an overarching personal value and to the latter in a nontechnical everyday sense. Other self-professed deep ecologists have also eschewed moral discourse and any formal approaches which claim to generalize the normative application of intrinsic value. Instead, they issue 'invitations' to experience a more expansive sense of self – the wider the identification of addressees, the more they will be naturally inclined to undertake benevolent acts (Fox, 1990, p 247):

> *[Given] a deep enough understanding of the way things are, the response of being inclined to care for the unfolding of the world in all*

its aspects follows 'naturally' – not as a logical consequence but as
a psychological consequence as an expression of the spontaneous
unfolding (development, maturing) of the self.

The validity of the intuition that all life is inherently valuable is defended,
but with recourse to the position that, ultimately, this cannot be determined
by discursive procedures. Indeed, Naess has consistently opposed attempts
to universalize the ultimate premises of his ecosophy as the philosophical
basis for radical environmentalism. On the contrary, at the level of ultimate
philosophies, a considerable diversity of religious and metaphysical views
is seen as compatible with the deep ecology movement (Drengson, 1997).
Their fundamentals, if articulated, have at most 'limited comparability' in
terms of cognitive contents. As long as they (intuitively) affirm the inherent
worth of nonhuman nature, any incompatibility of other fundamental
premises does not prevent agreement concerning priorities for significant
changes in environmental policy and common practical efforts to improve
ethical standards of human-environment interaction (Naess, 1992).[3]

Deep ecology nevertheless implies an incommensurability with dominant anthropocentric worldviews and this has important consequences for
wilderness preservation rationales. From our discourse ethics perspective,
deep ecological reasons for natural areas protection lack a secure communicative basis. Statements affirming an intrinsic moral sense of nature take
this fact as ontologically given or, in some of the more pantheistic positions,
as an 'act of faith' outside practical discourse (Kohak, 1984). Habermas
identifies immediate difficulties with such cosmological moral positions
(1982, pp 248–249):

> *[While] in our dealings with external nature we can indeed have*
> *feelings analogous to moral feelings, the norm-conformative attitude*
> *to this domain of external nature does not yield any problems suscept-*
> *ible to being worked up cognitively, that is, problems that could*
> *be stylized to questions of justice from the standpoint of normative*
> *validity.*

Of course, this restates the argument in Chapter 1 that led to the characterization of environmental democracy as a humanistic project: nonhuman
entities cannot pursue value-governed life projects or take part in communicative processes of civic self-determination. To repeat the conclusion there,
this does not mean that these entities – including ecosystems – cannot be
objects of moral consideration (there are very compelling reasons why they
are); it means that they cannot be subjects of a rights or justice discourse.
Environmental democracy rests on a shared notion of political autonomy
in which the addressees of duties are, in principle, authors of the rights
from which these duties arise. Deep ecology claims to find an inherent value
in nature yet moral valuation resides in *intersubjective* recognition with
reference to natural entities.

However deeply felt, wilderness activists in British Columbia who express a deep ecology motivation concede the problem in constructing a normative political position consistent with deep ecology. For example, a founding director of Friends of Strathcona Park (Vancouver Island) states:

> *Our argument is an awareness – a philosophical awareness that we do recognize that the world was not created for us, that we are a product of creation, and that we have to respect the Creation. And that is very difficult [to communicate]. . . . What I'm talking about are the values in life, not the values of economy and of jobs. These are the values of deep ecological existence, of spiritual values, of meaning.[4]*

Other preservation group leaders have stressed the need to encourage an emerging spiritual consciousness from the ecological consciousness apparent in public concern for natural areas protection.[5] But there is a marked incongruence between the personal attitudes of these wilderness activists and the arguments they put forward for their organizations. Not only are intuitive deep ecological feelings difficult to verbalize, they sit uncomfortably with power-orientated strategies and the communicative demands of the public policy community. Self-realization and ecological egalitarianism are ill-suited to discursive justification. Therefore, the generalizability of deep ecological values (the 'public interest') required by political decision-makers proves elusive. Not surprisingly then, it has proved more expedient for preservation groups to justify wilderness allocation in instrumental terms, appealing to anthropocentric values. Campaigns have historically emphasized scientific and economic benefits deriving from wilderness preservation, but often in conjunction with imagery that evokes a distinctive wilderness aesthetic (Searle, 1986; Careless, 1997).

Wilderness activists in British Columbia have favoured organized pressure groups as the primary means of attaining natural areas preservation and, like all public interest groups undertaking noninstitutional political action, this has implied appealing to a broad-based constituency through media-orientated campaigning (Pross, 1986, pp 108–129). Unlike older conservation organizations accepted in environmental policy-making circles (and sometimes in receipt of significant project-based funding from government sources), the preservationist groups have maintained a non-negotiable focus on wilderness protection. The establishment of the major multi-issue groups, from the British Columbia chapters of the Sierra Club (1969) and the Canadian Parks and Wilderness Society (1978) to the Valhalla Wilderness Society (1978) and the Western Canada Wilderness Committee (1980), has lent an institutional permanence to a movement comprised also of many smaller area-based preservation groups typically created in response to impending resource extraction threats, whether in old-growth forest areas (such as Friends of Carmanah/Walbran, 1991) or existing protected natural areas (such as Friends of Strathcona Park, 1987). While the central role of public opinion in noninstitutional environmental politics undermines any attempt to determine precisely the policy response of the political system to the explicit demands articulated by preservationist groups in the province, the wilderness protection movement has by no means been ineffective, pushing successive governments to protect key wilderness areas and, as evident by the participatory environmental negotiation exercise described in the last chapter, prompting the political system to accord a priority to anticipatory, sustainability-based land-use planning (however successful or not in practice). The key point here is that this has been accomplished by wilderness activists articulating natural areas preservation as a collective environmental good, recognizing that the bulk of public support for their aims connects to very real human benefits – recreation, environmental education, tourism dollars – as well as human (aboriginal) rights, even though their motivations have also been biocentric.

The major, multi-issue wilderness groups in British Columbia have thus maintained a pragmatic stance in employing normative claims to wilderness preservation, utilizing a wide range of anthropocentric arguments according to particular issues, and occasionally suggesting that an inherent value resides in wilderness. Behind their reluctance to formulate or articulate an explicit deep ecological platform lies a preference for leaving philosophical issues to individual activists, while concentrating group resources on strategically effective arguments in the political public sphere. Interviews this author conducted in British Columbia with over 30 leading preservationists in 1990–1991 and 1994 found that most group directors held beliefs akin to a deep ecological position. Alongside the key influence of Naess, several Canadian academics cited by these activists have contributed to the developing nonanthropocentric environmental philosophy. Among those closely associated with ideas of deep ecology are Alan Drengson, Neil Evernden, John Livingston and Stan Rowe.

Of the main provincial wilderness groups in British Columbia, the executive of the Canadian Parks and Wilderness Society – British Columbia chapter – has made the clearest effort to define a collective philosophical stance in terms consistent with the principles of deep ecology. This is, in part, a reflection of the relatively high proportion of intellectuals actively involved with the organization, both at the provincial and national level. The national executive has maintained the group's respectable public front, still prepared to mobilize preservation arguments which appeal to instrumental values; but provincial directors had already identified a shift of worldview by the early 1990s:

> There's been a revamping of our mandate to make it less anthropocentric, even more biocentric of an approach, reflecting an evolution in consciousness within the group itself. A lot of us have been very deeply influenced by the deep ecology movement. I think we find that rather unique insofar as environmental groups are concerned. And we have within our ranks quite a few people who, as Canadians, are

> *perceived as being at the forefront of deep ecology; for example, Stan*
> *Rowe, Ted Mosquin.[6]*

As expressed by wilderness preservationists in western Canada, deep ecology is perceived as being consistent with a progressive political philosophy. This sets some distance from the ideological polarization typically portrayed in American green politics between an idealistic deep ecology and social ecology – Murray Bookchin's influential notion of participatory ecological politics. Bookchin has led a trenchant critique of spiritual interpretations of deep ecology popular on the West Coast – formulations associated, for example, with institutions such as the Elmwood Institute in Berkeley and the radical wilderness group Earth First! (Bookchin, 1986; Merchant, 1990). Followers of social ecology in the US have commonly charged some deep ecologists with issuing authoritarian prescriptions for political change, attributing this to the lack of any historical and social analysis of ecological problems (Bradford, 1989; Elkins 1989–1990), although a *rapprochement* has been attempted (Chase, 1991). To be sure, the conservative currents of deep ecology articulated by some groups and individuals in the US are at odds with the particular ecosophy of Arne Naess, who advocates a democratic-participatory politics and a structural analysis of the production and consumption patterns behind present ecological problems. More relevantly, leading wilderness activists in British Columbia expressing sympathy for deep ecology have close connections with social justice issues and organizations, notably aboriginal interest groups. Deep ecology is seen as requiring democratic institutional reform, in line with the radical political platform of the Green party of British Columbia (formed in 1983 by prominent preservationists).

Nevertheless, the central normative claim of deep ecology remains problematic – that is, the authority of a perspective that lacks deep 'argumentation' concerning its own political morality. In a Canadian context, John Livingston has asserted that there exists no rational argument for conveying the inherent worth of nature, because this ultimately rests on experiential understanding of a state of being – 'the planetary biospheric self'. Indeed, Livingston envisages abandoning ethical concepts once this new 'natural' metaphysics is achieved (Livingston, 1981, pp 97–117; 1986). Communicative ethics exposes both the irrationality (the 'performative contradiction' of a moral argument for abandoning ethics) and potentially anti-democratic implications of such a recourse to a totalizing worldview. By spurning normative justification, it undermines the claims to generalizability of calls for wilderness preservation. Aside from tactical considerations, this type of deep ecological intuition is one reason for the non-negotiability of preservationist demands. This creates a tension between, on the one hand, the anthropocentric arguments utilized in the public sphere to champion the general interest of natural areas protection and, on the other, a philosophical motivation rooted in rejecting anthropocentric interests. This philosophically is untenable since the very imputation of ecological responsibility presupposes a demarcation between human valuation and nature (Soper, 1995, pp 160–161); insofar as deep ecology does not recognize the anthropocentric principles of justice and solidarity in its normative premises, it also lacks democratic legitimacy.

BIOREGIONALISM: NATURAL RIGHTS AND COMMUNITY CONTROL

This chapter will now discuss specific political implications arising from the contrast between a discourse ethics offering a procedural notion of justice and an environmental ethics (or deep ecological normative premise) oriented towards a concrete value order. These concern, in an empirical context, prescriptions for public (Crown) land-use reform presented by wilderness preservationists in British Columbia, notably the question of community empowerment with respect to forest resources. The link to deep ecology, and its basic norm of self-realization, is through deriving principles for self-determination of local communities – self-sufficiency, decentralization, autonomy (Naess, 1989a, pp 142–146, 204–206). A form of direct democracy is implied by these norms, but to what extent can they be justified through moral argumentation?

The major Vancouver and Victoria-based wilderness groups have developed a decentralist, localist perspective influenced greatly by the 'bioregionalism' of the broad-based alternative movement. Natural areas preservation has united the strategic agenda of urban environmentalists with the more radical concerns of revived 'back-to-the-land' communities in the Slocan Valley, the Cariboo, the Gulf Islands and Tofino. Rural preservation groups, such as the Valhalla Wilderness Society and the Friends of Clayoquot Sound (established 1979), express this overlap most clearly. In embracing decentralist themes they reflect a wider subculture in the Pacific North-West and coastal northern California, which has shaped the reception of deep ecology in North America: this is the continuing legacy of the hippie counterculture of the late 1960s. Bioregionalism has its roots in this way of life, although it was first popularized by Peter Berg of the San Francisco Planet Drum Foundation in the mid 1970s (Plant, 1990; Zuckerman, 1989, pp 50–53). Kirkpatrick Sale has offered a concise definition of 'bioregion' – 'a life territory, a place defined by its lifeforms, its topography and its biota, rather than by human dictates; a region governed by nature, not legislature' (Sale, 1985, p 43). Despite the original involvement of ecologist Raymond Dasmann in giving the term scientific meaning, bioregionalism has primarily become a moral philosophy inviting acceptance of a Leopoldian land ethic. Humans are portrayed as participants in a biotic community, with a responsibility to become knowledgeable ecological citizens. The process of learning to 'live in place' and developing bioregional identity is termed 'reinhabitation' (Berg and Dasmann, 1977; Berg, 1990).

In its prescriptions for the polity, bioregionalism draws upon the communitarian values of cooperation and participation favoured by deep ecology. As with Canadian readings of deep ecology, though, this has involved a moral abstention. The political resolution of environmental problems is accomplished by the recognition of – and identification with – natural regions and processes, even if the demarcation of these is problematic. What is the status, for example, of 'alien' individuals and communities (human and nonhuman)? Bioregional political philosophy claims to derive from ecological laws its normative principles of decentralization, complementarity and diversity. For wilderness in particular, Berg identifies a locus of ecological consciousness which will help transform environmentalism from a defensive preoccupation with protest toward proactive institutional reform (1990, p 25):

> *My own feeling is that the greatest shared value for the necessary upcoming ecological era is wilderness: because wilderness already embodies systems, designs, purposes that are workable, are demonstrably ecoenergetic-efficient in terms of using energy and resources and so on.*

Bioregionalism may be subsumed under the broad notion of deep ecology articulated by wilderness activists in British Columbia, although it carries a more explicit naturalistic stance. This presumes a political theory that begins from the discoverable 'truths' of natural law in order to evaluate existing institutions and policies, and initiate locally based bioregional mapping strategies (Aberley, 1993; 1994). Sale establishes the central principles of a 'bioregional paradigm' on this basis, which combines traditions of local natural wisdom with modern ecological knowledge. A more sophisticated expression of a communitarian perspective based on natural law has been presented by Michael M'Gonigle, a provincial environmentalist and professor in the faculty of law at the University of Victoria. For M'Gonigle, long-term social and ecological sustainability must ultimately be guided by the natural law of 'being in balance'. The 'natural self' or 'natural community' acknowledges the interrelatedness of all things in the biosphere, their spiritual unity and their intrinsic moral worth. Once again, natural laws are apprehended 'beyond rational thought' through personal experience of this balance. M'Gonigle endorses a bioregional programme of economic and political decentralization: local self-sustaining economies become a precondition for rooting participatory democracy in ecoterritorial communities. Empowerment at this local level is claimed to be the major structural reform serving the functional requirements of ecological sustainability (M'Gonigle, 1986; 1989–1990).

Bioregional thinking has marked a significant evolution in legal rationales for wilderness preservation. In the first place, it has reduced the reliance of preservation groups on centralized environmental protection legislation as the focus for lobbying efforts. This still assumes great strategic significance, and the bioregional perspective accedes to the continuing importance of provincial and federal powers for natural areas protection – as traditionally recognized by the wider conservation community – but it has informed a switch to ecological arguments for preservation. During the 1980s there existed a strong recreational lobby for US-type wilderness legislation in British Columbia, headed by the Federation of Mountain Clubs and the Outdoor Recreation Council. The recommendations of a provincial wilderness advisory committee in 1985 shared this enthusiasm for formal legislation, although the provincial government chose not to establish a wilderness act. Since then emphasis in legislative lobbying has shifted to the federal level, and provincial wilderness groups have supported nation-wide efforts to expand and strengthen national parks protection on grounds of biological diversity (Hummel, 1989). They have also fought for binding habitat protection provisions in the protracted development of Canadian endangered species legislation.

Existing attempts to aid wilderness preservation efforts by means of environmental law nevertheless sit uncomfortably with the moral frame-work of bioregionalism. Not only do they endorse a centralized political/legal structure, they imply a formal procedure divorced from any unquestioned metaphysical backing. This distinction must be emphasized. The moral legitimacy of modern legal procedures arises from employing principles of equity and impartiality, which distribute burdens of proof and set requirements for justification based upon the provision of good reasons. To be sure, legal regulation necessarily limits moral discourse because of obvious time and resource constraints, unburdening political and admini-strative decision-making from the need for continuous discussion. But moral justification is necessarily implied by the procedures of modern law, where normative conflicts are adjudicated in principle according to which competing interest lends itself to universalization (Habermas, 1996, pp 104–118). This idea of impartiality is violated by the substantive value premises of bioregionalism, which can be interpreted as reviving classical notions of 'natural right' – that is, the unfolding of natural entities as a source of moral value (Hinchman and Hinchman, 1989; M'Gonigle, 1986, pp 288–294).

Self-realization in its full ecological context points beyond civil law to the legislation of natural law. As expressed by Ted Mosquin, past president of the Canadian Parks and Wilderness Society, this implies a *moralization* of law (Mosquin, 1991, p 46):

> *A good legislated natural law would provide people with written codes to reaffirm a sense of right and wrong in our relations with the planet. Each written law would ensure that the norms of the ecosphere are valued and respected.*

The seminal statement on conferring legal rights to natural objects came from Christopher Stone (1972), who argued that human guardians or trustees could represent the interest of nonhuman entities in avoiding injury.

As a radical extension of existing human rights, this nevertheless retains the individualistic bias of conventional law (Elder, 1989). Furthermore, even American preservationists from a deep ecological perspective have recognized that legal arguments for wilderness 'rights' can only conceivably come from a consideration of human interests – for example, Thornton's (1997) case for wilderness protection informed by an environmentally based definition of mental health. Mosquin envisages a much more ambitious ascription of legal rights to life-supporting ecological functions and processes. This stands remote from current reform efforts in Canadian environmental law, where lawyers have argued for a recognition of citizen rights to a healthy environment. Lobbying has included attempts to enact a federal environmental bill of rights and to interpret the Canadian Charter of Rights and Freedoms in a manner that is sympathetic to environmental litigation. Both remain firmly in the realm of anthropocentric valuation and formal law: the right to environmental protection and enhancement is promoted as a public interest (Andrews, 1987; Muldoon, 1988). A consistent natural rights approach of the type advocated by Mosquin would paradoxically undermine the justification of wilderness preservation as a generalizable interest, because the rationale for natural areas protection would be tied to a specific naturalistic value order. Without reference to formal legal procedures ensuring impartial assessment across *different* value orientations, there would be little scope for moral argumentation to vindicate a wilderness act among those not sharing a belief in the intrinsic value of nonhuman nature.

The radical decentralization suggested by bioregionalism has led to wilderness activists in western Canada supporting legal assertions of aboriginal title. As articulated by M'Gonigle, the natural law perspective holds a key role for native title in British Columbia. Political struggles for native self-government are the clearest concrete examples of Canadian attempts to establish natural territorial structures for local governance. The traditional cultural values of native societies are seen as bound up with ecological awareness and adaptation. They express a collective identity based upon a continuing spiritual relationship to the land. North American environmentalists have long highlighted, often romantically, an aboriginal land wisdom symbolizing a life-affirming respect for nonhuman nature (Callicott, 1989; Booth and Jacobs, 1990). As a contribution to environmental sustainability, the accumulation of local ecological knowledge by aboriginal cultures has also been identified as invaluable by a Canadian standing commission on aboriginal affairs (1990, pp 16–17) and, more generally, the World Commission on Environment and Development (1987, pp 114–16). Provincial proponents of bioregionalism draw more far-reaching institutional lessons from native prescriptions for self-government. M'Gonigle describes the contours of a fundamentally new 'ecoconstitution' rooted in the social power of territorial communities. In line with his naturalistic perspective, native title retains historical authority as the model for an alternative conception of sovereignty. Against the centralized top-down powers of Canada's existing liberal constitution, the ultimate source of ecoconstitutional sovereignty is the naturally and culturally defined community (M'Gonigle, 1992).

Appreciation of traditional aboriginal use in wilderness areas is reflected in the legal recognition given to collecting and hunting activities in Canadian national parks. This divergence from the American notion of wilderness as 'empty' land – save for transitory visitors – was expressed most forcefully by Justice Thomas Berger in the 1977 report of the Mackenzie Valley pipeline inquiry.[7] Appointed in 1974 by the federal government to review the social, economic and environmental impacts of a proposed natural gas pipeline from the Alaskan and Canadian Arctic to southern metropolitan centres, Berger undertook numerous hearings throughout the western Arctic, recording testimonies on the traditional resource utilization and land stewardship of native peoples. His proposal that aboriginal people should share management responsibilities with the Canadian Parks service in national parks covering areas of aboriginal hunting and fishing was incorporated within national parks policy in 1979 (Berger, 1977; 1989). Within British Columbia, joint management agreements with native peoples in provincial parks had to wait until the second half of the 1990s, when the provincial government belatedly recognized the existence of aboriginal rights in protected natural areas.[8]

Berger's idea of wilderness as (aboriginal) *homeland* has proved influential among provincial environmentalists. This includes those key American emigrés who have been pivotal to the philosophical and strategic orientation of wilderness organizations, such as the founding director of the Western Canada Wilderness Committee:

> *My conception of wilderness has changed. I slowly realized that what we were trying to preserve was a network of natural ecosystems, and in many of those humans are a part of it – human use in a low impact way . . . aboriginal peoples have modified the landscape somewhat but they've kept the essence of the natural system there, and that's what we want to preserve. So this purist idea that I maybe came to to begin with was slowly replaced.*[9]

While acknowledging these common concerns, the catalyst for recent alliances between native peoples (First Nations) and environmentalists has been the convergence of short-term strategic objectives, notably opposition to logging operations in old-growth forests. For wilderness groups, the assertion of aboriginal title as a legal right has become a powerful challenge to the Crown-granted timber rights of resource companies. Beginning with Meares Island (1984–1985) and South Moresby (1985), this has effectively enabled them to block or delay a series of logging operations throughout the province, on the grounds that these would prejudice title negotiations. A more proactive series of legal challenges in the 1990s finally led in 1997 to the provincial Court of Appeal recognizing an aboriginal interest in forest resources and, more significantly, the Supreme Court of Canada judging that British Columbia has never had the jurisdiction to extinguish aboriginal rights, including aboriginal title to land.[10] However, as in the case of South Moresby National Park, successful campaigns for park *creation* have occasionally exposed differences between First Nations and wilderness preservationists, given that the designation of parks has created new third-party (conservation/recreation) interests potentially in conflict with the self-determination of native peoples. Forest and mining companies have attempted to capitalize on this tension by offering economic incentives to First Nations in exchange for their agreement to resource-extraction activities in areas subject to aboriginal title claims. The democratic self-identification of aboriginal people in relation to wilderness preservation has thus had to negotiate through a labyrinth of competing strategic considerations.

In this political context the bioregionalist endorsement of native self-government understandably stresses the primacy of aboriginal participation in resource and environmental decision-making. According to M'Gonigle, community control of local resource management may be achieved by means of local veto in a new third-level government (1989–1990, p 90):

> *The foundation for third-level government would ultimately be the recognition of regional title held by the people who live in the natural region, the title being historically rooted in the native community which has lived in the area from time immemorial. This title recognition amounts to an acknowledgement by the dominant culture of the fact of historic aboriginal territory 'ownership' and the need to negotiate a sharing of this territory with non-native society.*

An ecoconstitution would confer fundamental sovereignty on third-level government from which jurisdictional rights are delegated to other levels. This would authorize state jurisdiction to serve the large collective public interest in policy fields transcending natural regions, while the sharing of local title power with nonnative citizens would also emanate from these broader social responsibilities. Nevertheless, bioregional decentralization would be guaranteed constitutionally by awarding a political veto to third-level government, allowing it in principle to block developments threatening regional ecological sustainability. M'Gonigle's proposal has acquired additional saliency as a result of recent legal judgements building up justification for aboriginal title. That aboriginal title could apply to as much as 94 per cent of the province's land base indicates the potential scope of his model for local governance, not to mention its relevance to other jurisdictions where aboriginal title is applicable.

The key 1997 Supreme Court of Canada decision, Delgamuukw versus British Columbia, may finally accord a definitive legal weight to the rights to exclusive use and occupation of land pursuant to aboriginal title in the province (as opposed to the existing *constitutional* recognition of aboriginal rights under section 35(1) of the federal Constitution Act, 1982). Although the court declined to lay down any legal principles on rights to self-government, its declaration that aboriginal title confers a *sui generis* right to land places an obligation on provincial authorities, where such title has been successfully claimed, to respect the aboriginal practices on that land. The resonance with M'Gonigle's bioregionalist project is not only the grounding of aboriginal title on the physical occupation of land, past and present, but that this right to land recognizes also its 'inherent and unique value' (paragraph 129) for aboriginal cultures. In other words, the right to collective self-determination of aboriginal activities on such land is at once both procedural and substantive. This incurs duties on the provincial government, respectively, to include the prior interests of aboriginal rights holders in the process of environmental resource allocation and the actual allocation of those resources (paragraph 164). This may give legal authority to protecting aboriginal uses that are compatible with environmental preservation due to their cultural value. On the other hand, while certain environmentally destructive uses are deemed incompatible with aboriginal title (the example mentioned is strip mining), other potentially damaging uses (development of oil and gas reserves) are regarded as acceptable. Furthermore, against the bioregionalist model of third-level government, national and provincial policies can, given mechanisms of fair compensation, legitimately infringe on aboriginal title.[11]

The debates about aboriginal title are lively and complex. What this chapter stresses is that while this key statement by the Supreme Court of Canada conjoins aboriginal title to a physical and cultural relationship with the land (one, preservationists stress, that is typically more ecologically sound than non-aboriginal use of environmental resources), and sources this title partly in systems of aboriginal law predating British sovereignty, it remains firmly within modern legal discourse. In contrast with the bioregionalist view that aboriginal title should be evaluated exclusively in terms of aboriginal land traditions, the Supreme Court cites constitutional authority, common law and moral reasons for supporting title claims. A discourse theory of law, in keeping with the idea of environmental democracy advanced in this study, interprets such a judgement in terms of its independent communicative rationality: its normative appeal to all affected interests. I submit that particular moral force arises here from recognizing the social and economic injustices that have historically been borne by the First Nations of British Columbia – a human rights justification that can, if needed, cite pertinent articles of legally binding international covenants as well as customary law. The upshot is that the traditional relationship of aboriginal people to the land may provide *one* source for the legal recognition of their environmental interests (in keeping with aboriginal ethical valuations of nature), but that the bioregionalist argument puts too much of a burden on this communitarian aspect to legitimize both local governance and ecologically rational decision-making. A discursive legal framework is open to the many other, often separate, reasons in favour of (or against) both. It cannot, by definition, prejudge which would be the most relevant in any particular case, although the constitutional judgement discussed above will hopefully help entrench aboriginal rights and freedoms in land-use decision-making in British Columbia.

Another bioregionalist formula for power-sharing – with applicability outside areas of aboriginal title and to other jurisdictions – proposed by two members of the British Columbia Green party (Gray and Zammuto, 1997) imports directly an inverse-square rule from 'universal physical laws of nature' (gravity, heat, light) to demonstrate how local decision-making authority can be foregrounded but is still subject to checks, and is diminished by an inverse of the square of a nominal distance away from the community – taking in the region (1/2), the province (1/9), the nation (1/16) and the globe (1/25), all of which could be converted into local votes for local issues (the mechanics for achieving this are not given). This formulation, while revealing again a naturalistic understanding of democratic decision-making, nevertheless reflects the creative designs for environmental governance that is suggested by a grassroots movement for community control of natural resources in the province.

The seminal Slocan Valley Community Forest Management Project, undertaken during 1974 by a local citizens' group in the West Kootenays, has had an enduring influence on community forest proposals by environmentalists in the province, even though it was ignored by the provincial government. This innovative lay study, the culmination of two years' research and public input, called for the establishment of a local administrative system guaranteeing local community involvement in natural resource-use planning. A resource committee, comprised of local residents and representatives of public-resource management agencies, was recommended as the environmental resource decision-making authority within the relevant regional area of Crown forest land. Significantly, the project also endorsed the radical reallocation of timber cutting rights through a system of rural woodlots available to valley residents, and proposed that all Crown stumpage revenues (accruing to the state from timber extraction licences) from the region should be reinvested in local resource management activities (Slocan Valley Community Forest Management Project, 1974).

Community forestry studies and programmes gathered support in the 1980s and 1990s, as a growing number of water-use groups provided an additional rallying point for rural communities, under the umbrella of the British Columbia Watershed Protection Alliance. Wilderness activists, often involved in these local forestry and watershed networks, have endorsed their calls for the radical decentralization of the existing forest tenure system, away from the corporate control exercised by a few major multinational companies. These campaigns continue to challenge the very limited legal basis for community involvement, and promote a low-impact, labour-intensive 'ecoforestry' compatible with large-scale wilderness protection (M'Gonigle and Parfitt, 1994; Cooperman, 1996). However, in the face of only marginal improvements to the very limited basis for local municipalities and regional districts to regulate resource development and protect environmental quality, western Canadian bioregionalists have intensified collaboration with like-minded US groups within the 'Cascadian North-West' to push a transboundary agenda of massive wilderness protection – through the Greater Ecosystem Alliance (Friedman and Lindholdt, 1993) – and ecoforestry management – through the Pacific Certification Council (Simpson, 1995). These transnational efforts have still to generate widespread public awareness or support, and are actively opposed by corporate forestry and mining concerns; however, they represent a cross-border political mobilization to keep up with, and challenge, the investment reach of those corporate interests.

WILDERNESS PRESERVATION AND ENVIRONMENTAL DEMOCRACY

Discourse ethics – the major moral philosophy underpinning this book's understanding of environmental democracy – helps locate a central tension in wilderness preservationist politics: that is, between a *naturalistic* perspective and the *universal* orientation implicit in its appeals for democratic decision-making. While my observation in this geographical context – that deep ecology has been intuitively presumed by many advocates – may not be representative of other streams of the deep ecology movement, commentators have noted more generally the neglect of politico-practical guidelines within deep ecology (Sylvan, 1985, pp 14–15). It has been argued in response that, as a philosophy, deep ecology is excused from the responsibility of developing a political strategy (Gottlieb, 1995, p 43) or that, as long as it supports democratic political means, there is no need to prescribe any definite kind of governmental form (Naess, 1995, pp 147–148). Similarly, wilderness advocates are not normally obliged to present detailed moral arguments in defence of their prescriptions for natural areas protection. But without public justification of their intrinsic value premises, the more radical preservationist arguments which embrace ecosovereignty lack democratic legitimacy. If deep ecology is characterized by deep argumentation, such reasoning needs to include a critical examination of the social and political implications of its central ethical imperative.

A communicative ethics rejects the notion that any moral philosophy holds a privileged access to particular moral truths, preferring instead to clarify a procedure for the questioning and justification of normative validity claims. It claims to encourage forms of moral self-determination governed by critical but abstract principles of justice and solidarity – the content of moral choices is up to individuals in specific social contexts drawing reflectively upon their own cultural traditions and personal values. While this opposes naturalistic philosophy, it offers a more consistent democratic grounding of progressive environmental politics. Therefore, to return to the principle of sovereignty, environmental democracy (supported by discourse ethics) views the sovereignty of the people as comprising the essential conditions enabling processes of free and open public deliberation (Habermas, 1996, pp 463–490; see this book's conclusion) – a notion which is more appropriate to our highly complex and interdependent societies than the location of sovereignty within a biophysically and culturally defined local community. Critics have objected that such universal ideas isolate a communicative moral theory from the competing perspectives of actual political actors (Honneth and Joas, 1988, pp 152–167). Yet it is the existence of democratic rules and principles – equal respect and rights for the individual, protection of minorities and, as will be highlighted, collective rights to environmental quality – that protects increasingly diverse forms of cultural and moral identification (Habermas, 1993, pp 90–91). Deep ecology is, of course, one legitimate source of moral self-identification and ethical self-realization, but its claims to rightness in the public sphere can only be justified through argumentation. This is why it needs to clarify a defensible political morality, as Naess has more recently conceded (Light, 1997, pp 79–80).

Discourse ethics, the moral philosophical counterpart to our discourse theory of democracy, thus issues the challenge to wilderness preservationists to demonstrate their political legitimacy – to make crystal clear their attachment to principles of justice and solidarity, and to show why environmental justice is not possible without this support for radical, environmental democracy. This would reinforce the rational grounding for environmentalists who demand the open justification of policy decisions in all areas and the extension of public participation in administrative decision-making. To recall a core argument for environmental democracy, to the degree that political (and economic) institutions approximate the principles of free discourse among equals, the reasons for identifying the protection of critical biophysical processes as a generalizable interest become clearer and more convincing, because the social and ecological costs of advanced capitalism become more transparent. However, while the freedom to participate in social decision-making may help foster ecologically responsible attitudes and behaviour, this falls short of the guarantees sought by preservationists. Are there sufficient *universalist* grounds for wilderness preservation?

Here we seem to reach the limits of the Frankfurt school of moral theory. The communicative moral perspective characterizing discourse ethics is opposed to a wilderness ideology based on deep ecology. There are no moral grounds for *intersubjective* validity within the substantive ethical maxims of deep ecology, because valid norms – and consequent duties of interaction – can only be recognized and agreed upon by subjects capable of speech and action. Normative statements, in other words, can only be tested in rationally motivated human deliberation.[12] This is a claim, sensitive to the quality and distinctiveness of human needs, that unravels the most intricate ecocentric philosophies as soon as practical questions enter the frame. To be sure, Habermas concedes that, insofar as certain sentient creatures are drawn into social interactions, humans have a 'quasi-moral responsibility' towards animals based upon a shared potential for harm. But that moral justification is not possible for the preservation of plants and general biodiversity, because duties of interaction are plainly inapplicable. Instead, he suggests, there are good ethical and aesthetic reasons that could be marshalled in favour of natural areas protection – cultural reasons related to historical traditions and psychological health at a time when humans are modifying the environment on a global scale (Habermas, 1993, pp 105–111; Passmore, 1995).

Any ethical justification for wilderness preservation that draws upon cultural preferences must, of course, reckon with the powerful post-colonial critique of the wilderness idea – one that moves from its modern origins, through the national park movement, within the racially framed American exceptionalism of the late 19th century (Cosgrove, 1995), to its imperialistic complicity in the dispossession and genocide of indigenous peoples that accompanied the creation of nature reserves in colonial territories (Callicott, 1994–1995; Guha, 1989). As the Burmese example at the beginning of this book makes clear, the forcible eviction and slaughter of ethnic peoples in the name of natural areas protection has a chilling contemporary relevance, exposing the danger of a preservationist ideology divorced from a democratic self-understanding of human autonomy and self-determination. The contention that their biodiversity mapping and conservation activities somehow remained immune from the human rights atrocities being conducted by the Burmese government – a 'value-free' scientific endeavour detached from the forced relocation and killings – invites the strongest moral indictment against *that* purist preservationist philosophy.

A wilderness ideology impervious to social justice considerations will never achieve the generalizability of interests necessary to justify natural areas protection as critical in tackling the global biodiversity crisis. While a conservation-biology platform provides compelling scientific reasons for increasing the size and number of large protected natural areas, as habitat provision for viable populations of native species and as space for the operation of evolutionary processes (Noss, 1991; Grumbine, 1992, pp 184–228), a rationale for wilderness preservation informed by ecological metaphors alone lacks democratic legitimacy.

There are at least two sources for presenting natural areas preservation as a candidate which meets the principle of generalizability contained in discourse ethics. Firstly, following the interpretation in Chapter 1 of the universalistic message of environmentalism, we can classify wilderness as a collective ecological good where discourse ethical principles regarding the equitable distribution of environmental benefits among present generations can only be secured by paying prior attention to fairness in the collective provision of that good (Eder, 1996, pp 164–165, 183–186). Wilderness is a finite, nonrenewable and nonsubstitutable common property resource imparting public environmental benefits at a variety of geographical scales: from the regulation of essential life-support processes and living resource pools (Dearden, 1989), to the provision of irreplaceable sacred space (Graber, 1976). Fairness in the contribution of everybody to maintaining that common good, for present and future generations, requires a discursive interrogation of its collective values. As mentioned above, this open scrutiny of social and ecological values is facilitated by democratic institutions, aiding the public sphere of debate, with the result that a shared, pancultural (Henberg, 1995) idea of wilderness may emerge with wide-spread assent (a precondition for this is the development of democratic mechanisms of international environmental governance, such that the environmental benefits and costs are shared fairly between countries). Insofar as wilderness becomes a widely accepted metaphor for essential environmental health, the protection and restoration of natural areas is a universal element of ecological sustainability which, though ill-defined, already commands transnational support.

Related to the above, secondly, is the claim that intersubjective discourse presupposes ecological as well as linguistic standards. The biosphere makes possible and maintains a physical environment fit for human moral agents, so that healthy ecological systems represent a general material precondition for any linguistic communication – discursive or otherwise (Dryzek, 1990c). Although logical consistency demands that any moral theory restricts the notions of right and duty to human interactions, these ecological conditions of existence prioritize human responsibility to nature within discourse ethics. Indeed, as already noted in Chapter 1, in his discourse theory of democracy Habermas states that basic rights to ecologically secure living conditions are essential to exercising civil and political rights in modern democratic states (1996, pp 123, 445–446). The recasting of wilderness as protected natural areas in a more flexible manner than its purist North American expression, denoting areas relatively rich in biological diversity – both terrestrial and marine – might well secure its more extensive accept-ance as a critical component of biospheric health, and therefore part of a cosmopolitan human right to a safe environment. Again, the moral impetus is required at a global level to protect environmental quality; and the democratic legitimacy of international environmental decision-making is paramount. Coordinating efforts for natural areas protection must command widespread support within and between societies. This international level of environmental governance will be discussed later in the Conclusion.

5 Trade Unions and Environmental Democracy: A Study of the UK Transport and General Workers' Union

Environmentalists in the UK have not traditionally been sympathetic to the union movement, locating union concerns within a productivist ideology indifferent to the negative ecological consequences arising from economic growth. The British doyen of ecocentric environmentalism, Jonathon Porritt, has claimed that trade unions are unwilling to think in terms other than 'full-time jobs for full-time men' (Porritt and Winner, 1988, p 171). Similarly, Dauncey has suggested that the decline of trade union membership in Britain will continue if unions continue to be preoccupied with wages and working conditions. Instead, he offers them salvation in a green version of human resource management encompassing profit-sharing, productivity bonuses, flexible work patterns and one-union companies (1988, pp 156–157). Unions have also been chided for their failure to follow the fashionable advocacy of market-based environmental policy instruments in areas affecting their members (Gee, 1995, p 31). Against this criticism, David Pepper has rightly pointed to the long-standing struggles for social (and economic) equality conducted by the unions, and offered the historical characterization of organized labour as an environmental protest movement, exerting collective power to secure better living and working conditions (Pepper, 1995, p 63).[1] This continues to be the case.

At the same time as the environmentalist challenge to the union movement, the very structures and practices of organized labour have been charged as inimical to the freedom of individual workers, challenging the traditional socialist self-understanding of unions as champions of economic democracy. The neoliberal critique is well known: that union organization, by imposing codes of collective discipline on union members, prevents or impedes individual workers from realizing their own private interests regarding pay and working conditions. As will shortly be outlined, this outlook informed two decades' worth of anti-union legislation in Britain. And while the Labour government elected in 1997 has proposed a statutory right to trade union membership (provided majority support is forthcoming from at least 40 per cent of a workforce), allied with a commitment to reverse some of the more malicious aspects of Conservative legislation against organized labour (UK government, 1998), its deference to business interests translates into an acceptance of the neoliberal tenet that labour contracts are a matter of voluntary agreement between the employer and the employee. There is no sense of the odds stacked against the former, and no appreciation of the simple power-based rationale for collective action on behalf of the worker.

Coming from a participatory democratic perspective, the criticisms of those political philosophers sympathetic to organized labour means, however, that we cannot merely dismiss the democratic questioning of unions as neoliberal dogmatism. Here the observation that collective bargaining does not represent an unqualified advance for individual employees relates to the problem of balancing private autonomy (individual liberties) with collective self-determination (Habermas, 1996, p 413). How can we be sure, in other words, that the gains of collective bargaining justify the continuance of social roles for individual workers that may leave little room for them to question their very dependence upon the workplace, and the form that this takes? Think, for example, of the relation of wage labour to domestic labour, or the insulation of managerial sovereignty from democratic (worker and community) influence. This is not to claim that unions are not capable of airing such issues, but that they are typically sacrificed to very pressing (and legitimate) industrial relations concerns which, in the interests of collective power, often place a priority on membership passivity and conformity. The apparent contrast here is with a discourse theory of democracy that stipulates that individuals (and groups) have the freedom to interpret and deliberate on their interests in an active fashion. How else can individuals become aware of the ecological consequences of industrial processes and how these affect their interests – in the workplace, the home, the neighbourhood and so on?

The purpose of this chapter is to establish the role of trade unionism in environmental democracy, both in extending ecological regulation in industrial relations and in expanding the public discourse of ecological politics. It will ultimately present an environmental justice agenda for unions that, firstly, demonstrates how they can articulate interests on quality of life and equity that feed into their members' concerns beyond the workplace; secondly, it will demonstrate how the collective power of organized labour is necessary to the meaningful realization of individual autonomy. There are still substantial political and economic constraints facing unions in the UK, indicated by flexible production systems, declining union membership and the neoliberal 'reprivatization' of the labour market. However, in response to new patterns of work and global technological risks, some unions are constructing a distinctive politico-ecological role for organized labour. This has included broadening workplace health and safety concerns, and political campaigning around local and national environmental issues. Particular attention will be paid to the Transport and General Workers' Union (T&G, formerly TGWU) – the second largest union in the country, comprising 882,000 members. As a general union, the T&G's

involvement in environmentally related issues has been wide ranging, addressing issues within and between the trade and industry sectors represented by its members, while it also lays claim to a participatory democratic organizational structure.

ORGANIZED LABOUR AND NEOLIBERALISM: UNIONS IN RETREAT?

Given almost two decades of an unrelenting state onslaught on union rights and activities, the expectation that unions in Britain could play a proactive role in environmental politics seems at best misplaced. The sheer weight of anti-union measures supports the claim that the influence of unions in their traditional areas of concern – industrial relations policy and practice – was significantly reduced after 1979. According to a series of authoritative workplace industrial relations surveys, the number of workplaces, across all sectors, with recognized unions fell from 52 to 40 per cent between 1984 and 1990, primarily as a result of active derecognition and a lower likelihood of newer workplaces recognizing unions. From a peak of 13.3 million in 1979, union membership fell to 7.2 million by 1996, with union density declining to 31 per cent of the workforce – the lowest level for 50 years (Millward, 1994, pp 119–121; Cully and Woodhead, 1997).

Conservative policy targeted the traditional structures of collective bargaining which had enabled unions, in the voluntarist system of British industrial relations, to represent their members' interests concerning wages and working conditions. Unions were promptly excluded from national forums on economic policy and industrial training, and then were subjected to a series of legislative measures designed to deregulate the labour market. These included the weakening of individual employment protection, statutory support for nonunionism – including derecognition, the banning of closed shops and secondary picketing, mandatory strike ballots and other legal interference in internal union affairs. In addition, the historical immunities enjoyed by unions for breach of contract (through withdrawal of labour) were progressively restricted in order to undermine their collective power. For the Conservative administrations, the cumulative effect of this series of acts was intended to reassert the dominance of capital, reducing labour costs in line with the perceived supply-side needs of a competitive economy. The 'reprivatization' of the labour contract (Simitis, 1987, p 127) – through the reimposition of individual employment agreements and the decline of national or sectoral-level bargaining – demonstrated their ideological commitment to free market forces, even if, in practice, this entailed expanding the reach of trade union law and high-profile struggles with public sector unions (Deakin, 1992).

Notwithstanding the stark statistics of decline, predictions of a terminal collapse of unionism proved premature (Purcell, 1993). In the first place, political conflict between unions and the state in Britain was hardly novel; the state's willingness to take on the unions has historically relieved employers of the need to combine their forces (Fulcher, 1991, pp 312–327).[2] The 'new realism' adopted by the Trades Union Congress (the national federation of unions) in the 1980s denoted a conciliatory stance based more on tactical regrouping than unconditional surrender.

Secondly, the enthusiasm for radical industrial relations reform by the Conservatives did not uniformly find favour with employers, who had to cope with the day-to-day realities of the shop floor. As Marsh has argued, the top-down view of policy-making informing Conservative legislation on industrial relations precluded consultation even with employers, so that its effectiveness was compromised by a failure to appreciate that the preferences of the latter were often for stability in negotiations with labour rather than managerial militancy. Others have confirmed the resultant continuity in shop-floor industrial relations in both the public and private sectors – the bargaining strength of labour has traditionally drawn on the largely autonomous workplace characterizing British unionism. The decline in bargaining clout of national union officials was not mirrored, therefore, by a similar fall in the influence of unions at company and plant level (Marsh, 1992, pp 245–249).

Finally, trade union organization has proved resilient in its geographical heartlands, despite extensive job losses accompanying the deindustrialization of heavy manufacturing industry. The changing geographical landscape of unionization militates against nation-wide generalizations; the focus of attention must be on both processes of economic restructuring and local traditions of organized labour. What is clear is that trade union membership is now more widely dispersed; but unions have made little headway in organizing for new growth sectors, and are concentrated in the public, manufacturing and transport sectors (Martin, Sunley and Wills, 1996, pp 40–82).

Extensive merger activity within these sectors in the 1980s allowed unions such as the T&G to limit membership contraction. In fact, other unions copied the decentralized organizational structure of the T&G to offer more autonomy to incoming unions in what has been labelled a 'transport & generalization' movement (Undy et al, 1996, p 54). Moreover, in the case of the T&G, the Conservative objective of removing left-wing union leaderships through the requirement of periodic postal ballots – under the terms of the Trade Union Act 1984 and the Employment Act 1988 – actually backfired. Rather than herald a more moderate leadership, postal ballots have consistently reappointed Broad Left candidates, with an enhanced democratic legitimacy. The Conservative aim of undermining union strength by imposing on them new representative voting structures ignored the fact that British unions have always been governed by a workplace-based democratic self-understanding. As with other major British unions, instead of weakening organizational autonomy, the political assault on union government unintentionally strengthened the national leadership of the

T&G (Undy, Fosh, Morris, Smith and Martin, 1996, pp 260–262). This enhanced its ability, as we shall see, to professionalize its environmental policy commitments, as the union centralized control in areas outside wage bargaining.

The neoliberal *economic* goal of a more efficient labour market, facilitated by a weakened workforce, failed to achieve forecast gains in productivity and investment. Although capital increased its share of national income during this period, the real earnings of employed workers actually rose, running ahead of the small growth in average productivity (Hutton, 1995, pp 95–105). The shift to capital was achieved through the accelerated externalization of social and ecological costs, evident in long-term unemployment, job insecurity, family and community breakdown, widening material inequalities, environmental despoliation, urban air pollution, and a heavy 'ecological footprint' on the rest of the world. Faced with a growing internationalization of product markets, the neoliberal down-market plunge, touting the UK as the 'Hong Kong of Europe' with cheap, compliant labour and minimal social and environmental regulations, conceded full economic sovereignty to capital interests. For all the discussion on the end of 'Fordist' production systems – and there is evidence from collective agreements of a major shift to 'flexible' working practices, as demonstrated by job descriptions, grading structures and other workplace arrangements (Dunne and Wright, 1994) – this strategy in fact reinforced the traditional 'Taylorist' distinction between mental and manual labour. Unions presented an obstacle to this project.

James O'Connor's presentation of the 'second contradiction of capitalism' pinpoints the self-destructive effects of capitalist production in its ever-expanding demands on 'conditions of production' – labour, nonhuman nature, urban infrastructure and space. This is compounded by its internal crisis-tendency to overproduction where the lowering of individual capital costs undermines market demand and, ultimately, profits (O'Connor, 1988; 1991). For O'Connor, the labour movement now faces a double weakness determined, firstly, by a deregulated capital market and international division of labour indifferent to collective labour power in any one location, and, secondly, by the shift in focus by capital and social movements from conflict over production to production conditions (1991, p 9). As Beck has observed, this creates new social cleavages even within the structure of wage labour (1995, pp 146–147):

> *The lines of conflict in wage labour – in so far as the repercussions of industrial hazards and devastation are moved into the centre of the picture – [can] . . . then no longer be attached to the criterion of non-ownership of the means of production, but to whether one's job is in parts of the economic system that profit from risk or in those that are endangered by it.*

If Beck typically overstates the weakening class character of organized labour, it remains true that unions are no longer able to rely upon workplace production-related categories as the sole basis of membership identity. Moreover, the political potential for unions to challenge the capitalist restructuring of production conditions rests on their ability to recruit and solicit support from a far wider constituency. Examples of local and regional union alliances with employers against ecological interests, based on the perceived employment needs of their members, have often fuelled the scepticism of environmental campaigners (Pepper, 1986, p 129). However, as the 20,000 strong March for Social Justice in London in April 1997 demonstrated, alliances between trade unionists, civil rights campaigners and radical environmentalists are possible. Is this where organized labour must look for a new political relevance? It is now time to turn to the environmental policy and activities – within and outside the workplace – of the T&G in order to address this question.

THE T&G AND THE ENVIRONMENT

Policy-making within the T&G is facilitated by the union's decentralized organization. The main point of contact for the membership is the branch. Open to all members, its organization is largely autonomous and branch meetings can discuss whatever the membership considers appropriate (industrial, political, etc). In addition, the branch has the responsibility of nominating candidates to the first level of the union's internal structure – trade groups – who then stand for election across that grouping. The 14 trade groups allow the equitable representation of all industrial sectors within the union (whatever their membership strength). Like all of the T&G's committees, these are wholly based on lay member participation and have a remit similar to the branch. They also have the duty to elect members to both regional committees and national trade group commit- tees.[3] The union is divided into eight administrative regions, and the eight regional committees deal with issues of administration, politics and policy. In addition, there are 14 national trade group committees, whose remit is to address issues directly applicable to their industry domains. Union-wide policy can be determined by a general executive council – a lay member body tying together the policies of the regional committees and national trade committees – but primarily takes place through the biennial delegate conference. This constitutes the major union policy-making forum. It meets every two years to debate motions sent from the branches which, if agreed by a simple majority of the delegates, become T&G policy. Delegates to the conference are nominated from the branch level (open to anyone with at least two years' membership), thus reinforcing the workplace-based demo- cratic structure of the union.

The T&G has been involved in many environmentally related issues reflecting the concerns of members, although they have not necessarily been identified as such. For example, T&G transport policy in the mid 1970s was framed in distributional terms when the 1975 biennial conference called for a cessation of motorway-building until societal benefits could be measured against a public transport policy inclusive of all modes of travel. However, by the 1991 biennial conference the environmental influence was clearly apparent in the following motion passed, albeit without obscuring the social dimension:

> *Market forces and competition have produced more congestion on the roads and more pollution to the detriment of society as a whole. Road pricing is just another market solution that offers no solution to our members.*

The rejection of market-based economic instruments represented the union's consistent stance that transport policy should remain an area of collective provision and collective responsibility. At the 1997 biennial delegate conference this entailed overwhelming support for a motion endorsing national and local proposals for road traffic reduction. Again, the union noted both the negative environmental effects of road traffic growth (atmospheric pollution, increased carbon dioxide emissions and loss of countryside) and social externalities (for example, the restrictions on, and dangers to, children's play). However, this motion had been preceded by an internal T&G conflict over road-building, stoked up by the contentious road construction programme of the Conservative government. On one high-profile project, the Newbury bypass, the pro-environmental Rural, Agricultural and Allied Workers Trade Group, opposing the scheme, clashed openly with the Road Transport Commercial workers. The national leadership weighed in behind the latter trade group in supporting the project on obvious sectional grounds, thereby antagonizing environmentalists and anti-roads activists.

A significant challenge facing the T&G arises from divergences of opinion within its wide membership. There are clear political factions in the union and while the left has held sway over the trade groups and central office in recent decades – through the Communist party–Labour left caucus during Jack Jones's term as general secretary (1968-1979) and since the mid 1980s by the Broad Left grouping – there have been ideological differences. The concentration of moderate opinion in particular regions, coordinated by the Centre faction, has led to significant tensions between head office and these regions. Environmental conflicts of interest have tended to cut across these broad factions; one notable example is the union's position on nuclear power. In 1981 a motion was put to conference that opposed the nuclear programme and called for the use of conventional energy generation supplemented by alternative sources. It cited concerns over worker safety and, wider still, asserted:

It is morally wrong to produce large quantities of nuclear waste which will be a hazardous burden for future generations.

On the recommendation of the general executive council, expressing doubt about the scope for alternative energy supplies to meet the needs served by nuclear energy, the conference rejected this view and the motion was defeated. This sat uncomfortably with the union's strong unilateralist stance on nuclear disarmament – an unprecedented 34 resolutions on nuclear weapons were tabled at the very same conference, as a number of regional committees publicly backed the resurgence in the early 1980s of the Campaign for Nuclear Disarmament (CND). Even though the nuclear power motion noted that 'the continued development of nuclear power hastens the proliferation of nuclear weapons', the union executive was not willing to make the same connection, reluctant to offend fellow workers in the atomic energy industry. Only when the Labour party had come out clearly against nuclear power and, following Chernobyl, public disquiet had reached new heights, did the 1985 biennial conference reflect this mood by accepting motions calling for opposition to nuclear power.

Blanket environmental policies have not historically generated comparable conflict within the union, inviting substantial support across the membership and the organized factions. At the 1973 biennial delegate conference the T&G committed itself to taking an 'active part in combating all forms of environmental pollution and contamination', again in line with public opinion at the time; nevertheless, it took the next wave of environmental concern from the late 1980s, along with greater direction from central office, before the union institutionalized this commitment.

Following biennial conference calls for a high priority to be given to environmental issues, in 1990 the union executive created a Working Group on Environmental Action (ENACT), charged with defining a role for the T&G in proactive environmental protection measures (TGWU, 1991). The group's recommendations, published as a draft policy document and carried unanimously at the 1991 biennial conference, related to internal union organization, networking with groups outside traditional trade union circles, and lobbying for new environmental legislation. The first two areas included establishing a specialist T&G environmental action group, environmental education of members (for example, on 'how to complain' about environmental damage inside and outside the workplace), and an emphasis on building links with supportive environmental groups and local authorities. On the need for new UK environmental legislation, ENACT suggested creating an environmental conversion agency to assist in extending sustainable methods of production, and also in widening the remit of union health and safety representatives to include environmental risk. The significance of these recommendations within the T&G will now be examined, outlining their practical application and appraising their wider political purchase.

WORKPLACE HEALTH AND SAFETY

Attaching environmental concerns to health and safety standards is the most obvious way British unions have located workplace environmental issues within their remit. With this association established by the union's environmental policy, the T&G began a concerted effort in the 1990s to negotiate the application of environmental protection to the conventional responsibilities of union health and safety representatives. Across the 14 trade groups there are approximately 10,000 T&G health and safety representatives, empowered by the 1974 Health and Safety at Work Act to represent employees, receive training and consult with employers in this area. A union survey of 1048 of them in 1996 revealed that 75 per cent would like the legal right to to be involved in environmental issues – as safety, health and environmental representatives.[4]

The regulation of occupational health and safety in Britain, through the legislative provision for appointing workplace representatives (and also establishing safety committees), has long been characterized by a pragmatic, consensual philosophy. New legislation on health and safety is developed by a state Health and Safety Commission whose governing body has an equal number of representatives from the Trades Union Congress and the Confederation of British Industry – a tripartite structure repeated in the sector-based advisory committees and technical working groups. The functional effectiveness of this system, where the workplace committees on health and safety ensure local negotiations over standards, training and enforcement, contrasts with the adversarial wrangling over the US Occupational Safety and Health Act and, until 1994, even insulated it from the deregulatory zeal of Conservative ideologues (Williams, 1995; 1997). As with collective bargaining, though, the political compromise that fashioned the system of health and safety in Britain belies the asymmetrical structure of power in the employment relationship. Trade unions have had to struggle to force employers to accept healthier and safer production methods because employees are assumed to have 'freely contracted' to work-related risks. T&G health and safety representatives still experience this reality daily, evident in the continuing toll of industrial accidents (including fatalities, notably in the construction and agricultural sectors) and work-related illnesses.

It is widely accepted within the T&G that the policy priority given to environmental issues must be supported by union-wide publicity and educational resources. The rationale that unions will increasingly have to represent the interests of members in environmental quality has therefore informed the development of T&G national and regional environmental courses and relevant booklets and briefings.[5] Ron Todd, the previous T&G general secretary, actively supported this educational strategy, providing input into an innovative Trades Union Congress guide on improving environmental conditions within the workplace (Trades Union Congress, 1991). Unlike the legislative support already won for health and safety training, though, both employers and the government have proved resistant to institutionalizing environmental education for union members. Indeed, a government decision in 1993 to withdraw public funding for trade union health and safety training has forced unions to devote more resources to maintaining their levels of training provision in traditional safety areas. Nevertheless, the T&G general executive council agreed in September 1996 to incorporate environmental training within the T&G training of health and safety representatives, and committed itself at the 1997 biennial delegate conference to expanding this environmental education programme. A significant result of this commitment is an innovative handbook on safety, health and environmental issues for union health and safety representatives (T&G, 1998).

The union has also sponsored broad-based seminars on key health, safety and environmental issues affecting its members. An instructive example is the major seminar, organized by the T&G in July 1996, on the burning of chemical waste-based secondary liquid fuel (SLF) by the cement industry, bringing together shop stewards (from every cement plant in the country), employers, government officials and environmentalists (T&G, 1996).

At the seminar, the T&G national secretary for the cement industry, Len McCluskey, identified the health, safety and environmental concerns of their members as both workers in the industry and as members of (mainly) rural communities where most cement kilns are located. The varied toxic sources of SLF have required site-based authorization and regular workplace and environmental monitoring, with repeated claims by environmentalists that lower emission standards have been applied to cement plants compared to conventional waste incineration plants (Hellberg, 1995). The three unions at the seminar – the T&G was joined by representatives from the General, Municipal and Boilermakers' Union and the Amalgamated Engineering and Electrical Union – agreed to push for more stringent health and safety standards regarding the use of SLFs, a joint industry and union medical study of employees, and the development of a joint union code of practice on the safe use of SLFs. However, reassured by the risk assessments undertaken by the Health and Safety Executive and the Environment Agency, the unions decided not to oppose the burning of hazardous waste in cement kilns, despite the vociferous opposition of environmentalists. There was strong shop steward support for this position; indeed, environmental groups campaigning against SLF burning had antagonized local union representatives at several cement plants by both refusing to meet them and including the workers in their high-profile blanket condemnations of the industry. Not for the first time in Britain, environmentalists had missed an opportunity for early dialogue with affected unionists, failing to recognize their health and safety concerns – and first-hand knowledge – as relevant.

This example seems to indicate an inconsistency between the T&G's public support of the environmental movement generally and the stance of the workplace representatives, who expressed satisfaction with the cement companies in supplying all information requested on health, safety and environmental matters: a classic case of local class alliances of capital and labour against ecological interests (Harvey, 1985)? What it, in fact, demonstrates is how the 'consensual' approach to health and safety regulation effectively militates against the inclusion of wider environmental concerns.

The risk assessments required for SLFs under the Control of Substances Hazardous to Health Regulations (1988) are undertaken by the cement companies themselves, although scrutinized by the Health and Safety Executive, with stipulations for exposure monitoring, health surveillance and employee training. Trade union involvement is secured by the Health and Safety at Work Act, but there is no general legislative obligation to consult more widely than with the employees. Similarly, the separate authorization to burn industrial waste needed from the Environment Agency (inheriting in 1996 the regulatory functions of Her Majesty's Inspectorate of Pollution, HMIP) is subject to the use of the best available technology not entailing excessive costs (BATNEEC). The difficulties in placing monetary values on many environmental benefits and costs in this case has left much discretionary scope for local agreements between industry and government. The risk assessment methodology employed by the Environment Agency (best practicable environmental option) for SLF burning has lacked both openness and consistency (House of Commons Environment Committee, 1997, pp xlv–xlvii). Furthermore, cement companies have been able to suppress data on emission concentrations by citing 'commercial confidentiality'. In a situation where information concealment has been the norm for third parties, environmentalists have faced an onerous burden of proof to denote a significant risk to health from the burning of SLFs – hence their reliance on the mass media, national campaigns and legal challenges.[6]

Clearly, the unions in this case, notwithstanding the unwillingness of environmentalists to meet with local shop stewards, failed to appreciate the obstacles to environmental groups in ascertaining the facts about the burning of hazardous wastes. It was not enough for the T&G to claim to represent the interests of 'the population in general and...the environment' (T&G, 1996, p 47). But the union deserves credit for its commitment to democratize debate about SLFs outside the workplace. It was the T&G that exposed most starkly the scale of regulatory capture in this area by forcing the government, following complaints by the union's national health and safety coordinator to the parliamentary ombudsman, to reveal in 1995 the membership of department of the environment working parties on environmental standards in industry. The committee responsible for determining pollution limits for the cement industry included representatives from three cement industry associations and four major cement companies.[7] As confirmed by the House of Commons Environment Committee, the Environment Agency had been lax and secretive in controlling emissions from cement kilns, leading to its 'failure to regulate the cement industry properly' (1997, p xlviii). In its response, the newly elected Labour government promised to promote more openness and public involvement in SLF authorization procedures, but shied away from any regulatory reform of industrial pollution control processes (UK government, 1997).

Access to information about the ecological effects of production processes has become a priority for the T&G's coordination across its trade groups. The right to know about products and processes necessarily entails 'whistle-blower' protection. Within the UK, disclosure of concerns about health and safety issues rates amongst the safest legal exemptions from the contractual duties of confidentiality placed on employees, buttressed by their rights under the Health and Safety at Work Act, the Safety Representatives and Safety Committee Regulations (1977), and a clear public interest in promoting safe working practices. Yet, the historical absence of general statutory protection for whistleblowing entailed no *automatic* protection from dismissal, or action short of dismissal, for workers disclosing information about unsafe working conditions (Vickers, 1995, p 23). This protection also strictly limited health and safety issues to the workplace, preventing any extension to the health effects of production processes beyond the plant. A Labour government commitment to a new legal right of workers to disclose employment-related information in the public interest, including concerns about health, safety and environmental dangers, saw the passing of the Public Interest Disclosure Act in 1998, broadly supported by the unions. Whether this will enable unions to enhance their growing role as environmental watchdogs remains to be seen.

Equipped with legal rights over health and safety, unions in Britain have understandably not wanted to cede any control in this area to organizations outside the workplace – hence the real potential for antagonism with environmental groups when they perceive this authority to clash with their interests.[8] To be sure, union defensiveness is warranted since British management has recently been reasserting its prerogative to deal with health and safety issues unilaterally, while the Health and Safety Inspectorate remains understaffed and excessively deferential to employers (Millward, Stevens, Smart and Hawes, 1992, p 162). Health and safety norms and practices constitute a hard-fought arena between capital and labour, with material consequences for the social organization of production. The continuation of bipartite bargaining ensures stability, but prevents more fundamental questioning over the *production* of risks. As Beck has observed, the result is a technocratic monopoly on hazard definition and management, prompting environmentalists to argue that unions should not be entrusted with representing the more general interests of those affected by high-risk technologies. Significantly, Beck rejects the argument that unions are functionally incapable of such an appreciation, but issues them the political challenge to support the 'demonopolization' of environmental risk management through a more democratic determination of risk attributes and liabilities (1995, pp 173–180). This would entail public disclosure of relevant information and the regulatory invocation of a precautionary principle to reverse the burden of proof regarding environmental damage. According to this stance, unions would have to be prepared to place themselves at the vanguard of ecological and technical criticism of the company.

While the T&G has taken the first steps towards extending health and safety definitions to include environmental concerns, this falls short of the participation in product policy envisaged by Beck as a prerequisite for greening the trade union movement. Two tendencies that seem to point in this direction originate from the European Commission: the ecomanagement and audit scheme (EMAS) and employment-related health and safety directives. Both, though, afford little room for optimism.

T&G support of EMAS reflects the growing involvement of British unions in ecoauditing. EMAS, a voluntary environmental management system introduced across the European Union in 1995, provides an organizational framework for companies to commit themselves to improving environmental performance – albeit one that fails to prescribe any external performance standards beyond legislative compliance. However, the regulation introducing EMAS stipulates that employee consultation and training is required of companies participating in the scheme. The T&G has a representative on the UK advisory group for implementing EMAS and points to five of the nine companies awarded EMAS accreditation in the scheme's first year as T&G organized – this input included a significant involvement of T&G health and safety representatives.[9]

To its proponents, EMAS ascends the virtuous spiral of ecological modernization (see Chapter 2), where increasing efficiency – through cost savings on materials and energy use – promises enhanced competitiveness and new jobs. The positive-sum rhetoric has yet to attract many corporate takers in the UK, though, where the most important reason for implementing the scheme, given by the initial round of companies accredited in 1996, was its positive spin for public relations (Strachen, Haque, McCulloch and Moxen, 1997). Furthermore, companies opting to develop their own environmental strategies independent of EMAS have often proved hostile to union participation.[10] T&G concern with the effectiveness of EMAS led in 1996 to the union's general executive council call for the scheme to become mandatory. More seriously for unions generally, attempts to harmonize EMAS with the new international standard for environmental management systems, ISO 14001, threaten to weaken the nominal commitment to worker participation (and openness with environmental information) in the former. The International Standards Organization (ISO) developed ISO 14001 in closed negotiations with industry, rejecting trade union participation – a position publicly condemned at the 16th World Congress of the International Confederation of Free Trade Unions (ICFTU) in June 1996 (Gereluk and Royer, 1997, p 138; Krut and Gleckman, 1997). The price for union support of EMAS, despite its corporatist sheen, may well be to reduce the long-term regulatory scope of public authorities to protect labour from new health, safety and environmental risks. Self-regulation is ultimately incompatible with the democratic determination of product policy and environmental standards.

More firmly within the European Community's institutional structure has been enactment of employment-related health and safety directives, such as those involving pregnant workers, young people and working time. All have been issued under article 118a of the Single European Act (1986), which allows directives for the purpose of 'encouraging improvements, especially in the working environment, as regards the health and safety of workers'. The Working Time Directive, issued in 1993, warrants commentary due to its unsuccessful challenge to its validity by the UK government, forcing the European Court of Justice to define the reach of article 118a.

Less important here than the directive's substantive provisions on workers' rights to minimal breaks, rest periods and leave is the court's rejection of the narrow interpretation of the 'working environment' – referring strictly to workplace conditions and risks – offered by the UK government. Instead, in line with the World Health Organization's (WHO's) holistic definition of health, the court emphasized a broad integration of health and safety covering all conditions of work – an area of social policy, moreover, where member states cannot invoke the principle of subsidiarity to avoid their obligations (Fitzpatrick, 1997). Some industrial relations authorities have concluded that the new legal regime for the working time directive offers unions the opportunity to assert broader, environment-related definitions of health and safety, through enforcement efforts on behalf of their members and derogations from the directive by way of enhanced collective bargaining (Fitzpatrick, 1997, p 131; Ewing, 1996, pp 241–242, 324) – a view shared by the T&G and British unions generally. It seems more likely, given the numerous other derogations stated in the directive that work against the interests of labour (for example, the provision that allows workers to 'contract out' of health and safety protection), that the European Commission is not serious about the rights of workers. Article 118a, after all, is one of the very few provisions of the Single European Act not explicitly geared towards market integration, while the convergence criteria for European monetary union rule out the public expenditure necessary to raise health, safety and environmental standards.

As will be argued shortly in relation to European works councils, EU efforts to standardize regulation of the labour market may well leave unions out in the cold. European Community law on workforce consultation favours universal mechanisms of representation in order to include non-union workers. To conform to this position in Britain, the Health and Safety (Consultation with Employees) Regulations 1996 require employers to consult employees not covered by union-appointed health and safety representatives. But true to the neoliberal form of an outgoing Conservative administration, these regulations remain devoid of any adequate enforcement, employer support and wider employee representation links. It has been suggested that unions could benefit from this implementation deficit by creating 'roving safety representatives' and extending their recognition (James and Walters, 1997). Indeed, the T&G has successfully experimented with roving safety representatives within the Rural, Agriculture and Allied

Workers Trade Sector and has suggested creating roving union-appointed environmental representatives able to ascertain *ecological* problems across a range of workplaces. The latter would represent an important instrument for widening environmental democracy in industrial relations, and could be facilitated by an extension of health and safety legislation.

In a hostile domestic political context, union support of environmental management systems and the health and safety statements of the EU made clear tactical sense. With a Labour administration committed to a statutory recognition of organized labour, and after signing up to the European Social Chapter and the Working Time Directive, British unions are, arguably, now in a position to lead the type of proactive environmental challenge to product policy envisaged by Beck. T&G efforts to redefine health and safety in an ecological fashion point to an alternative form of environmental problem definition – one that draws directly upon the first-hand understandings of workers, questioning the epistemic monopoly of expert systems associated with capital, the state and institutional science. Democratic deliberation over the environmental risks of production processes must also, however, include the participation of lay publics (Wynne, 1996). And it is here that unions need to demonstrate a principled commitment to more transparent and inclusive negotiations over environmental regulation. In this they would find natural allies in existing environmental groups.

EXPANDING THE PUBLIC SPHERE OF ECOLOGICAL POLITICS

T&G efforts to include environmental issues within the prevailing structure of health and safety have, as shown above, prioritized wider discussion on key concerns, inviting the participation of ecological groups even though the union has resisted the opening up of bargaining over workplace-based environmental protection. The fact that union influence in this area is enhanced when organized labour combines existing health and safety activism with parallel public debates or campaigns is confirmed by recent research on German industrial relations (Hildebrandt, 1995). British unions, of course, can draw on a tradition of broader political campaigning and struggle, historically through their close links with the Labour party and with their interventions in the public sphere of ecological politics, where environmental problems are thematized. Such activity may have little bearing on the workplace, serving instead to meet the general ideological goals of the unions involved. Conservative legislation in 1984 which was designed to undermine such social unionism, by requiring confirmatory ballots on political funds, failed to appreciate the grassroots support for political campaigning within unions. A Trade Union Coordinating Committee, comprising 37 unions – including the T&G – successfully lobbied the members of all its constituent unions to vote to retain political funding, and actually encouraged the creation of new political funds in the wider union movement (Barrows, 1997, pp 129–140).

The T&G has consistently maintained its traditional funding support for the Labour party. At the same time, however, the union has rarely shied away from supporting political courses often at odds with the parliamentary Labour party or other major unions. It was the leftward shift in the T&G, presided over by Frank Cousins, that informed the union's consistent support of unilateralism since the late 1950s. While Labour party policy on nuclear disarmament wavered, the T&G maintained a strong backing of the Campaign for Nuclear Disarmament. This proved particularly significant to the second wave of unilateralism in Britain 20 years later, when T&G opposition to nuclear weapons found deep public resonance after the decision to locate cruise missiles in Britain. In the early 1980s, the union successfully carried unilateralist motions at Trades Union Congress (TUC) conferences, with the T&G general executive council actively backing the mass campaign against cruise. Moreover, holding the largest block vote at the annual Labour party conference, the union threw its weight behind the unilateralist resolutions that finally secured an electoral commitment by Labour to unilateral nuclear disarmament (Pimlott, 1982). To the current parliamentary party leadership, it was this sort of intimate union involvement in Labour policy that consigned the Labour party to the political wilderness for so long; but the principled T&G opposition to nuclear weapons contrasts markedly with Labour's vascillations on this issue.

Away from its links with the Labour party, the T&G has contributed positively to the vitality of noninstitutional environmental politics. Historically, this would include its high-profile campaigns in the 1980s against the use of pesticide 2,4,5-T (alongside the Association of Scientific, Technical and Managerial Staff and the Fire Brigades Union), and the joint campaign with the National Union of Seamen and the train drivers' union ASLEF to ban the dumping of nuclear waste at sea, both of which were successful (Cook and Kaufman, 1982; Slater, 1986). The latter campaign triggered a worldwide union boycott on ocean dumping led by the International Transport Workers' Federation. More recently, there has been a boycott of Shell on grounds of derecognition of T&G workers, linked with the Ogoniland campaigns organized in Britain by The Body Shop and Greenpeace. Finally, the Rural, Agriculture and Allied Workers Trade Group (25,000 members) has been actively liaising with a number of environmental organizations campaigning for environmentally safe agricultural production systems. As a member of the Sustainable Agriculture, Food and Environment Alliance, it has supported a blanket ban on agricultural biotechnology.

While supportive of the environmental movement in Britain, recognizing the distinctive campaigning strengths of existing pressure groups, the T&G has avoided more systematic linkages. This, as the union claims, may reduce duplication of effort, but the cost of the issue-based alliances with environmental activists remains a huge untapped potential for wider networking. Some prominent environmentalists have identified the potential for cross-fertilization, suggesting T&G sponsored positions at environmental groups and the use of well-established T&G communication links for campaign publicity.[11] In some instances, the union's caution is justified; for example, the T&G has faced continued opposition from Greenpeace UK in attempting to organize its workers. In 1995 the union recruited 60 members, representing 90 per cent of the paid staff at Greenpeace UK. However, despite being led by a Labour peer, the environmental group has still refused to recognize the union, implying that this is not possible until the T&G's environmental position reflects more faithfully the objectives of Greenpeace – an objection violating the basic human right of free association in the workplace (a failure to recognize unions shared in Britain with The Body Shop). This obstruction is sadly symptomatic of the widespread myopia afflicting British environmental groups with regard to industrial relations. Nevertheless, the current general secretary of the T&G believes that the union should be prepared to work with green groups on issues of common interest and pass over, for the moment, areas of conflict.[12]

The differences with environmental organizations also extend to internal decision-making procedures. Many greens would argue that union policy processes – such as the policy-making structure of the T&G – are slow and, at times, cumbersome (Porritt and Winner, 1988, p 41). For the T&G, these procedures represent an organizational prerequisite for according an equal voice to its wide diversity of members – a democratic bottom-up approach that is at the heart of the union's ethos. This contrasts with the hierarchical structures typically underpinning British environmental groups, who trade in democratic accountability for strategic responsiveness (Lowe and Goyder, 1983, pp 50–56) – an option inappropriate for the internal ways of reaching understanding within large unions. Of course, embroiled in bargaining processes with capital, under strongly asymmetrical relations of power, the *external* behaviour of unions is governed by a strategic rationality; but even here collective bargaining has democratic legitimacy on the basis of the self-organization of the union. If there is to be meaningful cooperation between environmental groups and unions, one critical task for the former is to develop a mature appreciation of the distinctive contours of industrial democracy.

At the international level, trade unions are, of course, one of the 'major groups' included in Agenda 21, the programme for sustainable development agreed upon at the UN Conference on Environment and Development in 1992. Chapter 29 of Agenda 21 is devoted to strengthening the role of workers and their unions in the pursuit of sustainable development (United Nations, 1993, p 235):

> ... *trade unions are vital actors in facilitating the achievement of sustainable development in view of their experience in addressing industrial change, the extremely high priority they give to the protection of the working environment and the related natural environment, and their promotion of socially responsible and economic development.*

The Commission on Sustainable Development (CSD), the UN body responsible for monitoring and promoting the implementation of the agreements reached at Rio, has institutionalized procedural openings for nine stakeholder groups. For example, at the fourth annual session of the CSD in 1996, a 'Day of the Workplace' allowed the International Confederation of Free Trade Unions (ICFTU) to publicize examples of union–management agreements in support of Agenda 21 – from ecoauditing (Finland) and ecolabelling (Sweden) to training partnerships (North America) and environmental collective agreements (the Philippines). In their links with nongovernmental organizations and state actors, both the ICFTU and the International Labour Organization have reminded the international environmental community that ecologically benign development is irrelevant without a strong element of social justice; and in embodying this approach, trade union action thereby represents a 'paradigm for sustainable development' (Gereluk and Royer, 1997, pp 134–136).

This is a worldview that had no purchase on the Conservative government in the UK, whose national sustainable development strategy, published in response to Agenda 21, omitted any mention of organized labour despite the CSD request that countries include information on worker participation in sustainable development reports. In its bland blend of market environmentalism and voluntarism, the UK strategy remained oblivious to notions of social justice and participatory democracy (UK government, 1994). Outside government, the national coordinating body, the UK Round Table for Sustainable Development – which includes, as its single union representative, the deputy general of the TUC – offered no corrective to this sustainability perspective and had no discernible influence on Conservative government policy. From a union perspective, then, the formation in July 1998 of a separate Trade Union and Sustainable Development Advisory Committee (which includes the T&G general secretary as one of 14 TUC representatives) signalled a welcome Labour commitment to incorporate trade unions more meaningfully within a national sustainable development strategy.

On the sustainable development front, more activity has taken place at the local level in Britain under Agenda 21 (see Chapter 6). In the case of Local Agenda 21, the UK Local Government Management Board (LGMB) has supported and coordinated the diverse range of local consultation processes underway; and while none of the recognized LGMB guides highlight a role for organized labour, the LGMB has invited trade union input from the TUC. For whatever reason, the unenthusiastic response from the TUC was a missed opportunity for the union movement to shape national guidance of local sustainability plans at this key coordinating level. Local Agenda 21 offers unions an audience base in the wider community, beyond the labour and green movements, that is receptive to arguments about quality of life. Trade unions need both to demonstrate their achievements in this area and to become involved at the Local Agenda 21 grassroots level. If a contribution from the labour movement is to be of value in influencing local sustainability plans, it must, of course, be informed. The T&G emphasis on environmental education and training provides a positive example here. In 1995 the T&G region 1 education department released a guide on Local Agenda 21 for active members, while T&G health and safety training courses often include briefings on Agenda 21 (Morter, 1995).

UNIONS AND ENVIRONMENTAL JUSTICE

The notion of unions as environmental actors raises the question of a formal coalition between trade unionists, environmental activists and social justice campaigners – a prospect raised at the Green Left conference in London in November 1996 and tentatively developed by such groupings as the Green Socialist Network, the Red-Green Network and the Socialist Movement. However, the possible role of the labour movement in forging such a coalition has tended to invite scepticism even from socialist writers, who point to the fragmented nature of unions and industrial relations in Britain (Kelly, 1988, pp 303–304).

Similarly, in North America, despite examples of 'worker environmentalism' within the grassroots environmental justice movement – such as the Workers Against Toxic Chemicals (WATCH) campaign formed by General Motors' employees in Lordstown, Ohio, and the Carolina Alliance for Fair Employment (Dowie, 1995, pp 157–160; Gardner and Greer, 1996) – the convergence of interest between organized labour and community campaigns against toxic waste has not been substantial or systematic enough to ignite the broader movement for social justice anticipated by some observers. One reason for this, resulting from a preoccupation with the policies and programmes of regulatory agencies, remains the reluctance of environmental justice activists to engage with the production decisions of capital in generating environmental risks (Field, 1997; Lake, 1996). Nevertheless, the multiracial, working class composition of the environmental justice movement, and its nonnegotiable forms of collective protest, suggest a real potential for radical alliances with an organized labour movement prepared to challenge production decisions on social and environmental grounds. Without assuming any simple transfer of political choices, several strategic options for unions in Britain are suggested by such a coalition of interests.

Unions as Supporters of Environmental Rights

In Britain links are being made between issues of environmental ill-health, poverty and social injustice, and democratic reform. In April 1996 the launch of Real World, a coalition of 32 nongovernmental organizations, represented the most public initiative so far to publicize an environmental justice agenda (Jacobs, 1996a). What Real World has prioritized is the modernization of the British political system through a written constitution, a codified bill of rights, the reform of parliament and a participatory notion of citizenship – all needed to reverse the erosion in recent years of civil freedoms. This democratic renewal is correctly identified as a necessary precondition to achieving environmental sustainability and social justice. And yet this 'politicization' (Jacobs, 1996b) of the UK nongovernmental sector, for all its strong ethical concern, stops far short of a radical environmental justice agenda. The Real World manifesto contains no discussion of labour rights – an omission all the more worrying given that workers in the UK still have no positive rights to associate or take part in industrial action (notwithstanding Labour's promise to give union membership a statutory basis). Furthermore, this failure to include workers as legitimate bearers of social and environmental rights betrays a liberal political economy. Without recognizing the potential role of unions to promote changes in political consciousness and behaviour by helping to challenge capital, it misses a central source of collective action in addressing social injustices and ecological degradation.

Workers, as individuals, are bearers of environmental and social rights, while unions represent and further the *collective* force of workplace-related rights. There is also no compelling reason why unions, as coherent and democratically governed organizations, could not be holders of collective environmental and social rights. As noted in Chapter 1, the increasing attention paid to the connections between human rights and environmental rights has gained international currency through the final report of the UN Subcommission on Human Rights and the Environment, which asserts 'the right to a secure, healthy and ecologically sound environment' (cited in Boyle, 1996, p 66). Of particular relevance here is its inclusion of the right to a safe and healthy working environment (principle 2.9), which complements the campaign of the International Labour Organization to press countries for ratification of 'core' labour standards as basic human rights. In addition, trade unions across the world have participated in developing an independent international convention, the Charter of Rights Against Industrial Hazards, Part III of which includes specific workers' rights to a working environment free from hazards.

In Britain, the incorporation of the European Convention of Human Rights (ECHR) into UK law promises, for the first time, to attribute positive civil rights to individuals. However, there are no express environmental rights in the ECHR, despite efforts to 'green' some of its existing provisions. It may be that the most effective formal means of promoting environmental justice interests in this case, as in human rights law more widely, is through an emphasis on procedural rights, such as the right to information, the right to participate in decision-making, and the right of administrative and legal redress (Desgagné, 1995; Douglas-Scott, 1996). But in the case of the ECHR these are procedures designed to protect *individual* rights (including individual employment rights), as opposed to collective rights. It also may be that, in Britain, the anticipated recasting of the legal aid system, in terms of a community legal service, could broaden access to environmental and social justice activists (Dunkley, 1997). With legal protection of employee rights secure, unions might be encouraged to test their standing in environmental law regarding concerns that collectively affect their members – that is, unions as bearers and champions of environmental rights. Again, though, a radical environmental justice project would go further, facing up to social and economic inequality through 'democratic participation in the capital investment decisions through which environmental burdens are produced and by which communities are affected' (Lake, 1996, p 171). In such a scenario, in order to thrive, unions could not avoid engaging with – and representing – the social, economic and environmental needs of their members.

Unions as Sources of Cosmopolitan Collective Identities

The notion of a cosmopolitan democracy (Held, 1995), mentioned in Chapter 1, identifies the need for a more cosmopolitan civil society as a base of egalitarian democracy, although its main theorist has said little on the cultural (re)sources available for constructing critical collective identities. Environmental democracy, by incorporating the interests of a wide range of active and informed citizens in discursive debate and decision-making, is, in principle, receptive to those affected negatively by environmental and social costs. It registers, for example, the disproportionate impact on ethnic minority and working class communities of these externalities – something mapped out starkly by environmental justice activists in the US (Szasz and Meuser, 1997). For unions to find relevance here means striking a resonance with the everyday experiences of those members inside and outside the workplace subject to incursions on their quality of life on the basis of gender, race, disability and age, while also celebrating the social and cultural diversity of that membership.

Of course, the associative action of organized labour in Britain has always had to accommodate a heterogeneity of worker interests, which have been reconciled democratically to support the collective bargaining and political campaigning of unions. What British unions, including the T&G, have recognized is the further potential for union growth with groups traditionally underrepresented in organized labour. For example, the increased unionization of women is one reason why British unions initially broadened their perspective on working conditions (Hunt, 1984); and the T&G has targeted recruitment campaigns and community outreach activities at women, beginning to redress the gender imbalance in its membership (most successfully in the Administrative, Clerical, Technical and Supervisory Trade Group, where 44 per cent of members were women in 1997, compared with 21 per cent across all trade groups). The T&G, and the Trades Union Congress generally, are also working to redress the continuing underrepresentation of ethnic minority members in the British union movement, especially at executive body level. It is the argument here that environmental justice issues offer a renewed source of interest for unions in attracting a diverse membership, encompassing both workplace-related environmental concerns and wider quality of life anxieties. And that source of interest *generalization*, as the general secretary of the T&G has observed, inevitably includes a class perspective: 'it's a reflection from where we are'.[13] A progressive cosmopolitanism necessarily includes a critical attitude towards the social and ecological injustices generated by private production and capital.

Unions as Loci of Extralocal Mobilization

What chance of advancing labour and environmental rights in an era of global economic liberalization, when transnational capital has seemingly eroded even the power of nation states to maintain social and ecological standards? While efforts by advanced capitalist countries to create a globally binding multilateral agreement on investment may not yet have succeeded, the deregulation of international capital flows has continued apace, restricting the scope for countries freely to determine economic policy priorities. Moreover, the International Confederation of Free Trade Unions (ICFTU) has long found accommodation with trade liberalization, concentrating on lobbying for the inclusion of labour clauses in World Trade Organization rules (ICFTU, 1996).

At the European level, British unions have similarly embraced the establishment of European works councils (EWCs), under a 1994 European Union directive, which involve new structures of worker representation in multinational companies operating across member states. For the T&G, which came to one of the first EWC agreements with Coates Viyella, the works councils offer formal channels for transnational consultation over union concerns, including workplace safety, health and environmental conditions (T&G, 1997a). One British authority on European labour law has argued that unions can strengthen their transnational influence through EWCs, noting that EU national governments are legally obliged 'to intervene in the internal management structures of multinationals to secure compliance [with the directive]' (Bercusson, 1997, p 43). As an instrument for securing worker representation and the mobilization of work-related environmental concerns across Europe, EWCs are, however, still chronically weak. Not only can management simply opt-out from the directive itself, but even those companies which create works councils are not required to consult independent trade unions. Indeed, many multinationals have used EWCs as a method of union exclusion. Finally, such is the balance of bargaining power weighted in the hands of management, that those trade unions drawn into the process may well face enforced passivity, rendering them inadequate protectors of worker interests (Wedderburn, 1997).

The effective pursuit of an environmental justice agenda by unions at a transnational level calls for an extralocal mobilization that refuses to accede to the demands of capital. And the only proven negotiating currency for organized labour over working conditions is the prospect of industrial action. Pan-European cooperation over the withdrawal of labour, as first undertaken in 1995 against the telecommunications company Alcatel, offers such a model, although international labour solidarity can, of course, draw upon a century of experience. At this level, the ICFTU rightly supports the recognition by national systems of labour law of the right to organize and participate in transnational, collective industrial action. Yet this does not remove the need for a broad-based sustained resistance to the accelerated commodification of labour and nature. In order to track the scale and allocation of capital accumulation, activist coalitions are required at different levels of geopolitical aggregation in order to exert democratic controls on private investment decisions (Gould, Schnaiberg and Weinberg, 1996, pp 181–186, 196–203). The organizational infrastructure developed by the US environmental justice movement demonstrated how national and regional groupings could empower – and radicalize – local efforts, but this formal support structure has been disabled by internal divisions and financial exigencies (Gardner and Greer, 1996, p 176).

Unions possess the experience of extralocal activism, along with the organizational continuity, to serve, in a nonexclusive way, as vehicles of political mobilization for environmental justice. By combining their knowledge of extralocal management intentions with member expertise on particular production processes and their environmental impacts, they could serve as key loci within broader federations of social and environmental justice groups. This is not an automatic step for unions; it remains a political choice – one which calls for a greater effort on their part to reach out both to those workers who are poorly represented in trade union structures and to the great number in the developing world not represented by unions who suffer some of the worst excesses of labour exploitation (Moody, 1997; Williams, 1998).

Unions as Instruments of Economic Democracy

Whatever their position on environmental justice, unions know that, in an era of flexible labour markets, their long-term representative capacity will depend upon their appeal to those workers subject to short-term contracts and peripheral employment status. And this entails giving 'a higher priority to social wage issues, including environmental protection and shared entitlement to social benefits, by those in regular and non-regular forms of employment' (Standing, 1997, p 31). To bargain effectively with capital on more than money wages and workplace conditions, therefore, necessitates close links with those community groups, nongovernmental organizations and local state agencies committed to redistributive justice. Standing's notion of *community unions* (1997, p 31) captures this social embeddedness well. In Britain, the last two decades have witnessed a remarkable growth in social economy enterprises providing for local needs – food cooperatives, organic food-box schemes, community land banks, local energy production, credit unions, and so on (Douthwaite, 1996). Often located in deprived urban areas, these structures of local provision are sometimes completely detached from the money economy – for example, the barter-based local exchange trading schemes (LETS) (Pepper, 1996, pp 309–316). While having at best a marginal relationship with the dominant system of wage labour, and largely ignored by unions, they illustrate direct forms of participation in economic decision-making, helping to recast ideas about industrial democracy.

The T&G is not unfamiliar with suggestions for the democratic reform of corporate governance. General Secretary Jack Jones played a major role in shaping the final recommendations of the Labour Committee of Inquiry into Industrial Democracy in 1977 (the Bullock Report), which proposed the election, by trade unionists, of worker directors onto the boards of companies having 2000 or more employees. Worker directors would have representational parity with company directors elected by shareholders, while a smaller, third group of independent directors would represent consumer and community interests. The anticipated employer opposition to these proposals proved forthcoming; but it was the deep divisions in the union movement that allowed a loss of nerve by the Labour government, consigning the report to ineffectuality.[14] This cemented the hold of a British field of 'industrial relations' divorced from production interests. Management thus continued with its unbridled economic sovereignty, resisting any encroachments on its strategic decision-making authority, even when these did not challenge underlying ownership structures or the profit motive. The T&G discovered this with its interventions in the aerospace and defence industries over arms conversion proposals, most notably the Lucas Aerospace alternative production plan, in 1976 and 1983, drafted in association with workplace shop stewards (Wainwright and Elliot, 1982; TGWU, 1987). Yet, while the suggestions – for the production of socially and environmentally useful technologies – were flatly rejected by management, they have inspired further workplace experiments in alternative production, such as the Bhopal alternative plan (Pepper, 1986, p 135) and the Green Work Alliance in Ontario, Canada (Keil, 1995).

Prospects for ecoconversion initiatives in Britain may seem bleak in manufacturing industry, where the new imperatives of staff efficiency have pulled even left-inclined unions such as the T&G into human resource management deals (for example, the T&G's 'new deal' with Rover), which further consolidate employer powers. In this situation, the extension of an environmental remit to health and safety representatives appears a substantial objective.[15] In the growth of social economy enterprises, however, is prefigured a different landscape of economic governance, populated by a plurality of self-organized economic associations. For those unions interested in redefining work in democratic terms, sponsorship of – and involvement in – these forms of socially and environmentally useful production is an important first step.

CONCLUSION

The T&G's claim to be 'the UK's greenest union' (T&G, 1997b, p 5) rests on its recent development of an environmental strategy prioritized, at the policy level, by the union's general executive council. This includes, as has been noted, the incorporation of environmental education within the T&G training of health and safety representatives, lobbying to extend an environmental remit to these representatives, and support for the European Union ecomanagement and audit scheme (EMAS) to become part of the collective bargaining agenda in all workplaces. Membership backing for these measures is beyond doubt and branches are constantly pressing the union executive on its environmental policy commitments. While the national leadership has not delivered on all fronts – for example, the permanent environmental action group recommended at central office level by ENACT has not been established – the union's environmental drive is singularly noteworthy within British unionism. But has any fundamental interrogation of union interests taken place?

The T&G has framed its workplace environmental commitment in the positive-sum language of ecological modernization, where the use of clean production and ecoefficient technologies promises new green jobs; and this technocratic preoccupation with productivity and competitiveness is entirely compatible, of course, with traditional imperatives of capital accumulation (Christoff, 1996, p 485). In this it is not alone. Other major British trade unions, notably Unison and the GMB, have been collaborating with environmental groups on proposals for green taxes. However, when ecological constraints not amenable to technological fixing impinge upon profitability, unions will need to be in a position to negotiate more far-reaching issues around alternative production or they will face deteriorating pay and conditions for their members. Here, though, unions will require the support of a legal and institutional framework conducive to the democratic negotiation of production choices. The political will for democratization of corporate decision-making is still absent from mainstream party agendas in Western democracies, but it is certainly being aired by environmental justice groups across the world. This deliberation on the social and ecological taming of private investment decisions awaits a meaningful union input.

At the same time, as the cement industry example highlighted – in the case over toxic emission standards and noninclusive procedures for ascertaining environmental risk – conflicts of interest between unions and environmentalists may be accentuated by the regulatory failure of state institutions. Where the T&G deserves credit in this respect is its commitment to democratizing environmental policy. The union has been at the forefront of campaigns on access to environmental information, equitable representation in policy-making, and making transparent the distributional consequences of policy outcomes. It is partly the secrecy of governmental decision-making on the environment that has made it difficult to identify shared social and ecological interests between unions and environmental groups. Pushing environmental policy-making in a more deliberative, democratic direction is thus necessary to support the role of unions as environmental actors.

What of the vaunted democratic nature of the union itself? Within the T&G in recent years, there have been complaints that the national leadership has neglected the particular interests of rank and file members, and that the lay member general executive council has not been effective in representing regional and trade group concerns. Nevertheless, these objections have not called into question the decentralized structure of the union itself, and are perhaps related most clearly to competing political factions within the T&G. On environmental issues, the Rural, Agriculture and Allied Workers Trade Group has demonstrated that both the autonomy accorded to trade groups in terms of policy development and the ability of the union itself to respond to these innovations are proven. Indeed, the lay member model of union self-organization long associated with the T&G has provided a discursive democratic template which the more top-down unions in the UK have, under increasing pressure to adapt to the changing preferences of their members, become interested in. Its decentralized structure is more likely to represent effectively the diverse range of work-related environmental interests expressed by members.

There has also been the external charge that the T&G is out of touch with the 'business unionism' of the day. In an era of declining union membership, this refers to an emphasis on a wide service delivery role as a way to attract and retain members, and some unions – for example, the Manufacturing, Science and Finance Union – have advertised extensively the individual benefits available on enrolment, such as tax and legal advice, insurance cover and financial assistance. From their historical origins as friendly societies, trade unions have always been service providers for their members, so this may seem uncontentious. However, the danger posed by business unionism is that this will lead to a depoliticization of union activity. The T&G has continued to stress the need to retain a primary focus on collective bargaining to improve terms and conditions at work, recognizing the danger that concentration on individual material benefits may under-mine the collective gains made for members. The call by the Fabian Society for unions to regard members 'as customers, not activists' (1996, p 54) ignores this simple fact. Business unionism as a rationale for union existence predicated on a *client* understanding of private autonomy precludes any role for unions as actors for environmental democracy.

While recognizing the proud social unionist traditons of the T&G, this chapter has argued that the union needs to establish a more proactive environmental stance across its recruitment, bargaining and campaigning agendas. The environmental justice platform outlined above is no more than a preliminary sketch offered to those unions who seek a worker citizen-ship model for the new millennium. However, its normative implications are clear – that an international unionism should promote the institutional conditions for equal individual rights to environmental health and for a collective determination of social and ecological needs. Discursive democracy, in the theoretical statements of its philosophical proponents, has noted how much personal self-determination is necessary for political self-determination (Habermas, 1996, p 417). The argument here serves as a partial corrective to this – a reminder of how collective power, here in the form of organized labour (but applicable to the environmental justice movement generally), often facilitates the real freedom to exercise individual capabilities. In a world shot through with gross inequalities and asymmetries of power, there is often no alternative to social movement activism to push forward social and ecological freedom (Moody, 1997).

For unions like the T&G this still implies a significant radicalization of aims and strategies – not in an atavistic manner indifferent to current realities, but tied to a democratic realization that any realistic challenge to capitalist imperatives and structures of power cannot avoid political mobilization based, at least in part, on *class* interests. (Harvey, 1996, p 401). All those marginalized by the unbridled commodification of labour and nature must be able to participate in constructing countervailing power, articulating shared social and ecological interests. Over 100 years ago, by means of social solidarity, unions helped to forge those conditions in the community that allow the realization of personal autonomy (Webb and Webb, 1965, p 847). That enabling role remains. Unions, then, must be attuned to individual concerns, and open to the heterogeneity of worker-citizen interests around quality of life. As enablers of environmental justice, they can then help to make the type of society that has been the goal of the labour movement for a century.

6 AGENDA 21 AND LOCAL DEMOCRACY: A BRITISH SEARCH FOR NEW PARTICIPATORY FORMS

For ordinary citizens in Western democracies, the highly abstract debates on democratic participation animating the academy have had little impact on their notion of what it means to be involved in political behaviour. This is not necessarily a case of an expert knowledge domain remote from the understanding of the lay public. Ideas of 'democracy', 'government', 'politics' and so on have their own meanings and dynamic in the public arena, which is by no means insulated from the claims of social sciences. Research findings are often reported in the media; professional politicians and political commentators fix onto fashionable academic buzzwords; and academics fulfill their pedagogic role in educational institutions and beyond. However, for all the attention usually given to national politics, citizen action – directed in some way or another at public authorities – is, most of the time, a matter of local concerns. In Britain comprehensive surveys of citizen political activity have consistently revealed the strongly 'place-based' nature of public action (see Parry, Moyser and Day, 1992). For reasons of immediacy and accessibility, the local political realm is where democratic norms and practices are worked out. Environmentalists have long understood the importance of 'thinking locally': it is only in recent years, however, that they have begun to take seriously the challenge of urban issues. And this has led to a particularly creative source of dialogue with local government on grassroots public participation.

Under the Agenda 21 umbrella, emanating from the programme for sustainable development agreed at the 1992 Rio Earth Summit (United Nations, 1993), UK local government has embraced the project of public consultation over social and environmental needs. As will be discussed, Local Agenda 21 has provided an important focus for new participatory ideas about environmental decision-making. It has also locked into wider British debates about restructuring local governance. The anticipation by local authorities of growing environmental responsibilities has afforded them an important raison d'être in an antagonistic contest with central government over their political autonomy. In the relentless erosion of local government in the past 20 years by an unprecedented barrage of central government legislation, we can observe the classic democratic danger of the Westminster parliamentary model – a political executive, aided by a compliant legislature, able at will to make changes of a far-reaching constitutional nature. We can also observe the imposition of a neoliberal understanding of democratic governance, where the state is rolled back and public sector norms are replaced by market ones. This involved, in practice, a shift for local authorities from direct service provision to service purchasing and residual regulation. Accountability was defined in terms of private, contractual relationships rather than public responsibilities. It is no wonder, then, that local environmental decision-making acquired a sharpened political saliency when projected into this context of central-local government relations.

The political visibility of local environmentalism, including its overlap with debates on local democratic reform, has, if anything, been enhanced since Labour's election to power in 1997. In New York in June of that year, at the special session of the United Nations General Assembly to review global implementation of Agenda 21, Prime Minister Blair announced the target that all UK local authorities will have a Local Agenda 21 in place by the year 2000. On the question of sustainable development, the collaboration between the Labour government and local authorities has offered an encouraging area of intergovernmental discussion. For Labour, though, this is only one component of a far-reaching agenda to modernize local government in Britain. Alarmed by low electoral turnouts, public apathy, and a significant incidence of local authority corruption, Labour suggested a more participatory model of local government, where local councils engage directly with their communities, involving local people in decision-making (Department of Environment, Transport and the Regions, 1998b; 1998c). This agenda of democratic renewal strikes out boldly in its consideration of discursive methods for involving the public, suggesting such consultative mechanisms as citizens' juries, focus groups and deliberative opinion polls, alongside ideas for public participation in decision-making through standing citizens' panels and forums. The embrace of the discourse principle seems also to concern fairness in decision-making, ensuring that under-represented groups are taken into account. And given the dependence of disadvantaged groups upon local public goods for maintaining at least a minimal quality of life (they cannot buy themselves out of pollution), the government commitment to place on local authorities a duty to promote the economic, social and environmental well-being of an area promises to give a statutory boost to integrating environmental concerns within sectoral decision-making.

From its origins in Rio, Local Agenda 21 has highlighted the need for consensus-based, inclusive approaches to develop local sustainability strategies.[1] Of the various 'major groups' or stakeholders identified as pivotal to the long-term success of sustainable development, it is the involvement of disadvantaged groups, notably women, young people and ethnic minorities, which will determine the legitimacy of this democratic process. The egalitarian, participatory intent of Agenda 21 is certainly evident in the rhetoric of many UK local authorities (and their associations), as well as in their experimentation with a wide range of community participation techniques. Local Agenda 21 provides a valuable learning experience for extending democratic practices and norms, spiralling out from the initial preparation of sustainablity strategies. Furthermore, in contrast to the previous government's confinement of this activity to community voluntarism, the Labour administration has expressed a willingness to consider *statutory* instruments as a means of facilitating new political and administrative structures. There is, then, a commitment to support increased public participation with the necessary institutional capacity.

The language of democratic renewal featuring in the policy and practical expressions of Local Agenda 21 has thus found a receptive audience with those formulating an alternative political project to neoliberalism. Stephen Young (1996; 1997) views the process as at least providing the civic foundations for citizen empowerment in local governance. He identifies a discourse of active citizenship, recovering the idea of public participation in local debate and decision-making. This is also an unashamedly justice-based agenda concerned with local social and ecological rights which, set against increasing income inequality in Britain, implies prescriptions for redistributional policies. It is therefore also consistent with the discourse theory of environmental democracy. In the terms of the latter, Local Agenda 21 anticipates, for local decision-making, the participation of all relevant parties and the increased use of deliberative techniques to help identify common interests and values. It means extending existing liberal norms of equal treatment (such as equal opportunities) to social and ecological wellbeing. To recall from Chapter 1, if, according to the idea of environmental democracy, there should be rights to decent social and ecological conditions of life alongside universal civil and political freedoms, then any pronounced inequalities in the former means that there are individuals and groups unable to realize their freedoms. Environmental well-being (in the broad social and ecological sense) and citizen empowerment are intimately linked: that, in short, is the message of Local Agenda 21.

Of course, this is a radical reading of how the Agenda 21 process locally can take on the socially inclusive and just principles of environmental democracy. But it is one that this chapter will show has at least some empirical purchase in the democratic practice of an inner London local authority. After outlining something of the local government context of Agenda 21 in the UK, this chapter summarizes Local Agenda 21 practice in London, and then draws on a case study (the London Borough of Islington) to examine several community participation initiatives orientated towards inclusiveness and public deliberation in determining local environmental needs. I have here to declare a personal involvement in some of the projects mentioned. The insight hopefully obtained from such experience must be measured against conventional academic demands for objective judgement. With this in mind, there is something of a constructive dialogue within the chapter; in particular, a series of criticisms from commentators sympathetic to the sustainability agenda are considered – these criticisms are, in effect, that the intellectual and policy discourse on Local Agenda 21 in the UK is deeply flawed (Marvin and Guy, 1997). For them, this process expresses a 'new localism' tied to inward-looking and unexamined assumptions about political agency, rather than creating democratic practices and identities. This new localism has generated a series of 'myths' or framing narratives which prevent a more rigorous explanatory account of the local transition to sustainable development. In what follows, this chapter elaborates upon, and engages with, some of these objections, relating them to empirical instances of sustainability planning.

STRUCTURAL CHANGES IN LOCAL GOVERNMENT: THE POLITICAL CONTEXT OF LOCAL AGENDA 21 IN THE UK

Few things are more predictable in UK local government than the fact, or imminent prospect, of institutional change. This reflects, in part, the lack of constitutional autonomy for local political authorities which, constrained by parliamentary statutes and central directives, are therefore subject to the whims of national government.[2] It is also explained over the past few decades by a series of reforms that attempted to rationalize a patchwork of different local authority forms, but failed to keep up with increasing financial demands and social pressures (such as growth in welfare provision). Since 1996 an increase in the number of single-tier, unitary authorities has continued this search for a 'structural solution' (Wilson, 1996) to the modern challenges of local government, identifying larger authorities as the answer to more cost-efficient, responsive local service provision. One of the results of this has been a decline in the number of elected authorities and councillors (elected members), which has raised the concern that local democracy is being traded for reasons of administrative efficiency. Since British local government has traditionally been based upon representative political structures, the increase in the number of residents served by each councillor in the new unitary authorities appears to mark an erosion in democracy.

As David Wilson (1996, p 443) argues, though, a preoccupation with the changing territorial boundaries of local authorities in Britain has tended to mask more far-reaching shifts in power within local government. For the Conservative administrations that introduced these changes to the internal structures of local public decision-making, the 'enabling authority' was the goal – local government where services were contracted out to the private sector (or internal council organizations on competitive terms), with the authority overseeing standards. Through the increased use of market incentives in service delivery, the council would be more accountable to individual residents' preferences. An obvious drawback to this in environmental terms is the downgrading of those collective benefits (such as clean air and open space) not reducible to customer-based monetary evaluation. More widely, there was a dramatic transfer of power from democratically elected authorities to centrally appointed quangos (quasi-autonomous nongovernmental organizations) who took over service delivery responsibility in such areas as education, transport and economic regeneration. Their democratic legitimacy proved to be virtually nonexistent. Established without explicit public debate, inconsistency and secrecy in their standards led to the popular perception that they were mechanisms of political patronage (Hirst, 1994, p 343). Reduction in the democratic autonomy of local government was reinforced by the capping of local tax levels, alongside the removal of other revenues (business rates and capital receipts) from local control.

Attributing all responsibility to central government for the democratic deficit in British local governance became a favourite charge of many hard-pressed local authorities; but this is not wholly accurate. The independent Commission for Local Democracy, in an assessment of the state of local governance in England and Wales, found that the *party politicization* of local authorities – the increased role of the national political parties in local politics – was undermining the public accountability and transparency of council decision-making; for example the way in which local parties prearrange the voting of elected members prior to council meetings and the increasing intervention of councillors in local authority management structures:

> *The system encourages political parties to continue the private informal management of councils and grants them inordinate power. The basis of local administration is secretive in itself and confusing for the bulk of local people. From that confusion arises apathy and cynicism towards local democracy (Commission for Local Democracy, 1995, pp 16–17).*

Interestingly, the new Labour administration's white paper on modernizing local government is indebted to the Commission for Local Democracy in calling for the clarification of executive and management structures. Furthermore, the commission's suggestion for more public accountability in local authority decision-making is reflected in the commitment to create a statutory duty on councils to consult their local publics (Department of Environment, Transport and the Regions, 1998c).

How has structural change been manifested in environmental decision-making within local authorities? First of all, despite established statutory responsibilities for land-use planning and environmental health, the very emergence of 'environment' as an area for corporate action only took place since the mid 1980s (Agyeman and Evans, 1994, pp 4–8). As a result of public ecological concern, environmental pressure group campaigns and the role of key 'policy entrepreneurs' within local government, institutional commitment to environmental sustainability from local authorities acquired momentum (Ward, 1993). A Friends of the Earth document, *Environmental Charter for Local Government* (1989), played a key role in guiding local authorities on drafting environmental plans and strategies, due in part to the concerted lobbying of local Friends of the Earth groups. In addition, local authority associations – notably the Association of Metropolitan Authorities, the Associations for County Councils and District Councils and the Local Government Management Board – served as important networks for the establishment of good practice in local environmental policy-making. The result of all this has been a proliferation of environmental policy instruments – environmental action plans, state of the environment reports, environmental auditing and, more recently, environmental management systems. It is possible to interpret this activity, which has encompassed ecological issues outside local authority control, as a defence and extension of the public service role of local government in the face of a hostile central government (Ward, 1993, pp 465–468). Whatever the force of this political rationale, local authorities institutionalized their expanding environmental remits in new corporate structures, most often overseen at the councillor level by an environment committee. The more ambitious greening across local policy processes has proved more hard going, although models of good practice have emerged (Hams et al, 1994).

Of all local authority functions, the one most amenable to integrating environmental interests would seem to be land-use planning. The British planning system has international status for its long-standing claim to strategic foresight and regulatory control. In this policy area, where local government has significant discretionary power, central government has conceded the crucial role of the former in promoting sustainable development. This has been reflected in the green recasting of the planning policy guidance (PPG) notes for local authorities. For example, PPG 1 frames local development plans as instruments for sustainable development, while PPG 12 requires local authorities to carry out an environmental appraisal of these development plans. To be sure, the non-local impetus for the greening of spatial planning has come from the European Union, notably the Fifth Environmental Action Plan, which has offered UK local government an additional source of legitimacy for its environmental responsibilities. And planners have not hesitated to interpret in these moves an important professional challenge to translate the idea of sustainability into practice (Blowers, 1993; Buckingham-Hatfield and Evans, 1996). It is not possible here to convey the richness of the proposals generated. What we can note is their general appeal that central government enables local authorities to move towards more participatory and integrated environmental policies. Key to implementing effectively sustainable development at the local level is the consistent support that these proposals express for the Rio principle of *subsidiarity* – that planning and management responsibilities should be delegated to the lowest effective public authority consistent with effective action (United Nations, 1993, p 67).

However, by the democratic standards of the discourse principle, the realignment of local planning for sustainable development faces major institutional obstacles. Firstly, the commitment to balance social, environmental and economic needs in planning decisions cannot disguise a structural bias inherent in the system. Susan Owens (1997, p 299) captures well the deference planners must show to existing structures of property rights and the ideology of economic growth:

> *. . . [this] means that applicants for planning permission do not normally have to prove the need for their proposed development because of the normal presumption of allowing planning applications unless there are sound planning reasons for refusal – a presumption which would seem to weight the much-advocated 'balance' in favour of development.*

Demands for environmental quality, she continues, almost invariably fare poorly when taking them into account would imply the curbing of 'essential' economic investment (such as minerals extraction and road development). Therefore, until the politically taboo subject of ecological constraints on certain productive and consumptive activities is broached, a more effective integration of environmental interests in British planning decisions is not possible.

This asymmetry, secondly, is at the expense not only of ecological interests but also those socially disadvantaged groups highlighted in Agenda 21. In contrast, as we shall see, to Local Agenda 21, central government statements on planning and sustainability have been conspicuous by their neglect of the issue of social equity. Since 1997, when Labour came to power with a high-profile commitment to tackle 'social exclusion', the distributional consequences of policy and planning processes have at least reached the political agenda. And professional planners had already begun to address these issues – for example, on the need for planning authorities to monitor the implications of their policies on ethnic minorities (Thomas, 1997, p 203). Yet, the continuing unwillingness of central government to address the pro-growth, private property bias at the heart of the land-use planning system prevents any meaningful response at protecting the environmental well-being of vulnerable and disadvantaged groups. The sincere commitment to equal opportunities of many local planning authorities is inadequate to tackle the economic and social causes of their disempowerment (such as poverty, unemployment and discrimination). Without security of property or income, these groups are likely to suffer disproportionately the negative social and ecological consequences of major development proposals in their localities. That is the nature of environmental injustice.

Lastly, the institutional failing here from an environmental democratic perspective is not just that the land-use planning system is not fully representative of all interests, but also that its consultative forms are not sufficiently deliberative. Marvin and Guy (1997, pp 314–317) observe that the new discourse of planning for sustainability has tended to retain a technocentric preoccupation with redesigning urban forms – for example, energy-efficient buildings, renewable technologies and public transport innovations. The set of new environmental policy instruments is therefore geared to a 'physicalist' notion of localities, where appropriately engineered designs will effectively remove threats to local environmental well-being. Their claim that this preoccupation with physical solutions has neglected the local knowledge of other actors has some validity. Insofar as certain local authorities have approached these concerns solely in a top-down engineering framework, only those clued into the technical formulation of sustainability have been able to articulate their interests in the relevant technical language. Rendering sustainable development only as an expert knowledge precludes alternative, nonprofessional conceptualizations of quality of life – especially those based on shared ethical and aesthetic judgments (Owens, 1997, p 302). Once again, some British planners have been responsive to exposing technical discourse to local needs determination; 'planning through debate' as an approach to local land-use decision-making has made explicit connections with Habermasian theory (Healey, 1992). In environmental practice, the requirement to subject local development plans to environmental appraisals has recently seen many local authorities undertake discursive consultative exercises. Nonetheless, environmental democracy implies *regular* deliberative input into local planning decisions, of which Islington council's experiment with delegated neighbourhood planning (see below) has been among the most noteworthy.

Of course, the thrust of Local Agenda 21 has been to promote public involvement in negotiating programmes for sustainability, and it is here that UK local government has grasped the opportunity for institutional innovation and community outreach. By 1997, on the basis of nation-wide surveys, it was estimated that at least 73 per cent of UK authorities acted as coordinators for Local Agenda 21 (Local Government Management Board, 1997). That this was ahead of Local Agenda 21 development in any other country generated international interest. One reason given for this remarkable uptake – for what, after all, is an area of nonstatutory activity – is the effective national coordination provided by a joint national steering group composed of representatives from the Rio major groups as well as local authority associations. In creating new integrative and participative structures, UK local authorities have drawn heavily upon the national guidance sponsored by this group. Amidst the diverse Local Agenda 21 strategies, this has encouraged the core adoption of common institutional responses – corporate sustainability strategies, interdepartmental officer working groups and the integration of sustainability concerns across council committees. There have also been institutional adaptations tailored to individual authority needs, although the actual location of staff with Local Agenda 21 responsibility (whether newly appointed or internally seconded) has overwhelmingly been in environment-related departments (Tuxworth, 1996). Perhaps the major concern with these coordinators vis-à-vis internal council decision-making has been their distance from those private party-aligned meetings where councillors make key political choices. More generally, as Tuxworth notes (1996, p 295), there has remained a troubling gap between officer enthusiasm on Local Agenda 21 and the interest of elected members. The possibility of falling political support for this process within local government is unlikely, however, to reverse the partial but important incorporation of sustainability concerns in decision-making structures that has already occurred.

Moreover, the political benefits of local authorities being seen to engage with their communities in Local Agenda 21 consultation exercises are significant. This partly explains why, in a context in which local government has been forced to reduce expenditure on nonstatutory activities, Local Agenda 21 has still received financial commitment from authorities. The diversity of community outreach forms indicates the role of local authorities as facilitators of *participatory voluntarism*. A 1996 local government survey revealed that two-thirds of all authorities are adapting existing participation structures – community forums, area local-service committees and planning consultation procedures – to Agenda 21 needs, while three-quarters of all authorities have developed one or more new participation structures (Tuxworth, 1996, pp 286–288). It is noteworthy that the new participation forms have been characterized by deliberative, consensus-based structures – for example, community visioning, action planning and local sustainability modelling. Their diffusion has been facilitated by local government associations and the UK Community Participation Network (Bishop, 1994; New Economics Foundation, 1998). Of the more permanent consultative structures, notably Local Agenda 21 forums, most have been administered by local authorities with the active involvement of many local government officers. Much effort has gone into formulating Local Agenda 21 programmes, usually informed by cross-sectoral working groups who deal with particular issues. As these bodies move from the agenda-setting stage to overseeing the implementation of local sustainability plans, difficulties are emerging: nevertheless, regarding their relationship with local authority decision-making structures (Sharwood and Russell, 1997).

This last point reveals unresolved questions about the democratic legitimacy of the new participatory forms engendered by Local Agenda 21. What is their relationship to existing local structures of representative democracy? One of the concerns about the sustainability project has been that its rhetoric of inclusiveness has not translated into incorporating all relevant interests. Within local authorities, the integration of sustainability principles has still to influence, and be influenced by, educational policy, social services and anti-poverty and welfare strategies (Local Government Management Board, 1998). Similarly, Local Agenda 21 consultation procedures, however innovative in their deliberative forms, have often still been perceived by non-participants as preoccupied only with environmental amenity concerns. A consequence of the initial awareness-raising emphasis of Local Agenda 21 processes is that they are not yet able to demonstrate a strong link to collective environmental benefits. To be sure, in terms of disadvantaged groups, such as ethnic minorities, much existing local authority practice encompasses sustainable development even if the Local Agenda 21 label is not attached (Agyeman, 1997, p 4). The challenge then is to show how existing norms and practices of equal treatment can be strengthened by a sustainability focus on social and ecological well-being. This chapter will now elaborate on this claim by way of reference to Agenda 21 initiatives within London, firstly across the capital and then in an inner London borough.

LOCAL AGENDA 21 IN LONDON

As with the rest of the UK, London local government has taken an active role in coordinating Local Agenda 21 initiatives. Of the 33 London municipalities (boroughs), only two had no Local Agenda 21 consultation exercise underway by 1997. Also in line with the national pattern, 20 of the boroughs had each created a Local Agenda 21 forum as the institutional focus for their public involvement. An independent survey of the London boroughs nonetheless revealed important differences in membership and purpose between these forum structures (Centre for Environmental Initiatives, 1997). A contrast can be drawn, on the one hand, between the more council-driven forums (such as Havering, Merton, Sutton) and, on the other hand, those more autonomous forums, typically chaired by a community representative, where borough-wide consultation and partnership building has been a priority (such as Lambeth, Islington, Tower Hamlets). The former forum types are in the minority in not having membership open to the general public; instead they maintain a traditional local authority preference for engaging at the coordinating level only with representatives of key stakeholders.

This formal consultative approach has facilitated a more professional development of local sustainability strategies. Yet, most boroughs, in opting for community-based forum evolution, have allowed Local Agenda 21 development to be more participatory and drawn out in an attempt to increase community outreach. The democratic advantages of this latter approach must be weighed against the implementation difficulties encountered by several community forums, where their local sustainability proposals have clashed with local authority priorities.

The Centre for Environmental Initiatives survey of Local Agenda 21 processes in the London boroughs uncovered, in addition, over 150 working groups who were dealing with specific sustainability issues:

> *Much of the work on Local Agenda 21 in London has been undertaken by these working groups. Groups in various boroughs have been responsible for researching and writing substantial parts of their Local Agenda 21 documents and strategies. Many play a coordinating and developmental role, producing sustainability indicators and action plans (Centre for Environmental Initiatives, 1997, p 4).*

Overwhelmingly, these working groups have been open to the involvement of all interested parties, drawing in a diverse range of community and voluntary groups (the major exceptions being the authority-driven working groups in Merton and a working group in the City of London comprising solely corporate interests). They give a useful picture of the key sustainability concerns across London as expressed by the Local Agenda 21 processes. The 1997 survey recorded 22 London-wide working groups on transport and also on sustainable land use and nature conservation, with high levels of activity also on energy (19 groups), waste minimization (18 groups) and pollution (14 groups) (Centre for Environmental Initiatives, 1997, p 19). Moreover, they also reveal specific local concerns – evident, for example, in Southwark's pedestrian rights group and Islington's nuclear trains working group (concerned with the cross-borough transport of nuclear waste).

That the London boroughs have been the organizing areas for Local Agenda 21 attests to the role of these local authorities as the most important level of democratic decision-making within the capital. Their present form goes back 35 years to the 1963 London Government Act, though they have historical roots to previous forms of London local government and civic identity. The central government's undermining of municipal autonomy, already mentioned as a reason for local government interest in Agenda 21, applies to London. What has made it even more salient in the capital is that since the abolition of the Greater London Council in 1986, London has lacked a democratically elected city-wide authority. For a city of seven million people, this resulted not only in a sweeping democratic disenfranchisement (with no constitutional comeback), but a confusing and inefficient fragmentation of London-wide functions. The overriding political motive of the Conservative government in removing the Labour-controlled Greater London Council is widely acknowledged, for even the Conservatives struggled to rationalize the bureaucratic quagmire that became London governance, with the overlapping administrative responsibilities between national government, various quangos and joint committees of the London boroughs (Hebbert, 1995).

In the early 1990s the creation of a Government Office for London and a cabinet subcommittee for London represented a belated recognition of the strategic failings of this arrangement, but did nothing to correct London's democratic deficit. Londoners consistently registered substantial support in opinion polls for the return of a democratic authority – something Labour made much political capital from in its 1997 manifesto commitment to create, if supported by London residents, a directly elected mayor and assembly. And following a London-wide referendum in 1998, the capital will now have a Greater London Authority and mayor by 2000.

For 15 years, then, the boroughs have had to address the social, economic and environmental challenges to a capital city without effective cross-borough coordination of strategic functions. Here the gap between the sustainability rhetoric of the Conservative government and the Agenda 21 principle of subsidiarity was particularly jarring. To take the key area of cross-sectoral planning, national government enjoined the boroughs to place their planning activities within the context of sustainable development, including Local Agenda 21 (Government Office for London, 1996, pp 9–10). Yet, as elsewhere in the country, this was in the context of onerous financial restrictions on local government expenditure and the removal or contracting out of numerous service functions. In difficult circumstances, cross-borough collaboration on sustainability planning has been rare. The notable exception has been the London Planning Advisory Committee, comprising planning officers from individual boroughs, which produced a landmark State of the Environment Report for London in 1995 and has commissioned research on integrated transport planning. As its name implies, though, the advisory committee has no decision-making authority, and is restricted by the national government to a monitoring and reporting role. For the range of growing social polarization and environmental degradation in London – such as widening income inequalities, increasing air pollution and traffic congestion, and homelessness – subsidiarity implies effective governance, assisted by national government, at the regional scale. Proposals for the new Greater London Authority recognize that its city-wide functions will include strategic planning, transport and environmental protection strategies, as well as economic regeneration (Department of Environment, Transport and the Regions, 1998a). Above all, the proposals place a statutory duty on the executive to promote sustainable development.

The Greater London Authority will coordinate Local Agenda 21 in the capital. In that task, it will be able to draw upon the development, since 1995, of a London-wide Agenda 21 by the capital's local authority network – the Association of London Government (ALG). A body composed of elected councillors, the ALG has been the self-proclaimed 'democratic voice of London' in the absence of a metropolitan authority. The Agenda 21 process sponsored by the association has logically focused upon strategic, cross-borough issues. It has been overseen by a London Agenda 21 steering group encompassing representatives from those key stakeholder groups identified at Rio – local government, women, young and older people, ethnic minorities, the private and voluntary sectors, and trade unions.[3] Indeed, representative consultation has characterized the detailed thematic work of stakeholder participants. According to the ALG, this was to avoid duplicating the direct community consultation work undertaken by the borough councils under the Local Agenda 21 banner (Association of London Government, 1996, p 4). What can also be read into this London-wide process is a reassertion of representative structures in the face of participatory democratic suggestions from groups such as the Institute of Community Studies (White and Young, 1996, pp 62–63) and the London Community Alliance that decision-making authority in the capital should be devolved down to urban parish councils or community assemblies.[4] Not surprisingly, the ALG has rejected the idea that subsidiarity might mean the abolition of the current boroughs.

To be sure, the London Agenda 21 Steering Group has discussed strategies to increase civic engagement in the capital, defined as 'the need to engage Londoners both in the Agenda 21 process and in wider decision-making processes' (Association of London Government, 1997, p 6). Its Civic Engagement Task Group reviewed a range of consultative and participative mechanisms for improving public involvement in decision-making, including existing borough experiments with community planning, citizens' juries and Local Agenda 21 forums. Although the group endorsed this development of civic engagement, it recommended that innovative forms of public involvement be maintained as voluntarist tools, supplementing the more important representative work of the forthcoming London-wide elected authority. Perhaps symptomatic of this belief that creating the Greater London Authority would be the single most important action to improve political participation, a planned London-wide survey of civic engagement in 1997–1998 by the ALG failed to find the necessary funding. Enabling new forms of public participation in London decision-making has proved not to be a priority for the Association.

While certainly deliberative, the London Agenda 21 process disappointed many nongovernmental groups across the capital with what they claimed was its lack of inclusiveness. In some cases, this reflected no more than a dissatisfaction with not being invited to any of the stakeholder discussions, and it is difficult to conceive of how the ALG, even if it had the will, could have found the resources to finance a more inclusive, bottom-up consultation process on London-wide sustainability issues. There are 30,000 voluntary organizations based in the capital, even before we consider the question of underrepresentation of certain interests. What *is* clear is that the London Agenda 21 process was not able to achieve full representation even within its own consultative parameters. Representatives of younger and older people were not able to attend all the 11 stakeholder meetings, while, more seriously, no ethnic minority representatives (though invited) attended any of these meetings. In fact, a similar pattern of underrepresentation of these groups has also been a problem for the Local Agenda 21 processes facilitated by the borough councils. With nonwhite residents making up a quarter of the population of London, the low involvement of ethnic minority communities in London's Agenda 21 initiatives represents the greatest challenge to the democratic credentials claimed by these processes. It is fair to say that Local Agenda 21 practices in the capital have not tackled the issues of social and economic marginalization affecting ethnic minorities. From one London-wide black perspective, only when Local Agenda 21 activity is coordinated by the Greater London Authority will the black community be able to have a meaningful say as a stakeholder group (Black Londoners for a Strategic Authority, 1997, p 14).

The absence of a democratically elected London authority has accentuated inequalities in the city-wide representation of interests. Without a metropolitan body able to represent, however imperfectly, the concerns of disadvantaged communities and groups across the capital, their interests have been systematically neglected. After the abolition of the Greater London Council, the increasing administrative role of central government in the capital's decision-making cleared the way for a laissez-faire approach to economic investment, with its misconceived assumptions about 'trickle-down' of benefits to the less fortunate. The only noteworthy locale of strategic planning, the Docklands, saw a centrally appointed London Docklands Development Corporation with no local accountability or community regeneration remit, and a Docklands transport steering group created to reassure private capital interests that property investment in the area would be supported by an adequate transport infrastructure. And the heart of London saw the continuation of the City's local authority – the Corporation of London – where most council members are appointed for life (by means of uncontested elections) on the basis of a voting system that enfranchises the traditional financial services sector over and above local residents (and other companies). The global preeminence of London's financial markets, generating 75 per cent of the country's income from that sector, has secured for the City its enduring immunity from any form of social and ecological accountability (both locally and globally).

This last point throws into perspective the immense institutional constraints weighted against those Londoners who want to improve the inclusiveness of public decision-making in the capital, even with the Greater London Authority in place. Its elected representatives will still be subject to the lobbying of powerful economic development interests with national and international clout. With this in mind, the idea of strengthening the political voice of voluntary and community groups has recently gained currency. The London Voluntary Service Council (1997) has recommended creating a civic forum for London, composed of representatives from nongovernmental groups, to act as a deliberative space for civic groups and to advise the Greater London Authority. Similarly, the Sustainable London Trust (1996, pp 37–39) has proposed a London citizens' forum to coordinate and strengthen the political influence of voluntary and community activity in the capital. Both suggestions were influenced in part by the London Local Agenda 21 processes. Indeed, in a clear challenge to the legitimacy of the ALG-led Agenda 21 consultation, the Sustainable London Trust claimed that a London citizens' forum is the most appropriate source for coordinating a London-wide Local Agenda 21. While the citizens' forum has still to materialize, a fledgling Agenda 21 grouping has emerged as part of the grassroots UK Sustainability Network. Launched in April 1998, London 21 has given itself the major aim of increasing involvement of Londoners in Local Agenda 21 processes, particularly young people.

In contrast with the formal London Agenda 21 process steered by the ALG, London 21 has embraced a radical agenda of social and environmental justice. It also represents an alternative, participatory vision of democratic governance influenced by proposals for community assemblies within the capital. Both representative and participatory conceptions claim allegiance to the Rio project of sustainable development and the principle of subsidiarity (which is made possible by the political ambiguities of Agenda 21). Are new forms of public participation in sustainability decision-making compatible with both? And what is their relationship to democratic and deliberative norms? In particular, Marvin and Guy claim to identify in dominant 'localist' prescriptions for sustainability decision-making a 'powerful homogenizing ethic and a strong sense of social control' (1997, p 316). Is there lurking behind the democratic rhetoric of local sustainability a wish by proponents to impose green lifestyles on individuals? It is at this point that we need to look at some examples of innovative democratic practice to work through these questions. All relate to an inner London borough where an interest in improving public involvement in local government predates Local Agenda 21.

DEVELOPING ENVIRONMENTAL DEMOCRATIC FORMS: THE ISLINGTON EXPERIENCE

With a population of 164,686 (1991 Census) and an area of 5.75 square miles (14.89 square kilometres), the London Borough of Islington is one of the most densely populated areas in London. It is also one of the most mixed in terms of ethnicity (almost 19 per cent of the population is composed of ethnic minority groups) and, like much of the capital, expresses some marked polarities in income and housing conditions. Nonetheless, on the basis of a range of deprivation indicators – including mortality rates, over-crowded and unsuitable accommodation, low educational attainment, income support and unemployment – the borough has been rated as the fourth most deprived in the country, with all of its 20 electoral wards within the 10 per cent most deprived English wards (Department of the Environment, 1995, p 97). It sits in an inner-east London belt of high deprivation, alongside Hackney, Tower Hamlets and Newham, which reveals an enduring pattern of low economic activity and state dependence. And in all these boroughs unemployment levels are highest among ethnic minority groups, who suffer also disproportionately from poor housing. Islington scores badly on several additional environment-related quality-of-life measures – a deficiency in recreational open space, poor air quality, rising asthma levels for local residents, high local suicide rates, and a demand for mental health services above the London average (London Borough of Islington, 1996).

Improving environmental (social and ecological) well-being is therefore an immediate, pressing concern for its population and has been a preoccupation of Islington's Local Agenda 21 process. What makes the borough distinctive is that it has long facilitated novel methods of political participation and communication to address issues around quality of life. The Agenda 21 consultation exercise in Islington must be understood in the context of this willingness to experiment with participatory forms. This section addresses first, therefore, the importance of neighbourhood democracy in the borough, before commenting on the environmental democratic potential of the Local Agenda 21 process, and then linking this to community-based urban regeneration. In each of these cases, the community identification of – and deliberation on – local needs has ultimately exposed the current limitations of representative democratic structures. And the local authority has actually supported the devolution of environmental decision-making to enable a more participatory structure of local governance. The general claim here is that Marvin and Guy's criticism that local sustainability norms are onerous is redundant in this case, because environmental well-being is linked to new spaces of citizen participation in local decision-making.

Neighbourhood democracy

As a way of meeting local needs, the *decentralization* of services was one of the recurring motifs of UK local government thinking in the 1980s. Its functional promise of more responsive and accessible service delivery was usually combined with a political belief that decentralization would enhance the accountability of local government structures. By means of neighbourhood-based committees or forums, local service delivery could be improved with increased citizen participation in decisions affecting their interests. More involved and informed citizens would bolster the democratic legitimacy of local authority decision-making. Widespread though the rhetoric was, few local authorities committed themselves to far-reaching decentralization in practice. The Labour council elected to office in Islington in 1982 actually pioneered such a programme, followed in London by Tower Hamlets and Kingston. In Islington, after an extensive round of public consultation, 24 neighbourhoods were initially established across the borough, each charged with delivering a cluster of key services – housing, social services, environmental health and some of the administrative functions of the chief executive's department. Since that time, as a consequence of various structural and staffing changes, the number of neighbourhoods has been reduced to 11 (see Figure 6.1) along with, as we shall see, their service functions.

Once decentralized service delivery had been established in Islington, the council moved to set up a parallel network of 24 advisory councils, neighbourhood forums, to involve local residents in deliberations over neighbourhood services and issues. After a progressive rationalization of local service provision in the 1990s, this shrank to 11 forums, in line with the reduction of neighbourhoods. However, the core forum functions have been maintained over this period of change. The forums continue as important instruments of democratic oversight and debate. The local authority has, under existing powers, been able to delegate planning authority to three forums while all forums are able to distribute small grants allocated to them for local projects. In essence, though, forums are not vested

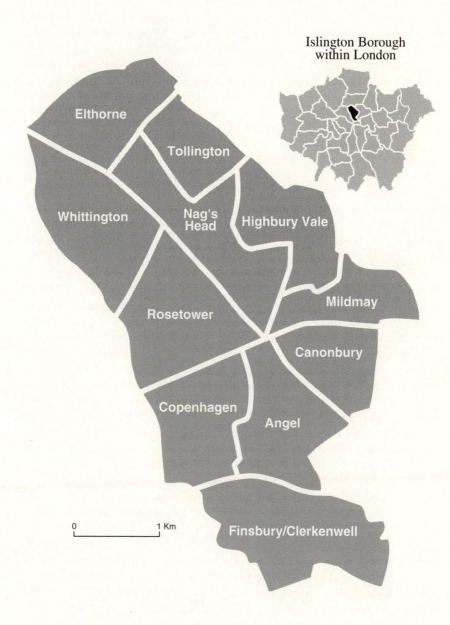

Figure 6.1 *Neighbourhoods in Islington*

with formal decision-making powers, because to do so would have transformed them into statutory committees with local ward councillors retaining authority for decisions. It was to avoid replicating representative local authority committees at a neighbourhood level, and to enhance participatory democracy, that the forums were created (Burns, Hambleton and Hoggett, 1994, p 183). They are therefore comprised, in part, by members elected locally and separately from local councillors (who sit on the forums as ward members with no voting rights). Furthermore, and this is the most important contribution of the neighbourhood system to combining deliberation with *inclusiveness*, the forums also have group members appointed by community associations and section members from underrepresented sections of the community – young people under 21, black and ethnic minorities, people with disabilities, women with caring responsibilities, and people of pensionable age.

According to Burns, Hambleton and Hoggett (1994, p 200), there are good grounds for claiming that the system of neighbourhood democracy pioneered by Islington has gone further than any other council in the UK in deepening public involvement in local government decision-making. Forums are representative, active bodies and 'have been successful in spreading information about political choices affecting the future quality of life in the neighbourhoods' (1994, p 197). They are also noted as having increased the responsiveness of council services by holding neighbourhood staff and council officers to account. Against this positive assessment, a more recent and influential review of the neighbourhood system by Capita Management Consultants (1997a) reaches very different conclusions. Here the forums are viewed as not fully representative of their local communities, since they depend upon an 'activist model' of political communication which gives disproportionate influence to those championing sectional interests. Instead of rational deliberation over local needs, forum discussion is subject to the self-selection of those with preset agendas. In addition, the forums are portrayed as having very limited influence on council decision-making, lacking formal channels for feeding their views into corporate and departmental policy-making. Forum input is limited to forum chairs who communicate in an ad hoc manner to service directors about particular issues (Capita, 1997a, pp 29–31).

These divergent appraisals are as much a result of different understandings of local governance as objective changes in the performance of the neighbourhood system. The first is sympathetic to the participatory political goals of the decentralization project; the second is informed by a managerial worldview preoccupied with the efficiency of local service provision. Exposed to standard local-authority performance indicators, the service quality record of decentralized structures has indeed not been good. External agencies have been particularly critical of Islington's child protection services and housing allocations at the neighbourhood level. And the neighbourhood structure itself has been implicated in these service delivery failings, due to the spread of professional expertise across the system, a lack of central coordination and confused accountability structures (Capita, 1997a, pp 25–35). From our perspective, the discourse principle implies norms of equal treatment, which are undermined by deficiencies in central control if residents in different neighbourhoods encounter significant variations in service provision. In Tower Hamlets the loss of corporate direction in the 1990s was even more marked, leading to serious failings with its neighbourhood system. Given the explicit aim of decentralization to improve service quality, and the need to demonstrate to local populations connections between neighbourhood forum deliberations and service provision decisions, the problems in Islington seem to throw into doubt the role of neighbourhood democracy in enhancing quality of life. According to some Islington councillors, the local authority's inward concern with decentralized service delivery rendered it ill-prepared for the market-based 'contract culture' (Capita, 1997b, Appendix F, p 2).

However, far from discrediting the decentralized neighbourhood system, the weaknesses identified in Islington attest to a participatory experiment that has not yet gone far enough and, notwithstanding managerial failings, has for most of its duration faced major financial and political controls imposed upon the local authority by central government. Nowhere has the participatory potential of, and constraints to, the neighbourhood forum structure been more apparent than in environmental decision-making. Traffic and environmental issues make up 20 per cent of the concerns raised at neighbourhood forum meetings (Capita, 1997a, p 30), indicative of their impact on local populations. Yet these recurrent issues – street cleansing and maintenance, traffic management, footway repairs, etc – relate to services not managed through the neighbourhood offices (and, in the case of strategic roads, not even controlled by the local authority), though relevant staff are designated to liaise with the neighbourhoods.[5] The keen interest of neighbourhood forums in environmental matters has been recognized by Islington Council, which has established consultative channels between the forums and its environment committee. Since 1989 the local authority has also allowed several neighbourhood forums, through planning subgroups, to consider planning applications affecting their locality – a unique planning innovation in the UK. This successful devolution of planning authority, at the limit of the legal powers of the council, has only been possible by delegation via the chief officer, with the proviso that ultimate authority remains with the council planning committee. As nonstatutory bodies, neighbourhood forums lack the formal powers to translate broader environmental concerns effectively into collective binding decisions.

A major restructuring of the neighbourhood system in 1997–1998, sparked by the Capita report, allowed Islington Council to reaffirm its commitment to neighbourhood democracy, with measures to improve and increase community participation in local decision-making. For the 11 neighbourhood offices this has meant, firstly, the development of a new information and access role for all council services; the local authority is to widen the opportunities for local monitoring of service provision. Secondly, one of the primary tasks for a new network of neighbourhood quality managers, appointed in June 1998, has been to develop and implement *local democracy strategies*. Central to these plans is the strengthening of neighbourhood forums, broadening their membership, terms of reference and format in a proactive manner. In response to the Capita observation that the forums have had limited impact on council policy, new formal consultation channels and roles have been created. But just as important is the intention for forums to foster increased civic participation, widening their connections with local residents and community organizations (London Borough of Islington, 1997b, p 15). The vision is of forums as facilitators for neighbourhood deliberation on all issues affecting the social and ecological well-being of local residents. Significantly, the forums themselves have relayed the view to the council that a precondition for more effective participation in local governance on their part is civic education and training. Revitalizing civic activity as a community-wide priority therefore raises challenges to actors and institutions outside the local authority.

The national government's proposals for local democratic renewal have raised expectations within Islington Council that the long-standing commitment of the borough to *empower* citizen participation in local decision-making may finally be politically feasible. Furthermore, there is the expectation that the potential for realizing environmental democratic forms is finally opening up. When the neighbourhood forums were originally set up, the idea was floated that some might eventually evolve into decision-making neighbourhood councils. Only since the election of the Labour government have supportive signals emerged from Whitehall, though, regarding enabling legislation for devolving local decision-making powers. Labour's general election manifesto in 1997 included support for the principle of subsidiarity and the piloting of new methods of local governance. Within Islington Council members have endorsed the principle of subsidiarity in decision-making, noting that this implies devolution of powers to local people on many environmental issues affecting their neighbourhoods.[6] The council has therefore lobbied the government to instruct the secretary of state for environment, transport and the regions to allow London boroughs to set up urban parish councils, as originally suggested by the Commission for Local Democracy (1995, p 51). There has been significant support for the parish council model from the neighbourhood forums in Islington, who view this as necessary to encourage greater participation in local governance (London Borough of Islington, 1998a, Appendix B). These urban parish councils, if agreed to in local referenda, would be able to exercise a range of powers over maintaining the neighbourhood environment, would have at least consultative rights over planning applications and would be able to raise a local tax.

Of course, the notion of subsidiarity still leaves extra-local representative structures to deal with decisions requiring higher levels of coordination and control (such as statutory obligations over environmental health provision). Islington Council has understandably not followed the radical recommendations of the community assembly movement, who see no need for borough councils between urban parish councils and a strategic London authority. The onus of proof is very much on those who see borough structures as redundant to demonstrate why this is the case, just as any prescription for annexing existing democratic forms has a moral obligation to convince all those affected of the merits of such a move. Significantly, Islington Council's support for creating urban parish councils sits alongside other proposals for devolving powers to neighbourhoods and involving local communities. Of the other options explored for devolving powers to neighbourhoods, only creating neighbourhood committees, under the control of local ward committees, is possible under existing powers. Additional neighbourhood innovations – delegating executive capacity to local elected members, to a majority party, or electing a neighbourhood mayor (London Borough of Islington, 1998b) – would have been possible under a Local Government (Experimental Arrangements) Bill supported by Labour in the 1997–1998 session of parliament; but this failed to be enacted.[7] This leaves local authorities dependent upon national government for new legislative proposals for modernizing local government. Other local democracy initiatives suggested by Labour – deliberative opinion polling, citizens' juries, focus groups and conferences – have already been employed by Islington Council. However, these are all relatively uncontroversial consultative innovations: the scope of London local authorities to devolve decision-making powers remains the true litmus test of the national government's commitment to renewing local democracy.

Islington Local Agenda 21

For Marvin and Guy (1997, pp 312–313), a central framing narrative of the new localism is to represent local government as the best suited to tackling local environmental problems. That local authorities are key actors in delivering local sustainability strategies is, of course, taken as given by Chapter 28 of Agenda 21. Even after the loss of many service provision functions, local authorities in the UK continue with extensive service delivery and regulatory roles, and these activities impact directly upon the living conditions of local residents. Above all, local government is the focus for democratic representation and legitimacy at this level of governance. As a result, the attribution of lead agency status to local government in the coordination of Local Agenda 21 strategies is hardly surprising. What Marvin and Guy question is the taken-for-granted preeminence of local authorities in the 'new local environmentalism', which, in their opinion, has oversimplified the diverse, contested sources of political agency and identity – many of which cross over local boundaries. This reinforces their claim that local prescriptions for sustainability, as encouraged and facilitated by local authorities, are foisting environmentalist norms onto individuals in a manner far from consensual.

The Islington Local Agenda 21 process has certainly featured an active role for the local authority, and this has evolved out of the council's various environmental initiatives. In an approach that corresponds with the general direction of local authority decision-making noted earlier in the chapter, Islington Council set up an environment committee and a joint environment advisory committee in 1989. That same year, it adopted the Friends of the Earth environmental charter prior to launching its own environmental policy and action plan, subsequently updated in 1995. From the beginning Islington Council has emphasized its commitment to nurture environmentally responsible behaviour within the borough. Alongside reforms to internal decision-making, it has therefore developed community-based initiatives encompassing environmental education and awareness raising, and support for voluntary activity. None of these interventions in local civil society can be construed as colonizing public space occupied by existing civic activism, nor can any be charged with imposing environmental norms. Rather, they have overwhelmingly involved measures designed to enable community voluntarism – notably, establishing the Islington Community Environmental Trust as a focus for environmental grant applications and funding an environmental development officer. The council's own environmental action plan has also been firmly tied to its participatory democracy initiatives – for example, by enhancing the role of neighbourhood forums in environmental decision-making and integrating environmental objectives within Islington's race and women's equality action plans.

As Islington has moved to address the challenge of sustainable development, the council has undertaken political management reforms designed to institutionalize a top-level commitment to sustainability. At the corporate level, the council agreed a council charter for a sustainable future in 1995, informed by four principles (London Borough of Islington, 1995):

- the encouragement of individual and collective responsibility for the environment;
- the creation of a viable system for protecting the environment;
- equal access for all to a good-quality environment;
- the promotion of a healthy and safe environment.

Political support for this charter from the majority Labour group ensured that it was incorporated within the strategic deliberations of council committees: the key Policy and Resources Committee agreed in December 1996 to instruct officers to formulate a council sustainability action plan to merge the environmental action plan with broader sustainability objectives. This action plan, informed by the results of the Local Agenda 21 consultation process, is the key local authority policy statement on sustainability, with clearly defined staff responsibilities and targets (London Borough of Islington, 1997a). It is reviewed by the top policy-making committee every six months. Furthermore, all council committees have since 1996 been required, where relevant, to note the environmental implications of their decisions. To secure the integration of sustainability concerns across all policy areas, the council has declared its intention to broaden these out to sustainability implications, but this has still to be realized.

In a review of Islington's approach to delivering local sustainability, the independent district auditor noted the strength of its management arrangements (Gott and Dobson, 1998, p 2). The survey highlighted as good practice the cross-council Local Agenda 21 officers group, which helps translate corporate sustainability commitments into concrete actions. Chaired by the assistant chief executive, with officers from all service departments and technical staff conversant with specialist environmental management areas, the officer group maintains an integrated approach at the service level. The deliberative space provided by this group has proved invaluable for the local authority (although it has not always met regularly). Its issue-specific sessions (on traffic and air pollution, awareness raising, built environment and housing), as well as a visioning exercise geared towards developing long-term objectives, have shaped the council's action plan for sustainability. To be sure, the district auditor observed scope to generalize this type of interdepartmental working within the local authority, and also identified specific policy areas where outcomes could be improved (energy and waste consumption, recycling); but overall Islington has compared favourably with other local authorities subject to the same auditing methodology.

The important contribution of Islington to sustainability planning has been in combining a high-level corporate commitment to environmental sustainability with a community-led Local Agenda 21 process. To recall the dual perspective of environmental democracy, deliberative communication about public concerns is likely to be most open and inclusive when a participatory division of labour between the state and civil society is maintained. In other words, the formal decision-making powers of the state, resting largely on representative political structures, can be made more democratic by empowering individuals and communities to become involved in the key decisions affecting their lives and living conditions. However, these new participatory forms are dependent upon a healthy civil society of autonomous public debate and associative activity. In Britain, in recent years, both sides at the local level have been battered. Central government has simultaneously eroded the freedom of local authorities to determine local priorities and also some of the vital freedoms on which civic self-determination relies (such as the freedom of public association including, as noted in the last chapter, freedom of association in the workplace). This is the context in which local authority support for community-based Agenda 21 initiatives has acquired important political weight – as the local state fostering the democratic capacity of civil society.

In the case of Islington, the Local Agenda 21 planning process has been led by a borough-wide Agenda 21 forum, chaired by the Member of Parliament for Islington North. The forum is essentially a round table comprising a range of community representatives from the council, neighbourhood forums, local businesses and public sector organizations, and voluntary groups. Acknowledging the significance of existing working relationships on environmental concerns, the forum was established in 1996 by broadening out the terms of reference and membership of the local authority's joint environment advisory committee (JEAC). This transformation was approved by the representatives on that consultative body, although the insistence of local environmentalists that the forum retain the accountability function of JEAC – quizzing the local authority on its environmental record – has given the forum a schizophrenic character, switching uneasily (and often in the same meeting) between questioning council members and officers and discussing community sustainability concerns. Ironically, if this has sometimes led the forum to be more preoccupied with local authority business than constructing a local sustainability strategy, as Marvin and Guy claim is the pattern with the new localism, this has reflected the wishes not of the council but environmental group representatives. It is clear that the council has devoted the bulk of the resources to support the forum, although this burden has been shared with other bodies, such as the University of North London and the Chamber of Commerce. In addition, strategic guidance for the forum is provided by an Islington Agenda 21 steering group, a management body also made up of various local stakeholders, independent of local authority decision-making structures.

The community-led nature of the Islington Agenda 21 process is also evident from the rest of its organizational infrastructure. A Local Agenda 21 coordinator position, though funded since September 1996 by the council, is unique in the UK in being based at a local university (the University of North London) and includes explicit sustainability awareness raising and outreach responsibilities. This partnership approach was established when the university hosted a public conference on Agenda 21 in May 1995, organized in association with the local authority, Islington Voluntary Action Council and the Islington Environment Forum. Over 180 people attended the conference; workshop discussions on a variety of topics set in motion several working groups, including transport and pollution, energy conservation, waste minimization and recycling, mental health, nuclear trains, sustainability indicators and Whittington Neighbourhood Agenda 21. Most of these groups have been chaired by community representatives, although council officers have also participated. Supported and advised by the coordinator, the working groups have undertaken the bulk of the detailed work on Islington's Local Agenda 21, with forum meetings serving to publicize this work and seek further community input. Some of their recommendations pertinent to council business have been incorporated within the local authority action plan for sustainability, while the council received the full combined working group reports as the borough's Local Agenda 21 strategy document in spring 1998.

My involvement in the Islington process has been through membership of the steering group and as convenor of the Sustainability Indicators

Working Group. In what follows, the intention is not to summarize the content of the borough's Local Agenda 21, but rather to offer some comments on the environmental democratic potential of its experience with public participation techniques – that is to say, the extent to which they have encouraged inclusive deliberation on concerns about life opportunities and conditions. Have these forms served as a catalyst for the democratic articulation of a local sustainability strategy?

A first point to note is that the terms of reference for the borough-wide Local Agenda 21 forum encourage it to ensure that the widest possible range of interests is involved in preparing a sustainability strategy and action plan. Furthermore, not only must there be appropriate representation of Islington's communities and local interests, these must be brought together to achieve a consensus on the way forward. The open model of forum membership, extending in practice beyond forum group representatives to all attendees of forum meetings, reflects this desire to invite all interested parties. Efforts to maximize accessibility of meetings have included varying their locations and times, although there have been recurring concerns that they have not been publicized widely enough. Early on in the process, attendance at forum meetings peaked at around 40 to 50 individuals, though this has since declined by about a fifth. It has become clear that the deliberative space represented by forum meetings is their most important property, and those interactive meetings where participants have engaged directly with defining sustainability goals or targets have been the most successful. Yet those opportunities have sometimes been relegated down busy forum agendas in favour of requests to question council members and officers on current sustainability issues – the residual JEAC function already mentioned. Loading the forum with this accountability role has maintained a valuable communicative link with council decision-making, but seems to have led to the localist frame of reference observed by Marvin and Guy (1997), making it more difficult to encourage consensus-based, future-oriented discussions on quality of life in the borough.

The procedural openness of the Islington forum model, laudable in democratic terms, must be considered alongside the input of those groups with guaranteed representation, since the legitimacy of the process also depends upon involving these existing community interests. In terms of neighbourhood-based representation within the borough, the involvement of the neighbourhood forums (with fixed membership of the Local Agenda 21 forum) is, of course, crucial in reinforcing the council's own goal of more effective participation in environmental decision-making. And to encourage neighbourhood forum participation in the Islington Local Agenda 21 process, the council has given presentations at neighbourhood forum meetings. In practice, neighbourhood input into the borough-wide forum has been far from comprehensive. This has also proved to be the case with the working groups, from a few with no formal neighbourhood representation (business and economy, nuclear trains) to those with substantial neighbourhood forum participation (energy conservation, transport and pollution).

Neighbourhood forum involvement has been most pronounced from those neighbourhoods with active environmental subgroups, notably Elthorne and Whittington. Indeed, Whittington Neighbourhood set up its own Agenda 21 group in January 1996, and its impressive pilot work on recycling and energy conservation has been incorporated within the council's sustainability action plan. The Whittington example points to the value of neighbourhood-based deliberations on social and ecological needs, feeding into borough-wide discussions. However, the fact that it is only those neighbourhood groups already active in environmental issues who have become engaged in the Local Agenda 21 process reveals the continuing deficit in active interest-based representation from the other neighbourhoods. And even the neighbourhood forums undertaking Agenda 21 work have struggled to maintain their momentum in the context of the recent neighbourhood reorganization and budget cuts.

The mixed neighbourhood involvement in the Islington Agenda 21 process reveals the biggest challenge to ensuring an appropriate representation of interests – existing imbalances in community voluntarism will tend to be replicated by new associative networks unless considerable effort is devoted to bringing underrepresented groups within the process. Even guaranteed representation for such groups, as in the Islington Agenda 21 forum for women, ethnic minorities, youth, pensioners, and people with disabilities, is often not enough to secure their involvement. The plain reason for this is that these groups, typically weak in their organizational presence, lack the resources, confidence or time to participate, or perhaps even the inclination. The tendency for Local Agenda 21 processes to attract 'the usual suspects' has been an issue for Islington as elsewhere in the UK. The forum and working groups have attracted predominantly white middle-class professionals, comfortable with the consultative rules of the game from their voluntary activity in other areas. In fact, this propensity to conform to existing patterns and habits of civic activity may not necessarily be healthy for Local Agenda 21 processes where the goal is creative, shared articulation of a community-wide vision. The discourse principle stipulates that all affected interests have the opportunity to participate in determining local needs, regardless of income, age, ethnicity, educational attainment and so on. Local Agenda 21 processes are therefore hopelessly stranded in democratic terms if they cannot effect this wide-ranging representation. It means, therefore, that they must also be part of wider strategies of political empowerment and civic education.

On a small scale, community outreach work by two of the Islington Agenda 21 working groups has demonstrated the value of two participatory techniques in reaching those groups neither active in the Agenda 21 process nor whose particular interests seem to have been taken into account. These methods are focus groups and community visioning.

In the Sustainability Indicators Working Group, we developed an open-ended question schedule for identifying local concerns and how they might be tackled. We then invited Islington's Women's Equality Unit and Race

Equality Unit to facilitate focus groups, on the basis of a short questionnaire, with members of the community they judged not to have been involved in the Local Agenda 21 process. In trying to reach individuals and groups whose priorities had until then not been addressed, the intention was to create informal, discursive spaces, guided by an agreed facilitator, to decide on key concerns. Most of the focus groups featured individuals not active in voluntary organizations, and took place at locations in the community (such as local cultural centres). Between September 1996 and February 1997 six of these deliberative sessions took place with the following groups: unemployed women, Greek-Cypriot women, Chinese women, the Islington Pensioners Forum, the Forum of Ethnic Minority groups in Islington, and Turkish/Kurdish women. Significantly, these focus groups generated concerns which corresponded with borough-wide Agenda 21 forum priorities – such as air pollution, crime and street cleanliness – but they also generated particular issues that might otherwise have been neglected – for example, the availability of council literature in non-English languages and the education of children from ethnic minority groups. The feedback from these focus groups informed the council's sustainability action plan and Islington's Local Agenda 21, while the focus group technique has been incorporated within the former as an ongoing consultative tool for identifying sustainability concerns with groups unlikely to be effectively represented by other mechanisms.[8]

The Whittington Neighbourhood Agenda 21 Group has pioneered a local outreach project to widen participation in its own neighbourhood sustainability plan. Since 1997 this has centred on a community visioning initiative designed to enable local community groups and organizations to engage in discussions about sustainability. It has been explicitly influenced by a variety of visioning models publicized by the UK Community Participation Network, notably 'future search' conferences and 'planning for real' exercises – both geared towards creating shared visions of the future in a non-confrontational way (New Economics Foundation, 1998, pp 39–42; 75–78). Having received external funding, the Whittington project is coordinated by a formal management group, although it still has to rely on substantial voluntary involvement. Visioning has entailed intensive work with selected groups in assisting them to represent their concerns about quality of life. The first local groups to participate were a primary school, an Afro-Caribbean women's group and a youth club, giving an idea of the transferability of the approach. The ultimate aim of the project is to produce a visioning pack, informed by the experience of the visioning sessions, which will serve as a creative resource for local residents in articulating their needs and interests. What makes it particularly noteworthy from an environmental democratic perspective, apart from its bottom-up development via the participation of underrepresented groups, is its aim of identifying common social and environmental interests across the neighbourhood (and beyond; visioning places the neighbourhood in a global sustainability context). As we shall now see, this type of collective needs determination

also applies to local areas where social exclusion and economic marginalization have chronically weakened community networks.

Community-led Regeneration Planning

Environmental democracy offers a principle – the discourse principle – for
determining the fairness of actions and norms – which can be termed 'just'
when all affected persons agree on these actions and norms as participants
in rational dialogue. This places the onus on Local Agenda 21 processes,
which claim to be democratic and deliberative, to demonstrate equal access
to identifying new social and ecological norms of sustainability. Yet, it is
clear that there are sharp asymmetries in society regarding the opportunities
for contributing effectively to such discussion – for example, unequal
distribution of information, civic abilities, time, etc. The most serious, and
most threatening to the well-being of disadvantaged groups, are those deep-
seated material inequalities which have become more pronounced in the
UK in recent years, especially in urban areas. For the poorest 20 per cent of
society, articulating common environmental interests over the long term
is sidelined by everyday survival strategies orientated towards meeting
immediate needs. An unfortunate consequence of this for a deliberative
theory of democracy is that even if institutional opportunities are extended
so that the interests of the poor can be articulated, it is likely that their
expectations will be adjusted downwards because of that deprivation (Sen,
1992, pp 149–150). In other words, sustainability action norms may well
still be skewed to favour the interests of relatively privileged groups with
a greater sense of political possibility.

Although they have a benign view of the effects of market forces on
local environments and communities, Marvin and Guy (1997, p 316) rightly
identify an understanding of extra-local production and consumption cycles
as a conspicuous absence in much urban environmentalism. Islington's
Local Agenda 21, like most in London, has not directly addressed the
challenges to local sustainability strategies arising from the negative social
consequences of capital disinvestment. This seems surprising because the
Labour government has made tackling 'social exclusion' a defining project
during its period in office. A social exclusion unit, reporting directly to the
prime minister, was established in December 1997 to address the enduring
multiple deprivation affecting certain groups and areas. Government
pronouncements on social exclusion have been characterized by a clear
communitarian agenda. Community voluntarism, as represented by 'social
entrepreneurs', has been promoted as empowering disadvantaged people
– developing associative networks as a result of the failure of both the
market and the state to meet local needs. The emphasis is on an 'ethic of
responsibility' and avoiding welfare dependency, allied with a scepticism
of redistributional programmes.

Islington, like most inner London boroughs, has areas of high deprivation – neighbourhoods with inadequate housing, high crime, stubborn long-term unemployment and poor amenities. One of the first priorities of the social exclusion unit was to develop integrated and sustainable approaches to solving the problems of the 1370 'worst estates' in England, seeking examples of innovative neighbourhood strategies designed to involve the private and voluntary sectors. Since the preliminary identification of the 'worst estates' focused on tenure characteristics of accommodation, the most deprived areas were associated, above all, with concentrations of council (social) housing, with London having the highest share of deprived council estates (Lee and Murie, 1998, p 91). In Islington, south Tollington Neighbourhood contains the largest concentration of social housing in the borough – over 1600 residential units, housing 5500 people, centred on the Andover and Six Acres estates. This area has for some time faced severe social and environmental problems. The indicators of multiple deprivation are alarming. Over 50 per cent of adult residents are economically inactive (through unemployment, long-term illness or disability), 44 per cent of households are in receipt of welfare support, and there is double the London average for lone parent families (Thake, 1998, p 8). The physical conditions of the estates are poor, compounded by vandalism, graffiti and the abandonment of communal spaces. Camden and Islington health authority found high levels of heroin and crack cocaine use and dealing, feeding rampant juvenile crime. For vulnerable groups, such as the elderly, one consequence is widespread fear and depression.

However, though dissatisfaction with the local authority is rife, community bonds have not completely fractured. Tenant associations, youth and senior groups, and other informal networks have maintained important neighbourhhood links. When invited by Islington Council to investigate with the residents and other relevant bodies possible ways of regenerating the area, the University of North London decided, firstly, to undertake a community planning exercise; this provided the means for residents discursively to articulate their concerns and suggestions. As a participatory tool, community or action planning involves the structured facilitation of community discussion on physical planning and urban design issues (New Economics Foundation, 1998, pp 11–14). The Tollington community planning week, covering two weekends in January 1998, employed a multidisciplinary team of facilitators to enable resident deliberation on a series of topics. These 15 workshops covered living on the estates (children/youth, elderly, disabled, ethnic minorities), life outside the home (culture and religion, leisure and recreation, health, community care, alcohol and drugs), education (early years to secondary, adult, special needs/out of school), and work (unemployment and training, voluntary action, economic activity). Workshops were open to all, as were participatory design sessions based upon a model and large map of the area, which allowed residents to attach written suggestions without having to engage in debate. This last technique illustrates the need to include those not wishing, at that time, to present their views verbally. Community planning techniques strive to avoid listening only to the confident and articulate.

The community planning week set in motion a series of follow-up consultative activities in the Tollington area – questionnaires, interviews, focus groups – organized by six theme groups (children and families, quality of life, lifetime learning, economic activity, physical issues, governance). Just as Islington Agenda 21 highlighted the need to assist underrepresented groups to express their concerns, so – on a larger scale – the Tollington initiative arranged outreach events to hear those voices, such as a children's day and sessions with black and ethnic minority residents. Within Islington, Tollington Neighbourhood has the highest proportion of ethnic minority residents (30 per cent of the local population), with the local authority allocating social housing in recent years to refugees from Somalia and Eritrea. Underinvestment in the Andover and Six Acres estates, coupled with economic disenfranchisement and social dislocation for many residents, has helped to stir up racism towards the recent African arrivals as well as other minority groups. One of the most important contributions of the Tollington initiative to combat the presence of such destructive social attitudes has been to carry out a contemporary history project based upon the self-descriptions of a diverse group of residents. While this has revealed a profound sense of helplessness (Thake, 1998, p 8), it has, nevertheless, created a valuable community resource for recognizing, and making sense of, the richness of residents' biographies and cultural ties. It may be merely a modest step to enable the construction of a shared sense of place; but, like the wider planning initiative itself, its role in rebuilding community solidarity promises to be positive.

There is still one obvious precondition – that the communities living on the Andover and Six Acre estates are able to take a meaningful part in the regeneration of their neighbourhood. In summer 1998, following the extensive consultation and dialogue with residents and other actors, the university was able to present a masterplan for regeneration of south Tollington. The major institutional innovation proposed was to create a partnership comprising residents' representatives, Islington Council, the local health authority, the police, business representatives and the voluntary sector. If approved in a local referendum, the idea is that this Tollington partnership would be delegated the authority from national and local government to coordinate substantial physical investment in the housing stock and physical infrastructure of the area. It would also oversee a diversification of service delivery agencies – each accountable to a local user committee – responsible for housing repairs and maintenance, health services, youth and elderly services, and training. It was recognized that resident participation in the partnership would have to be supported by a community capacity-building programme to strengthen and extend neigh-bourhood-based associative activity. An autonomous community associ-ation was suggested as the umbrella body for facilitating the participation of local residents, commanding an independent income base from the

commercial development of underutilized estate assets – such as the allocation of some housing units to workshop use and the sale of parking
franchises. Indeed, it would be a responsibility of the Tollington partnership
to encourage new businesses in the area, where possible meeting the
training and employment needs of local residents.

The Tollington proposals for self-directed community renewal, still to
be endorsed by the local authority and dependent upon grant support either
from central government or the European Union, are not without precedent
in London. Other social housing estates in the capital, such as Broadwater
Farm in Haringey and Lea View in Hackney, have seen successful regeneration projects featuring community participation and regeneration partnerships. However, the Tollington initiative has generated crucial questions
about local governance, which have exposed limitations to the official
discourse of social exclusion. The six months of consultation and community
dialogue leading up to the Tollington regeneration proposals broadened
the project beyond a focus on the 'worst estates' in terms of social housing.
The social and environmental concerns recorded revealed a knowledgeable
local population anxious to reclaim control of their life opportunities and
quality. In attaching deprivation indicators too readily to social housing
concentrations, the Labour government fell prey to stereotypical views of
'problem' or 'sink' estates (Lee and Murie, 1998), and were divorced from
appreciating the role of structural economic and social inequalities. For all
the rhetoric of community involvement and fairness, the national social
exclusion agenda labours under moralistic assumptions about 'perverse
incentives' which undermine individual responsibility, rather than engaging
with the relations of gender, class and racial domination which breed
antagonistic social relations. To do so would be to radicalize a social
exclusion debate so far silent on relations of power.

The step in this direction represented by the Tollington initiative is
linking democratic needs determination with institutional prescriptions for
community empowerment. This moves us back to the question of devolved
decision-making, though community-led regeneration planning points to
instances where civic self-determination requires strategic support and
community capacity-building. It usefully corrects the tendency of Local
Agenda 21 planning processes to assume that all citizens are on a level
playing-field regarding their ability to express, individually and collectively,
their social and ecological interests. Above all, it demonstrates that community voluntarism, faithful to the discourse principle, will require formal
institutional support for those people underrepresented by existing associative networks. For the state this presents far-reaching challenges – negotiating rights and responsibilities between communities and government, and
working out new relationships between representative and participative
governance structures: in short, what Stephen Thake (1995, p 72) terms the
need for a new democratic settlement. The proponents of social inclusion
have still to grasp this nettle.

CONCLUSION

This chapter has made extended reference to a variety of deliberative democratic forms orientated towards enabling local populations to identify common social and ecological interests – Local Agenda 21 forums and working groups, neighbourhood forums, focus groups, community visioning and community planning. Most of these have operated as temporary consultative structures designed to supplement existing local representative polities, although the Islington Neighbourhood system institutionalizes some degree of resident participation in decision-making over local service delivery. And in the context of a Labour commitment to democratic renewal, for the first time in years a national government has declared an interest in creating a political infrastructure which supports these local experiments in participatory practice. However, those anticipating a far-reaching democratization of local government may well be disappointed. In spite of Labour's strong rhetorical commitment to community involvement, including the UK Local Agenda 21 process, the government seems to be drawing back from anything which implies the local devolution of political power. Even in London, with a new capital-wide authority imminent and borough councils likely to have a greater executive decision-making autonomy, the creation of urban parish councils is looking less and less likely – even if, as in Islington, there has been local authority and citizen support for such a move, especially in the area of environmental decision-making.

What this means is that the potential for developing local environmental democracy has become lop-sided in metropolitan areas. On the one hand, there is a flurry of associative activity in civil society which communicates public social and ecological concerns, and is likely to be strengthened by a new statutory duty on councils to consult with their populations as well as a power to hold local referenda. In addition, the duty on councils to promote the economic, social and environmental well-being of their areas promises to make them more receptive to proposals for improving urban sustainability. On the other hand, though, the programme for the 'radical' modernization of local government presented by the Labour government relegates decentralization to the status of one of several political management options available to councils. The new models for local governance designed to give a bigger say to local people – a directly elected mayor with a cabinet, a cabinet and council-elected leader, and a directly elected mayor and council manager – are designed to be compatible with delegating executive responsibilities to council officers who act under guidance from local councillors and/or a neighbourhood forum (Department of the Environment, Transport and the Regions, 1998c, 3.48). However, there is no proposal for devolving political authority in urban areas where local communities have expressed a preference for more direct participation in decisions affecting their interests. The heightened democratic expectations arising from Local Agenda 21 exercises may not be satisfied by reforms rooted so firmly within representative notions of political governance.

Yet, this is perhaps why Labour is more comfortable with a communitarian agenda that is more explicit about responsibilities than rights. Such an agenda enjoins people to become engaged in voluntary initiatives – such as Local Agenda 21 – to improve the environmental well-being of their communities, but without the necessary means to steer productive and consumptive activities within their localities (for example, through devolved authority over planning, transport and economic development). The democratic identification of local social and ecological needs over the long term only becomes viable if communities are able to make collectively binding decisions to those ends. For those disadvantaged and vulnerable groups in particular who are typically frozen out of the political market place of competing demands, only the institutionalization of participatory structures with real decision-making authority (such as that envisaged for the Tollington partnership) is likely to secure them an effective input into the decisions affecting their life chances and quality of living. Taking deliberative and democratic norms seriously at the local level means being prepared to redistribute power.

Conclusion: Global Environmental Democracy

The previous chapters have elaborated upon the notion of environmental democracy, combining theoretical and empirical claims across a range of examples where environmental interests have been developed with explicit reference to participatory democratic norms. Environmental democracy as an *explanatory* term proposes that those existing democratic practices and institutions which further environmentalist ideas in an inclusive manner are more likely than market-based or bureaucratic decision-making models to generate decisions which are strongly responsive to social and ecological concerns. Informed by local knowledge and experience, they actively transform environmental preferences through open communication in order to reveal shared interests. They are also more likely to lead to durable commitments to environmental sustainability insofar as decisions significantly affecting community interests are 'owned' by those involved. Today, the political scope for extending such collective decision-making remains to be seen. The institutional tendencies towards environmental democracy summarized at the state level in Chapter 2 are still emerging, even for those European neocorporatist countries judged to have come furthest. The full social and ecological effects of decision-making which approximate environmental democracy will only become apparent in the early decades of the 21st century if, firstly, its institutional forms are generalized and if, secondly, an uptake of quality-of-life measures generates more systematic analyses of the causal links between institutional structures and decision outcomes.

This presumes that current tendencies towards environmental democracy are at least maintained – in other words, allowed political space to demonstrate their positive social and ecological value to citizens. Even for the advanced liberal democracies of the global North, where the benefits of extending participatory decision-making are expected to be registered by large constituencies, this is not, of course, guaranteed. The interaction of biophysical and social systems, managed through the unpredictable bargaining and negotiation of political elites, generates numerous uncertainties, forever recasting environmental interests in the light of contingent events. It is sobering that none of the case studies, all selected initially as promising forms of collective communication favouring environmental democracy norms, have so far triggered a meaningful governmental commitment to the one common political goal they all share: the decentralization of environmental decision-making authority – whether in terms of rural land use (Chapters 3 and 4), urban community planning (Chapter 6) or the workplace (Chapter 5). Since neither the Canadian nor the UK political systems qualify as 'ecological corporatist' according to the structuralist perspective in Chapter 2, so extra attention must be given to individual environmental democratic forms, as in the case studies, and their relationship to wider state regimes. These case studies assessed the concrete arguments and practices for generalizing environmental interests and, as a preliminary selection, indicated the diversity of participatory forms encompassed by the notion of environmental democracy.

There is scope for much work investigating the explanatory relevance of environmental democracy at the national and subnational level. As noted in this book's introduction, the case studies discussed in this work are not necessarily representative of environmental democracy. They are particular networks of social interaction, from formal institutional to voluntarist, that claim to be faithful to the discourse principle – equal respect for all. Taking this principle seriously entails accounting for practical instances where the principle informs action, and evaluating these examples according to its own demanding criteria of impartiality and inclusiveness. This book has attempted to do this with the case studies, trying to remain sensitive to their different contexts of action, while also maintaining that the discourse principle carries a universalist *normative* message concerning environmental interests. It holds that civic self-determination – as opposed to, say, elite political bargaining or market choices – is the most legitimate means of generalizing environmental interests in a democratic fashion. As a political project, this points to the strengthening of citizen autonomy in decision-making by extending existing liberal rights to encompass the social and ecological conditions of democratic communication. Environmental democracy is located at the convergence of (human) environmental rights and deliberative procedures of decision-making.

The normative evaluation of the participatory forms covered in Chapters 2 to 6 addressed, above all, the *moral* justification of their environmental choices – the democratic legitimacy of state-led or sponsored environmental decision-making judged fairly according to all relevant interests (Chapters 2 and 3); and the potential role of nongovernmental action in furthering societal norms of equal treatment by representing views otherwise neglected by dominant groups. For the former, those institutional conditions surveyed at the state level (Chapter 2) highlighted various ways of constructing and considering shared environmental interests, while Chapter 3 covered an impressive Canadian exercise in environmental deliberation that operationalized notions of administrative fairness. In terms of nongovernmental action, the case studies are, again, not indicative of all those environmental interests which would otherwise fall by the political wayside without collective political mobilization. However, they do suggest the range of such concerns – wilderness values (Chapter 4), workplace-related environmental health (Chapter 5) and quality of life in inner-city communities (Chapter 6). Within

the real world of power politics, it would be naive to expect the nongovernmental groups which promote such interests to be free of strategic motives
or organizational hierarchies. After all, their environmental justice credentials
rest both on their commitment to egalitarian (social and ecological) objectives and their *effectiveness* in achieving these. The chapters scrutinizing the
moral discourse of wilderness preservation groups, organized labour and
urban community groups found differing strengths and weaknesses in their
various normative claims. What is beyond doubt is that each instance of
collective action advances vital environmental interests.

Up to this point, this book's concern has been with environmental
democracy in several advanced capitalist countries, partly as a methodological choice reflecting my own geographical location as a researcher but
also because the liberal democracies of the global North are associated with
the deepest institutionalization of environmental decision-making (related,
of course, to their advanced stage of industrialization and historic legacy
of environmental despoliation) and the existence of political cultures open,
at least in principle, to the expression of environmental concerns. In other
words, there are established democratic institutions and standards of
fairness which suggest the possibility of transforming social preferences
towards a more inclusive and effective consideration of environmental
interests. However, if the discourse principle embodies a moral universalism, this must extend to all humanity, regardless of political boundaries.
While citizenship is overwhelmingly associated with membership of nation-
states, environmental democracy should also make sense for civic self-
determination between and through states.

After first examining the relationships between countries and the more
diffuse notion of global civil society, this Conclusion examines how the
democratization of state and market sovereignty gives a global purchase
to environmental democracy. A return to the Burmese case outlined at the
beginning of the book marks out at least one transnational strategy for
furthering human environmental rights, recasting democratic accountability
in a way that makes demands on us all as citizens and consumers.

INTERNATIONAL ENVIRONMENTAL REGIMES AND GLOBAL CIVIL SOCIETY

Behind the rapid growth in recent years of international environmental
agreements is the realization among many states that current human activities generate ecologically damaging effects which, at their most severe,
are disrupting those life-support systems upon which we all depend. In
particular, we can point to the rapid depletion of global biodiversity and
productive land, as well as the overexploitation of common environmental
'sinks' – the waste absorption function of global atmospheric and hydrological
systems. Scientific understanding of global environmental degradation has

advanced to the point where there is a strong consensus about the transboundary effects triggered, for example, by chlorofluorocarbons or rising greenhouse gas emissions, even though there are still uncertainties about precise causal pathways. Prompted above all by environmental interest groups, the liberal democracies of the global North have perceived the need for coordinated action to address these environmental challenges. There is also no doubt a strategic appreciation among these states that, in an interdependent world, the offloading of environmental costs across borders is a potential source of serious geopolitical tensions.

Over the past 15 years, research on global environmental cooperation has been dominated by regime analysis which, following the influential formulation of Stephen Krasner (1983, p 2), has addressed the principles, norms, rules and decision-making procedures shaping actors' interactions in various environmental issue areas. These issue areas may be defined by their geographical extent, jurisdictional attributes and nature of resource use. Regime analysis encompasses work both on the explicit rule systems structuring environmental treaties (for example, Mitchell, 1994, on international oil pollution conventions), as well as a recognition of the role of implicit principles and norms governing actor behaviour in international environmental decision-making (Vogler, 1995). A recent survey of the field notes its theoretical heterogeneity and pragmatic orientation, offering a broad range of explanations for the processes underlying regime formation, transformation and effectiveness (Stokke, 1997). There is no space here to convey the richness of this research; instead this chapter will highlight that branch of regime analysis – labelled 'process-oriented' regime theory – that I take to be most sympathetic to the conceptual framework of environmental democracy. In its sensitivity to situational context and the intersubjective nature of regimes, the process-oriented approach investigates how environmental regimes collectively define and transform environmental interests.

Where might the discourse principle of environmental democracy enter here? Between states negotiating international environmental agreements, there are clearly relevant questions about procedural fairness. Whatever the ecological problem generating the need for collective action, deliberation and negotiation over environmental norms rely upon the voluntary consent of sovereign states: hence the crucial importance of legitimacy – whether those states affected by proposed new international rules see themselves as obliged by them according to sound reasons rather than coercive ones (Stokke, 1997, p 48). The more the procedures shaping a suggested new environmental regime are open, inclusive and based upon consent between all affected sovereign states, the more new agreed obligations can claim to embody procedural fairness. However, these demanding procedural requirements carry the danger that the only collective measures agreed upon will be limited to those acceptable to the least enthusiastic party – what Underdal calls the 'law of the least ambitious programme' (1997, p 254). In practice, as regime analysts have shown, this has meant an increasing emphasis in international environmental regimes on nonbinding instruments (informal agreements, voluntary protocols and resolutions) and 'escape clauses', which they have welcomed as incorporating a necessary flexibility into environmental agreements, enabling regimes to be more inclusive over the long term (Raustiala and Victor, 1998, pp 693–694).

Whether inclusive environmental regimes are also 'effective' – in terms of positive behavioural change and ecological outcomes – has been a central question for regime analysis; given the recent creation of most of these regimes, the conclusions are as yet inconclusive. The explanatory value of the discourse principle thus lies not only in exploring the causal significance of procedural fairness in promoting voluntary consent but also the equitability of outcomes – whether an environmental agreement is perceived by those affected parties as distributing fairly the costs and benefits of signing up. For global environmental regimes, this is typically the greatest challenge, in particular allocating burdens of compliance between the advanced industrialized countries and the rest of the world. In the Montreal Protocol (on stratospheric ozone depletion), for example, a multilateral ozone fund and technology transfer agreement, allied with compliance delay rights for developing countries, is designed to ensure fair compliance conditions (Vogler, 1995, pp 127–136). For the United Nations Framework Convention on Climate Change, the historical responsibility of advanced industrialized countries in producing the bulk of greenhouse gas emissions is recognized by their onus to reduce emissions. All international environmental regimes are, of course, shot through with strategic power considerations. The discourse principle can serve as a critical tool in uncovering the role of sectional interests in unfairly skewing compliance tasks and responsibilities.

Application of the discourse principle to environmental regimes raises, in addition, the obligation actively to involve nonstate actors in negotiating and implementing environmental agreements. If the democratic legitimacy of environmental norms rests on their exposure to the consent of significantly affected parties, there is no logical reason to exclude nongovernmental groups which represent transnational interests. To be sure, only states are the formal signatories to international treaties. States are the sovereign actors at the international level, with the legal responsibility to represent their respective jurisdictions in regime negotiations, and then to implement agreed treaties through their own domestic political and administrative systems. Nation states therefore remain powerful actors in international environmental policy-making (Economy and Schreurs, 1997), which is reflected in the state-centred perspective of most regime analysis.

At the same time, however, process-oriented regime theorists have started to detail the activities of nonstate actors in shaping environmental regimes. Multinational corporations are an important source of political lobbying across national boundaries, although there is a divergence of opinion on how far the internationalization of economic activity has extended their global political influence. The question of corporate social and ecological accountability will be returned to later. More space has been devoted in regime analysis to the role of nongovernmental environmental groups in transforming international environmental agreements through mobilizing public opinion. The shift to a preservationist stance within the International Convention for the Regulation of Whaling and the 1993 London Convention ban on the dumping at sea of radioactive waste are examples of such influence (Vogler, 1995, pp 51–64). Less well known is the potential role of nongovernmental organizations in implementing environmental regimes through compliance monitoring – for example, the work of the World Wildlife Fund, which feeds monitoring information to the Convention on International Trade in Endangered Species of Wild Fauna and Flora.

Recent research on environmental regime implementation undertaken by the International Institute for Applied Systems Analysis (IIASA) has shown that even though environmental interest groups are increasingly participating in negotiating international environmental commitments, facilitated by greater procedural access, their input is proving difficult to maintain at the implementation stage. They often lack the resources and technical capability to track policy and behavioural responses to new environmental norms (Victor, Raustiala and Skolnikoff, 1998, pp 23–24). The overlap here with the participatory intent of environmental democracy is in explaining the nature of nonstate actor involvement in regime formation and implementation, with the aim of recommending ways of encouraging more inclusive and deliberative structures. Many international environmental agreements now rely upon the early and close participation of 'target groups' – those sectional interests (typically corporations) directly affected by new rules and norms – in their negotiation, with the risk that government commitments to collective ecological benefits are diluted to assuage target group concerns about regulatory burdens. A key finding of the IIASA work across many environmental regimes is that the effectiveness of international commitments is enhanced when target group involvement is counterbalanced by the participation of public interest groups (Victor, Raustiala and Skolnikoff, 1998, p 310).

Of course, this involvement would be encouraged over the long term by the formal recognition of participation rights for nongovernmental organizations (NGOs) in global environmental governance. Progress has already been made in strengthening the consultative status of NGOs in intergovernmental decision-making forums. The United Nations Conference on Environment and Development in 1992 is often cited as a catalyst in this respect, where NGO networking and financial support enabled 1400 NGOs to attend the conference as UN-recognized participants. Furthermore, Chapter 27 of Agenda 21 – the programme of sustainable development agreed upon at the conference – endorsed an enhanced role for NGOs in developing and implementing policy actions at all scales. And since the Rio meeting, NGO input in intergovernmental implementation of sustainability actions has been formalized through the NGO steering committee of the UN Commission on Sustainable Development (Mucke, 1997). These advances made in environmental NGO representation have set the agenda for a review within the United Nations system of the role of NGOs in intergovernmental decision-making. Formal consultative status for international NGOs has been available since 1968 through accreditation by the UN Economic and Social Council, but this mechanism has not been widely employed until recently. UN consultative status is accorded to those NGOs of 'international standing' who are representative of relevant fields of competence and are democratically constituted. This has thrown up questions about representative parity in the UN system between Northern NGOs and those resource-poor groups from the global South often struggling to survive in hostile domestic political contexts. Regional criteria for NGO representation, such as those developed by the Commission on Sustainable Development, present one way of guaranteeing Southern NGO input into intergovernmental forums; however, there remain unresolved questions concerning NGO capacity-building in the global South.

At the global level, NGOs are advancing the democratization of environmental governance. They are clearly opening up deliberation on environmental norms, transposing domestic techniques of public mobilization across national borders. Their growing consultative status in international environmental forums is allowing them to disseminate important information and hold (inter)governmental institutions accountable to the public (Bichsel, 1996, p 252). Some place them at the vanguard of a new global civil society – the space of voluntary activity in pursuit of collective aims below and across state boundaries (Wapner, 1997, p 66). Associative activity is no longer confined to domestic political contexts; for example, global electronic communications networks are extending social dialogue on environmental interests across the planet. There are also other nonstate actors actively discussing social and ecological concerns – for example, the so-called 'epistemic communities' of experts and scientists addressing environmental problems in a professional fashion, often feeding into intergovernmental decision-making forums. However, it is, above all, the social justice-oriented NGOs who do the most to make good, in global civil society, the environmental democratic principle that environmental norms are generalized by means of a noncoercive discourse open to all affected parties. They apply the democratic criteria of transparency, accountability and inclusiveness to promote the transformation of collective environmental preferences.

Regime analysts have proposed an internal connection between democratic legitimacy and regime effectiveness that is consistent with the communicative thrust of environmental democracy. To recall from Chapter 1, deliberative structures and practices are encouraged by the interplay of participatory decision-making with the open expression of collective preferences in civil society. Oran Young (1997, pp 291–299) presents a similar thesis at the level of global governance, suggesting that the success of international and transnational environmental agreements is, to a large extent, a question of the interplay of regime structures and the effective participation of nonstate actors. This holds, he claims, across many different regime areas for the same overarching reasons relayed in Chapter 1 – that open and inclusive dialogue about environmental interests brings more information, motivation and understanding to the decision-making forum. Again, there are no guarantees that ecologically rational outcomes will result; but the contention of regime theorists is that the liberal democratic states offer the most promising political framework conditions for global environmental management challenges:

> *Compared with cooperation involving nonliberal states, [environmental] cooperation among liberal states is* deeper, *in the sense of involving greater attention to domestic activities,* more demanding, *in terms of substantive commitments, and* more intrusive, *in that cooperation among liberal states is more likely to feature scrutiny behind the border as well as limitations on the externalities that liberal states can impose on each other (Raustiala and Victor, 1998, p 697).*

Any triumphalist note that this thesis might strike is soon silenced by the recognition that this achievement is relative, and that liberal states still have far to go to realize their incipient tendencies towards environmental democracy. The demanding challenges to democratizing global environmental governance posed by state and market sovereignty will now be outlined, but in a way that suggests that they are by no means intractable.

HUMAN RIGHTS AND GLOBAL ENVIRONMENTAL DEMOCRACY

Environmental democracy expresses at its centre the notion that collective decision-making with environmental implications is a matter of open and inclusive deliberation; that the impartiality of this decision-making is best expressed by a range of citizenship rights; and that, in order sustainably to support citizen self-determination, these rights must include socially and ecologically secure living conditions. Chapter 1 outlined the case for such human environmental rights, noting how this implies a universal application to a common humanity in line with existing human rights discourse. The idea of universal civil and political rights already has legal currency in the international community (the International Covenant on Civil and Political Rights entered into force in 1976); and, as Ingram notes, even if states disagree in their interpretation of rights, they nevertheless 'share a practice of intersocietal evaluation in human rights terms' (1994, p 200). The argument here is that this shared space of intelligibility is the basis for advancing an environmental rights project – one therefore resonant with existing norms of international justice but which extends these norms in an ecological and social direction.

International law, as embodied both in customary behaviour between states and their collective interpretation of treaties, already recognizes democratic rules and norms as the most legitimate justification for systems of governance (Franck, 1991). The 'right to democratic governance' is increasingly informing the architecture of international environmental regimes – for example, as noted above, through the rule of voluntary consent for states and the participation of nongovernmental groups. International environmental law is by no means a clear-cut field. The recent growth in environmental treaties alone has fast been generating new rights and obligations; and to these we must add the more diffuse body of 'soft law' comprising legally nonbinding but influential resolutions, declarations and principles (Caldwell, 1996, p 148). While treaties tend to be issue-specific, they may well make reference to, and develop, the environmental obligations expressed in soft environmental law. One such norm is the precautionary principle – the obligation on states to address threats of serious environmental damage even if there is a lack of full scientific certainty regarding causal pathways. This principle is now incorporated within several international environmental conventions, pushing forward a preventative norm of environmental protection. Cameron (1994) observes in the development of the precautionary principle the articulation of a transnational environmental interest, autonomous from state-centric concerns and the cost-benefit criteria of private investment decisions. If environmental rights and obligations are to assume transnational legal authority, converging with an inclusive human rights discourse, they must nevertheless engage with these major ordering principles of international society – in other words, the dominant norms of state sovereignty and market sovereignty.

State Sovereignty

The development of international law is still based on the mutual recognition between states of exclusive political autonomy over the populations within their own territories, along with their rights and obligations as members of the international community. States participate in international treaty-making as holders of 'sovereign rights' regarding their entitlements to political authority (Young, 1997, p 7). International environmental norms, in order to become legally binding, must therefore be accepted by sovereign states within this international system. Much has been made of the tension between state sovereignty and the transboundary scale of serious environmental problems – whether originating within or outside national borders. Global environmental democracy suggests the need for collective decision-making forums to defend ecologically and socially secure living conditions across borders, with the distinct possibility that state sovereign rights might sometimes have to defer to environmental ones. Yet, all international environmental regimes accept the dominant fact of state sovereignty, typically relying upon the domestic political authority of states to implement agreed actions. At the same time, while state sovereignty might seem to adhere to the discourse principle on one level – recognizing other states as equals in international law – this is not the inclusive moral community envisaged by environmental democracy. The international system accords sovereign rights only to nation states, and those states give citizenship rights only to their own inhabitants. The criteria for including states as members of international society, and citizens as members of states, are not those of the discourse principle – 'all affected interests' – but those of a territorially defined community.

How, then, can we recast state sovereignty in discursive democratic terms? As mentioned at the end of Chapter 4, the discourse principle supports an alternative 'procedural' notion of sovereignty that is not fixed by location or territory, but refers to democratic justification – whether collective decision-making authority is anchored in processes of free and inclusive deliberation (Habermas, 1996, pp 486–490). Within their borders, therefore, the expectation on nation states is that political authority is only legitimate if it is clearly related to participatory procedures of collective decision-making. This is not to argue that sovereignty becomes detached from the state, but that the connection assumes an unambiguous moral basis. States will long remain the foremost law-making authorities within international society; but by recasting arguments for sovereign rights in procedural democratic terms, there are less convincing political reasons for them to avoid responsibility for exercising sovereignty collectively in international environmental decision-making. If the discourse principle spells out in an environmental issue area that the equitable participation of all affected parties encompasses various state and nonstate actors crossing over sovereign jurisdictions, the onus is on democratic polities to cooperate effectively.

There are many different suggestions for democratizing international environmental decision-making, and there is no space here to assess the competing blueprints. However, the general characteristics of global governing institutions which are consistent with the participatory intent of environmental democracy may be broadly stated. One strength of the current structure of international environmental regimes, focused as they are on specific issue areas, is that they constitute a flexible, decentralized system of administrative arrangements able to specialize in the problems identified (Young, 1997, p 279). The marriage of *decentralization* with the communicative expression of environmental interests has been a recurring theme throughout this book. Those collective decision-making systems responsive to locally expressed social and ecological preferences are in a better position to address the causes and impacts of environmental degradation than are hierarchical bureaucratic forms or the abrogation of political responsibility through private market choices. At the international level, this endorses the current trend for environmental regimes to be more open and inclusive; and the most effective way to further that democratic space is the entrenchment of human environmental rights in international law, applying to all institutional loci of collective decision-making with environmental implications. Commentators have noted the growing acceptance of environmental rights by state authorities, particularly as embodied in international environmental agreements (Cameron and Mackenzie, 1996). Furthermore, as noted in Chapter 1, the extension of generic human rights to environmental protection gives a strong moral authority to those general interests agreed by democratic communities to be necessary for human well-being. Locating these claims in human rights discourse, and emerging (binding) principles of international law, is perhaps the only means in the foreseeable future where environmental interests could conceivably impinge upon state sovereignty.

The recognition of environmental rights in international law would have to be accompanied by improved mechanisms for democratic accountability within the United Nations system. David Held's (1995, pp 267–286) proposals for democratizing intergovernmental institutions deserve consideration in this context, since they are explicitly informed by a rights-based, participatory notion of global governance. His 'cosmopolitan model' of democracy includes numerous recommendations for strengthening the institutional autonomy of the UN as well as establishing new deliberative bodies for interest representation across states – for example, a new independent assembly of democratic peoples (serving initially as a 'second chamber' to the UN General Assembly) and a network of directly elected continental parliaments. The legal recognition of environmental interests could be enhanced by a revived UN environment system (with a broader remit covering the human and nonhuman environment) that operates in a decentralized manner to address the concerns raised by the continental democratic assemblies – perhaps by linking these assemblies with UN regional commissions (see Vavrousek, 1995). Held envisages a deliberative, inclusive structure for the new global bodies and, in line with the arguments of earlier chapters in this book, points out that their embrace of participatory norms can be informed by, and complement, the deepening of democracy at local levels. The two are mutually reinforcing paths to the democratic conditioning of state sovereignty.

Institutional recommendations for global environmental democracy, in promoting the noncoercive resolution of social and ecological interests, cannot also avoid addressing the historical association of state sovereignty with a territorial monopoly over military security. International environmental agreements testify to the importance of interstate cooperation and the employment of peaceful instruments in tackling ecological problems, along with their social consequences. The proposition of the regime theorists that there is an internal connection between liberal political systems and effective environmental cooperation rests, in part, on the assumption that liberal democracies are essentially pacific, resorting to military force only as a means of self-defence or under UN auspices (as both justified in international law). Liberal states, self-defined as rights-protective and democratic, make a claim to strong observance of nonaggression in the international system. It may be that this 'pacific liberalism' has only been achieved historically by military conquest and coercive policies (Mann, 1996), and there is surely a moral responsibility on these countries to lay open their involvement in past militarism; but this does not irreparably compromise the liberal discourse of human rights and democracy: 'It is a mistake to throw out the language of self-determination and autonomy because of its contingent association with historical configurations of Western power' (Held, 1995, p 282). Indeed, the opposite is the case.

For the project of environmental democracy, the political priority regarding state sovereign rights to the use of force is to place them in a broader context of global security, attuned as much to the security of people and the environment as the traditional focus on state security (Commission on Global Governance, 1995, pp 78–85). The independent Commission on Global Governance has shown how this expands on norms of international security by recognizing human rights to secure living conditions, which, of course, agrees with the core notion of environmental rights advanced in this study. Geopolitical tensions over environmental resources and pollution are likely to be major sources of conflict in the 21st century. Given global ecological interdependence, there is an immediate need to integrate environmental considerations within the UN system of collective security. And in accord with many green arguments, there is a need to promote demilitarization of the international community, including, of course, nuclear disarmament.

International acceptance of the universal human right to socially and ecologically secure living conditions would question the monopoly of states to determine security priorities. Among the reforms to the UN system recommended by the Commission on Global Governance in order to establish a preventative approach to collective security, two reforms challenge state sovereignty – the proposal, firstly, that the UN charter is revised to allow a more representative security council to authorize intervention *within* countries if the security of their people is being violated extensively, and, secondly, that nonstate actors are given the right to petition the UN Security Council to address grave threats to social and ecological security (Commission on Global Governance, 1995, pp 88–93, 260–263). Both proposals would restrict the scope of state sovereign rights to non-intervention in their affairs, but are wholly consistent with accepting a global human right to a secure existence. A right of petition would formally recognize that nonstate actors may sometimes represent the security interests of citizens against their domestic political authorities (even if the latter claim to be democratic). It therefore identifies more generally the important role of global civil society in feeding social and ecological concerns into intergovernmental forums. Human rights and environmental interest groups have often exposed liberal state complicity in irreversible environmental degradation and military conflict (for example, through arms sales). Any acceptance of an enlarged concept of security by states is likely to be grudging and minimal. The hope is that by opening up the UN system to public security concerns, there will be a reorientation of the global security system from a state-centric preoccupation with external military defence to an acknowledgement that the threats to global political stability arise, as well, from social inequality and ecological risks.

Market Sovereignty

By 'market sovereignty' is meant the economic authority of institutions governed by distinctive proprietary freedoms. A defining feature of liberalism is its association of rights with exclusive forms of property ownership. At its apex is the freedom of individuals to do as they lawfully please – own property, exchange goods and generally conduct economic relations independent of government interference. The state is granted the residual role of protecting property rights and maintaining social order. This in essence continues to be the core ideological belief of free market apologists, and dominates the policy prescriptions of the modern neoliberals. More significantly, the vigorous defence of private property rights and commercial freedoms underpins the increasing global integration of national economic systems which are driven by private investment flows. Recent international agreements on trade liberalization – notably the Uruguay Round of the General Agreement on Tariffs and Trade (GATT) which led in 1994 to the creation of the World Trade Organization (WTO) – have given free trade norms a binding global authority. In this institutional context, the negative libertarian view of rights articulated by economic liberalism, which rejects social and ecological checks on market choices, conflicts with any political project that seeks to realize environmental rights. And unlike state sovereignty, the contractual authority of corporate actors is both less transparent and less accountable to democratic scrutiny.

The central challenge to environmental security arising from inter-national trade is that there is a structural incompatibility between environ-mental regimes and current world trade rules. According to the free market rationale of WTO/GATT, increased trade liberalization motors economic growth through improved efficiencies as countries specialize production in areas where they have a comparative advantage. The anticipation of increased global welfare rests, of course, on the assumption that there are no uncompensated external costs, whether social or ecological. Yet the very expansion of international environmental regimes attests to the growing ecological degradation, and attendant social dislocations, resulting from markets which generate environmental externalities. The core trade rules structuring the WTO/GATT system are the so-called nondiscrimination principles of most-favoured-nation status and the national treatment provision. Their combined effect is to entrench, in international law, equality of treatment for internationally traded products. However, this undermines the ability of democratic governments to introduce environmentally based distinctions in trade policy, discriminating against products deemed to be ecologically harmful (von Moltke, 1997, pp 252–253). To be sure, article XX of GATT, allowing conditional exceptions to WTO/GATT obligations, includes scope for states to appeal to human, animal or plant health and natural-resource conservation reasons to justify trade restrictions, while a committee on trade and environment was established by the WTO in 1994 to integrate international trade and environmental regime rules. In practice, though, the WTO has steadfastly defended the core principle of nondiscrimination, opposing environmental interpretations of article XX (the US cited these provisions in defence of its blanket prohibition on tuna harvested by fishing methods that are destructive to marine mammals – an argument rejected by a GATT dispute resolution panel; see Schoenbaum, 1997, pp 273–280). The alarming result is that the legal authority of all those international environmental regimes with trade-restrictive provisions has been thrown into doubt (Charnovitz, 1996).

Paralleling the liberalization of trade has been the increasing deregulation of international capital markets. Over the past two decades numerous bilateral and regional investment agreements have facilitated a rapid expansion in international capital flows, under the neoliberal assumption that financial liberalization, like free trade, will improve conditions for economic growth. The champions of open investment regimes are, of course, the advanced capitalist countries, constantly seeking new outlets and markets for their powerful financial service sectors. Under their membership of the OECD, the push to establish an all-encompassing global investment regime manifested itself in negotiations over a multilateral agreement on investment, which folded when the French withdrew in October 1998. The multilateral agreement on investment would have imported the nondiscrimination principle from the WTO/GATT system to foreign investment flows, implying legally binding rules over national authorities. This remains the aim of the OECD states, and negotiations over a world investment regime are likely to reemerge within WTO. It is also probable that, like the world trade regime, any multilateral investment agreement will allow exceptions (such as a recurrent US demand in trade policy to buttress its state sovereignty in selected areas), but that these will pay only lip service to environmental concerns (before their collapse, no formal environmental exceptions were agreed upon in the negotiations over the multilateral agreement on investment). With unencumbered market sovereignty planned globally for finance capital, the scope for effective environmental regimes at all scales will certainly be reduced substantially. Financial markets, now dominated by short-term, speculative transactions, will, in that case, continue to operate oblivious to their negative effects on communities and ecological conditions of life.

The challenge to environmental democracy arising from international economic liberalization seems daunting. How can its ubiquitous market rationality be forced to address public environmental concerns? Neoliberal ideology casts the liberalization process as inexorable, properly outside discursive forums and nonmonetary environmental preferences, while even many critics of globalization have fatalistically concluded that there is no alternative. Paul Hirst and Grahame Thompson (1996) have convincingly rejected the claim that the international economy is beyond democratic accountability, drawing attention to the many ways markets and companies still depend upon public authorities, nationally and internationally, to protect commercial freedoms (pp 183–189). Ironically, in the wake of the Asian financial crisis, multinational companies are among the more vocal groups lobbying governments and international regulatory agencies to stabilize exchange rates and capital markets. The fact that international trade and financial agreements extend the role of international law actually reinforces the sovereign legal authority of nation states (Hirst and Thompson, 1996, p 194). If we recognize this interdependence between state sovereignty and commercial rights, then the environmental democratic breaching of market sovereignty becomes a political possibility.

In the first place, *existing* norms of international law theoretically allow states to take unilateral action against economic activity deemed to violate multilateral environmental agreements or even emerging customary environmental principles. The doctrine of 'opposability' enables a state to assert interests recognized as having currency in international society, if not yet incorporated within binding agreements (such as environmental policy actions informed by the precautionary principle). Furthermore, countermeasures taken by a state can be justified against an economic or political agent if that agent, ignoring requests for redress, continues to violate an international environmental norm (such as the doctrine of equitable use of shared water resources). Schoenbaum (1997, pp 299–301) encompasses both under the label 'creative unilateralism' to argue that, subject to clear violations of customary environmental law and rules of proportional action, trade-related restrictions to protect environmental interests are legitimate state actions. To accord with international law, the WTO/GATT system must therefore concede, in principle, the possibility of such unilateral state measures. As a defence of environmental interests, these measures are dependent, of course, upon state sponsorship and an international state system open to the equitable representation of environmental concerns. In reality, strategic motives, both within and between states, often override consideration of social and ecological problems – hence the immediate need to entrench environmental rights in international law. Already, in the increasing spread of international environmental law, and the expression of social and ecological concerns by global civil society, there is increasing scope to support states who are prepared to take a lead in promoting environmental sustainability in international politics. The global recognition of environmental rights would strengthen that possibility.

A second path to making the international economic sphere more accountable to democratic constituencies is the reform of the WTO and the establishment of a new global economic forum. To take the former, the lack of openness and accountability within the WTO has become most obvious with regard to its dispute-resolution mechanism. A number of high-profile WTO dispute-resolution panel rulings have struck down the legality of several US and European environment-related import bans. These panels fall outside acceptable procedural norms of fairness and representation; for example, there are no rights of intervention for interested parties (governmental or nongovernmental) and no structures of public scrutiny for the appointees of the dispute-resolution panels. Even where attention to environmental interests is incorporated within the WTO – through the Committee on Trade and Environment – there has been little progress. The committee has met periodically with environment and development NGOs, who have consistently and unsuccessfully called for permanent access to WTO proceedings. Significantly, prominent WTO member states have now recognized the inability of the WTO to integrate environmental considerations within world trading rules (even though sustainable development is set out as a goal in its founding charter – the 1994 Marrakesh Agreement). Pressure for reform, therefore, comes both from states and global civil society.

The lack of structural links between the WTO and the United Nations system has accentuated the general democratic deficit here. There is no deliberative, inclusive international forum scrutinizing the WTO. In its report, the Commission on Global Governance proposed the creation of a UN economic security council, in part to establish oversight over the WTO and the Bretton Woods institutions (the World Bank and the International Monetary Fund), and also in part to draft a strategic policy framework for integrating environmental interests within the international economic system (Commission on Global Governance, 1995, pp 155–162). The idea of such a forum undercuts the political influence of Western-dominated economic forums (OECD, G8), which is why it is still far from being realized. Whether or not this new international agency is created, moving to a fairer system of global economic deliberation, the immediate imperative remains the environmental democratic reform of the WTO.

Finally, the most important route – albeit the most difficult politically – to bringing the international economic sphere under environmental democratic control is to expose corporations to effective mechanisms of social and ecological accountability. While we might recognize the value of the various voluntary social and ecological auditing schemes subscribed to by companies in relation both to their production processes and products, the discourse principle of environmental democracy stipulates a more universal, binding means to ensure that all parties affected by significant resource allocation decisions are able to negotiate their concerns. David Korten's (1995, pp 308–312) suggestion that a commitment to serving public needs is incorporated within national systems of corporate law, subject to approval and revision by popular referendum or legislative/judicial action, is a first step towards ensuring that environmental rights recognized by states have purchase in the economic sphere. He then recommends a raft of financial instruments to internalize social and environmental costs in production processes, and to foster community enterprises (such as prefer-ential treatment of community banks, worker and community buyout options, environmental taxes). Obviously the taxation of multinational companies can only be successfully coordinated at an international level; likewise, any reform of corporate law to allow worker and community influence on private investment decisions must be locked into an inter-national framework of regulatory authorities and environmental rights-protective law.

The democratic conditioning of market sovereignty in this way is not completely beyond the realms of political possibility. The idea of a global tax on foreign currency transactions (the Tobin tax) to discourage damaging speculative trading is on the agenda, while the Commission on Global Governance (1995, pp 217–221) has recommended charges for the use of the global commons (such as an airline ticket surcharge, ocean fishing user fees and a charge on ocean maritime transport). These new global revenue sources could usefully be channelled, under the guidance of democratic funding bodies, into social development and ecological restoration projects across the world. As noted at the end of Chapter 2, these intermediate support bodies, standing between state institutions and firms, should function at the lowest possible effective level to best meet social and ecological needs. By supporting community enterprises and alternative production systems, they would both democratize and institutionally diversify the economic sphere with existing corporate forms; these forms would be forced to adapt to meet their new legal responsibilities to public-needs determination. Such a project must, of course, be subject to democratic negotiation along the lines of the discourse principle, and within human rights parameters. Going back to the example featured in the Introduction, the next section will show how the liability of transnational private-investment decisions is transformed by taking human environmental rights seriously.

TRANSNATIONAL LIABILITY FOR ENVIRONMENTAL HARM

International liability for environmental harm is a recognized norm of action under customary international law. This was first established by an international tribunal set up in 1935 to arbitrate claims made by the US regarding transboundary pollution damages, traced to the discharges of a metal refinery in western Canada. The ensuing Trail Smelter decision established the legal precedent that states have a duty to prevent serious environmental harm to their neighbours; this was formally adopted as a general liability rule at the 1972 Stockholm Conference on the World Environment (as principle 21 of the Stockholm Declaration; Caldwell, 1996, pp 150–151). It has also been articulated by the International Court of Justice

– the judicial arm of the United Nations – in its Corfu Channel decision and in an advisory opinion on the legality of the threat or use of nuclear weapons (Schoenbaum, 1997, p 300). This harm prevention doctrine is clearly a principle of international liability, pertaining only between sovereign states who are legally responsible for addressing environmental concerns through national policy-making. As Penz (1998) argues, there are structural reasons why even liberal democratic states may not actively protect their citizens against external environmental harm – for example, their willingness to discount trade-related environmental costs for shared economic benefits arising from that trade, or the overriding of harm considerations by strategic interests. Developing the harm principle, therefore, partly depends on communicating more clearly the benefits of harm prevention and promoting a right to compensation of parties who are affected by environmental damage.

It is not difficult to identify occasions where more coercive remedies are necessary, which leads to the notion of state or corporate criminal accountability. Crimes against the environment, as noted by Caldwell (1996, p 153), acquired international saliency following the firing of Kuwaiti oil wells by the Iraqi army during the Gulf War. This revived proposals to create a permanent international criminal court, previously considered in the context of genocide, terrorism and drug trafficking, but now also including environmental criminality. The International Law Commission subsequently developed the proposals for an International Criminal Court (ICC) which, after tortuous negotiations in Rome in mid 1998, led to an enabling treaty signed by 30 countries. The ICC can come into existence only when 60 states have ratified the treaty, which is likely to take several years. It is significant that the US strongly opposed the formation of the ICC, rejecting any incursion on American sovereign powers (American commitment to international law is, at best, inconsistent; for example, in 1986 the US rejected the jurisdiction of the International Court of Justice after the court judged as unlawful the American mining of Nicaraguan ports). Alongside the refusal of China to sign the Rome treaty, the US commitment to challenge the establishment of the ICC presents a substantial obstacle to strengthening human rights across the globe.

It is too early to assess the potential role of the ICC in dealing with environmental crimes. In Rome a compromise on jurisdiction means that only those prosecutions referred by the UN Security Council or by directly affected states will be considered, undermining an International Law Commission recommendation that other parties, including individuals, could submit cases directly to the ICC. Indeed, consistent with environmental democracy would be a recognized human right to corporate or state criminal accountability, according all affected parties who suffer demonstrable (social and ecological) harm a right to a criminal investigation, first at a national level or, if domestic courts are unwilling or unable to act, by the ICC.

The environmental norms seeping into international law have tended originally to come from proposals and debates featuring environmental NGOs, who have directed attention to transboundary ecological problems and their social consequences. These norms typically make a public claim to embrace common environmental interests, justifying associated regulatory prescriptions to protect them from harm. They are presented as being in the interest of all, though international law vests sole responsibility with states to consider their validity and value. In this book the claim has been advanced that the institutionalization of environmental interests by states is more likely to happen effectively if decision-making is deliberative and inclusive. We might also expect those states who internally espouse environmental democracy to assert equitable environmental interests in international political society. What, though, if states are reluctant or unwilling to indicate violations of environmental rights in other jurisdictions? In particular, what if these environmental harms fall within the sphere of transboundary economic activity, where corporations are adept at bypassing high social and ecological standards? The discourse principle makes no distinction between affected parties based on state or market sovereignty. It submits all collectively binding decisions to the same moral test – that their authority is democratically justified only to the extent that all affected parties could rationally agree on them as participants in their formulation. What this means is that states cannot *legally* monopolize the global representation of environmental concerns; these concerns may be better expressed as transnational interests (beyond state borders) rather than as international ones (between states). Is there any space in the state-centric realm of international law for nongovernmental parties to establish a *transnational* liability for environmental rights violations covering individuals, states and corporations?

One emergent area of judicial activity which is receptive to nonstate actors seeking redress for human rights violations under international law is what has become known as 'transnational public law litigation' (Koh, 1991). This entails individuals (and also governments) presenting suits in national courts with extra-jurisdictional content, bringing together domestic and international law, even if both plaintiffs and defendants are nonresidents. As outlined by Koh, transnational public law litigation nominally involves plaintiffs who seek retrospective redress for alleged serious harm, but it also carries an important prospective aim: 'to provoke judicial articulation of a *norm* of transnational law, with an eye towards using that declaration to promote a political settlement in which both governmental and nongovernmental entities will participate' (1991, p 2349). In other words, by asking domestic courts to explain and assert norms of global conduct, this type of legislation can promote the universalization of human rights – including the right to democratic governance. Transnational public law litigation has evolved furthest in the US, activated above all by the Alien Tort Claims Act which has encouraged federal courts to proclaim on violations of customary international norms (Walker, 1997). Of key relevance here, American courts have declared both state and nonstate actors liable under this act. In the latter category, a 1997 preliminary ruling by a Californian federal court, Doe versus Unocal, has for the first time held that the act applies to private corporations (Aceves, 1998; Greer, 1998).

Doe versus Unocal returns us to the construction of the natural gas pipeline in Myanmar (Burma), mentioned in the introduction to this book. The plaintiffs in the case are 14 farmers from the Tenasserim region, bringing a class action against Unocal, Total, Myanma Oil and Gas Enterprise and the military government. Their lawsuit contends that the defendants are responsible for, or complicit in, serious human rights violations associated with developing the Yadana pipeline. These alleged abuses include slave labour, forced relocation, torture and violence against women – all directly undertaken by Myanmar military personnel. The alleged culpability of the oil companies, Unocal and Total, rests on their financing the military to secure the pipeline route and to provide local labour and materials (Aceves, 1998, p 310). Both Unocal and Total have vigorously contested the charges in the lawsuit, claiming that the communities in the vicinity of the pipeline have provided labour willingly and have generally benefited from invest-ment in the region. Significantly, they sought to dismiss the litigation as 'private actors' unconnected from any jurisdiction under the Alien Tort Claims Act, prompting the court in an initial ruling to clarify nonstate liability for violations of international law.

This preliminary ruling unambiguously stated that private corporations have both rights and responsibilities under international law, making them liable for charges under the Alien Tort Claims Act in spite of the widely acknowledged principle of limited liability in corporate governance. It stressed, however, that justiciable allegations must relate to legal norms universally accepted in the international community (*jus cogens* norms), restricting consideration to those rights violations with this well-established moral pedigree – in particular, claims of forced labour and torture (clearly covered in the legally binding Convention 29 of the International Labour Organization and the International Convention against Torture; Aceves, 1998, p 311). The testimonies of refugees from the Tenasserim region provide the primary evidence for these abuses, although the plaintiffs' legal team also cited numerous human rights reports from governmental and non-governmental organizations. It is also noteworthy, in addition, that the US Bureau of International Labor Affairs has independently found substantial corroboration of refugee accounts of forced labour from Total documents and the field observations of US embassy staff in Myanmar – at least during the early stages of the Yadana pipeline project (Bureau of International Labor Affairs, 1998, p 26).

If transnational public law litigation is fostered by the existence of *jus cogens* norms, such as well-established civil and political rights, this still leaves a question over consideration of environmental norms. Many of the principles generated by international environmental law – including norms embodied in multilateral treaties – have not yet accumulated the necessary historical and geographical currency to qualify as universally accepted. The environmental case against the Yadana pipeline project has been clearly laid out by EarthRights International, one of the human rights groups responsible for serving the litigation in Doe versus Unocal on behalf of the plaintiffs. This account contends a complete absence of environmental accountability and regulatory oversight concerning the pipeline development in Myanmar, and criticizes the oil companies for not making public their own environmental impact assessments (EarthRights International, 1996, pp 54–64). Of clearest resonance with the discourse principle of democracy is the alleged violation of the right of those affected by the pipeline to participate in decisions concerning its social and ecological implications. The relevant international norm cited by EarthRights International is principle 10 of the Rio Declaration on Environment and Development (1992), stating that environmental issues require the participation of all concerned citizens, facilitated by access to information. While principle 10 may be interpreted as a clear procedural environmental right approaching international consensus (Cameron and Mackenzie, 1996, pp 134–135), it is arguably still some distance from *jus cogens* status. It is no coincidence that violations of environmental rights do not explicitly feature in Doe versus Unocal and that EarthRights International has directly lobbied the UN Human Rights Commission to build up state support for environmental rights (Greer, 1998, p 37).

Human rights and environmental groups may still have much work to do in pressing for the global recognition of human environmental rights; but transnational public law litigation at least provides a procedural form for addressing these problems in any democratic state with a rights-conversant judiciary. In principle, it meets discursive democratic conditions of equitable participation, interest generalization and reasoned judgement (albeit of the adjudicative kind rather than consensus-based deliberation). Moreover, the precedent set by the Doe versus Unocal ruling on corporate liability for human rights violations arising from foreign investment activities may have important implications for corporate environmental accountability. The more environmental norms attain national and international legal endorsement, reaching the threshold of rights status, the greater their transnational legal scope for interrogating the activities of multinational companies. Corporate transnational liability for serious environmental harm is, due to the tireless efforts of NGOs, now on the rights agenda. It will require continued application by many individuals and associations in global civil society to give it bite as a technique of democratic scrutiny.

Transnational public law litigation thus offers at least the potential to serve as an environmental democratic check to economic power, and in a way that would universalize liability for environmental rights violations. This liability would also encompass governmental action, though here state sovereignty also raises the test that challenges must pertain to *jus cogens* norms. Under the act of state doctrine, widely acknowledged in customary international law, states should typically refrain from judicial judgement on governmental acts within sovereign territories. National statute law may sometimes reinforce the act of state norm. In this way the US Foreign Sovereign Immunities Act led to the dropping of the Myanmar governmental actors as defendants in Doe versus Unocal, declaring for this case their immunity from American courts (Aceves, 1998, p 311). However, the scope of state sovereign immunity in relation to human rights violations seems to be gradually eroding, as recently witnessed by the treaty of the International Criminal Court and the judgement of the UK Law Lords on extra-territorial jurisdiction over General Pinochet for human rights abuses. Might the 21st century see governmental and corporate actors called to account transnationally for environmental rights violations? Are we near to empowering individuals and communities, wherever they are in the world, with the global rights to protect the social and ecological conditions of their existence?

GLOBAL ENVIRONMENTAL CITIZENSHIP

Building up legal capabilities to assert environmental rights – of which transnational public-law litigation stands as only one suggestive pathway – cannot be divorced from wider questions about citizenship. The discourse principle informing the approach taken in this book holds that collectively binding decisions are democratically justified to the extent that all affected persons could, in principle, give their rational assent to them following an open, inclusive decision-making process. As outlined in the introduction to this book, the freedom to participate as equal citizens in such self-determination is nominally protected in Western democracies by civil and political rights, while the notion of environmental rights extends that protection to satisfactory social and ecological conditions of life.

Environmental democracy implies an active notion of citizenship, inviting citizens not only to interrogate existing institutional designs and governance justifications according to its principles, but also to experiment with participatory forms of decision-making. This notion faces at least three substantial challenges from dominant understandings of citizenship. Firstly, to support an active idea of citizen involvement, there is an onus on the state to guarantee collective ecological and social goods (such as clean air and water, cheap public transport, welfare support, universal education and public health care). This conflicts with recent trends in the advanced democracies to cut back on social provision, with citizenship reduced to private expressions of client satisfaction or complaint. Citizen action in support of shared environmental interests involves, secondly, claims which cross national borders; yet citizenship is still overwhelmingly linked to membership of a nation state. Finally, strong environmental rights imply correspondingly high citizenship obligations, notably regarding the restraining of consumerist expectations in Western democracies. However, these run up against the entrenched ethos of a consumer society seemingly oblivious to social and ecological costs. Each of these three areas casts doubt on the potential of the more demanding, other-regarding way of identifying ourselves as citizens suggested by environmental democracy. This chapter will now offer a few final comments on how environmental citizenship could help to wean democratic identities away from self-interest, nationality and consumerism.

Self-interest

The wide-ranging influence of neoliberalism as an economic ideology which shapes governmental choices in the advanced capitalist countries has directly challenged equality as a social goal, reviving the classic liberal understanding of citizenship as private self-determination with minimal obligations to others. Chapter 1 mentioned the neoliberal response to ecological problems, including its distinctive wise-use political agenda to roll back all environmental regulations. Neoliberalism has no time for environmental democracy. The progress of deliberative environmental decision-making forums depends upon the support of states subscribing to more egalitarian notions of democratic governance. Chapter 2 cited empirical support for advanced environmental capacity-building in the European social democracies. Although these states may still be some way from comprehensively institutionalizing participatory environmental decision-making, there seems to be a plausible causal link between their inclusive political forms and their environmental policy achievements. Moreover, their receptiveness to collective environmental interests belies domestic political cultures which are more open and responsive to other-regarding concerns.

Thomas Janoski (1998, pp 133–139) observes in the European social democratic countries a high level of (civil-political and socio-economic) rights and obligations, with many citizens members of – and active participants in – nongovernmental associations. Compared to 'liberal' states, such as the US and Japan, which maintain low levels of rights and obligations, the social democracies maintain strong notions of citizenship supported by relatively high equality and social welfare provision. Citizens participate actively both in corporatist policy forums and voluntary associations, encouraging the type of communicative interplay between state and civil society that fosters generalizable interests. Democratic deliberation and fair bargaining over environmental interests appears to be more possible in this type of political system. This does not mean that innovative participatory forms cannot be found in other countries; the case studies attest to that. Moreover, social movement activism can generate strong rights claims in spite of, as well as because of, national political cultures. The point is that participatory environmental governance, if it is to be enduring, requires sympathetic state support and active citizenship involvement. And the social democracies continue to embody the clearest form of active citizenship consistent with a strong collective provision of social and ecological welfare. They are the starting point for an environmental democratic political culture. Transferring this model to other countries, of course, is by no means straightforward, but the spread of the neoliberal alternative has already impoverished other-regarding norms of citizenship across the global North.

Nationality

If social democratic principles are the starting point for enhancing citizenship rights within states, where their adoption would signal a revival of legitimate income redistribution and active regulatory defence of environmental interests, environmental democracy pushes further still in a more egalitarian, transnational direction. However enlightened the prevailing notion of citizenship might be in a country, its attachment to the state – typically the nation state – necessarily excludes all those outside from full membership. The association of citizenship with national identity is historically contingent upon, and ultimately inconsistent with, the open-ended moral reach of the discourse principle, where a reciprocal recognition of equal treatment between individuals and groups depends upon universal rights and duties. The restriction of citizenship entitlements on the basis of ethnicity, religious affiliation, gender or territorial community identities violates the simple egalitarian premise of this principle. Already Western democracies are having to accommodate the fact that promoting equality amongst their increasingly multicultural populations may require protected rights for minority groups (Kymlicka, 1995). The long-term reconciliation of ethnic-cultural diversity, inside and outside national borders, with environmental citizenship is through universal human rights to decent social and ecological living conditions. While membership of a state will continue to be the main source of citizenship, since its legal recognition rests firstly with national governments, making claims on and fulfilling obligations to the state, being an environmental citizen increasingly means exercising rights and responsibilities that have transnational scope.

From experiments in local environmental self-governance and the mobilization of transnational environmental interests by NGOs, strong candidates for universal rights consideration are emerging – at their most general, these include the right to a secure, healthy and ecologically sound environment and the right to participate in decisions affecting ecological and social interests. As the UN *Ksentini Report* laid out, these basic substantive and procedural rights give rise to more specific entitlements and duties. It is only from this rights status, I contend, that environmental principles – marshalled to protect social and ecological interests in practice (such as the precautionary principle and ecological sustainability) – might carry the necessary weight when placed against competing social claims.

Their universal political character, tying ecological and social well-being to the conditions for autonomous, democratic decision-making, makes environmental citizenship less a property of national identity than of common humanity. This is in keeping with the general call from the Commission on Global Governance (1995, pp 55–57) for a global citizenship ethic of common rights and responsibilities, and also with David Held's notion of cosmopolitan democracy. For Held, the exercise of political autonomy by individuals and groups within and beyond nation states 'must be conceived as based on the *multiple lodging* of the rights and obligations of democratic law in the organizational charters of the agencies and associations which make up the spheres of politics, economics and civil society' (1995, p 277). In this sense we can speak of global environmental citizenship to refer to the plurality of decision-making spaces where environmental rights and obligations are applicable.

Consumerism

Global environmental citizenship balances a strong notion of rights with heightened expectations of environmental responsibility. Perhaps the key litmus test for the latter is the curtailing of unrestrained consumer demands, particularly in the global North. For neoliberal thinkers, who define rights above all by self-ownership of goods and free consumer preferences, this is where environmental norms are exposed as hostile to individual liberty. The type of regulatory controls environmentalists claim are necessary to protect social and ecological well-being (such as prohibitions, licences and taxes) may indeed curb consumer freedom of choice. But if these conditions of life are indeed critical to the continuation of autonomous decision-making, then these controls warrant serious consideration. What the discourse principle adds here is that collective subscription to any such restrictions must be according to open and inclusive deliberation. What if individuals or communities still want to ignore potentially irreversible environmental costs for short-term material benefits? In short, this may not be possible. Environmental rights status means that critical components of social and ecological well-being carry a far higher threshold of protection than political and economic systems of choice routinely allow. They cannot be overturned simply by majoritarian preferences or by an economic cost-benefit calculus, even when both claim adequately to incorporate environmental values. The democratic negotiation of environmental interests should thus proceed on the basis that some social and ecological interests have very strong (legal) claims to protection, and that those who wish to diminish them would need at least to demonstrate an overriding public-interest justification.

Perhaps even more problematic than agreeing upon and institutionalizing controls on environmentally damaging economic interactions is addressing the ecologically unrealistic material expectations of Western consumerism. The cultural influence of mass consumption colours our identity as citizens in a restrictive way by excluding the economic sphere from principles of democratic participation and accountability. Yet, at the same time the neoliberal understanding of citizenship appraises the legitimacy of the state on the basis of its ability to guarantee market conditions which are conducive to free investment and high economic growth. As citizens, our loyalty to the state is linked to our individual material prosperity. Environmental charges and taxes may make visible some of the ecological costs associated with many consumer goods, but they tend not to provoke reflection on wider lifestyle choices. Fortunately, ecological economists are already developing alternative indices of societal well-being (such as the index of sustainable economic welfare) which call into question traditional governmental representations of national prosperity, such as gross national product (GNP), by including measures of environmental deterioration, social welfare and income inequality. These alternative indices clearly mark out the gap between GNP trends and socio-economic sustainability (see Max-Neef, 1995). Their political value is convincingly articulated by Michael Jacobs (1997) as drawing attention to how our well-being depends upon the collective provision of social and ecological goods. This is an important means of communicating the generalizability of environmental interests in the political public sphere, with the aim of redefining quality of life.

The unceasing reminder to environmental politics represented by the discourse principle is that maintenance of decent social and ecological conditions of life not only supports, but is facilitated by, equal respect for all vital interests. Reciprocal recognition and protection of those interests is served by the ascription of rights. Environmental rights give a strong moral authority to those claims to quality of life which enable us to keep open the fullest range of options for the future while meeting fairly the needs of everyone in the present. The echo here with the global norm of sustainability and its commitment to intra- and intergenerational justice is deliberate. However, unlike the largely voluntarist language of sustainable development, environmental democracy as a political project looks to the explicit recognition of environmental rights in national and international law. With these rights, environmental values and interests might acquire more gravity in collective decision-making, while meaningful participatory opportunities could open up in state and market institutions. Of course, this depends upon collective political action. Have we the right to expect that a new generation of environmental citizens is empowered to reverse the global spiral of ecological degradation and social inequality in which we currently find ourselves?

NOTES

CHAPTER 2

1 The basic criteria identified by Dahl are: effective participation, voting equality at the decisive stage, enlightened understanding, and control of the agenda (1989, pp 115–118). This specification of decision rules contrasts with Ingram's broader emphasis on principles of self-government: rule of democratic law, limited moral establishment, publicity, integrity, moral rights against the state, and strong social provision (1994, pp 171–188). The defining characteristics of democratic governance can therefore be presented in a minimal or maximal fashion.

2 New institutionalists make a formal distinction between public goods and common-pool resources (CPRs). Both share the problem of nonexcludability – potential beneficiaries cannot be prevented, at reasonable cost, from using the environmental good/resource. However, public goods in theory are not subtractable (use by one does not impact upon the use of another), whereas with CPRs use by one individual may result in a qualitative or quantitative depletion of the resource – as is the problem with many renewable and nonrenewable environmental resources. For any particular resource, the public good-CPR distinction will vary according to the nature of its abundance and use (Keohane and Ostrom, 1995, pp 13–15).

3 The key academic centres associated with the Berlin school are the Environmental Policy Research Unit at the Free University of Berlin, headed by Martin Jänicke, and the Social Science Research Centre, Berlin – although comparative research shaped by this research draws in a global network of social scientists. See the various contributions in the recent *festschrift* for Jänicke (Mez and Weidner, 1997).

4 There have been other experimental forms of participatory decision-making, such as citizens' panels and community planning initiatives; but the development of regulatory negotiation in the US has received particular impetus from a federal executive order and memorandum in 1993 (Fiorino, 1995, p 225).

5 The selection of environmental indicators by the Berlin researchers – sulphur dioxide (SO_2), nitric oxide (NO_x) and carbon dioxide (CO_2) emissions, population served by sewage treatment plants, municipal waste and fertilizer consumption per capita, and major protected areas (Jänicke and Weidner, 1997, pp 317–320) – is by no means exhaustive. It is possible to question their representativeness of environmental quality. However, the environmental quality trends are mapped out according to acknowledged international data sources (UNEP, OECD, FAO) and present at least an acceptable starting point for cross-national comparisons.

6 The immediate catalyst for this policy swing in the US was Reagan's Executive Order 12291, compelling all environmental rule-making authority to have a narrow cost-benefit justification. In Britain a similar administrative directive – which also stipulates that proposed regulatory measures must be subject to cost-benefit analysis – had to wait until the UK 1995 Environment Act. However, this was preceded by a series of anti-regulatory policies, from the privatization of utilities to contracting out requirements for local authorities.

7 However, an important subsidiary hypothesis is that Green parties, which emerged in Western Europe from social movement activism, would be expected to be stronger in countries – such as Germany and France – that are less responsive to anti-nuclear demands (Kitschelt, 1986, pp 83–84). Of course, there are many other socio-economic and political factors that need to be taken into account when exploring the dynamics of Green party politics (see O'Neill, 1997).

8 Unconventional actions, defined as 'demonstrative' or 'confrontational' or 'violent', are recorded according to coded analyses of national newspaper reports in the four countries over the period 1975–1989 (Heijden, 1997, p 47, no 6).

9 The environmental quality indices are calculated from data contained in the World Resources Report (1992–1993) and the United Nations Human Development Index.

CHAPTER 3

1 The commission was established by the Commissioner on Resources and Environment Act, Statutes of British Columbia, 1992, Chapter 34.

2 The recent growth of multipartite land-use negotiations in British Columbia predates, and extends beyond, the CORE processes. Successful attempts include the Western Strathcona Land Advisory Council on Vancouver Island, which formulated a strategy for the sustainable use of the area's natural resources, and the Height-of-the-Rockies Task Force, responsible for defining the boundaries of a wilderness area. For an indication of the range of initiatives see CORE (1995a, pp 48–52).

3 Revised Statutes of British Columbia, 1979, Chapter 140.

4 Revised Statutes of British Columbia, 1979, Chapter 272.

5 Interview with Stephen Owen, Commissioner on Resources and Environment; Victoria, British Columbia, September 1994.

6 This recommendation was not novel in a provincial context. The Royal Commission on Forest Resources, appointed in 1975, had made the same point following its examination of forest policies in the province (Royal Commission on Forest Resources, 1976, p 265).

7 Western Canada Wilderness Committee versus Minister of Environment, Supreme Court of British Columbia. Vancouver Registry A880554, 7 March, 1988, 11 pages. The court applied a precedent-setting Supreme Court of Canada judgement, Finlay versus Canada (1986), which extended a rule allowing public interest standing in constitutional cases to nonconstitutional ones challenging a statutory authority for administrative action.

8 Interview with Allan Lidstone, Land-Use Planning Supervisor, Ministry of Forests; Victoria, British Columbia, September 1994.

9 Interview with Stephen Owen, Commissioner on Resources and Environment; Victoria, British Columbia, September 1994.

10 Fourteen of these goals – those pertaining in particular to settlement planning and regional growth strategies – were incorporated in the Growth Strategies Statutes Amendment Act (section 942.11(2)), passed by the provincial legislature in May 1995.

11 The commissioner had met cabinet on a regular basis. During 1994 this 'open channel of communication' meant meetings every couple of weeks. According to the first commissioner, there proved to be 'a lot of respect in the cabinet for the independence of the commission and the values it represents' (personal interview, September 1994). Owen served as commissioner until 1 August 1995, when he was appointed deputy attorney general. Former assistant deputy minister for fisheries and food, Stuart Culbertson, replaced Owen as acting commissioner of CORE until the disbanding of the commission in 1996.

12 Interview with Kaaren Lewis, Senior Policy Analyst, Land-Use Coordination Office; Victoria, British Columbia, September 1994.

13 An organizational template for the formalization of LUCO is an earlier environment and land-use committee secretariat, created in 1973 by the first New Democratic Party administration under the provisions of the 1971 Environment and Land-Use Act. Responsible for a series of innovative land-use investigations and resource management studies, recommendations from the secretariat proved instrumental in the inception of regional resource planning in British Columbia in the late 1970s. Regional resource management committees, established in 1978, served as a model for the CORE proposals on strengthening interagency regional planning in the province. For an illustration of the organization and roles of the original secretariat, see Environment and Land-Use Committee (1976, pp 8–57).

14 Interview with Stephen Owen, Commissioner on Resources and Environment; Victoria, British Columbia, September 1994.

15 These points were developed in a letter to Commissioner Owen from Carol Reardon, a barrister and solicitor at the West Coast Environmental Law Association, dated 7 October

1993. In his reply, dated 30 November, Owen claimed that the absence of settled government policy had hampered the substantive negotiations, while noting that the tables had requested an extension to their original deadlines (subsequently agreed to by cabinet). On the matter of resource requirements, he added that interministerial technical working groups had improved the information and technological assistance available to all stakeholders. Both letters are on file at the West Coast Environmental Law Association, 1001–127 West Hastings Street, Vancouver.

16 Interview with Paul George, Founding Director, Western Canada Wilderness Committee; Vancouver, British Columbia, September 1994.

17 Following a long-standing refusal to recognize the existence of aboriginal rights, the government in British Columbia reversed its policy in the early 1990s by creating a treaty commission to oversee negotiations with First Nations over self-government, including land and resource rights. Resolution of aboriginal ownership and jurisdiction in these areas, likely to take decades, will have profound implications for forest land decision-making in the province. For an understanding of the historical background to this fundamental policy shift, see Tennant (1990).

18 The respective totals in the government land-use plans are 11.3 per cent for the West Kootenay/Boundary region and 12 per cent for the Cariboo-Chilcotin. These compare with protected areas designations of 13 per cent for Vancouver Island and 16.5 per cent for the East Kootenay region. For a comparative synopsis, see CORE (1995c, pp 40–43).

19 These regional-scale resource management lands represent the most restrictive gradation of three integrated resource management zones forming the forest land reserve. The other two, general forest areas (GFAs) and high-intensity areas (HIAs), have a more intensive resource development and management emphasis (Low Intensity Area Review Committee, 1995, pp 2–3).

20 Interview with Brian Gilfillan, Vice-President (Forestry), Council of Forest Industries; Vancouver, British Columbia, September 1994.

21 Interview with William Cobb, Mayor, Williams Lake; Vancouver, British Columbia, August 1994.

22 Interview with Ken Sumanik, Environment and Land-Use Director, Mining Association of British Columbia; Vancouver, British Columbia, September 1994.

23 Across Vancouver Island, CORE estimated that in the short term, as a result of its land-use zoning recommendations, 900 jobs would be lost, over Cdn$42 million in annual wages and salaries would be forgone, and the province would lose between Cdn$15 and 18 million in annual tax revenues (CORE, 1994a, pp 194–196). In response to this scenario, while still creating 46 new provincial parks to complete the protected areas strategy for Vancouver Island, the provincial government signalled a continuing commitment to resource development activities by zoning 81 per cent of the land base as a forest land reserve.

24 Interview with Paul George, Founding Director, Western Canada Wilderness Committee; Vancouver, British Columbia, September 1994.

CHAPTER 4

1 Of course, *aesthetic* representations are too dependent upon individual subjective preferences and particular cultural contexts to achieve universal purchase; but shared reflections on the aesthetic experience of external nature may guide an intersubjective recognition of its transformative value. This contrasts with those ecocentric thinkers who emphasize a positive aesthetic of nature based on its 'objective' ecological properties – from Aldo Leopold (1966, pp 256–269) to Holmes Rolston (1989, pp 232–245).

2 It should be noted that some environmental philosophers have developed an ecocentric ethic at odds with the holistic perspective of deep ecology. For example, Paul Taylor offers a nonanthropocentric rationale for wilderness preservation centred on the inherent worth of each living thing. Preservation is supported by the principled requirements of 'distributive' and 'restitutive' justice toward wild communities of *individual* plants and animals (Taylor, 1986, pp 99–168, 191–192, 305–306).

3 I acknowledge, therefore, that Naess is by no means representative of all deep ecological positions, even if his way of thinking has proved influential in this regional context.

4 Interview with Dr Marlene Smith, Director, Friends of Strathcona Park; Errington, British Columbia, August 1990.

5 Interview with Paul George, Founding Director, Western Canada Wilderness Committee; Vancouver, British Columbia, September 1994. The Western Canada Wilderness Committee has been the most successful wilderness preservation group to emerge in British Columbia. Within ten years of its founding in 1980, the committee had over 30,000 members and an annual income in excess of Cdn$2.8 million. While the 1990s have seen a stabilization of membership and income at less heady levels (in 1995 membership stood at 21,000 and revenue at Cdn$1.9 million), the group has justified the global environmentalist recognition given to its high-profile, innovative campaigns for wilderness preservation. Some of the internationally significant wilderness areas protected, for which the committee can take significant or major credit, include South Moresby (1987), the Carmanah Valley (1990–1994), the Khutzeymateen Valley (1992), the Tatshenshini (1993), the Skagit Valley (1995) and the Stein Valley (1995).

6 Interview with Rick Searle, Chair, Canadian Parks and Wilderness Society – British Columbia chapter; Victoria, British Columbia, March 1991.

7 This is not to deny the historical and continuing influence in Canada of North American 'purist' notions of wilderness. Indeed, a comprehensive public review and planning process conducted by Parks Canada in the mid 1980s (Heritage for Tomorrow), canvassing citizens' views across the country, found strongest support in British Columbia for the classical concept of large wild or 'empty' areas (Nelson, 1989, pp 95–96). A more recent province-wide survey (The British Columbia Parks Legacy Public Consultation Project), conducted in 1997–1998 by the parks division of the British Columbia Ministry of Environment, Lands and Parks, also noted a strong preservationist sentiment for parks as protected natural areas.

8 By 1998 there were ten such joint management agreements in place, including – to illustrate the range of protective designations – the Huchduwachsdu Nuyem Jees/Kitlope Heritage Conservancy, the Stein Valley/Nlaka'pamux Heritage Park and Say-Nuth-Khaw-Yum/Indian Arm Provincial Park.

9 Interview with Paul George, Founding Director, Western Canada Wilderness Committee; Vancouver, British Columbia, September 1994.

10 Delgamuukw versus British Columbia, Supreme Court of Canada, File No 23799, 11 December 1997.

11 Ibid, para 165: 'the development of agriculture, forestry, mining, and hydroelectric power, the general economic development of the interior of British Columbia, protection of the environment or endangered species, the building of infrastructure and the settlement of foreign populations to support those aims, are the kinds of objectives that are consistent with this purpose and, in principle, can justify the infringement of aboriginal title'. Note the recognition of environmental protection as a legitimate policy objective that might override local or regional title, which suggests a potential source of tension between preservation groups and aboriginal people.

12 Against critics of this (post-Kantian) ethical position (Johnson, 1991, pp 60–74; Plumwood, 1993, pp 165–171), I would argue that 'correct' moral valuing presupposes communicative competence and is therefore necessarily human based. This is not the same as 'species chauvinism' because it does not preclude a benign attitude towards nature. As Kate Soper argues, by recognizing the 'otherness' of nonhuman nature, this approach may actually be less 'arrogant' than those naturalist accounts that unreflectively project onto other creatures analogies to human needs, desires and capacities (1995, pp 170–171). In addition, *within* human societies the communicative notion of rationality that informsi discourse ethics by no means excludes moral feelings such as care, respect and sympathy. These feelings are central to judging the appropriateness of moral norms in concrete situations (Günther, 1993, pp 137–153). The point is that such feelings cannot be the '*final* reference point' for judging moral phenomena according to a principle of generalizability (Habermas, 1993, pp 174–175).

CHAPTER 5

1 One of the many examples that could be cited here is the London matchgirls' strike in 1888: B Webb and S Webb (1920, pp 402–404).

2 The overt class bias of action has ranged from straightforward coercion (1926 general strike) to the statutory wage controls and union regulation put in place by the 1970–1974 Conservative government. That employers can draw political strength from the *weakness* of their interest organizations, on account of their market power, is indicated more widely by Streeck (1992, pp 76–104).

3 This method of representation was devised in 1922 by Ernest Bevin, the first general secretary of the TGWU (now the T&G), as part of the union's founding rule book: Stephens (1981, pp 48–56). The 14 trade groups are as follows: Administrative, Clerical, Technical and Supervisory; Building, Construction and Civil Engineering; Civil Air Transport; Chemical, Rubber, Manufacturing and Oil Refining; Docks and Waterways; Food, Drink and Tobacco; General Workers; Passenger Services; Power and Engineering; Public Services; Road Transport Commercial; Rural, Agriculture and Allied Workers; Textiles; and Vehicle, Building and Automotive.

4 The survey was undertaken by the T&G national health and safety coordinator; T&G (1997b, p 13).

5 Interview with John Fisher, T&G Director of Education; London, June 1995.

6 In Britain this information secrecy even applies to emergency planning provisions with regard to major industrial hazards. A European council directive (82/501 – the 'Seveso' directive) on the major accident hazards of certain industrial activities had originally planned to include an obligation to inform citizens about safety procedures in the event of accidents. However, this was removed after political pressure from member states. This secrecy contrasts strongly with the American Emergency Planning and Community-Right-to-Know Act, 1986, which creates rights for citizens and local governments to obtain information about potential threats in their localities involving hazardous chemicals.

7 T&G, 'Come clean on pollution!' *T&G Health and Safety Record*, no 1, winter 1996. The chair of the cement industry working group was the chairman of Ready Mixed Concrete, one of the largest cement firms in Britain. He has since been appointed to the board of the Environment Agency. For a general account of the closed, bilateral negotiations between government and business prevalent in the UK pollution control sectors see Smith (1997, pp 53–81).

8 However, there are industrial sectors where, for 'national security' reasons, these key rights have been abrogated, notably the nuclear sector (Lewis, 1978). Between 1984 and 1994,
for similar reasons, mere membership of a union was declared illegal by the Conservative government for workers at the intelligence-gathering government communications headquarters in Cheltenham. Those workers refusing to leave their union were sacked (Barrows, 1997, pp 241–246).

9 For example, at the chemical firm Rhone Poulenc, the T&G managed to negotiate that health and safety representatives are allowed the same rights on environmental issues as their legal entitlements over health and safety.

10 A T&G survey of the Confederation of British Industry green company listing in 1996 discovered that only one of 25 UK companies producing annual environmental reports had active union involvement in compiling the report. Personal communication with Alan Dalton, T&G National Health and Safety Coordinator, November 1996.

11 Interview with Angela Mawle, Director, Women's Environmental Network; London, May 1995.

12 Interview with Bill Morris, General Secretary of the T&G; London, November, 1995.

13 Interview with Bill Morris (as above).

14 While the then TGWU endorsed the report (TGWU, 1978), it was vehemently opposed by the General and Municipal Workers' Union and the Electrical, Electronic, Telecommunications and Plumbing Union: Kelly (1988, pp 209–210).

15 This may yet, however, also be an achievable objective. In its current review of UK health and safety legislation, the Labour government is actively considering such an option. At a TUC environment conference in London in October 1998, in response to a question from the T&G national health and safety coordinator, Deputy Prime Minister John Prescott declared his personal support for extending environmental rights to health and safety representatives: 'I'm convinced of this argument.'

CHAPTER 6

1 According to Chapter 28 of Agenda 21, the Programme for Sustainable Development agreed at the United Nations Conference on Environment and Development: 'Each local authority should enter into a dialogue with its citizens, local organizations and private enterprises and adopt "a local Agenda 21". Through consultation and consensus-building, local authorities would learn from citizens and from local, civic, community, business and industrial organizations and acquire the information needed for formulating the best strategies' (United Nations, 1993, p 233).

2 Local authorities in Britain are executive rather than legislative bodies (their powers to pass byelaws are minimal and firmly controlled by central government). Decisions are taken according to majority voting of members at council meetings.

3 The nongovernmental organizations represented on the steering group are Age Concern London, the Black Environmental Network, the National Union of Students (London Region), London First (business), the London Voluntary Services Council, the South and Eastern Region Trades Union Congress, and the Women's Environmental Network. The steering group is chaired by Councillor Tony Coleman, MP, from the London Borough of Merton.

4 According to the London Community Alliance, elected community assemblies, representing between 10,000 and 15,000 people, could be enabled by an act of parliament and local referenda. Should these referenda demonstrate majority support for community assemblies, it is envisaged that each London borough might contain up to 12; London Community Alliance, 'Power's coming home!', December 1997.

5 Under the Road Traffic Act, 1991, and schedule 5(5) of the Local Government Act, 1985, the secretary of state for transport is able to designate strategic 'red routes' and 'designated roads' which come under the traffic management responsibilities of a centrally appointed bureaucrat – the traffic director for London.

6 One of the key supporters of this was the chair of the environment committee. See Councillor Andrew Bosi, 'Subsidiarity in decision-making on the environment', London Borough of Islington, Environment Committee Consultative Meeting, 18 February 1997, item 5(ii).

7 The Local Government (Experimental Arrangements) Bill, 1997, if enacted, would have allowed local authorities, subject to national government approval, to carry out time-limited innovations in their executive decision-making. However, as a private member's bill supported – rather than initiated – by the Labour government, there was no legislative priority attached to it and it ran out of time in the 1997–1998 parliamentary session. Local authorities wishing to make innovations in democratic governance remain with their hands tied behind their backs.

8 It should also be noted that the Technical and Environmental Services Department, Islington Council, conducted a separate consultation exercise with six ethnic minority groups as part of the local authority's 1996–1997 Race Action Programme. While the focus was on the department's work, the meetings were also used to promote Islington's Agenda 21 planning process. The council officer involved reported little interest from the groups in Local Agenda 21 as a process, but received a clear expression of their immediate socio-economic and environmental needs. Personal communication with Geoff Rudd, Policy, Development and Quality Manager, Technical and Environmental Services Department, 17 June 1997.

REFERENCES

Aberley, T (ed) (1993) *Boundaries of Home: Mapping for Local Empowerment*, Gabriola Island, British Columbia, New Society Publishers

Aberley, T (ed) (1994) *Systems by Design: The Practice of Ecological Planning*, Gabriola Island, British Columbia, New Society Publishers

Aceves, W J (1998) 'Doe v Unocal', *American Journal of International Law*, Vol 92, pp 309–14

Achterberg, W (1993) 'Can liberal democracy survive the environmental crisis? Sustainability, liberal neutrality and overlapping consensus' in A Dobson and P Lucardie (eds), pp 81–101

Achterberg, W (1996a) 'Sustainability and associative democracy' in W M Lafferty and J Meadowcroft (eds) pp 157–74

Achterberg, W (1996b) 'Sustainability, community and democracy' in B Doherty and M de Geus (eds) pp 170–87

Agyeman, J (1997) *Ethnic Minorities and Sustainable Development: Local Agenda 21 Roundtable Guidance 14*, London, Local Government Management Board

Agyeman, J and B Evans (eds) (1994) *Local Environmental Policies and Strategies*, Harlow, Longman

Alexy, R (1994) 'Basic rights and democracy in Jurgen Habermas's procedural paradigm of the law', *Ratio Juris*, Vol 7, pp 227–38

Amnesty International (1996), *Myanmar. Kayin (Karen) State: The Killings Continue*, London, Amnesty International

Amnesty International (1997a) *Amnesty International Report 1997: Myanmar*, London, Amnesty International

Amnesty International (1997b) *Myanmar: Ethnic Minority Rights under Attack*, London, Amnesty International

Amnesty International (1997c) *Myanmar: A Challenge for the International Community*, London, Amnesty International

Amnesty International (1998) *Myanmar: Atrocities in the Shan State*, London, Amnesty International

Anahim Round Table (1994) *Anahim Round Table Resource Management Plan*, Anahim Lake, British Columbia, Anahim Round Table

Andersen, M S (1997) 'Denmark' in M Jänicke and H Weidner (eds) pp 157–74

Anderson, M R (1996) 'Human rights approaches to environmental protection: an overview' in A E Boyle and M R Anderson (eds) pp 1–23

Andrews, W J (1987) 'The public interest perspective' in D Tingley (ed) *Environmental Protection and the Canadian Constitution*, Edmonton, Environmental Law Centre, pp 20–25

Andrews, W J (1993) *Comments on the Schwindt Report*, Vancouver, West Coast Environmental Law Association

Andrews, R L (1997) 'United States' in M Jänicke and H Weidner (eds) pp 25–43

Apel, K-O (1990) 'Is the ethics of the ideal communication community a utopia? On the relationship between ethics, utopia, and the critique of utopia' in S Benhabib and F Dallmayr (eds) *The Communicative Ethics Controversy*, Cambridge, Mass, MIT Press, pp 23–59

Apffel-Marglin, F (1998) *The Spirit of Regeneration: Andean Culture Confronting Western Notions of Development*, London, Zed Books

Association of London Government (1996) *An Agenda 21 for London: Reports from Working Groups of Key Stakeholders*, London, ALG

Association of London Government (1997) *An Agenda 21 for London: Sustainability Indicators, Targets and Action Plans*, London, ALG

Atkinson, A (1991) *Principles of Political Ecology*, London, Belhaven

Baker, S (1996) 'Environmental policy in the European Union: institutional dilemmas and democratic practice' in W M Lafferty and J Meadowcroft (eds) pp 213–33

Bankes, N (1993) 'Ethics and resource takings: The Schwindt Report', *Resources*, No 41, pp 1–7

Bandi, G (1996) 'Financial instruments in environmental protection' in G Winter (ed) pp 201–17

Barrows, C (1997) *Industrial Relations Law*, London, Cavendish

Baumann, R J (1994) 'Exotic expropriations: government action and compensation', *The Advocate*, Vol 52, No 4, pp 561–79

Beck, U (1992) *Risk Society: Towards a New Modernity*, London, Sage

Beck, U (1995) *Ecological Politics in an Age of Risk*, Cambridge, Polity

Beehler, R (1983) 'The concept of fairness' in Evangeline S Case et al (eds) pp 1–14

Benhabib, S (1994) 'Deliberative rationality and models of democratic legitimacy', *Constellations*, Vol 1, No1, pp 26–52

Benton, T (1989) 'Marxism and natural limits: an ecological critique and reconstruction', *New Left Review*, No 178, pp 51–86

Benton, T (1993) *Natural Relations: Ecology, Animal Rights and Social Justice*, London, Verso

Bercusson, B (1997) *European Works Councils - Extending the Trade Union Role*, London, Institute of Employment Rights

Berg, P (1991) 'What is bioregionalism?', *The Trumpeter*, Vol 8, pp 6–8

Berg, P and R Dasmann (1977) 'Reinhabiting California', *The Ecologist*, Vol 7, pp 399–401

Berger, T R (1977) *Northern Frontier, Northern Homeland. Volumes I and II. The Report of the Mackenzie Valley Pipeline Inquiry*, Ottawa, Minister of Supply and Services

Berger, T R (1989) 'Opening remarks' in R Searle (ed) *Wilderness, Parks and Native Land Claims*, Victoria, Canadian Parks and Wilderness Society, pp 3–19

Berking, H (1996) 'Solidary individualism: the moral impact of cultural modernisation in late modernity' in S Lash, B Szerszynski and B Wynne (eds) pp 189–202

Beuermann, C and B Burdick (1997) 'The sustainability transition in Germany: some early stage experiences', *Environmental Politics*, Vol 6, pp 83–107

Bichsel, A (1997) 'NGOs as agents of public accountability and democratization in intergovernmental forums' in W M Lafferty and J Meadowcroft (eds) pp 234–55

Bishop, J (1994) *Community Participation in Sustainable Development: Local Agenda 21 Roundtable Guidance 1*, London, Local Government Management Board

Black Londoners for a Strategic Authority (1997) *New Leadership for London*, London, BLSA

Block, W E (ed) (1990) *Economics and the Environment: A Reconciliation*, Vancouver, British Columbia, The Fraser Institute

Blowers, A (ed) (1993) *Planning for Sustainable Development*, London, Earthscan

Bobbio, N (1987) *The Future of Democracy*, Cambridge, Polity

Bodansky, D (1994) 'The precautionary principle in US environmental law' in T O'Riordan and J Cameron (eds) pp 203–28

Boehmer-Christiansen, S (1994) 'The precautionary principle in Germany – enabling government', in T O'Riordan and J Cameron (eds) pp 31–60

Bohman, J F (1990) 'Communication, ideology, and democratic theory', *American Political Science Review*, Vol 84, No 1, pp 93–109

Bookchin, M (1982) *The Ecology of Freedom: The Emergence and Dissolution of Hierarchy*, Palo Alto, CA, Cheshire

Bookchin, M (1986) 'Freedom and necessity in nature: a problem in ecological ethics', *Alternatives*, Vol 13, pp 29–38

Bookchin, M (1990) 'Ecologizing the dialectic' in J Clark (ed) *Renewing the Earth: The Promise of Social Ecology*, London, Green Print, pp 202–19

Bookchin, M. (1995) 'Communalism: the democratic dimension of anarchism', *Democracy and Nature*, Vol 3, No 2, pp 1–17

Booth, A L and H M Jacobs (1990) 'Ties that bind: Native American beliefs as a foundation for environmental consciousness', *Environmental Ethics*, Vol 12, pp 27–43

Botkin, D (1990) *Discordant Harmonies: A New Ecology of the Twenty First Century*, New York, Oxford University Press

Bourdieu, P (1990) *In Other Words: Essays Towards a Reflexive Sociology*, Cambridge, Cambridge University Press

Bourdieu, P (1998) 'A reasoned utopia and economic fatalism', *New Left Review*, No 227, pp 125–34

Bowler, P J (1992) *The Fontana History of the Environmental Sciences*, London, Fontana

Boyle, A (1996) 'The role of international human rights law in the protection of the environment' in A E Boyle and M R Anderson (eds) pp 43–69

Boyle, A E and M R Anderson (eds) (1996) *Human Rights Approaches to Environmental Protection*, Oxford, Clarendon Press

Bradford, G (1989) *How Deep is Deep Ecology?* Novato, California, Times Change Press

Bramwell, A (1989) *Ecology in the 20th Century: A History*, New Haven, Yale University Press

Brenneis, K (1991) 'An evaluation of public participation in the British Columbia Ministry of Forests', *Forest Resources Commission Background Papers*, Vol 1, Victoria, British Columbia Forest Resources Commission

Bressers, H Th A and L A Plettenburg (1997) 'The Netherlands' in M Jänicke and H Weidner (eds) pp 109–31

Brunet, R (1994) 'Their jobs, their homes, their lives', *British Columbia Report*, Vol 5, No 27, pp 18–23

Buckingham-Hatfield, S and B Evans (eds) (1996) *Environmental Planning and Sustainability*, Chichester, John Wiley

Buckle, L G and S R Thomas-Buckle (1986) 'Placing environmental mediation in context: lessons from "failed" mediations', *Environmental Impact Assessment Review*, Vol 6, No 1, pp 55–70

Bureau of International Labor Affairs (1998) *Report on Labor Practices in Burma*, http://www.dol.gov/dol/ilab/public/media/reports/ofr/burma/main.htm

Burns, D, R Hambleton and P Hoggett (1994) *The Politics of Decentralisation: Revitalising Local Democracy*, London, Macmillan

Cabinet Planning Secretariat (1993) 'Proposed forest sector strategy action plan', *Forest Planning Canada*, Vol 9, No 3, pp 12–16

Cahn, M A (1995) *Environmental Deceptions*, Albany, State University of New York Press

Caldwell, L K (1990) *Between Two Worlds*, Cambridge, Cambridge University Press

Caldwell, L K (1996) *International Environmental Policy: From the Twentieth to the Twenty-First Century*, Third Edition, Durham, Duke University Press

Callicott, J B (1987) 'The conceptual foundations of the land ethic' in J Baird Callicott (ed) *Companion to a Sand Country Almanac*, Madison, University of Wisconsin Press, pp 186–217

Callicott, J B (1989) 'American land wisdom? Sorting out the issues', *Journal of Forest History*, Vol 33, pp 35–42

Callicott, J Baird (1994–95), 'A critique of and an alternative to the wilderness idea', *Wild Earth*, Vol 4, No 4, pp 54–59

Cameron, J (1994) 'The status of the precautionary principle in international law' in T O'Riordan and J Cameron (eds) pp 262–89

Cameron, J and R Mackenzie (1996) 'Access to environmental justice and procedural rights in international institutions' in A E Boyle and M R Anderson (eds) pp 129–52

Capita (1997a) *Review of the Neighbourhood Office System. Volume 1: Final Report*, London, Capita Management Consultants

Capita (1997b), *Review of the Neighbourhood Office System. Volume 2: Appendices*, London, Capita Management Consultants

Careless, R (1997) *To Save the Wild Earth: Field Notes From the Environmental Frontline*, Vancouver, British Columbia, Raincoast Books

Carson, R (1962) *Silent Spring*, Boston, Mass, Houghton Mifflin

Carter, N (1996) 'Worker co-operatives and green political theory' in B Doherty and M de Geus (eds) pp 56–75

Case, E S et al (eds) (1983) *Fairness in Environmental and Social Impact Processes*, Calgary, Faculty of Law, University of Calgary

Castoriadis, C (1995) 'The problem of democracy', *Democracy and Nature*, Vol 3, No 2, pp 18–35

Centre for Environmental Initiatives (1997) *The Potential for Local Links: Local Agenda 21 in London*, Carshalton, CEI

Chambers, S (1996) *Reasonable Democracy*, Ithaca, NY, Cornell University Press

Chapman, G, K Kumar, C Fraser and I Gaber (1997) *Environmentalism and the Mass Media: The North–South Divide*, London, Routledge

Charnovitz, S (1996) 'Multilateral environmental agreements and trade rules', *Environmental Policy and Law*, Vol 26, pp 163–69

Chase, S (ed) (1991) *Defending the Earth*, Boston, Mass, South End Press

Christoff, P (1996) 'Ecological modernisation, ecological modernities', *Environmental Politics*, Vol 5, pp 476–500

Cohen, J L and A Arato (1993) *Civil Society and Political Theory*, London, MIT Press

Cohen, J and J Rogers (eds) (1995) *Associations and Democracy*, London, Verso

Commission for Local Democracy (1995) *Taking Charge: The Rebirth of Local Democracy*, London, Municipal Journal Books

Commission of Inquiry into Compensation for the Taking of Resource Interests (1992) *Final Report*, Victoria, Queen's Printer

Commission of the European Communities (1997) 'Proposal for a Council Directive on the assessment of the effects of certain plans and programmes on the environment', *Official Journal of the European Communities*, C 129, pp 14–18

Commission on Global Governance (1995) *Our Global Neighbourhood*, Oxford, Oxford University Press

Commission on Resources and Environment (1993a) *Tatshenshini/Alsek Land Use*, Victoria, CORE

Commission on Resources and Environment (1993b) *1992/93 Annual Report*, Victoria, CORE

Commission on Resources and Environment (1993c) *Aboriginal Participation in Regional Planning Processes*, Victoria, CORE

Commission on Resources and Environment (1994a) *Vancouver Island Land Use Plan*, Victoria, CORE

Commission on Resources and Environment (1994b) *Cariboo–Chilcotin Land Use Plan*, Victoria, CORE

Commission on Resources and Environment (1994c) *1993/94 Annual Report*, Victoria, CORE

Commission on Resources and Environment (1994d) *Provincial Land Use Strategy, Volume 1: A Sustainability Act for British Columbia*, Victoria, CORE

Commission on Resources and Environment (1994e) *Provincial Land Use Strategy, Volume 2: Planning for Sustainability*, Victoria, CORE

Commission on Resources and Environment (1995a) *Provincial Land Use Strategy, Volume 3: Public Participation*, Victoria, CORE

Commission on Resources and Environment (1995b) *Provincial Land Use Strategy, Volume 4: Dispute Resolution*, Victoria, CORE

Commission on Resources and Environment (1995c) *British Columbia's Sustainability Strategy, Report to the Legislative Assembly, 1994–95*, Victoria, CORE

Cook, J and C Kaufman (1982) *Portrait of a Poison: The 2,4,5-T Story*, London, Pluto Press

Cooperman, J (1996) 'Ideas on tenure reform', *British Columbia Environmental Report*, Vol 7, pp 8–9

Cormick, G (1989) 'Strategic issues in structuring multi-party public policy negotiations', *Negotiation Journal*, Vol 5, No 2, pp 125–32

Cosgrove, D (1995) 'Habitable earth: wilderness, empire and race in America' in David Rothenberg (ed) pp 26–41

Cotgrove, S and A Duff (1981) 'Environmentalism, values and social change', *British Journal of Sociology*, Vol 32, pp 92–110

Crawford, S E and E Ostrom (1995) 'A grammar of institutions', *American Political Science Review*, Vol 98, No 3, pp 582–600

Crenson, M A (1971) *The Un-Politics of Air Pollution*, Baltimore, Johns Hopkins University Press

Cully, M and S Woodhead (1997) 'Trade union membership and recognition', *Labour Market Trends*, Vol 105, pp 231–40

Curtice, J and R Jowell (1997) 'Trust in the political system' in R Jowell et al (eds) pp 89–109

Dahl, R A (1989) *Democracy and its Critics*, New Haven, Yale University Press

Dahl, R A (1991) *Modern Political Analysis*, Fifth Edition, London, Prentice Hall

Dalton, R J and M Kuelcher (eds) (1990) *Challenging the Political Order: New Social and Political Movements in Western Democracies*, Cambridge, Polity Press

Dauncey, G (1988) *After the Crash: The Emergence of the Rainbow Economy*, London, Green Print

Deakin, S (1992) 'Labour law and industrial relations' in J Michie (ed) *The Economic Legacy 1979–1992*, London, Academic Press, pp 173–94

Dearden, P (1989) 'Wilderness and our common future' *Natural Resources Journal*, Vol 29, pp 205–21

Dennett, D C (1995) *Darwin's Dangerous Idea: Evolution and the Meanings of Life*, London, Allen Lane

Department of the Environment (1995) *1991 Deprivation Index: A Review of Approaches and a Matrix of Results*, London, HMSO

Department of the Environment, Transport and the Regions (1998a) *A Mayor and Assembly for London*, Cm 3897, London, Stationery Office

Department of the Environment, Transport and the Regions (1998b) *Modernising Local Government: Local Democracy and Community Leadership: Consultation Paper*, http://www.local.doe.gov.uk/sponsor/democrac.htm

Department of the Environment, Transport and the Regions (1998c) *Modern Local Government: In Touch with the People*, http://www.local-regions.detr.gov.uk/lgwp

Desgagné, R (1995) 'Integrating environmental values into the European Convention of Human Rights', *American Journal of International Law*, Vol 89, pp 263–94

Devall, B and G Sessions (1985) *Deep Ecology: Living as if Nature Mattered*, Layton, Utah, Gibbs Smith

Dobson, A (1990) *Green Political Thought*, London, HarperCollins

Dobson, A (1996a) 'Democratising green theory: preconditions and principles' in B Doherty and M de Geus (eds) pp 132–48

Dobson, A (1996b) 'Representative democracy and the environment' in W M Lafferty and J Meadowcroft (eds) pp 124–39

Dobson, A and P Lucardie (eds) (1993) *The Politics of Nature: Explorations in Green Political Theory*, London, Routledge

Dodds, F (ed) (1997) *The Way Forward: Beyond Agenda 21*, London, Earthscan

Doern, G B and T Conway (1994) *The Greening of Canada: Federal Institutions and Decisions*, Toronto, University of Toronto Press

Doherty, B and M de Geus (eds) (1996) *Democracy and Green Political Thought: Sustainability, Rights and Citizenship*, London, Routledge

Dorcey, A H J and C L Riek (1987) *Negotiated Settlement of Environmental Disputes: An Analysis of Canadian Experience*, Report prepared for the Canadian Environmental Assessment Research Council

Douglas-Scott, S (1996) 'Environmental rights in the European Union – participatory democracy or democratic deficit?' in A E Boyle and M R Anderson (eds) pp 109–28

Douthwaite, R (1996) *Short Circuit: Strengthening Local Economies for Security in an Unstable World*, Totnes, Green Books

Dowie, M (1995) *Losing Ground: American Environmentalism at the Close of the Twentieth Century*, Cambridge, Mass, MIT Press

Drengson, A R (1990) 'What is ecosophy?', *The Trumpeter*, Vol 7, pp 1–2

Drengson, A R (1997) 'An ecophilosophy approach, the deep ecology movement and diverse ecosophies', *The Trumpeter*, Vol 14, pp 110–111

Dryzek, J S (1987) *Rational Ecology*, Oxford, Basil Blackwell

Dryzek, J S (1990a) 'Designs for environmental discourse: the greening of the administrative state' in R Paehlke and D Torgerson (eds) pp 97–111

Dryzek, J S (1990b) *Discursive Democracy*, Cambridge, Cambridge University Press

Dryzek, J S (1990c) 'Green reason: Communicative ethics for the biosphere', *Environmental Ethics*, Vol 12, pp 195–210

Dryzek, J S (1995) 'Political and ecological communication', *Environmental Politics*, Vol 4, No 4, pp 13–30

Dryzek, J S (1996) 'Political inclusion and the dynamics of democratization', *American Political Science Review*, Vol 90, pp 475–87

Dryzek, J S (1997) *The Politics of the Earth: Environmental Discourses*, Oxford, Oxford University Press du Bois, F (1996) 'Social justice and the judicial enforcement of environmental rights and duties' in A E Boyle and M R Anderson (eds) pp 153–75

Dunn, J (1993) *Western Political Theory in the Face of the Future*, Cambridge, Cambridge University Press

Dunne, S and M Wright (1994) 'Maintaining the "status quo"? An analysis of the contents of British collective agreements, 1979–1990', *British Journal of Industrial Relations*, Vol 23, pp 95–105

Dunsmuir III Steering Committee (1997) *Dunsmuir III: Moving Forward Together – Consolidating Progress on a Provincial Land Use Strategy*, Victoria, British Columbia, Trafford Publishing

EarthRights International (with Southeast Asian Information Network) (1996) *Total Denial: A Report on the Yadana Pipeline Project in Burma*, EarthRights International

Eckersley, R (1992) *Environmentalism and Political Theory: Toward an Ecocentric Approach*, London, UCL Press

Eckersley, R (1995) 'Liberal democracy and the rights of nature: the struggle for inclusion', *Environmental Politics*, Vol 4, pp 169–98

Eckersley, R (1996) 'Greening liberal democracy: the rights discourse revisited' in B Doherty and M de Geus (eds) pp 212–36

The Ecologist (1972) 'Blueprint for survival', *The Ecologist*, Vol 12, pp 1–43

Economy, E and M A Schreurs (1997) 'Domestic and international linkages in environmental politics' in M A Schreurs and E Economy (eds) *The Internationalization of Environmental Protection*, Cambridge, Cambridge University Press, pp 1–18

Eden, S E (1993) 'Individual environmental responsibility and its role in public environmentalism', *Environment and Planning*, Vol 25, pp 1743–58

Eder, K (1996) *The Social Construction of Nature*, London, Sage

Elder, P S (1989) 'Legal rights for nature: the wrong answer to the rights question' in R Bradley and S Duguid (eds) *Environmental Ethics 2*, Burnaby, British Columbia, Simon Fraser University, pp 107–19

Elkington, J and T Burke (1987) *The Green Capitalists*, London, Gollancz

Elkins, S (1989–90) 'The politics of mystical ecology', *Telos*, No 82, pp 52–70

Elster, J (ed) (1998) *Deliberative Democracy*, Cambridge, Cambridge University Press

Environment and Land Use Committee (1976) *Report of the Secretariat*, Victoria, Queen's Printer

Ewing, K (ed) (1996) *Working Life: A New Perspective on Labour Law*, London, Institute of Employment Rights

Fabian Society (1996) *Changing Work*, London, Fabian Society

Field, R C (1997) 'Risk and justice: capitalist production and the environment', *Capitalism, Nature, Socialism*, Vol 8, No 2, pp 69–74

Finkle, P (1983) 'New approaches to fairness: the bureaucracy responds' in E S Case et al (eds) pp 29–38

Fiorino, D (1995) 'Regulatory negotiation as a form of public participation' in O Renn, T Webler and P Wiedemann (eds) pp 223–37

Fishkin, J L (1991) *Democracy and Deliberation: New Directions for Democratic Reform*, New Haven, Yale University Press

Fitzpatrick, B (1997) 'Straining the definition of health and safety', *Industrial Law Journal*, Vol 26, pp 115–35

Flader, S (1974) *Thinking Like a Mountain*, Columbia, University of Missouri Press

Forest Resources Commission (1991) *The Future of Our Forests*, Victoria, British Columbia Forest Resources Commission

Fotopoulos, T (1997) *Towards an Inclusive Democracy: The Crisis of the Growth Economy and the Need for a New Liberatory Project*, London, Cassell

Fox, W (1990) *Towards a Transpersonal Ecology: Developing New Foundations for Environmentalism*, Boston, Shambala

Franck, T M (1992) 'The emerging right to democratic governance', *American Journal of International Law*, Vol 86, pp 46–91

Frankel, B (1987) *The Post-industrial Utopians*, Cambridge, Polity

250 *Environmental Democracy*

Fukuyama, F (1992) *The End of History and the Last Man*, London, Hamish Hamilton

Fulcher, J (1991) *Labour Movements, Employers, and the State: Conflict and Cooperation in Britain and Sweden*, Oxford, Clarendon Press

Furze, B, T de Lacy and J Birckhead (1996) *Culture, Conservation and Biodiversity*, Chichester, John Wiley

Gamble, A, G Kelly and D Kelly (eds) (1997) *Stakeholder Capitalism*, New York, St Martin's Press

Gardner, F and S Greer (1996) 'Crossing the river: how local struggles build a broader movement', *Antipode*, Vol 28, pp 175–92

Gee, D (1995) 'Making pollution pay', *New Statesman and Society*, 14 April, p 31

Gereluk, W and L Royer (1997) 'Trade union action: a paradigm for sustainable development' in F Dodds (ed) pp 125–45

Giannis, D and P Liargoras (1998) 'Focusing regional and environmental policies in the European Union through the development of environmental quality indices', *European Environment*, Vol 8, pp 86–93

Giddens, A (1984) *The Constitution of Society*, Cambridge, Polity

Giddens, A (1990) *The Consequences of Modernity*, Cambridge, Polity

Giddens, A (1991) *Modernity and Self-Identity: Self and Society in the Late Modern Age*, Cambridge, Polity

Giddens, A (1994) *Beyond Left and Right: The Future of Radical Politics*, Cambridge, Polity

Goldblatt, D (1996) *Social Theory and the Environment*, Cambridge, Polity

Goldsmith, E (1992) *The Way: An Ecological Worldview*, London, Rider

Goodin, R E (1992) *Green Political Theory*, Cambridge, Polity

Gott, M and M Dobson (1998) *Environmental Stewardship: London Borough of Islington Audit 1996/97*, London, District Audit

Gottlieb, A M (ed) (1989) *The Wise Use Agenda: The Citizen's Guide to Environmental Resource Issues*, Bellevue, Washington, The Free Enterprise Press

Gottlieb, R (1995) 'Spiritual deep ecology revisited', *Capitalism, Nature, Socialism*, Vol 6, pp 41–45

Goudie, A S (1997) *The Human Impact Reader: Readings and Case Studies*, Blackwell, Oxford

Gould, C C (1988) *Rethinking Democracy: Freedom and Social Cooperation in Politics, Economy, and Society*, Cambridge, Cambridge University Press

Gould, K A, A Schnaiberg and A S Weinberg (1996) *Local Environmental Struggles: Citizen Activism in the Treadmill of Production*, Cambridge, Cambridge University Press

Government Office for London (1996) *Strategic Guidance for London Planning Authorities*, London, GOL

Graber, L (1976) *Wilderness as Sacred Space*, Washington, DC, Association of American Geographers

Grant, M (1996) 'Environmental liability' in G Winter (ed) pp 219–37

Gray, N and Z Rick (1997) 'Environmental democracy: the missing agenda', *Green Party News*, No 38, pp 6–8

Greater Ecosystem Alliance (1994) *The Big Picture: Protecting Biodiversity in BC*, Nelson, British Columbia, The Greater Ecosystem Alliance

Greer, J (1998) 'US petroleum giant to stand trial over Burma atrocities', *The Ecologist*, Vol 28, pp 34–37

Grumbine, E (1992) *Ghost Bears: Exploring the Biodiversity Crisis*, Washington, Island Press

Grundmann, R (1991) 'The ecological challenge to Marxism', *New Left Review*, No 187, pp 103–20

Guha, R (1989) 'Radical American environmentalism and wilderness preservation: a Third World critique', *Environmental Ethics*, Vol 11, pp 71–83

Günther, K (1993) *The Sense of Appropriateness: Application Discourses in Morality and Law*, Albany, NY, State University of New York Press

Gunton, T (1993) 'Crown-land planning in British Columbia: managing for multiple use' in M A Fenger et al (eds) *Our Living Legacy: Proceedings of a Symposium on Biological Diversity*, Victoria, Royal British Columbia Museum, pp 275–93

Habermas, J (1982) 'A reply to my critics' in D Held and J Thompson (eds) *Habermas: Critical Debates*, Cambridge, Cambridge University Press, pp 219–83

Habermas, J (1987) *The Theory of Communicative Action. Volume 2: A Critique of Functionalist Reason*, Cambridge, Polity

Habermas, J (1989) 'Towards a communication concept of rational collective will-formation. A thought experiment', *Ratio Juris*, Vol 2, pp 144–54

Habermas, J (1989–90), 'Justice and solidarity: On the discussion concerning "Stage 6"', *The Philosophical Forum*, Vol 11, pp 32–52

Habermas, J (1990) *Moral Consciousness and Communicative Action*, Cambridge, Polity

Habermas, J (1992a) 'Further reflections on the public sphere' in C Calhoun (ed) *Habermas and the Public Sphere*, Cambridge, Mass, MIT Press, pp 421–61

Habermas, J (1992b) *Postmetaphysical Thinking*, Cambridge, Polity

Habermas, J (1993) *Justification and Application: Remarks on Discourse Ethics*, Cambridge, Polity

Habermas, J (1996) *Between Facts and Norms: Contributions to a Discourse Theory of Law and Democracy*, Cambridge, Polity

Haddock, M (1995) *Forests on the Line*, Vancouver, Sierra Legal Defence Fund

Haigh, N (1994) 'The introduction of the precautionary principle in the UK' in T O'Riordan and J Cameron (eds) pp 229–51

Hajer, M (1995) *The Politics of Environmental Discourse: Ecological Modernization and the Policy Process*, Oxford, Oxford University Press

Hams, T et al (eds) (1994) *Greening Your Local Authority*, Harlow, Longman

Haraway, D (1989) *Primate Visions: Gender, Race and Nature in the World of Modern Science*, London, Routledge

Hardin, G (1993) *Living Within Limits: Ecology, Economics, and Population Taboos*, Oxford, Oxford University Press

Harding, S (1986) *The Science Question in Feminism*, Milton Keynes, Open University Press

Harvey, D (1985) 'The geopolitics of capitalism' in D Gregory and J Urry (eds) *Social Relations and Spatial Structures*, London, Macmillan, pp 128–63

Harvey, D (1996) *Justice, Nature & the Geography of Difference*, Oxford, Basil Blackwell

Hatch, R B (ed) (1994) *Clayoquot and Dissent*, Vancouver, Ronsdale Press

Hay, P R and M G Haward (1988) 'Comparative green politics: beyond the European context?', *Political Studies*, Vol 36, pp 433–48

Hayek, F A (1988) *The Fatal Conceit: The Errors of Socialism*, London, Routledge

Healey, P (1992) 'Planning through debate: the communicative turn in planning theory', *Town Planning Review*, Vol 63, pp 143–62

Hebbert, M (1995) 'Unfinished business: the remaking of London government, 1985–1995', *Policy and Politics*, Vol 23, pp 347–58

Heidegger, M (1977) 'The question concerning technology' in *The Question Concerning Technology and Other Essays*, London, Harper & Row, pp 3–35

Heijden, H-A van der (1997) 'Political opportunity structure and the institutionalisation of the environmental movement', *Environmental Politics*, Vol 6, pp 25–50

Held, D (1995) *Democracy and the Global Order: From the Modern State to Cosmopolitan Governance*, Polity, Cambridge

Hellberg, T (1995) 'Incineration by the backdoor: cement kilns as waste sinks', *The Ecologist*, Vol 25, pp 232–37

Henberg, M (1995) 'Pancultural wilderness' in D Rothenberg (ed) pp 59–70

Hesse, M (1980) *Revolutions and Reconstructions on the Philosophy of Science*, Brighton, Harvester Press

Hilderbrandt, E (1995) 'Environmental achievements in enterprises – with special reference to industrial relations', in M Jänicke and H Weidner (eds) pp 317–24

Hilson, C and I Cram (1996) 'Judicial review and environmental law – is there a coherent view of standing?', *Legal Studies*, Vol 16, pp 11–26

Hinchman, LP and M G Hinchman (1988) '"Deep ecology" and the revival of natural rights', *The Western Political Quarterly*, Vol 42, pp 201–28

Hirst, P (1994) *Associative Democracy*, Cambridge, Polity

Hirst, P (1995) 'Quangos and democratic government', *Parliamentary Affairs*, Vol 48, pp 341–59

Hirst, P and G Thompson (1996) *Globalization in Question*, Cambridge, Polity

Hoban, T M and R O Brooks (1996) *Green Justice: The Environment and the Courts*, Second Edition, Boulder, CO, Westview Press

Hoberg, G (1993a) 'Environmental policy: alternative styles' in M Atkinson (ed) *Governing Canada: Institutions and Policy*, Toronto, Harcourt Brace Jovanovich, pp 307–42

Hoberg, G (1993b) 'Regulating forestry: a comparison of institutions and policies in British Columbia and the US Pacific Northwest', *Forest Economics and Policy Analysis Research Unit Working Paper* , No 185, Vancouver, FEPA Research Unit, University of British Columbia

Holland, A (1997) 'The foundations of environmental decision-making', *International Journal of Environment and Pollution*, Vol 7, pp 483–96

Honneth, A and H Jonas (1988) *Social Action and Human Nature*, Cambridge, Cambridge University Press

House of Commons Environment Committee (1997) *The Environmental Impact of Cement Manufacture, Third Report*, London, The Stationery Office

Howlett, M and K Brownsey (1988) 'The old reality and the new reality: party politics and public policy in British Columbia 1941–1987', *Studies in Political Economy*, Vol 25, No 1, pp 141–76

Hummel, M (ed) (1989) *Endangered Spaces: The Future for Canada's Wilderness*, Toronto, Ontario, Key Porter Books

Hunt, P (1984) 'Workers side by side: women and the trade union movement' in J Siltanen and M Stanworth (eds) *Women and the Public Sphere*, London, Hutchinson, pp 47–53

Hutton, W (1995) *The State We're In*, London, Jonathan Cape

Inglehart, R (1977) *The Silent Revolution*, Princeton, Princeton University Press

Ingram, A (1994) *A Political Theory of Rights*, Oxford, Clarendon

Ingram, D (1993) 'The limits and possibilities of communicative ethics for democratic theory', *Political Theory*, Vol 21, pp 294–321

Integrated Resource Planning Committee (1993) *Land and Resource Management: A Statement of Principles and Processes*, Victoria, Province of British Columbia

International Confederation of Free Trade Unions (1996) *The Global Market – Trade Unionism's Greatest Challenge*, Brussels, ICFTU

Jacobs, M (for the Real World Coalition) (1996a) *The Politics of the Real World*, London, Earthscan

Jacobs, M (1996b) 'Real World', *Environmental Politics*, Vol 5, pp 744–51

Jacobs, M (1996c) 'Sustainability and "the market": a typology of environmental economics' in R Eckersley (ed) *Markets, the State and the Environment: Towards Integration*, London, Macmillan, pp 46–70

Jacobs, M (ed) (1997) *Greening the Millennium: The New Politics of the Environment*, London, Blackwell

Jacobs, M (1997) 'The quality of life: social goods and the politics of consumption' in M Jacobs (ed) pp 47–61

James, P and D Walters (1997) 'Non-union rights of involvement: the case of health and safety at work', *Industrial Law Journal*, Vol 26, pp 38–50

Jamison, A (1996) 'The shaping of the global environmental agenda: the role of non-governmental organizations' in S Lash, B Szerszynski and B Wynne (eds) pp 224–45

Jänicke, M (1990) *State Failure*, Cambridge, Polity Press

Jänicke, M (1992) 'Conditions for environmental policy success: an international comparison', *The Environmentalist*, Vol 12, pp 47–58

Jänicke, M (1996) 'Democracy as a condition for environmental policy success: the importance of non-institutional factors' in W M Lafferty and J Meadowcroft (eds) pp 71–85

Jänicke, M (1997) 'The political system's capacity for environmental policy' in M Jänicke and H Weidner (eds) pp 1–24

Jänicke, M and H Weidner (eds) (1995) *Successful Environmental Policy: A Critical Evaluation of 24 Cases*, Berlin, Edition Sigma

Jänicke, M and H Weidner (eds) (1997) *National Environmental Policies: A Comparative Study of Capacity-Building*, Berlin, Springer

Janoski, T (1998) *Citizenship and Civil Society*, Cambridge, Cambridge University Press

Johnson, L E (1991) *A Morally Deep World*, Cambridge, Cambridge University Press

Jones, C E and C Wood (1995) 'The impact of environmental assessment on public inquiry decisions', *Journal of Planning & Environmental Law*, pp 890–904

Joppke, C (1991) 'Social movements during cycles of issue attention: the decline of the anti-nuclear energy movements in West Germany and the USA', *British Journal of Sociology*, Vol 42, pp 43–60

Jowell, R et al (eds) (1997) *British Social Attitudes: The 14th Report*, Aldershot, Ashgate

Keil, R (1995) 'The Green Work Alliance', *Capitalism, Nature, Socialism*, Vol 6, No 3, pp 63–76

Kelly, J (1988) *Trade Unions and Socialist Politics*, London, Verso

Keohane, R O and E Ostrom (eds) (1995) *Local Commons and Global Interdependence: Heterogeneity and Cooperation in Two Domains*, London, Sage

Kitschelt, H P (1986) 'Political opportunity structures and political protest: anti-nuclear movements in four democracies', *British Journal of Political Science*, Vol 16, pp 57–85

Koh, H K (1991) 'Transnational public law litigation', *Yale Law Journal*, Vol 100, pp 2347–402

Kohak, E (1984) *The Embers and the Stars*, Chicago, Chicago University Press

Kornov, L (1997) 'Strategic environmental assessment: sustainability and democratization', *European Environment*, Vol 7, pp 175–80

Korten, D (1995) *When Corporations Rule the World*, London, Earthscan

Kramer, L (1996) 'The elaboration of EC environmental legislation', in G Winter (ed) pp 297–316

Krasner, S D (ed) (1983) *International Regimes*, Ithaca, Cornell University Press

Krebs, A (1997) 'Discourse ethics and nature', *Environmental Values*, Vol 6, pp 269–79

Kriesi, H et al (1995) *New Social Movements in Western Europe: A Comparative Analysis*, London, UCL Press

Krut, R and H Gleckmen (1997) *ISO 14001: The Missed Opportunities*, London, Earthscan

Kuhn, T (1970) *The Structure of Scientific Revolutions*, Second Edition, Chicago, University of Chicago Press

Kymlicka, W (1995) *Multicultural Citizenship: A Liberal Theory of Minority Rights*, Oxford, Clarendon Press

Lafferty, W M and J Meadowcroft (eds) (1996) *Democracy and the Environment: Problems and Prospects*, Cheltenham, Edward Elgar

Ladeur, K-H (1996) 'Environmental constitutional law' in G Winter (ed) pp 15–34

Lake, R (1996) 'Volunteers, NIMBYs and environmental justice: dilemmas of democratic practice', *Antipode*, Vol 28, pp 160–74

Lambrechts, C (1996) 'Public participation in environmental decisions', in G Winter (ed) pp 63–79

Land Use Coordination Office (1997) *Resource Management Zones for Vancouver Island*, Victoria, British Columbia, Land Use Coordination Office

Lash, S, B Szerszynski and B Wynne (eds) (1996) *Risk, Environment & Modernity: Towards a New Ecology*, London, Sage

Law Reform Commission of Canada (1985a) *Crimes Against the Environment*, Ottawa, Law Reform Commision of Canada

Law Reform Commission of Canada (1985b) *Report on Independent Administrative Agencies: A Framework for Decision-Making*, Ottawa, Law Reform Commission of Canada

Lee, P and A Murie (1998) 'Targeting social exclusion', *New Economy*, Vol 5, pp 89–93

Leopold, A (1966) *A Sand Country Almanac*, New York, Oxford University Press

Levi, M (1997) *Consent, Dissent, and Patriotism*, Cambridge: Cambridge University Press

Levy, A, C Scott-Clark and D Harrison (1997) 'Save the rhino: kill the people', *The Observer*, 23 March, p 9

Lewin, L (1991) *Self-Interest and Public Interest in Western Politics*, Oxford, Oxford University Press

Lewis, M W (1992) *Green Delusions: An Environmentalist Critique of Radical Environmentalism*, London, Duke University Press

Light, A and E S Higgs (1996) 'The politics of ecological restoration', *Environmental Ethics*, Vol 18, pp 227–47

Light, A (1997) 'Deep socialism? An interview with Arne Naess', *Capitalism, Nature, Socialism*, Vol 8, pp 69–85

Litfin, K (1994) *Ozone Discourses: Science and Politics in Global Environmental Cooperation*, New York, Columbia University Press

Livingston, J A (1981) *The Fallacy of Wildlife Conservation*, Toronto, McClelland & Stewart

Livingston, J A (1986) 'Ethics as Prosthetics' in P P Hanson (ed) *Environmental Ethics*, Burnaby, British Columbia, Simon Fraser University, pp 299–322

Local Government Management Board (1997) *Local Agenda 21 UK Review: 1992–1997*, London, LGMB

London Borough of Islington (1995) *Islington Council Charter for a Sustainable Future*, London, LBI

London Borough of Islington (1996) *State of the Environment in Islington*, London, LBI

London Borough of Islington (1997a) *New Council Action Plan for a Sustainable Future*, London, LBI, Chief Executive

London Borough of Islington (1997b) *New Neighbourhoods, Housing and Social Services*, London, LBI, Chief Executive

London Borough of Islington (1998a) *Modernising Local Government – Local Democracy and Community Leadership*, London, LBI, Chief Executive

London Borough of Islington (1998b) *Neighbourhood Democracy Initiatives*, London, LBI, Chief Executive

London Voluntary Service Council (1997) *Enriching Democracy: A Civic Forum for London*, London, London Voluntary Service Council

Low Intensity Area Review Committee (1995) *Low Intensity Areas for the Vancouver Island Region: Exploring a New Resource Management Vision*, Victoria, LIARC

Lowe, P and J Goyder (1983) *Environmental Groups in Politics*, London, George Allen & Unwin

Lucas, A R (1987) 'Natural resources and environmental management: a jurisdictional primer' in D Tingley (ed) *Environmental Protection and the Canadian Constitution*, Edmonton, Alberta, Environmental Law Centre, pp 31–43

Lundqvist, L J (1997) 'Sweden' in M Jänicke and H Weidner (eds) pp 45–71

Macdonald, R A (1980a) 'Judicial review and procedural fairness in administrative law: I', *McGill Law Journal*, Vol 25, No 4, pp 520–64

Macdonald, R A (1980b) 'Judicial review and procedural fairness in administrative law: II', *McGill Law Journal*, Vol 26, No 1, pp 1–44

MacIsaac, R and A Champagne (eds) (1994) *Clayoquot Mass Trials: Defending the Rainforest*, Gabriola Island, British Columbia, New Society Publishers

Macnaghten, P and J Urry (1998) *Contested Natures*, London, Sage

Manin, B (1987) 'On legitimacy and political deliberation', *Political Theory*, Vol 15, No 3, pp 338–68

Mann, M (1996) 'Authoritarian and liberal militarism: a contribution from comparative and historical sociology' in S Smith, K Booth and M Zalenski (eds) *International Relations Theory: Positivism and Beyond*, Cambridge, Cambridge University Press, pp 221–39

Marchak, P (1986) 'The rise and fall of the peripheral state: the case of British Columbia' in R J Bryn (ed.) *Regionalism in Canada*, Richmond, Ontario, Irwin, pp 123–59

Marsh, D (1992) *The New Politics of British Trade Unionism: Union Power and the Thatcher Legacy*, London, Macmillan

Martin, R, P Sunley, and J Wills (1996) *Union Retreat and the Regions: The Shrinking Landscape of Organized Labour*, London, Jessica Kingsley

Martinez-Alier, J (1995) 'Political ecology, distributional conflicts, and economic commensurability', *New Left Review*, No 211, pp 70–88

Marvin Shaffer and Associates (1992) *Evaluation Methodology and Data Sources for Social and Economic Impact Assessment of Forest Land Management Options: Background Reports*, Victoria, Forestry Canada/British Columbia Ministry of Forests

Marvin, S and S Guy (1997) 'Creating myths rather than sustainability: the transition fallacies of the new localism', *Local Environment*, Vol 2, pp 311–18

Max-Neef, M (1995) 'Economic growth and quality of life: a threshold hypothesis', *Ecological Economics*, Vol 15, pp 115–18

McChesney, R W (1997) *Corporate Media and the Threat to Democracy*, New York, Seven Stories Press

McCormick, J (1989) *The Global Environmental Movement: Reclaiming Paradise*, London, Belhaven

McDade, G J (1993) *Report on Compensation Issues Concerning Protected Areas*, Vancouver, Sierra Legal Defence Fund

McDaniels, T L (1992) 'Structuring alternatives for forest land management planning' in Marvin Shaffer and Associates, pp 1–10

McInnis, J (1996) 'Keys to the boreal forest puzzle in Alberta', *International Journal of Ecoforestry*, Vol 12, pp 171–75

McIntosh, R P, (1985) *The Background of Ecology: Concept and Theory*, Cambridge, Cambridge University Press

Mellor, M (1992) *Breaking the Boundaries: Towards A Feminist Green Socialism*, London, Virago

Merchant, C (1990) 'Environmental ethics and political conflict: a view from California', *Environmental Ethics*, Vol 12, pp 45–68

Mez, L and H Weidner (eds) (1997) *Unweltpolitik und Staatsversagen*, Berlin, Edition Sigma

M'Gonigle, M (1986) 'The tribune and the tribe: toward a natural law of the market/legal state', *Ecology Law Quarterly*, Vol 13, pp 233–310

M'Gonigle, M (1989–90) 'Developing sustainability: a native environmentalist prescription for third-level government', *BC Studies*, No 84, pp 65–99

M'Gonigle, M (1992) 'Our home and native land? Creating an eco-constitution in Canada' in J Plant (ed) *Putting Power in its Place. Create Community Control!*, Gabriola Island, British Columbia, New Society Publishers, pp 49–58

M'Gonigle, M and B Parfitt (1994) *Forestopia: A Practical Guide to the New Forest Economy*, Madeira Park, British Columbia, Harbour Publishing

Middleton, N (1995) *The Global Casino: An Introduction to Environmental Issues*, Edward Arnold, London

Mills, M (1996) 'Green democracy: the search for an ethical solution' in B Doherty and M de Geus (eds) pp 97–114

Millward, N (1988) *The New Industrial Relations?* London: Policy Studies Institute

Millward, N et al (1992) *Workplace Industrial Relations in Transition: The ED/ESRC/PSI/ACAS Surveys*, Aldershot, Dartmouth Publishing

Ministry of Crown Lands (1989) *British Columbia Land Statistics*, Victoria, British Columbia, Ministry of Crown Lands

Ministry of Forests (1990) *Integrated Resource Management on Provincial Forest Lands: Ministry Policy*, Victoria, British Columbia Ministry of Forests

Mitchell, R B (1994) *Intentional Oil Pollution at Sea: Environmental Policy and Treaty Compliance*, Cambridge, Mass, MIT Press

Mon Information Service (1996) *French Total Co's and American Unocal Corp's Disastrous Gas Pipeline Project in Burma's Gulf of Martaban*, Bangkok, Mon Information Service, http://www.hcs.harvard.edu/~burma/mon.html

Moody, K (1997) 'Towards an international social-movement unionism', *New Left Review*, No 225, pp 52–72

Morter, N (1995) *Local Agenda 21: A Guide for Active T&G Members*, London, T&G

Mosquin, T (1991) 'Should natural laws be legislated?', *Borealis*, No 3, pp 46–47

Mucke, P (1997) 'Non-governmental organizations' in F Dodds (ed) pp 93–100

Muldoon, P (1988) 'The fight for an environmental bill of rights: legislating public involvement in environmental decision-making', *Alternatives*, Vol 15, No 2, pp 33–39

Myers, N (1985) *The Primary Source: Tropical Forests and Our Future*, New York, W W Norton & Company

Myers, N (1988) 'Threatened biotas: "hot spots" in tropical forests', *The Environmentalist*, Vol 8, pp 187–208

Myrick Freeman III, A (1994) 'Economics, incentives, and environmental regulation' in N J Vig and M E Kraft (eds) *Environmental Policy in the 1990s*, Washington, Congressional Quarterly Press, pp 189–208

Naess, A (1973) 'The shallow and deep, long-range ecology movement: a summary', *Inquiry*, Vol 16, pp 95–100

Naess, A (1989a) *Ecology, Community and Lifestyle*, Cambridge, Cambridge University Press

Naess, A (1989b) 'Self-realization: an ecological approach to being in the world' in J Seed et al (eds) *Thinking Like a Mountain: Towards a Council of All Beings*, Santa Cruz, New Society Publishers, pp 19–30

Naess, A (1992) 'The encouraging richness and diversity of ultimate premises in environmental philosophy', *The Trumpeter*, Vol 9, pp 53–60

Naess, A (1995) 'Deep ecology in the line of fire', *The Trumpeter*, Vol 12, pp 146–49

Nash, R (1982) *Wilderness and the American Mind*, Third Edition, New York, New Haven

Nash, R (1989) *The Rights of Nature: A History of Environmental Ethics*, Madison, University of Wisconsin Press

Nelson, J G (1989) 'Wilderness in Canada: Past, present, future', *Natural Resources Journal*, Vol 29, pp 83–102

New Economics Foundation (1998) *Participation Works! 21 Techniques of Community Participation for the 21st Century*, London, NEF

Nixon, B (1990) 'Principles of integrated management lack legislative authority in British Columbia, when compared with US forest law', *Forest Planning Canada*, Vol 6, No 6, pp 9–14

Norton, B (1987) *Why Preserve Natural Variety?* Princeton: Princeton University Press

Noss, R F (1991) 'Sustainability and wilderness', *Conservation Biology*, Vol 5, pp 120–22

O'Brien, M and S Penna (1997) 'European policy and the politics of environmental governance', *Policy and Politics*, Vol 25, pp 185–200

O'Connor, J (1988) 'Capitalism, nature, socialism: a theoretical introduction', *Capitalism, Nature, Socialism*, Vol 1, No 1, pp 1–19

O'Connor, J (1991) 'The second contradiction of capitalism: causes and consequences' in Conference Papers, *CES/CNS Pamphlet 1*, Santa Cruz, CA, pp 1–10

O'Connor, J (1997) *Natural Causes: Essays in Ecological Marxism*, New York, Guilford Publishers

O'Connor, M (1997) 'The internalization of environmental costs: implementing the Polluter Pays Principle in the European Union', *International Journal of Environment and Pollution*, Vol 7, pp 450–82

Oelschlaeger, M (1993) 'The idea of wilderness as deep ecological ethic', Paper presented at the Fifth World Wilderness Conference, Tromso, Norway, September

Offe, C (1985) *Disorganized Capitalism*, Cambridge, Polity

O'Hara, S U (1996) 'Discursive ethics in ecosystems valuation and environmental policy', *Ecological Economics*, Vol 16, pp 95–107

Ombudsman of British Columbia (1989) 'Victoria, Province of British Columbia', *1988 Annual Report to the Legislative Assembly*, Victoria, Province of British Columbia

O'Neill, J (1993) *Ecology, Policy and Politics: Human Well-Being and the Natural World*, London, Routledge

O'Neill, M (1997) *Green Parties and Political Change in Contemporary Europe: New Politics, Old Predicaments*, Aldershot, Ashgate

O'Riordan, T (1981) *Environmentalism*, Second Edition, London, Pion

O'Riordan, T (1989a) 'Best Practicable Environmental Option (BPEO): A case study in bureaucratic adaptation', *Environmental Conservation*, Vol 16, pp 113–22, 162

O'Riordan, T (1989b) 'The challenge for environmentalism' in R Peet and N Thrift (eds) *New Models in Geography: The Political Economy Perspective*, London, Unwin Hyman, pp 77–102

O'Riordan, T (1996) 'Democracy and the sustainability transition' in W M Lafferty and J Meadowcroft (eds) pp 140–56

O'Riordan, T and J Cameron (eds) (1994) *Interpreting the Precautionary Principle*, London, Earthscan

O'Riordan, T and A Jordan (1995) 'The precautionary principle in contemporary environmental politics', *Environmental Values*, Vol 4, pp 191–212

Ostrom, E (1990) *Governing the Commons: The Evolution of Institutions for Collective Action*, Cambridge, CUP

Ostrom, E (1995) 'Constituting social capital and collective action' in R O Keohane and E Ostrom (eds) pp 125–60

Owen, S (1993) 'Participation and sustainability: the imperatives of resource and environmental management' in S A Kennet (ed) *Law and Process in Environmental Management*, Calgary, Institute of Resources Law, pp 335–66

Owens, S (1997) '"Giants in the path": planning, sustainability and environmental values', *Town Planning Review*, Vol 68, pp 293–304

Ozawa, C P (1993) 'Improving citizen participation in environmental decision-making: the use of transformative mediator techniques', *Environment and Planning C: Government and Policy*, Vol 11, No 1, pp 103–17

Paehlke, R (1989) *Environmentalism and the Future of Progressive Politics*, New Haven, Yale University Press

Paehlke, R and D Torgerson (eds) (1990) *Managing Leviathan: Environmental Politics and the Administrative State*, London, Belhaven Press

Pahl-Wostl, C (1995) *The Dynamic Nature of Ecosystems: Chaos and Order Entwined*, Chichester, John Wiley

Palmer, V (1995) 'Forest policy expected to make communities suffer', *Vancouver Sun*, 26 January, A18

Parry, G, G Moyser and N Day (1992) *Political Participation and Democracy in Britain*, Cambridge, Cambridge University Press

Passmore, J (1995) 'The preservationist syndrome', *The Journal of Political Philosophy*, Vol 3, pp 1–22

Pearce, D (1992) 'Economics, equity and sustainable development' in P Ekins and M Max-Neef (eds) *Real-life Economics: Understanding Wealth Creation*, pp 69–76

Pearce, D and R K Turner (1990) *Economics of Natural Resources and the Environment*, London, Harvester

Penz, P (1998) 'Environmental victims and state sovereignty: a normative analysis' in C Williams (ed) pp 27–47

Pepper, D (1986) 'Radical environmentalism and the labour movement' in J Weston (ed) *Red and Green: The New Politics of the Environment*, London, Pluto Press, pp 115–129

Pepper, D (1993) *Eco-Socialism: From Deep Ecology to Social Justice*, London, Routledge

Pepper, D (1996) *Modern Environmentalism: An Introduction*, London, Routledge

Pimlott, B (1982) 'Trade unions and the second coming of CND' in B Pimlott and C Cook (eds) *Trade Unions in British Politics*, London, Longman, pp 215–36

Pitkin, H F (1967) *The Concept of Representation*, Berkeley, University of California Press

Plant, C (1990) 'In pockets of resistance: the back-to-the-land movement matures' in V Andruss, C Plant, J Plant, E Wright (eds) *Home! A Bioregional Reader*, Gabriola Island, British Columbia, New Society Publishers, pp 26–28

Plumwood, V (1993) *Feminism and the Mastery of Nature*, London, Routledge

Porritt, J and Winner, D (1988) *The Coming of the Greens*, London, Fontana

Price Waterhouse (1995) *Analysis of Recent British Columbia Government Forest Policy and Land Use Initiatives*, Vancouver, Forest Alliance of British Columbia

Pross, A P (1986) *Group Politics and Public Policy*, Toronto, Oxford University Press

Province of British Columbia (1993a) *A Protected Areas Strategy for British Columbia*, Victoria, Queen's Printer

Province of British Columbia (1993b) *Social and Economic Impact Assessment for Land and Resource Management Planning in British Columbia*, Victoria, Queen's Printer

Pulido, L (1994) 'Restructuring and the contraction and expansion of environmental rights in the US', *Environment and Planning A*, Vol 26, pp 915–36

Purcell, J (1993) 'The end of institutional industrial relations', *Political Quarterly*, Vol 64, pp 6–23

Ragin, C C (1992) '"Casing" and the process of social inquiry' in C Ragin and H S Becker (eds) *What is a Case? Exploring the Foundations of Social Inquiry*, Cambridge, Cambridge University Press, pp 217–26

Raustiala, K and D G Victor (1998) 'Conclusions' in D G Victor, K Raustiala and E B Skolnikoff (eds) pp 659–707

Rawls, J (1988) 'The priority of right and ideas of the good', *Philosophy and Public Affairs*, Vol 17, pp 251–276

Rayner, J (1996) 'Implementing sustainability in west coast forests: CORE and FEMAT as experiments in process', *Journal of Canadian Studies*, Vol 31, No 1, pp 82–101

Raz, J (1986) *The Morality of Freedom*, Oxford, Clarendon Press

Reardon, C (1993) 'Is the CORE process fair?', *West Coast Environmental Association Newsletter*, Vol 17, No 5, p 5

Red Green Study Group (1995) *What on Earth is to be Done?* Manchester, Red Green Study Group

Reich, R (1985) 'Public administration and public deliberation: an interpretive essay', *Yale Law Journal*, Vol 94, pp 1617–41

Renn, O, T Webler and P Wiedemann (1995) *Fairness and Competence in Citizen Participation: Evaluating Models for Environmental Discourse*, Dordrecht, Kluwer

Ridley, M (1995) *Down to Earth: A Cautious View of Environmental Problems*, London, Institute of Economic Affairs

Rolston, H (1988) *Environmental Ethics*, Philadelphia, Temple University Press

Rothenberg, D (ed) (1995) *Wild Ideas*, Minneapolis, University of Minnesota Press

Round Table on the Environment and the Economy (1991) *Reaching Agreement. Volume 1: Consensus Processes in British Columbia*, Victoria, British Columbia Round Table on the Environment and the Economy

Round Table on the Environment and the Economy (1994) *Public Involvement in Government Decision-Making: Choosing the Right Model*, Victoria, British Columbia Round Table on the Environment and the Economy

Round Tables on the Environment and the Economy in Canada (1993) *Building Consensus for a Sustainable Future*, Ottawa, National Round Table on the Environment and the Economy

Rouse, J (1987) *Knowledge and Power: Toward a Political Philosophy of Science*, London, Cornell University Press

Rowe, S (1990) *Home Place: Essays on Ecology*, Edmonton, NeWest Publishers

Royal Commission on Environmental Pollution (1976) *Air Pollution Control: An Integrated Approach*, Cmnd 6371, London, HMSO

Royal Commission on Forest Resources (1976) *Timber Rights and Forest Policy in British Columbia. Report of the Royal Commission on Forest Resources, Volumes 1 and 2*, Victoria, Royal Commission on Forest Resources

Sagoff, M (1988) *The Economy of the Earth: Philosophy, Law and the Environment*, Cambridge, Cambridge University Press

Sale, K (1985), *Dwellers in the Land*, San Francisco, Sierra Club Books

Saward, M (1993) 'Green democracy' in A Dobson and A Lucardie (eds) *The Politics of Nature*, London, Routledge, pp 63–80

Saward, M (1996) 'Must democrats be environmentalists?' in B Doherty and M de Geus (eds) pp 79–96

Schatzski, T R (1996) *Social Practices: A Wittgensteinian Approach to Human Activity and the Social*, Cambridge, Cambridge University Press

Schneider, S H and P J Boston (eds) (1991) *Scientists on Gaia*, Cambridge, Mass, MIT Press

Schoenbaum, T J (1997) 'International trade and protection of the environment: the continuing search for reconciliation', *American Journal of International Law*, Vol 91, pp 268–313

Searle, R (1986) 'Is there hope for big wilderness in Canada?', *The Trumpeter*, Vol 3, pp 38–39

Sen, A (1992) *Inequality Reexamined*, Clarendon Press, Oxford

Shapiro, I (1986) *The Evolution of Rights in Liberal Theory*, Cambridge, Cambridge University Press

Sharwood, M and S Russell (1997) 'A review of Local Agenda 21 fora', *EG*, No 3, pp 3–8

Sherrod, A (1993a) 'CORE processes: the little known threat to existing parks', unpublished manuscript, New Denver, British Columbia, The Valhalla Society

Sherrod, A (1993b) 'Flaws in the CORE process (as experienced by the wilderness conservation sector of the Slocan Valley Pilot Project)', unpublished manuscript, New Denver, British Columbia, The Valhalla Society

Simitis, S (1987) 'Juridification of Labour Relations' in G Teubner (ed) *Juridification of Social Spheres*, Berlin, de Gruyter, pp 113–61

Simonsen, K (1981) 'The value of wildness', *Environmental Ethics*, Vol 3, pp 259–63

Simpson, D (1995) 'The bioregional basis of forest certification: Why Cascadia?', *International Journal of Ecoforestry*, Vol 11, pp 140–43

Slater, J (1986) 'Dumping nuclear waste at sea' in E Goldsmith and N Hildyard (eds) *Green Britain or Industrial Wasteland?* Cambridge, Polity, pp 267–72

Slocan Valley Community Forest Management Project (1974) *Final Report*, New Denver, British Columbia

Smith, A (1997) *Integrated Pollution Control: Change and Continuity in the UK Industrial Pollution Policy Network*, Aldershot, Ashgate

Soper, K (1995) *What is Nature? Culture, Politics and the Non-Human*, London, Blackwell

Standing Committee on Aboriginal Affairs (1990) *Unfinished Business: An Agenda for all Canadians in the 1990s*, Ottawa, Queen's Printer

Standing, G (1997) 'Globalization, labour flexibility and insecurity: the era of market regulation', *European Journal of Industrial Relations*, Vol 3, pp 7–37

Stephens, M (1981) *Ernest Bevin, Unskilled Labourer and World Statesman 1881–1951*, London, TGWU

Stokke, O S (1997) 'Regimes as governance systems', in O R Young (ed) pp 27–63

Stone, C (1972) 'Should trees have legal standing? Toward legal rights for natural objects', *Southern California Law Review*, Vol 45, pp 450–501

Strachen, P, M Haque, A McCulloch and J Moxen (1997) 'The eco-management and audit scheme: recent experiences of UK participating organizations', *European Environment*, Vol 7, pp 25–32

Straaten, J van der (1992) 'The Dutch National Environmental Policy Plan: To choose or to lose', *Environmental Politics*, Vol 1, pp 45–71

Streeck, W (1992) *Social Institutions and Economic Performance: Studies of Industrial Relations in Advanced Capitalist Countries*, London, Sage

Stroup, R J and J A Baden (1983) *Bureaucratic Myths and Environmental Management*, Cambridge, Mass., Ballinger

Supreme Court of Canada (1997) *R. v Hydro-Quebec*, File No 24625, Ottawa

Susskind, L and J Cruikshank (1987) *Breaking the Impasse: Consensus Approaches to Resolving Public Disputes*, New York, Basic Books

Sustainable London Trust (1996) *Creating a Sustainable London*, London, Sustainable London Trust

Sylvan, R (1985) 'A critique of deep ecology', *Radical Philosophy*, Vol 41, pp 10–22

Szasz, A and M Meuser (1997) 'Environmental inequalities: review and proposals for new directions in research and theory', *Current Sociology*, Vol 45, pp 99–120

Szerszynski, B (1997) 'Voluntary associations and the sustainable society' in M Jacobs (ed) pp 148–59

Taylor, B (1997) 'Green in word...' in R Jowell et al (eds) pp 111–36

Taylor, P W (1986) *Respect for Nature*, Princeton, Princeton University Press

Tennant, P (1990) *Aboriginal Peoples and Politics*, Vancouver, University of British Columbia

Thake, S (1995) *Staying the Course: The Role and Structure of Community Regeneration Organizations*, York, Joseph Rowntree Foundation

Thake, S (1998) 'Making community-led regeneration work: the experience of the Tollington initiative', Public lecture, University of North London, 10 June

Thomas, H (1997) '"Ethnic minorities and the planning system": a study revisited', *Town Planning Review*, Vol 68, pp 195–211

Thompson, E P (1991) *Customs in Common*, London, Merlin

Thornton, J (1997) 'Wild nature, sanity, and the law', *The Trumpeter*, Vol 14, pp 137–42

Trades Union Congress (1991) *Greening the Workplace*, London, TUC

Transport and General Workers' Union (1978) *Industrial Democracy*, London, TGWU

Transport and General Workers' Union (1987) *Arms Jobs Conversion*, London, TGWU

Transport and General Workers' Union (1991) *ENACT: Environmental Charter for the TGWU*, London, TGWU

Transport and General Workers' Union (1996) *The Safety, Health and Environmental Implications of Burning Alternative Fuels in Cement Kilns: A Report of a T&G Organized Conference Attended by the AEEU and GMB*, London, T&G

Transport and General Workers' Union (1997a) *Safety, Health and Environmental Issues and European Works Councils*, London, T&G

Transport and General Workers' Union (1997b) *T&G Health and Safety Record*, No 3

Transport and General Workers' Union (1998) *Handbook on Safety, Health and Environmental Issues*, London, T&G

Trudgill, S and K Richards (1997) 'Environmental science and policy: generalizations and context sensitivity', *Transactions, Institute of British Geographers*, Vol 22, pp 5–12

Turner, R K (1995) 'Sustainability: principles and practices', in R K Turner (ed) *Sustainable Environmental Economics and Management*, Chichester, John Wiley, pp 3–36

Tuxworth, B (1996) 'From environment to sustainability: surveys and analysis of Local Agenda 21 process development in UK local authorities', *Local Environment*, Vol 1, pp 277–97

UK Government (1994) *Sustainable Development: The UK Strategy, Cm 2426*, London, HMSO

UK Government (1997) *Government Response to the Third Report of the House of Commons Environment Select Committee Session 1996–97, Cm 3692*, London, The Stationery Office

UK Government (1998) *Fairness at Work, Cm 3968*, London, The Stationery Office

Underdal, A (1997) 'Capacity for international environmental governance', in L Mez and H Weidner (eds) pp 252–57

Undy, R et al (1996) *Managing the Unions: The Impact of Legislation on Trade Union Behaviour*, Oxford, Clarendon Press

United Nations (1993) *Agenda 21: The United Nations Programme of Action From Rio*, New York, United Nations

Vanagas, S (1994) 'Culture of conflict', *British Columbia Report*, Vol.5, No 49, pp 18–22

Vance, J (1990) *Tree Planning: A Guide to Public Involvement in Forest Stewardship*, Vancouver: Public Interest Advocacy Centre

Vanderzwagg, D and L Duncan (1992) 'Canada and environmental protection: confident political faces, uncertain legal hands' in R Boardman (ed) *Canadian Environmental Policy: Ecosystems, Politics and Process*, Toronto, Oxford University Press, pp 3–23

Vavrousek, J (1995) 'Institutions for environmental security' in J Kirkby, P O'Keefe and L Timberlake (eds) *The Earthscan Reader in Sustainable Development*, London, Earthscan, pp 267–73

Vickers, L (1995) *Protecting Whistleblowers at Work*, London Institute of Employment Rights

Victor, D G, K Raustiala and E B Skolnikoff (eds) (1998) *The Implementation and Effectiveness of International Environmental Commitments*, Cambridge, Mass, MIT Press

Vogel, D (1986) *National Styles of Regulation: Environmental Policy in Great Britain and the United States*, Ithaca, New York, Cornell University Press

Vogler, J (1995) *The Global Commons: A Regime Analysis*, Chichester, John Wiley

Voisey, H and T O'Riordan (1997) 'Greening institutions for sustainable development: The United Kingdom's national level approach', *Environmental Politics*, Vol 6, pp 24–53

Von Moltke, K (1997) 'Institutional interactions: the structure of regimes for trade and the environment' in O Young (ed) pp 247–72

Wade, W and C Forsyth (1994) *Administrative Law*, Seventh Edition, Oxford, Clarendon Press

Wainwright, H and D Elliot (1982) *The Lucas Plan: A New Trade Unionism in the Making?* London, Allison & Busby

Walker, J M (1997) 'Domestic adjudication of international human rights violations under the Alien Tort Statute', *Saint Louis University Law Journal*, Vol 41, pp 539–60

Wapner, P (1997) 'Governance in global civil society' in O R Young (ed) pp 65–84

Ward, S (1993) 'Thinking global, acting local? British local authorities and their environmental plans', *Environmental Politics*, Vol 2, pp 453–78

Weale, A (1992) *The New Politics of Pollution*, Manchester, Manchester University Press

Weale, A (1997) 'Great Britain' in M Jänicke and H Weidner (eds) pp 89–108

Webb, S and B Webb (1920) *The History of Trade Unionism*, Second Edition, London, Longmans Green and Co

Webb, S and B Webb (1965) *Industrial Democracy* [1897], New York, A M Kelly

Webler, T (1995) '"Right" discourse in citizen participation: an evaluative yardstick' in O Renn, T Webler and P Wiedemann (eds) pp 35–86

Western Canada Wilderness Committee (1993–94) 'A conservation vision for Vancouver Island', *WCWC Educational Report*, Vol 12, No 7

Western Canada Wilderness Committee (1996) 'WCWC seeks 40 per cent wilderness preserved for future generations', *WCWC Educational Report*, Vol 15, No 15, p 1

Westra, L (1993) 'The ethics of environmental holism and the democratic state', *Environmental Values*, Vol 2, pp 125–36

Westra, L (1994) *An Environmental Proposal for Ethics: The Principle of Integrity*, Lanham, MD, Rowman & Littlefield

White, J and M Young (1996) *Governing London*, London, Institute of Community Studies

Wilderness Advisory Committee (1986) *The Wilderness Mosaic*, Victoria, British Columbia: Wilderness Advisory Committee

Wilkinson, D (1997) 'Towards sustainability in the European Union? Steps within the European Commission towards integrating the environment into other European Union policy sectors', *Environmental Politics*, Vol 6, pp 153–73

Williams, B A and A R Matheny (1995) *Democracy, Dialogue and Environmental Disputes*, New Haven, Yale University Press

Williams, C (1998) *Environmental Victims: New Risks, New Injustices*, London, Earthscan

Williams, D R (1994) 'Environmental law and democratic legitimacy', *Duke Environmental Law and Policy Forum*, Vol 4, No 1, pp 1–40

Williams, K (1995) 'Deregulating occupational health and safety', *Industrial Law Journal*, Vol 24, pp 133–40

Williams, K (1997) 'Making rules for occupational health in Britain, the USA and the EC', *Anglo-American Law Journal*, Vol 26, pp 82–110

Wilson, D (1996) 'Structural "solutions" for local government: an exercise in chasing shadows?', *Parliamentary Affairs*, Vol 49, pp 441–54

Wilson, E O (1993) *The Diversity of Life*, London, Allen Lane

Winter, G (ed) (1996) *European Environmental Law: A Comparative Review*, London, Longman

Witherspoon, S (1996) 'Democracy, the environment and public opinion in Europe' in W M Lafferty and J Meadowcroft (eds) pp 39–70

Wood, C (1995) *Environmental Impact Assessment: A Comparative Review*, London, Longman

World Commission on Environment and Development (1987) *Our Common Future*, Oxford, Oxford University Press

Wynne, B (1994) 'Scientific knowledge and the global environment' in M Redclift and T Benton (eds) *Social Theory and the Global Environment*, London, Routledge, pp 169–89

Wynne, B (1996) 'May the sheep safely graze? A reflexive view of the expert–lay knowledge divide' in S Lash, B Szerszynski and B Wynne (eds) pp 44–83

Young, O R (ed) (1997) *Global Governance: Drawing Insights From the Environmental Experience*, Cambridge, Mass, MIT Press

Young, S C (1996) 'Stepping stones to empowerment? Participation in the context of Local Agenda 21', *Local Government Policy Making*, Vol 22, pp 25–31

Young, S C (1997) 'Local Agenda 21: the renewal of local democracy?' in M Jacobs (ed) pp 138–47

Zuckerman, S (ed) (1989) *Third North American Bioregional Congress: Proceedings*, Lillooet, British Columbia, New Catalyst

INDEX

Finland 93
First Nations 118–19, 143–7
Fotopoulos, Takis 42–3
Framework Convention on Climate
    Change 216
France 77, 88
Frankel, Boris 43–4
Frankfurt School 128, 149
Friends of Carmanah/Walbran 137
Friends of Clayoquot Sound 140
Friends of Strathcona Park 137
Friends of the Earth 183–4, 200
Fukuyama, Francis 22
future generations 1, 31, 36–8, 40, 47, 62,
    126, 131, 151

General Agreement on Tariffs and Trade
    (GATT) 224, 226
    see also WTO
General Municipal and Boilermakers'
    Union (GMB) 161, 176
Germany
    constitutional commitment to
        environmental protection 76
    and ecological modernization 93, 94
    early ecologism in 32
    electoral system 66–7
    environmental activism in 88–9
    and environmental liability 96
    environmental policy 84–5
Giannis, Dimitrios 93
Giddens, Anthony 14, 19, 33
    on environmentalism 27–30
Goldsmith, Edward 33
Goodin, Robert E 39–40, 128
Gould, Carol 99
Greater Ecosystem Alliance 148
Greater London Authority 190, 192
Greater London Council 189, 192
Green parties 67, 147, 239
Greenpeace 167, 168
Grundmann, Rainer 44
Gundersen, Adolf 57
Günther, Klaus 128

Habermas, Jürgen 15, 52–3, 59, 128–31, 150
    on discourse principle 8, 10–11
    on environmentalism 27–30
Hajer, Maarten 12–13, 53, 94, 96
Hardin, Garrett 33
Harvey, David 44
health and safety 160–6
Heijden, Hein-Anton van der 89, 90
Held, David 52–3, 75, 222, 236
Higgs, Eric 57
Hirst, Paul 38, 226
Hobbes, Thomas 34

human rights 6–7, 40, 43, 59–63, 66, 171,
    219–3
    see also environmental rights

India 69
industrial democracy 168, 175
information
    access to 107, 163, 176
    right to 77, 78, 232
Inglehart, Ronald 27
integrated pollution control 80, 162
integrative capacity 65, 79–83, 88
International Confederation of Free Trade
    Unions (ICFTU) 169, 173, 174
International Convention for the
    Regulation of Whaling 217
International Court of Justice 228–9
International Criminal Court (ICC) 229, 233
international environmental agreements 19,
    69, 75, 214–19, 226
International Law Commission 229
International Panel on Climate Change 26
Islington see London Borough of Islington

Jacobs, Michael 49–50, 237
Jänicke, Martin 71–3, 79, 83, 92–3, 238
Janoski, Thomas 234
Jones, Jack 158, 175
jus cogens norms 231, 232

Korten, David 227
Krasner, Stephen 215
Ksentini Report 60–1, 235
Kyoto Climate Change Conference 60

Labour Party 166–7, 180, 198
Lambrechts, Claude 77, 78
Law Reform Commission of Canada 120
legitimation deficit 28, 104–5, 115
Leopold, Aldo 133–4, 140, 241
Levi, Margaret 98
Liargovas, Panagiotis 93
Light, Andrew 57
Litfin, Karen 12
Livingston, John 138, 139
Local Agenda 21 18, 49, 85, 169–70, 179–82,
    185–8
    in London 188–93, 199–206
local government (in UK)
    structural changes in 182–8
    environmental policy 179–82, 183–4, 200
Locke, John 34
London Borough of Islington 18, 181, 189,
    193–210
London (dumping) Convention 217
Lovelock, James 23
Luhmann, Niklas 66–8, 69